KU-519-011

Scandal

Scandal

A SCURRILOUS
HISTORY OF GOSSIP

Roger Wilkes

Atlantic Books
London

First published in Great Britain in 2002 by Atlantic Books,
an imprint of Grove Atlantic Ltd

Copyright © Roger Wilkes

The moral right of Roger Wilkes to be identified as the author of this work has been
asserted in accordance with the Copyright, Designs and Patents Act of 1988.

All rights reserved. No part of this publication may be reproduced, stored in a retrieval
system, or transmitted in any form or by any means, electronic, mechanical, photocopying,
recording or otherwise, without the prior permission of the copyright owner and the
above publisher of this book.

2 4 6 8 9 7 5 3 1

A CIP catalogue record for this book is available from the British Library.

ISBN 1 903809 63 0

Typeset by FiSH Books, London WC1
Printed and bound in Great Britain by Creative Print & Design (Wales) Ebbw Vale

Atlantic Books
An imprint of Grove Atlantic Ltd
Ormond House
26–27 Boswell Street
London WC1N 3JZ

Contents

List of Illustrations

young party in 1930 (Cartoon by Antony Wysard, originally for *The Tatler* reproduced by kind permission of James Wysard)

14. Marquess of Donegall in Hollywood with Carole Lombard and Fredric March (courtesy of Mrs Carolyn Tate)

15. Walter Winchell at his *New York Mirror* desk in the early 1930s (courtesy of Hal Layer, Professor Emeritus, San Francisco State University)

16. Marquess of Donegall and the Duchess of Windsor, the former Mrs Wallis Simpson (courtesy of Mrs Carolyn Tate)

17. Godmothers of gossip: Louella Parsons and Hedda Hopper (© Bill Ray)

18. Roy Blackman and the *Daily Mirror* gossip team of 1960 (© John Chillingworth Archive)

19. *Confidential*'s 1957 cover story exposing Liberace as a closet homosexual (courtesy of www.bobsliberace.com)

20. Fred Newman, gossip editor of the *Daily Sketch* in 1960, with Scottish stunt-girl Rosemary McLellan (© John Chillingworth Archive)

21. Jack Profumo as the scandal breaks in 1963. (© *Private Eye*)

22. Christine Keeler, the most photographed woman in Britain as Stephen Ward's trial opens (© Hulton Getty)

23. *Private Eye*'s Grovel, based on Nigel Dempster of the *Daily Mail* (© Fluck and Law. Photography by John Lawrence Jones, printed with permission from *Private Eye*)

24. Former beauty queen Joyce McKinney, star of the Mormon missionary 'sex-in-chains' case (© PA Photos)

25. Peter Bessell MP, star witness at Jeremy Thorpe's 1978 trial (by Srdja Djukanovic, *Daily Telegraph*, courtesy of Carol Djukanovic)

26. Lady Diana Spencer outside her Kensington flat in 1980 (© Hulton Getty)

27. Jeffrey Archer and Andrina Colquhoun (© Alpha Photo Press)

28. Monica Lewinsky at the height of the scandal over her liaison with President Clinton (© AP)

29. Matt Drudge, the original cyber gossip columnist. (© AP)

30. A troubled Princess of Wales on a visit to the ballet in 1996 (© Reuters)

Acknowledgements

I would like to thank Mrs Carolyn Tate for allowing me to peruse material by her stepfather, the late Marquess of Donegall, who wrote the 'Almost in Confidence' columns in the *Weekly Dispatch* during gossip's golden age in the 1930s. Mrs Tate's mother, Her Grace, Maureen, the Marchioness of Donegall, kindly loaned me several bound volumes of cuttings shortly before her death in 1999. I also thank Mrs Rosalie Edgar, widow of Donald Edgar, who wore the William Hickey mantle in the 1950s, and their daughter Deirdre Duff, for letting me see his collection of cuttings from the *Daily Express*. I am grateful to Bruce Hunter of David Higham Associates for permission to quote some extended passages from Tom Driberg's autobiography *Ruling Passions* (Quartet Books). I am also indebted in various ways to Francis Wheen, Tony Rushton and Hilary Lowinger of *Private Eye*, Robert M. Barnes, Scott Bennett, Piers Burnett, Paul Callan, John Chillingworth, Brian Coulon of the *Daily Telegraph*, Jonathan Goodman, Dr Michael Harris of Birkbeck College, London, Sarah Hepworth of *The Times* archive, John Lawrence Jones, Roger Law, John Lawrence, Hal Layer, Sam Leith, latterly Peterborough of the *Daily Telegraph*, Celia Levett, Janet McMullin at the library of Christ Church, Oxford, Brian Masters, Shelley Power, Bill and Marlys Ray, E. S. Turner, Katherine Whitehurst, Rebecca Wilson, James Wysard, staff at the Bodleian Library, Oxford, the London Library, and the Public Record Office at Kew. I also wish to thank Toby Mundy and Bonnie Chiang at Atlantic Books for their care and enthusiastic encouragement. Finally, my thanks to my wife for enduring the trials and torments of a gossip widow with fortitude and forbearance.

Introduction

Tho' these be trifles light as straws,
They show what wind is blowing!

OLD BALLAD

Everybody reads gossip, except the Queen. Of course, not everybody (and certainly not Her Majesty) would actually admit to peeking at the gossip column in the morning paper. But, hand on heart, how many of us honestly deny ourselves that delicious daily draught of disclosure? Gossip, once just humble grapeshot in the journalistic arsenal, has gone nuclear; it *is* the power of the press. As Harold Macmillan found to his dismay, newspaper gossip can topple governments; nearly forty years on, Jeffrey Archer discovered it had lost none of its potency to make or break marriages and careers, to precipitate scandals and to hurl its victims headlong towards perdition. When Britain's philandering Foreign Secretary Robin Cook awoke to find embarrassing and intimate details of his failed marriage blabbed across the papers, Prime Minister Tony Blair warned that unless we all concentrated on life's serious issues, British politics risked descending into 'a sort of gossip column'[1] as it had in America. But already, in the sex-sodden suburbs of Blair's Britain, the red-top tabloids – and, increasingly, the so-called serious broadsheets – have promoted tittle-tattle about sex and celebrity to screaming headline news, the mother-lode of millions of lives.

Journalist Paul Johnson once likened gossip columns to pornography: 'People turn to them, despite their better judgement, knowing that they are yielding to a sleazy impulse.'[2] Of course, by no means is it a modern impulse. Our grandparents yielded, and their grandparents before them. Then, as now, the themes were sex and power, who's in, who's out, the private pulse of public figures. The stories themselves are measured out like small change, jingling, meaningless and inconsequential. 'I've no idea how many of them are true,' says novelist Wendy

1

Holden of her favourite gossip column, 'but it always makes me start my day with a smile.'[3] Gossip is great to enjoy, but tougher to tolerate. 'I spend my whole life being annoyed by it,' complains actress Dervla Kirwan.[4] Most of us relish the froth and gulp it down, bubbles, bits and all – the half-truths, exaggerations, inaccuracies and downright lies – knowing that, at bottom, it's harmless enough. Sometimes, though, newspaper gossip casts a shadow, portends something more serious, points towards something darker and it is then that we catch the breath of scandal.

Like gossip, scandal sells. If there seems to be more of it about than ever, it's because over two tumultuous centuries our newspapers and other media have redefined the line between public and private life. A more prolific, less respectful popular press has meant that we have all become more visible; media scrutiny now extends into areas of our lives previously hidden from view, and people with something to hide now find it much harder to shroud themselves in secrecy.

Oscar Wilde, who perhaps understandably came to detest keyhole journalists ('In old days men had the rack. Now they have the press'),[5] drew a somewhat jaded distinction between gossip and scandal. 'Gossip,' he declares in *Lady Windermere's Fan*, 'is charming. But scandal is gossip made tedious by morality.' It was not long before Wilde found himself at the centre of one of Victorian London's most infamous scandals, a newspaper frenzy that fed what he had despairingly identified, five years ahead of Britain's first popular daily newspaper, as the nation's 'gross popular appetite'. Now, as then, the gossip columnist's calling is not perceived as a noble one. The term has became part of our modern lexicon of invective; when young TV historian Dr Tristram Hunt rubbished Dr David Starkey's racy programmes on Britain's kings and queens, he derided them as 'the work of a gossip columnist' who reduced history to the level of *EastEnders*.[6] But for more than three centuries, these Jimmy O'Goblins of journalism have been ladling both scandal and gossip down the throats of a seemingly insatiable reading public. It has become addictive. Even the scrofulous and prolific Samuel Johnson, one of Britain's first celebrities and as much gossiped about as gossiping, confided: 'I love a little secret history.'[7] These days, it seems, we all do.

Between the two world wars of the twentieth century, newspaper gossip enjoyed a certain glossy glamour. 'Nowhere else in Europe is gossip-writing a highly paid and creditable profession,' grumbled the writer Aldous Huxley. It was a last hurrah for the old class system, already creaking but still largely venerated in the British press, whose 'inordinate snobbery' Huxley found staggering. 'In no other country do so many newspapers devote so large a proportion of their space to a chronicle of the activities of the merely rich or the merely ennobled,' he spluttered. Huxley believed that the aspiring English middle classes derived a deep satisfaction from gossip columns. 'They are prepared,' he wrote, 'to listen to the privileged class congratulating itself.'[8] Today it is not snobbery but a fixation with synthetic celebrity icons that drives and feeds the paragraphists. Substitute the glitterati for the rich, ennobled or privileged, and Huxley's darts still hit home today. The novelist Simon Raven sneered that gossip writers sought to explain the supposed sophistication and glamour of high society to what he derided as 'gutter mentalities', but that was forty years ago, soon after the Fleet Street gossip trade had been discredited as an unsavoury, almost sinister, avocation.

The truth is that we are all gossip-guzzlers now. In Britain it has been a popular obsession since newspapers first appeared 300 years ago. Various individuals have laid claim to have invented the modern gossip column. In America, it was a cross-eyed Scot in the 1830s, and in Britain, a century later, a Canadian megalomaniac press baron. Thanks to them, from harmless beginnings, whispering in the wings of eighteenth-century public discourse, gossip has become a sulphurous brew that has long since burst the confines of traditional gossip columns and cascades over the daily newspaper diet of millions. In fact, few modern papers will now even lay claim to having such old-style gossip columns at all. Many have long since been rebranded as 'diaries', each with its own take on what constitutes good gossip, and all aiming for (though by no means always hitting) Francis Wheen's bulls'-eye definition of a perfect diary item: interesting, if true.

Gossip has few raw ingredients: scandal, rumour, glamour and scurrility. The best newspaper gossip is shot through with (preferably illicit) sex, a dose of disclosure and a distinct whiff of danger. Gossip writers offer us a warts-and-all snapshot of the age, a pin to see the peep-show. The gossip explosion can be traced back at least a hundred years to the Fleet Street revolution that spawned the popular press. But its real origins are older still. The story of gossip rattles along from Regency London, where muckraking scandal sheets were hawked in the streets, to the tower blocks and shopping malls of today's celebrity-obsessed Britain. For gossip is no longer idle chit-chat. It is a fully fledged newspaper commodity. Readers look to the tabloids in particular to dish the dirt as well as (sometimes even instead of) providing the news of the day. Gossip is the salt in the stew, without which, declared the Anglo-American editor R. D. Blumenfeld, 'life would be dull and inexpressive'.[9] As it casts its daily spell, gossip performs a social function, too, drawing millions of ordinary readers within a magic circle of exclusiveness. Gossip celebrates our fascination with the seven deadly sins, and our disregard for any number of commandments.

Many top-rank writers and journalists have devilled for gossip. Sacheverell Sitwell, who wore the secret mantle of Atticus for the *Sunday Times* in the early 1950s, likened his weekly task to a truffle hunt. Ian Fleming, who managed to get Sitwell fired for being too whimsical and literary, believed that, to be a good columnist, you had to be able 'to write something out of nothing across the maximum space in the minimum time'.[10] That is certainly a gift, but what strikes the non-gossip writer, observing the daily round of chaff on the wind, particularly the tabloid variety, is that so much effort achieves so very little. It seems like an exercise in futility, endlessly repeated, a ritual crunch through ground glass, apparently glittering with promise but on close examination virtually worthless. Although Malcolm Muggeridge eventually found life on the *Evening Standard*'s gossip page good money for scarcely no work, at first he confessed to finding it 'revoltingly futile, and...exhausting.'[11] Noel Coward assailed Harold Nicolson for constantly emptying his accumulators upon 'futile energies'; Nicolson himself, working for Beaverbrook, felt humiliated; he yearned to be out of it and not to feel that his batteries were wasted 'playing the spillikins of the Press.'[12]

Throughout history, there is evidence of an appetite for news. But the word itself is a stripling, only some five hundred years old. The *New English Dictionary* finds that 'news' was 'in common use only after 1500' and the earliest example cited is dated 1423. There are other words to describe the same concept, of which 'tydings' appears to be the earliest. Gossip, however, is much older, dating back to Biblical times.

Cuneiform tablets dating from 1500 BC chronicle a Mesopotamian mayor's affair with a married woman. In the 1920s, London hostesses complained that 'sneak guests' were leaking material to the gossip columns, but there was a sneak-guest controversy in ancient Rome, when Cicero railed against those who 'sinned against the salt'. The Bible, too, brims with good gossip items. The story of Belshazzar's feast, complete with the writing on the wall, is full of gossipy touches. 'Actually,' says the American historian Robert Wernick, 'there is gossip and, in perhaps its most elevated form, there is history.'[13] And maybe the historian, for his part, is merely what Ambrose Bierce characterized as 'a broad-gauge gossip'.[14]

Newspaper and magazine gossip provides a running footnote to events, giving us the spicy, spiky facets that get overlooked or squeezed out of news stories. Gossip is concerned with indiscretions, infelicities, infidelities, failings and foibles, follies and fatuities. T. H. White, chronicling the age of scandal in the eighteenth century, believed it was useless to gossip about an unknown character and impossible to tell a good story about a person without foibles, 'for it is the foible which gives the story point.'[15] An inveterate name-dropper, the gossip writer makes out that he knows not only everyone worth knowing but everything about them, and is pleased to be their confidant. In fact, most gossip journalists know very little about the people they write about, and print exactly as much as the gossiped-of (or their PR people) are prepared to feed them.

In medieval times the market place served as a focus for the exchange of news and gossip. Travellers were eagerly pumped for the news they brought from their journeys, and often imparted their tidings, great and small, in return for hospitality. These scraps of information were traded verbally, and were inevitably embroidered, refracted and distorted before vanishing on the wind. Today's trifles are trapped on the page. The modern newspaper contains news of course (in greater or lesser quantities), but it contains much else besides: advertisements, pictures (now often in full colour), comment, features, strips, puzzles and gossip. In contrast, the newsbooks of Charles I's reign, apart from an occasional crude woodcut, were devoted exclusively to news, or what passed for news in the 1600s. Elements of our modern newspaper can be traced back even further, to the sixteenth century. The equivalent of our gossip pages would have covered the social comings and goings of the court, tame and bland subjects by modern standards. But in the sixteenth century no one dared trifle with the names of the great and the good; and unless the news about them was favourable and couched in tones of deference, no one would risk printing it. Nevertheless, the common people were agog to know about who was doing what to whom in court circles. News of murders, miracles, monsters, plagues, prodigies, calamities and catastrophes, wonders, witchcraft and the weather would also have appealed to the equivalent of today's tabloid-toter. The earliest journalists in Elizabethan England possessed all the instincts of the modern gossip-grubber, and wrote up a good story 'for that the thing is so rare & notable that it shoulde not be kept from the posteritye' (this was 1564). They had no compunction either about breaching anyone's privacy, 'because I know certainly, that not a few, for their better satisfaction, are very desirous to understand the truth thereof' declared the author of *The Late Commotion of certaine Papists in Herefordshire* in 1605. Such stories, with their racy appeal, identified a new audience. Gossip made readers of people who had little or no interest in laborious accounts of diplomatic manoeuvres and who could muster only the faintest appreciation of courtly verse.

Gossip gets a bad press. Gossiping by word of mouth – the sort of chit-chat that everyone exchanges every day – is frowned upon as idle and trivial. The problem is that most oral gossip is traded furtively; it is, after all, nothing more than talking about other people behind their backs. In print, things are different. With the post-Restoration dawn of an organized press, the swarf of gossip was wrought into a potentially mighty political weapon. The literary world of the late seventeenth and early eighteenth centuries witnessed a remarkable transformation in which the oral culture of the old world coalesced with the print culture of the new. The printed discourse of Defoe's *Review*, Swift's *Examiner* and the multitude of journals, mercuries and intelligencers was a product of a timeless oral culture in which news and opinion was transmitted primarily by talk and gossip in the street, the market place and coffee-house. In the increasingly competitive literary market place in which such pamphlets and journals appeared, the fledgling press had to entertain as well as to instruct. The more gossipy and scandalous the content, the better the sales. To modern eyes, the non-stop mud-slinging, rudeness and outrageous libels that pour from these public prints seem astonishing, but these were no more than the early flexions of journalistic entrepreneurs. The rich mix of political argument and gossipy, personal jibes and jests satisfied an emerging desire for news as entertainment.

The word 'gossip' originally referred to a godparent and mutated to mean any close friend. In the seventeenth century, as the *Oxford English Dictionary* reminds us, one of the main definitions of a gossip was 'a woman's female friends invited to be present at a birth'. Dr Johnson, in his dictionary of 1755, defines a gossip as 'one who runs about tattling like women at a lying-in'. But this definition, drawing attention to gossiping as a predominantly female activity, wasn't new, even in Johnson's day. The figure of Mrs Noah in the medieval Chester mystery plays some four hundred years earlier shows us why. But as the printed word overtook the oral tradition, writers like Mrs Manley reinforced the stereotype, observing the 'merry up-sitting of the gossips'[16] at a birth in her *New Atalantis* and casting the midwife Mrs Nightwork as an inveterate tattle-tale in the tradition of Shakespeare's Mistress Taleporter in *A Winter's Tale*.

Scandal, gossip's flapping cloak, strikes a darker chord. What draws us is the sight of the hypocrite standing naked before us in the ruins of his reputation, and the reek of moral or social outrage in our nostrils. These are powerful journalistic engines. Revving them hard brings the readers flocking, the Pharisees holding aloft their gold coins of probity. But our Sabbath-breaking scandals, served in a stew of sex, sport and (increasingly) snort, have their roots deep in tradition, too. The *News of the World*, the Sunday scandal sheet with the biggest circulation on the planet, first appeared in the year of Dickens's *A Christmas Carol*. Its Augustan age spanned women's emancipation and the abolition of the hangman; one of its vintage episodes came in the mid-1880s with the jaw-dropping Campbell divorce case.

Like so many 'society' scandals, the Campbell affair began as a gossip paragraph. The Hon. Mark Bouverie, spotting Lady Colin Campbell in the waiting room at Fenchurch Street Station and, subsequently, with a man who was not her husband on the platform at Purfleet, spread the rumour that she had eloped with Lord Blandford, randy son of the Duke of Marlborough. The gossip columnist for a widely read society newspaper promptly printed the rumour as fact. From this tiny seed sprouted a monstrous growth, and in 1886 Lady Colin found herself at the centre of Britain's longest and most sensational divorce trial. One newspaper damned it as 'a flood of filth', another as 'immorality and obscenity without parallel'. The story had drama, mystery, suspense, love, sex, jealousy, revenge, humour and pathos. As the *News of the World* later famously exclaimed: 'All Human Life Is There', and it proceeded to anatomize exactly what it was and where, in shameless, not to say gynaecological, detail.

The case tainted almost everyone connected with it, but Lady Colin herself, who had been exposed as a glamorous nymphomaniac, derived from it a dangerous notoriety that appealed to the makers of the nascent popular press. When T. P. O'Connor MP revived a daily gossip column in the downmarket London newspaper, the *Star,* at the end of the nineteenth century, even the cerebral George Bernard Shaw nodded approval. 'T. P. rightly maintained,' Shaw noted, 'that washerwomen are as keen on society gossip as duchesses.'[17] It was O'Connor's master stroke to appoint his own (attractive American) wife as gossip editor, launching her first column with the arresting line: 'Lady Colin Campbell is the only woman in London who has her feet manicured.'[18]

Is there some theory that helps define the unstoppable growth of gossip? It is no less cruel than ever it was, but thanks to twitchier lawyers it is less personally vindictive and acrimonious. It is, however, no less intrusive: gossip-grubbers have pried, spied, probed, gaped and goggled for as long as there have been newspapers in print and curious people to read them, while the rest of us shrieked for stronger privacy laws. But the nature of gossip has changed; it has become more prurient (with sex no longer reportable from the divorce court, it dived headlong into the gossip columns just as the 1920s started to roar) and, with the death of deference, it is a good deal cheekier. Gossip has altered the nature of fame, connived indiscriminately at the glorification and destruction of people who deserved neither, and helped inflate a quite grotesquely distended cult and culture of celebrity. While busily putting down the mighty from their seats, postmodern gossip-gleaners have turned instead to fawn on the new phoney gods, the dreary, bleary nonentities of popdom and soapdom, 'buffoons' (as one indignant but disillusioned gossip groupie once put it) 'writing about baboons.'[19] But perhaps the biggest seismic shift in twentieth-century newspaper gossip is that, by the century's end, almost all of it was sealed with the imprimatur of legitimate journalism.

We can try to blame the Americans. Historians of Hollywood have traced our fascination with celebrity to the emergence of the film industry nearly a hundred years ago, which created, in the words of critic Richard Schickel, 'a lust for intimate knowledge'[20] of its stars and produced gorgons of gossip like Louella Parsons and Hedda Hopper to satisfy it. But it was only a generation ago, in the mid-1970s, that the media seriously began to promote celebrities and print tittle-tattle about them, following the yellow-brick road to Dumbed-Downsville. News of the glitterati now spills across the serious broadsheet press on both sides of the Atlantic, with the entire British contingent, for example, clearing their front pages (and many more inside) for the death of a Beatle[21] on a scale that, only a few years ago, would have been reserved for the Second Coming. In a new world of tabloid TV, day-long talk shows and proliferating soaps, celebrity gossip has become mainstream. We find ourselves gawping up at these stars, not just to drown out our own lives of quiet desperation, but because we are drawn by the unspoken, flickering hope that, like us, they might turn out to have feet of clay. Aaron Spelling, who created the first truly glamorous sex-and-shopping TV soaps in *Dallas* and *Dynasty*, put his finger on why we're all hooked: 'It's rich people having problems,' he explained, 'that money can't solve.'[22] Even politics, covered for years with a series of dull thuds by the sobersides of the Washington press corps, now gets the celebrity treatment, with the sizzle of sex and scandal the defining soundtrack to the Clinton presidency.

But it's happening in Britain too, where even the 'respectable' newspapers have fallen into the fervent embrace of the cult of celebrity. On the rim of the twenty-first century, gossip swamps our dailies with a motley mixture of trivia, telly, sex, crime, lottery, sport and a salivating chronicle of the fortunes and misfortunes of the royal, rich and famous. Real news, in the sense of events in context, is marginalized, and is often not covered at all by the tabloids. On 11 September 2001, not even the crack of Armageddon could stem the tide. Much hand-wringing accompanied the hasty and, it transpired, premature obituaries for modern celebrity culture. For a few tense moments, it seemed the landscape had changed. Had the appetite for fame evaporated? Had we heard the last of Posh and Becks? The world held its breath. In New York, within sight of Ground Zero, *Vanity Fair* editor Graydon Carter was proclaiming the 'death of irony' and promising 'a seismic shift in what we are doing'.[23] In Britain, irony was not dead, only sleeping. Within days, the trickle started. Was Liz Hurley pregnant? Two weeks later, the trickle had become a spate. Who was the baby's father? And as humankind tottered on the brink of the abyss, the *Sun* got down to some good corn-fed gossip, skittling all this to one side and soaring to the occasion with its front-page splash: QUEEN HAS RUBBER DUCK IN HER BATH. A classic diary paragraph, blown up (like the duck's crown) out of all proportion. But interesting. If true. Gossip was back, unchastened and by royal appointment.

Royal update: the telephone rings. Apparently, my usually reliable sources were wrong about the Queen not caring for gossip. According to the 'Peterborough' column in the *Daily Telegraph*, she loves to read tittle-tattle. Back in the 1970s, she discovered that the then Prime Minister, Harold Wilson, also liked to keep up with the latest scuttle-butt. On learning that Wilson had beaten her to the latest twist in a long-forgotten sex scandal that was splashed all over the *Evening Standard*, the sovereign seemed distinctly miffed and complained to her private secretary: 'Why didn't I have that edition?'[25]

1

Puffs, Parsons and Paragraphs

The harlots of Piccadilly hitched up their petticoats and stepped aside. Jostling pickpockets, hearing the commotion, were momentarily distracted, and carriage horses shied on the clattering cobbles. From his drawing room in Arlington Street, Horace Walpole was astonished to hear the sound of drums and trumpets; hurrying to his window he saw a procession carving a path through the crowd. At first, he thought it was a press-gang raising soldiery for the war in the American colonies, for this was the late autumn of 1776. It was a war of sorts, but Walpole noticed that the marchers were smartly groomed, 'dressed expensively, like Hussars, in yellow habits with blue waistcoats and breeches'. These were no warriors, but a hired band of street performers wearing masks, advancing to the beat of martial music and brandishing not muskets but coloured streamers and handbills, which they pressed into the hands of the gaping onlookers. On their high caps, picked out in braid, the words 'Morning Post' glinted in the watery sunshine. At the head of the procession, Walpole recognized the pugnacious and defiant figure of the young Revd Henry Bate, the editor of that notorious scandal sheet and renowned throughout London as 'the fighting parson'.

Walpole gazed down on 'this mummery' and despaired. 'What a country!' he twittered in one of his gossiping news-of-the-day letters. 'Is there any sense, integrity, decency, taste left? A solemn and expensive masquerade in defence of daily scandal against women of the first rank.'[1] Walpole had heard that the *Morning Post* had a rival, the new, but identically named, *Morning Post*, so packed with even more scandalous matter, he noted, that it 'exceeds all the outrageous Billingsgate that was ever heard of.'[2] The opening shots had been fired in London's first – and highly entertaining – circulation war. The battleground was the paragraphing trade, the inky ancestor of newspaper gossip.

Daring to be different, the original *Morning Post* was roughly the size of a modern tabloid, cheaper and smaller than the other journals hawked on the street corners of Georgian London by a raggle-taggle army of bugle-blowing postboys. Advertisements dominated the content; one in the first number in 1772 offered for sale a register of addresses of the strumpets of Piccadilly; another (accordingly) offered 'the famous Patent Ointment for the Itch'. For his morning threepence, the eager reader would also be regaled with a few items of foreign intelligence, news of the court, church appointments, borough elections, accounts of highway robbery, arrivals at the Bath spa, sporting intelligence and even some uplifting poetry. But what really sold the paper were its scandalous paragraphs, teeming with details of people's personal lives.

> The deserted state of the metropolis, at this season, is evident from the present solitary appearance of the Mall in St James's Park and forsaken walks of Kensington Garden, tho' both were wont to be enlivened by the perambulations of numberless beauties, neither of them is now frequented by scarce a single belle...
>
> A divorce, it is said, will take place early the next sessions, between a certain Irish Earl and his Countess, who are lately separated; in which case, the Lady, it is expected, will immediately espouse her most adorable gallant![3]

Although Henry Bate conducted this daily discourse with parsonical fastidiousness, he knew the risks and regarded the occasional challenge to a duel to the death as an irritating occupational hazard. Fortunately, Bate was a skilful duellist and was also handy with his fists; the gossip that he dished up with one he was well able to avenge with the other. While still in his twenties, Bate had abandoned his late father's rectory in Essex for the fleshpots of London and the charms of the *demi-monde*. His portrait shows a handsome Georgian squire puffing up his ruffled chest while his dog nuzzles him adoringly. Seeing the picture exhibited at the Royal Academy, one critic, possibly a target of a *Morning Post* squib, complained: 'The man wants execution and the dog wants hanging.'[4] But the diarist William Hickey (the original one) was impressed by Bate, 'a man of abilities and honourable sentiments, his person remarkably good'.[5]

The 'new and most infamous' paper, which had outraged Walpole and galvanized Bate into an extravagant show of journalistic promotion, had been launched early in November 1776 in a fit of pique. For some reason, the publisher of the original *Morning Post*, George Corral, had been summarily dismissed. He had sought revenge by rallying the printer, Edward Cox, to his cause and bringing out the upstart title, with the aim of confusing readers and denting sales. The result was such a thorough copy of the original 'as to deceive all but the very elect', and Bate swiftly persuaded the Lord Chancellor to grant an injunction banning the impostor. But Corral and Cox laughed at the law. They immediately renamed their paper the *New Morning Post* and continued to publish their counterfeit. Corral and Cox accused Bate of belonging to a gang of 'reverend parsonical banditti', for while he was not the only cleric to be associated with the newspaper trade, he was certainly the most belligerent. Bate's four-year editorship had been marked by several perilous encounters with the aggrieved and outraged victims of his scurrilous paragraphs. One of them, a swaggering man-about-town, Captain Croftes, challenged Bate to a duel. The paragraphing parson accepted, but while arrangements were being made, Fitzgerald, one of Croftes's cronies, insisted that Bate should first give satisfaction to 'his friend, Captain Miles'. Accordingly, Bate bared his fists and the pair set to for some twenty minutes, finally convincing the bellowing crowd (and particularly 'Captain Miles') that Bate, though the smaller man, was the better one. Bate claimed he never received one blow that he felt. 'Captain Miles', quickly unmasked as Fitzgerald's servant and a hired bully, was sent home in a coach, 'with his face a perfect jelly'. 'You, sir,' cried the humiliated Fitzgerald, 'thrive by scandal and live upon defamation.'[6] He was not wrong.

> The Duchess of D———, it seems, is fresh *moulted*, and sports now a higher topple crown than ever; – her nodding plumes and lappets, when she put her head out of her box at the opera house on Thursday evening last, excited universal pleasantry through the galleries and set all the risible muscles in the house at work; yesterday, such are the attractions of beauty, that her angelic features could not be concealed, even under all these paraphernalia of fashionable lumber; for not a soul that contemned her extravagant taste, but spoke at the same time in raptures of her person, and charms.[7]

The Revd Henry Bate was never one to choose his words with care. His savage onslaughts in the *Morning Post* prompted titters in club and coffee-house, but also put him in peril of his life. In 1777, a disreputable buck by the name of Captain George Robertson Stoney challenged Bate over a paragraph in the *Morning Post* reflecting on Lady Strathmore, a merry widow being courted by Captain Stoney. According to one report, Bate had failed to convince him that the offending paragraph had appeared without his knowledge. Stoney insisted on 'the satisfaction of a gentleman or the discovery of the author', an early, and certainly acute, example of a journalist protecting his sources. When the two men met by accident in the Strand a few days later, 'they adjourned to the Adelphi tavern, called for a room, shut the door, and being furnished with pistols, discharged them at each other without effect.' They then drew swords, each wounding the other, with Bate bending his blade on Stoney's breastbone in the process. While Bate tried to straighten the blade with his foot, the police broke the door down, 'or the death of one of the parties would most certainly have been the issue'.[8]

When Bate took the editor's chair in 1772, his trick was to concentrate the paper's news coverage on personalities, people 'conspicuous for folly, vice or some prominent absurdity'. For Bate was a showman, and what he injected into the *Morning Post* was entertainment. His weapon was society gossip, amusing, witty, often malicious. It played well with the reading public and the paper flourished as a result. The *Post* began selling 'puffs', because the owners realized the market value of damaging tittle-tattle, and by 1780 there was scarcely a paragraph in the paper that had not been paid for by someone. Furthermore, the *Post* profited from suppression fees, either to squash some embarrassing item altogether or to contradict one that had already been published.

Bate propelled the *Morning Post* to unprecedented success. Not only was he a dab hand at 'lively writing' but, as an inveterate diner-out and networker, he had the inside track on social gossip. He joined the Beefsteak Club where he met and cultivated Sheridan, Garrick and the other great wits of the day. He also wangled an entrée into the fashionable circles of Carlton House, where the Prince of Wales's cronies and sycophants fed him juicy morsels for his paper. 'There was a sportive severity in his writings,' declared one admirer, 'which gave a new character to the public press.'[9] Dr Johnson admired Bate's courage. 'We have more respect for a man who robs boldly on the highway,' he told Boswell, 'than for a fellow who jumps out of a ditch and knocks you down behind your back.'[10]

After Bate married in 1780, he decided to leave the *Morning Post* and to start a derivative rival, the *Morning Herald*. He reverted briefly to the role of showman, sending squads of boys in scarlet jackets and gold lace on their hats swarming through the streets of London, carrying placards promoting his new title. While promising that the *Herald* would be free of 'obscene trash and low invective', Bate swiftly introduced rebarbative doses of both and ran the paper along similar lines to the *Post*, careless of what he printed or wrote, in one observer's view, 'so long as it raised a laugh or sold a copy'.[11] But the fighting parson had exhausted his luck as a scurrilous paragraphist. The following year, he was jailed for twelve months for a libel on the Duke of Richmond, which had appeared (Bate claimed without his knowledge) in the *Morning Post* while he was still editor. 'Nothing could be more disgraceful,' shrilled Horace Walpole, hastening to record Bate's downfall in his journal. 'He was the worst of all the scandalous libellers that had appeared both on private persons as well as public.'[12] Bate emerged jauntily from prison to leave journalism and rejoin the Church. Riches and honours (he was created a baronet when he was nearly seventy) were heaped upon him, and he lived into his seventy-ninth year. Fighting Fitzgerald died an ignominious death, being hanged at Castlebar in 1786.

The chance episode in which their paths crossed was enough to establish Bate as a journalist of national repute. Although his reputation was founded on thousands of scurrilous paragraphs, he had single-handedly changed the character of the public press, transforming the 'dull, heavy and insipid' papers of Georgian London into something much more combative, lively and quintessentially English. By currying favour with the Prince of Wales, Bate had unprecedented access to the charmed royal circle, to the spluttering exasperation of his rivals. Macaulay, who had himself written for the *Post* as a young man, was appalled, considered Bate and his grubbing ilk to be beyond the social pale, and found it 'almost incredible... that any human being should ever have stooped to fight with a writer in the *Morning Post*'.[13] Bate may have crammed his unregenerate paper with buffoonery and scurrility; it may have reeked of scandal and verged on the obscene; but he did no more than anticipate modern tabloid taste by 200 years.

Grub Street was where gossip began to gurgle. As early as the 1690s, hack writers, the forerunners of modern journalists, were able to make a living by their labours. There was the 'jovial, brutal, vulgar, graphic' Ned Ward, whose columns in the *London Spy*, exposing 'the Vanities and Vices of the Town' between November 1698 and May 1700, fizzed with witty observations of Restoration London. He offered a sense of the pulsing low life of the capital as well as entertaining (and often coarse) accounts of the social trivia of the day. His description of a night in a sailors' tavern in Billingsgate glistens with gossipy reportage as a group of coarse fisherwomen, each with a 'Nipperkin of warm Ale and Brandy', exchange ribaldries with some seamen who come piling in, 'short Pipes in their Mouths, Oaken Truncheons in their Hands, Thrum Caps upon their Heads and Canvas Trunks upon their Arses'.[14] Between 1640 and 1660, before Ward's time, printed pamphlets had flourished but few newspapers. News was spread by newsletters, written by hand in London and sent to subscribers in the country who circulated them among their neighbours. During the Civil War, both Royalists and Roundheads recruited writers in the propaganda war. These proto-journalists were the first to define a role as opinion formers, in response to the demands of their readers. The crisis called for argument armoured with ridicule and abuse in a campaign of blood and thunder. Printed invective coursed like lifeblood. The stakes were high; criticizing the government might be construed as treason, a capital offence. News-sheets, like books and pamphlets, were rigorously censored.

These news-sheets were sold in the streets by characters known as Mercury women. Such a woman makes a brief appearance in Ben Jonson's play *The Staple of News*, asking for 'a groat's worth of any News, I care not what, to carry down this Saturday to our vicar'.[15] The Roundheads hired female spies to pose as Mercury women, infiltrating Royalist ranks, ostensibly to gather material for newsbooks but reporting the gossip so gleaned to Cromwell's henchmen. Those caught in the act were taken to the House of Correction and whipped. The most notorious was a fat old woman known as 'Parliament Joan', 'peeper' and 'whisperer' to the Council of State. 'O the mysterie of a little inck and paper,' one commentator jeered at these bustling women news-gatherers and their ceaseless scribblings. 'No rest day or night with these cursed caterpillars, *Perfect Passages, Weekly Occurrences, Scout, Spye, Politicus, Diurnal,* the Devil and his dam.'[16]

In Stuart London, the first recognizable British newspapers quickly grasped the public's appetite for scandal, despite official attempts to ban the printing of 'lewd and naughty matters' of the kind that would engross today's audience of *News of the World* readers. In 1681, the Tory newspaper *Loyal Protestant and True Domestick Intelligencer* reported a court case featuring an unusual *ménage à trois:* a mistress, her maid and a 'great Mastiffe'. The mistress had been observed 'Beast-like upon all Four, with her Posteriors Bare, and the Dog effectively performing'. According to the paper, the lady's explanation was that she had got drunk at a fair 'and suffered three or four men to enjoy her, by which Coition she got the Venerial Disease, and supposing with herself that Copulation would help her Malady, and not having the Convenience of a Man, she betook herself to this crime for Remedy.'

The following year, the same paper, ever-anxious to embarrass Puritans, made straight the way of our modern wayward vicars with the tale of the Dissenting minister who 'laid with two Wenches ten Nights at a Guinny a Night: that he exercised one while the other raised his Inclinations'.[17]

Thomas Nashe, an elusive Elizabethan lowlife and the first English journalist, would have known a few fornicating ministers. Dead at only thirty-three, Nashe spent the last ten years of his troubled life in the toils of Grub Street, struggling (and finally failing) to keep afloat. Nashe raked his world of hack-writers, printers, court hangers-on, spies and informers for gossip and intrigue. Shot through with a pouncing bohemian wit, Nashe's scurrilous pamphlets were a kind of *Private Eye* of the 1590s. *Pierce Penilesse,* his best-seller of 1592, was bursting with topical social comment as Nashe cast a roving eye around Tudor London and in a series of vivid cameos caught the follies, affectations and seamy pleasures of the capital. C. S. Lewis hailed him as 'undoubtedly the greatest of the Elizabethan pamphleteers, the perfect literary showman, the juggler with words who can keep a crowd spell-bound by sheer virtuosity'.[18] *Pierce Penilesse* was the first example of a journalist writing about real contemporary figures in a thinly veiled way. Nashe's catchy title attracted readers, and the paper became the most popular of Nashe's works.

With all its reckless jumble, the pamphlet wears the jaunty red nose of the modern tabloid. So Nashe writes of 'old hacksters . . . i n the wrinckles of whose face ye may hide false dice and play at cherrypit in the dint of their cheekes', and of younger women with lips 'as lavishly red as if they used to kisse an okerman every morning'.[19] He was totally over the top, mounting the first public display of journalistic fireworks, flinging new comic terms, monstrous caricatures and preposterous overstatements at his bemused readers. As in today's tabloids, the effect was extravagant and colloquial, but in Nashe's time it was a mail-fisted sensation.

Nashe, an unprepossessing, scrawny, snaggle-toothed gentleman-ragamuffin, prowled the precincts of St Paul's where London writers held court, picking up gossip of deals and assignations. Those precincts, attracting crowds of milling lowlifes, was clearly a place 'to learne some news', and Nashe recognized that such disreputable company was a rich source of material. With his journalistic antennae twisting this way and that, the result is that his writings smack of topical, cock-snooking reportage. Here is the Elizabethan pamphleteer *par excellence*, says his biographer Charles Nicholl, not because he writes *about* Elizabethan life, but because he writes from *inside* it.

Nashe's pages boil over with grotesque, wire-drawn images: 'an old straddling Usurer' with a 'huge woorme-eaten nose, like a cluster of grapes hanging downewardes'; a 'burliboand' Danish soldier with 'a flaberkin face, like one of the foure winds, and cheeks that sag like a woman's dugs over his chin-bone'; a gaggle of sixpenny strumpets and their 'cut-purse paramours'. This is high-voltage journalism from the age of doublet and hose, up close and personal. Flitting on the fringes of the court, Nashe offers glimpses of the Elizabethan great and good, the nobility who were the celebrities of their day and with whom Nashe rubbed shoulders. 'Ingeniously veiled satire on the great and powerful is one of his specialities,' reports Nicholl, 'libels none the less appetizing because based on some tittle-tattle he picked up from the Clerk of the

Kitchens or over dice with the "dapper Mounsier Pages of the Court".'[20] And yet Nashe took a jaundiced view of his fellow hacks, inveighing in *Pierce Penilesse* against 'such goose gyblets or stinking garbadge, as the ly[in]gs of newsmongers', the gossipings of such as 'a base Inck-dropper' or 'scurvie peddling Poet' in their 'dunghill papers'.[21]

But if Nashe with his muckraking invective was pre-eminent among 'the riffe-raffe of the scribling rascality',[22] he did not live to see the birth of the modern newspaper. Pamphlets of news, carrying word of events such as fire, frost and murders, were superseded in the 1620s by the first English-language corantos, single broadside sheets carrying reports of foreign news. Because of their format and regular appearance, these are regarded as the early forerunners of English newspapers. The idea was soon adapted for the dissemination of domestic news in quarto newsbooks. We know a lot about this style of newsmongering because Ben Jonson parodied the trade in 1626 in his comedy, *The Staple of News*. As a young actor, Jonson had counted Nashe among his acquaintances, but had since moved on to the elevated circles of the court, where his intimates, 'sealed of the tribe of Ben', included poets, writers and various men-about-town. Jonson's play ridicules the profession of newsgathering and the growing public appetite for news, this 'hungering and thirsting after published pamphlets of news, set out every Saturday, but made at home, and no syllable of truth in them; than which there cannot be a greater disease in nature, nor scorn upon the time'.[23] The main theme of Jonson's play anticipated the gossip-grubbing antics of twentieth-century Fleet Street by 300 years, for Jacobean journalists were the first to twig the idea of slipping paragraphs into the public prints that advertised smart restaurants and the smart nobodies using them.

The 'Staple of News' in Jonson's play was an imaginary news-agency, employing scouts to collect rare and startling intelligence from all parts of London. 'Sirs,' shouts the character Shunwell to the gossip scouts milling around the supper tables at the Apollo Rooms, 'you must get of this news, to store your office – who dines and sups in the town; where and with whom; it will be beneficial; when you are stored, and as we like our fare, we shall reward you.'[24] Jonson was fashioning a witty and topical satire on the prevalent London interest in newspapers, but his barbs on the business of 'who dines and sups ... where and with whom' would have hit home more than three centuries later. There is a modern ring, too, to the observation of a different character when he talks of the gossip service and the money sloshing within it as: 'A mighty thing; they talk six thousand a year.'[25]

The news-sheets satirized by Jonson were edited and written by young men in and around Paternoster Row, close to St Paul's; they would then be snapped up by news-boys, washerwomen and linkmen in the cathedral churchyard and hawked in the taverns and coffee-houses of Fleet Street, not yet the street of ink but the favourite resort of gentlemen of wit. In the closing years of the seventeenth century, a growing desire to know what was happening in 'the Establishment' took root and steadily grew. The newspapers began to chronicle more and more appointments and promotions – political, Church, military and civil. From this, explains the Restoration historian James Sutherland,

> it was an inevitable step to entertaining readers with intimate details about persons of quality; who had been married or was about to be married, who had got a son or a daughter, and who had died; what peer was travelling abroad, or visiting Bath or Tunbridge Wells in the summer, which peer had fought a duel with which gentleman, who had dined with the Lord Mayor or the sheriffs, or at one of the Inns of Court... The social column was well on its way to being born.'[26]

In London's inky trade, the reign of Queen Anne witnessed a grand awakening. The collapse of the Licensing Act in 1695 meant the end of censorship. Independent newspapers could flourish legally and their numbers grew so quickly that there were complaints of a glut. 'So many news papers (or so called) are daily published,' noted one newcomer to the capital in 1696, 'that it would seem needless to trouble the world with more.'[27] But the citizens were hungry for news, for discourse, for talking points and for novelty, and in 1704 Daniel Defoe, who went on to create Robinson Crusoe, seized the moment and devised the world's first informal, chatty newspaper column.

Unprepossessing in appearance (hooked-nosed with a dark, warty complexion), and having a self-confessed 'unhappy love of the bottle' as well as an irregular love life, Defoe was every inch a journalist. When not ranging across the kingdom on horseback as a spy, he was usually to be found in one of his favourite London coffee-houses, snatching at specks of information and intelligence. A natty, spare figure in his 'Beau Habit', long tasselled wig, iron-bound hat and blue cloak, a diamond sparkling on his little finger, he would observe 'some Going, some Coming, some Scribbling, some Talking, some Drinking, others Jangling, and the whole Room stinking of Tobacco'.[28] Twice clamped in the public pillory for publishing libels, Defoe, bankrupt businessman and pamphleteer, launched his *Review* as a means of making money on his release from Newgate Prison, where he had been incarcerated for sedition.

The *Review* aimed to explain what was happening in Europe, but Defoe added an 'entertaining part' in which he discoursed on the lighter side of life. 'After our serious matters are over,' he explained, 'we shall at the end of every paper present you with a little diversion, as anything occurs to make the world merry; and whether friend or foe, one party or another, if anything happens so scandalous as to require an open reproof, the world will meet with it there.'[29] Defoe's readers were largely middle class, together with tradesmen and Dissenters like Defoe himself. His targets were the *haute bourgeoisie* of the clergy and the professional idlers he met in the bawling coffee-houses of London. The *Review*'s circulation was small and most weeks could be reckoned only in hundreds. It was a political paper, 'Purg'd from the Errors and Partiality of News-Writers and Petty-Statesmen of all sides', 'a weekly history of Nonsense, Impertinence, Vice and Debauchery'.[30] In the second issue, Defoe introduced a new feature, a prototype gossip column, headed 'Advice from the Scandalous Club'.

Here he dispensed advice on morals and manners in a style mixing rectitude with ribaldry, ranging through the field of human frailty to cover such vices as duelling, swearing, and the lustful and drunken escapades of the clergy, particularly High Churchmen. Early numbers scrutinized the press, and in particular 'our News-Writers and daily complaints being still made of their Scandalous Mistakes, Ignorances and Contradictions'.[31] Defoe pioneered the technique of calumny by camouflage, identifying his victims but keeping their names secret:

One JP, a Reformer, brought a Drayman before the Club, for that he had scandalously been at Work with his Dray and Horses at the Vulgar

21

Employment of Carrying and Starting Strong Beer, on the 30th of January last, contrary to My Lord Mayor's Express Order for the Observation of that day.

The Fellow being taken in the Fact, had little to say as to that, but saucily told them they had nothing to do with him, for he belong'd to Sir J—n P—s.

The Society, in Respect to the Ruler of the People, presently dismist the Man, and Order'd him to let his Master know how Civilly they had used him.

But being at the same time Inform'd that several other Men had been severely Punish'd for Working on the same day; they made it be Noted down in their Book of Remembrance, How Beneficial a thing it is, to be a L—d M—'s Drayman.[32]

Defoe took the idea of a column of miscellany from a journal called the *Athenian Mercury*, published during the 1690s by an esoteric literary club, the Athenian Society, founded by the eccentric publisher John Dunton.[33] The *Mercury's* masthead promised erudite answers to 'all the most nice and curious questions propos'd by the ingenious'. The questions were, indeed, curious. 'Where had Adam and Eve their needles and thread to sew their fig-leaves together?' 'What sex was Balaam's ass of?' As a member of Dunton's Athenians, Defoe was a regular contributor to the *Mercury's* columns, impressing Dunton himself with such versatility as a journalist as to draw from him the accolade of 'a man of good parts, and very clear sense [who] can say what he please upon any subject'.[34]

Single-handedly, Defoe was chronicling the stirrings of a cultural revolution in England, a seismic power shift in which the Whigs, mainly middle class and commercial, were seizing the ascendancy from the upper class and the landed Tories. Defoe was among the first to see the old world through a pair of sharp modern eyes, the first, as the historian G. M. Trevelyan acknowledged, to have perfected the art of the reporter.[35] As a journalist observing the scene, Defoe was the perfect embodiment of the changing, seething society of the time, no 'base Inck-dropper' or 'riffe-raffe of the scribling rascality', but a new creature altogether, a columnist and commentator whose instincts and reflexes were essentially middle class. He had his pretentions, hankering always to be thought of as a gentleman, changing his name from Foe to the more aristocratic De Foe, and prefacing his collected writings in 1703 with a formal portrait complete with coat of arms and personal motto. As one of Defoe's biographers observed, 'Mr Review consciously sought to elevate himself in status; he was not to be dismissed as just another venal Grub Street journalist but respected as a gentleman.'[36]

The *Review* was a mouthpiece for the moderate Tory views of Defoe's patron, Robert Harley, Earl of Oxford and Speaker of the House of Commons. Its great rival was the *Observator*, appearing twice weekly since 1702, which championed the radical Whig point of view. The *Observator's* editor, John Tutchin, bore a grudge against Defoe, and, like a number of other journalists, ridiculed and attacked his claims to gentility. Their public exchanges, traded in their respective newspapers, are a pre-echo of the banter between tabloid newspaper diarists of today, the Dempsters and Bensons of the *Mail* and *Express*, twitting their 'so-called rivals'. Tutchin and another London editor, Joseph Browne, mocked Defoe in print in the 'most scurrilous manner', accusing him of lack of scholarship and pointing to his humble origins in trade, dismissing him derisively as no more than a 'mechanic' and 'a hosier's apprentice'. Defoe rallied to his own defence in the columns of the *Review*, assuring his readers that while he did indeed lack a classical education, he had 'more learning' because he had 'more manners'. Once, Defoe's vexation got the better of him, and he laid into Tutchin:

> As to his ill language, his profess'd resolution to expose me, his abusive treatment of me with his tongue, *for he dare not do it with his hands*, I'll finish all my replies of this sort with telling him a story; and if this won't do, I'll tell him another.
>
> Two dogs liv'd near one another, a Black and a Brown. Black, *that was more addicted to bark than to bite*, would always run baying and barking after Brown, whenever he went by; Brown took no notice of a long time, but being once more than usually teaz'd and provok'd, he gravely turn'd about, smells at Black, and finding him of a currish cowardly breed, and not worth his notice, very soberly and unconcerned, he holds up one leg, pisses upon him, and so goes on about his business. *And so do I.*[37]

Jonathan Swift also inveighed against Defoe, branding him one of those 'weekly libellers', a put-down suggesting that such scribblers and scribblings are beneath his contempt ('I know it may be reckoned a weakness to say anything of such trifles as are below a serious man's notice').[38] Like Defoe, Swift was also on the payroll of Robert Harley and the Tory ministry, but there was an important social difference: Swift served Harley as a pamphleteer and considered himself his social equal, while Defoe, with 'the bad standing of a pilloried journalist',[39] had to swallow his pride and content himself with the status of a tradesman at Harley's back door. In 1710, Defoe's resentment boiled over. In his paper, the *Examiner*, Swift rounded on both Defoe and Tutchin, 'two stupid, illiterate scribblers, both of them fanatics by profession; I mean the *Review* and *Observator*'. He loftily swept aside the *Review* as being 'of a level with great numbers among the lowest part of mankind', acknowledging, however, that Defoe had met with some success in reaching a large, if unrefined, readership.[40] Defoe's initial response in the *Review* was brief and cutting: 'If, Sir, you have so much learning, how came you to have so little manners?'[41] In subsequent issues, Defoe expanded his attack on Swift, excoriating Mr Examiner for '[m]uch powder, I say, much noise, much ill-language; much call-names, no argument'.[42]

The *Review* eventually became the best-selling periodical in London, and was read mainly by ordinary, uneducated people, the masses dismissed by Swift as 'great numbers of the lowest part of mankind'. Another literary figure, Charles Leslie of the High Tory paper, *Rehearsal*, observed that while most of them could not read, they would eagerly gather in the streets around someone who could, and who would read aloud from the latest copy of the 'bilingsgate' *Review*. A correspondent to another paper complained of 'how greedily the ignorant and inconsiderate crowd swallow [Defoe's] crude and indigent notions',[43] while Leslie, in desperation, advised Tory journalists to take a leaf out of the *Review*, the *Observator* 'and the rest of the scandalous club' by dumbing down their own writing so 'as to be intelligible to the meanest capacity … in small papers that may come out weekly and be dispersed in coffee-houses where the other pernicious papers spread their poison'. Defoe had spotted a mass market, which he worked assiduously to satisfy, but although his 'Advice from the Scandalous Club' was aimed at less-educated readers, it seems that the *Review* was devoured, too, by the intellectual elite. '[N]otwithstanding their mealy modesty,' lamented the Tory Charles Leslie, 'these dirty papers go on.'[44]

Defoe invented journalistic dodges still in use today. In his articles on the war in north-east Europe, Defoe always referred to Sweden as S—, because (as his readers knew) he had been threatened with imprisonment by the Swedish envoy in London for writing about the Swedish king. Defoe also devised the formula of circumlocution, as in the libel-proof phrases that used to litter *Private Eye* such as 'not a million miles from' and 'not unadjacent to'. Thus, in a *Review* paragraph in June 1707, Defoe writes of 'a Church of England parson not above 150 miles from Exeter', when, as everyone realized, he meant an Exeter parson.

He wrote entertainingly about life's vicissitudes. Occasionally, he would allow himself a short dissertation on social habits of the day, such as smoking among young people:

> Every body that Smoaks (secretly intimating that 'tis no Virtue at least) tells you he would not do it, but that he has some imperfection, either in his Eyes, or Teeth, or somewhere else; and what occasion is there of an Excuse, if there be no Fault committed? Truly, We are apt to believe, most that use it, have some Weakness; the Young in their Judgments, the Old in their Natures; but those particularly who take it for Diversion; some use it this hot Weather, because they find (as they say) a coolness by it; they can't endure the sight of a Chimney in a Coffee-House, but the Skreens are drawn before them, yet they will have both Fire and Smoak at their very Mouths, and this to cool them; but if they think so, let them enjoy the Nation, tho' we take the Reason to be this, That the Pipe disposes them to sit very quiet, hardly without any stirring; Now we believe, were they to sit so still, without a Pipe, they would cool as soon.[45]

Defoe was probably the most prolific writer in the English language, and his *Review* was one of the great achievements of early eighteenth-century journalism. He wrote it single-handedly while at the same time plunging into countless other literary projects, turning his pen to every conceivable topic. Almost his entire output was anonymous. As a journalist with a mission, Defoe hated social inequality and campaigned against it in his *Review*. One biographer doubts that for all Defoe's exertions the paper ever reached a circulation of more than a few hundred. It obviously had an influence out of all proportion to its meagre sales. In the coffee-houses of London, schools of wit and dialectic, the gossipy *Review* was eagerly scrutinized and passed round. Defoe himself joined other well-known writers for conversation and to peck for tittle-tattle, gleanings for the next issue.

Defoe wrote that he had devised his Advice from the Scandalous Club 'for examining and censuring Things Scandalous, and openly deserving Reproof'.[46] He was therefore dismayed when readers saw it as an all-purpose miscellany and began to write in with questions about life, love, politics and public controversies. The exhausted author of the *Review* found 'his Table spread with Cases of Conscience, Enigmas, Difficulties in Philosophy, in Politicks, in Ethicks, Economicks, and what not. Here are Questions in Divinity, Morality, Love, State, War, Trade, Language, Poetry, Marriage, Drunkenness, Whoring, Gaming, Vowing and the like.' What he really had in mind, Defoe explained, was '[a]ny thing Curious, any thing Experimental, either in History, in Politicks, in Physicks'. But there were two groups of readers to keep sweet: those with no relish of history who wanted the *Review* to concentrate on 'all Mirth, Pleasantry and Delight', and the others who 'frequently press us to leave off Jesting and Bantering', saying, ''Tis Pity it should be clog'd with the Impertinence and Nonsense of the *Scan. Club*.'[47]

Defoe made no bones about his design; the *Review* was intended to appeal to a wide readership, and he, as editor, intended to steer a middle course 'between these two Extremities', hoping that readers who preferred the serious, weighty half of the paper would bear with those who preferred the other half, 'the Merry Part', the Scandal Club with its gossip, chit-chat and snippets. Eventually this diverting feature overflowed into a short series of monthly supplements, and in the general election year of 1705 Defoe broke the Scandal Club free of his *Review* altogether and launched a new supplement, the *Little Review*, published on Wednesdays and Fridays between editions of the *Review*. But the innovation only lasted for a couple of dozen issues and the following year Defoe restored his original format. Although the 'Jesting and Bantering' of the Advice from the Scandal Club was the most popular of the *Review*'s features, Defoe took the bold stroke of replacing it with the far graver 'Miscellanea', in which he gave vent to his strait-laced views on manners and morals.

As a journalist, Defoe was something of a phenomenon, an editor and reporter with a highly developed eye and ear for what was wanted and the skill to write it quickly and in an entertaining way. He immediately grasped the selling power of sex. Some have accused him of treating it lightly (the House of Commons protested to the bishops about the *Review*'s licentiousness) but he was a fierce critic of debauchery, even though that may have been more for journalistic effect than from an inner conviction. 'The *Review* and its supplements must have been an important civilising force among simple readers,' says the American scholar Arthur Wellesley Secord who edited the standard facsimile edition of the paper in the 1930s. 'It is true they treat delicate matters in a merry tone, but their advice is sensible and probably more effective than if it had been presented gravely.'[48]

In a reading of his columns nearly three centuries later, Defoe emerges as a shrewd observer of the social scene. His journalism anticipates some of the themes he developed in his novels, written in later life, such as extramarital sex, women abandoned and betrayed, and the status of prostitutes:

A Poor Whore made a sad Complaint this Week at the Club, and demanded Justice against a Certain Eminent Citizen, who had exacted her Performance, but cheated her of her Wages.

The Society, resenting her Character, took her into Custody immediately, and began to talk of using her very Scurvily, being particularly offended at the Brass of her Countenance, and the Affront, as they took it, put upon their Society.

She told them plainly she was a Whore, and 'twas her Calling; ... She told them, That a Certain Citizen of London, living within a Mile of Threadneedle-Street, having agreed with her for a dark Affair, at the Price of a Guinea, had sham'd her off with a Halfpenny being in the Night, notwithstanding she had been so Honest to him, as not to pick his Pocket of 50 Guineas, which he own'd he had about him, contrary to the Duty of her Profession.

The Society told her, they would do here all the Justice they thought was due to her, which was to Summon the Man to appear at the next meeting, and demanded Directions how to send to him; she told 'em he might be heard of at the Sun Coffee-house behind the Exchange, provided the Notice was left with the Man of the House.[49]

Defoe succeeded in masking a private scandal of his own, concerning his mistress who apparently bore him a son. In his forties, Defoe took up with 'a Lady who vended Oysters', probably the wife of the weaver with whom he was living in 1702. In 1707, an irate reader wrote to Defoe complaining about the amount of repetition in the *Review*. 'I often read your Paper 'till I am sick,' the anonymous critic announced, 'and I have recommended it as a better Purge than Rhubarb, and a Vomit far exceeding that of Tartar Emetic.' The writer went on to refer to Defoe's relationship with the weaver's wife and his adventures in the 'Procreation Trade', suggesting that he believed he was on to something. Defoe was defiant. 'Rail on, Gentlemen,' he exclaimed, 'the Dirt you throw flyes back in your own Faces, and bears me sufficient Testimony, that the Physick works well, by the Vomit and Stink of the Patient.'[50]

There was much to report in the early years of the eighteenth century: increased party political activity, war on the Continent and growing prosperity at home. Information, comment and entertainment were in huge demand. The result was a bright flaring of public prints. Many guttered and died; a few, notably *Tatler* and *Spectator*, achieved an unprecedented status among the well-to-do and the upper classes. Both were the work of Joseph Addison and Sir Richard Steele, and neither came close to being what would now be called a scandal sheet. *Tatler* first appeared in April 1709 and was published thrice-weekly until it closed just twenty months later. It was a miscellany of features covering learning, poetry, 'Foreign and Domestick News' and accounts of 'Gallantry, Pleasure, and Entertainment', gathered together as 'The Lucubrations of Isaac Bickerstaff', Steele's pseudonym. *Tatler*'s tone was distinctly raffish (despite Bickerstaff's 'grave' persona), smacking of coffee-houses and ladies' assemblies, and was admired by the writer John Gay for 'a Style ever varying with the Humours, Fancies and Follies he describes'.[51] (Defoe himself remarked that *Tatler* was a continuation of his own efforts at social instruction in the Scandal Club essays, but he came to resent Steele for hopping aboard his bandwagon without an invitation.) *Tatler*'s early numbers were chattier and more personal than later ones, with stories fizzing with what Coleridge described as Steele's 'pure humanity'. He ridiculed the follies and weaknesses of the age, in sketches of fops, wags and coquettes.

As a rake among men is the man who lives in the constant abuse of his reason, so a coquette among women is one who lives in continual misapplication of her beauty. The chief of all ... is pretty Mrs Toss: she is ever in practice of something which disfigures her, and takes from her charms; though all she does, tends to a contrary effect. She has naturally a very agreeable voice and utterance, which she has changed for the prettiest lisp imaginable. She sees what she has a mind to see, at half a mile distance; but poring with her eyes half shut at every one she passes by, she believes much more becoming.[52]

When *Tatler* folded on the second day of 1711, Steele disappointed not only a growing readership but also those coffee-houses where Bickerstaff's gossipy lucubrations 'had brought them more Customers than all their other News Papers put together'.[53] The *Spectator* first appeared two months later and ran until December 1712. (Defoe's *Review* outlived both, finally folding in 1713.)

The *Spectator* was obviously from the same Addison–Steele stable, but was presented in an altogether more sober, reflective tone. Nevertheless, Gay was impressed, confessing himself 'Surpriz'd all at once by ... such a noble profusion of Wit and Humour'.[54] In an early *Spectator*, Addison announced that while women were sending him letters stuffed with gossip by the bundle – tales of fallen virgins, faithless wives or amorous widows – 'it is not my Design to be a Publisher of Intreagues and Cuckoldoms'.[55] Instead, the journal served up a vivid picture of ordinary daily life, recreating the London of Queen Anne with paragraphs on fashions for women and men, notes on interior decor and design, new recipes, health and beauty tips. 'The world of eighteenth-century London passes before our eyes,' says Donald Bond, the *Spectator*'s chronicler:

the hackney coachmen and the street hawkers, the knife-grinders and the sow-gelders, the lacemen and the bellows-menders, the pastry-men and the street jugglers ... Natural science, classical learning, the theatre, the world of books, philosophy, religion, art and music ... The variety of subject-matter and the freshness of its treatment help us to understand why the *Spectator* was such a tremendous success in its day and why it continued to be read through the century.[56]

Its notes and observations derived from the table-talk of the seventeenth century and belonged to the journalistic literature of the Restoration. But its sheer range and glittering style, its exuberance and knowingness, place the *Spectator* of Addison and Steele at the fountainhead of the modern newspaper diary column.

2

The Bubble of the Rabble

In Britain in the early eighteenth century, 'the national taste,' complained the Victorian antiquary Thomas Wright, 'had become as vulgar as the national manners.' Journalists and writers plied their trades with a coarseness of expression that was characteristic of the age. As Wright pointed out, the most popular and widely read literary works were 'scandalous memoirs, secret history, surreptitiously obtained... and ill-disguised obscenity'.[1] In the newspapers, adulteries, elopements and the sexual shenanigans of prominent people were given blanket coverage, fuelled by the salacious details offered in evidence during adultery cases in the House of Lords. So Georgian readers were fed a constant diet of high jinks in high places: the admiral's wife discovered in a Charing Cross brothel in 1771, the Countess of Eglinton's adultery in 1788 and that of Lady Abergavenny in 1729. 'Private persons have not escaped the notice and censure of our licentious press,' lamented Robert Trevor, 'nor can even the grave bury poor Lady Abergavenny's shame, every sillable of whose name, and every particular of whose life are hawked about the streets as articulately as old cloaths etc.'[2] It was a familiar complaint from the ruling class about the prurient reading habits of the lower orders. 'The pen,' sniffed one, 'is become the bubble of the rabble.'[3]

But sex and scandal sold famously, and plainly appealed as much to the leisured classes as to the masses. Women in particular thirsted for the latest society frisson, and feasted on the revelations of two of the most successful gossip-grubbers of the age, Della Manley and Eliza Haywood. As well as writing books, they dabbled in journalism and occupied editorial chairs when to be a female professional writer was unusual and socially frowned upon. Mrs Mary Delariviere Manley was the uncrowned queen of gossip. In 1709 her scandalous and erotic best-selling romance, *Secret Memoirs*

31

and Manners of Several Persons of Quality of both Sexes from the New Atalantis, caused a sensation with its tittle-tattle about real society people masquerading under fictitious names. 'She removed his head from her lap,' ran a typically trembling vignette, 'and reposed it on a height of cushions that rested upon the couch where she was setting, and cast herself upon her knees in the same posture he was with her beautiful face to his... He clasped himself about her with all the force of love and, lengthening out the ravished kiss she gave, wounded the lovely lips to which he had owed his delight!'

Mrs Manley was the first recorded woman editor of the British press. In 1709 she launched the *Female Tatler,* a thrice-weekly gossip sheet masquerading as a journal of serious discourse. Styling herself 'Mrs Crackenthorpe, A Lady that knows everything', she was also the original Agony Aunt, dispensing advice to readers on how to conduct themselves in public. In an issue dated October 1709 Mrs Manley called attention to the current fad of women smuggling themselves into men-only venues in disguise: 'The young lady in the Parish of St Laurence near Guild Hall, that lately went to the Coffee House in Man's Cloathes with two 'Prentices, called for a Dish of Bohee, smoak'd her Pipe, and gave herself an abundance of Stroddling Masculine Airs, is desired to do so no more.' A few days later, Mrs Manley, 'resenting the affront offered to her by some rude citizens', resigned without warning.

Mrs Manley and Richard Steele of *Tatler* disagreed on the morality of personal satire. Steele had written in *Tatler* that 'where crimes are enormous, the delinquent deserves little pity, but the reporter less.'[4] In the *New Atalantis,* Mrs Manley excelled at precisely the kind of scandalum magnatum that Steele despised. Indeed, in the first volume of her infamous book, she pillories Steele, with whom she appears to have had some sort of on-off relationship, having, in Leigh Hunt's words, 'loved and lampooned' him by turns. A grudge grew between them, based on Steele's refusal to lend money to Mrs Manley, even though she had baled him out in earlier, straitened times 'when I was going to my ruin'. Swift, who visited Mrs Manley a year or two after her book was published, found her in low spirits, and very ill with dropsy and a sore leg. He reported that she was 'about forty, very homely and very fat', and self-effacing when discussing her own charms, she agreed that her perfections 'are not of the sort that inspire immediate delight and warm the blood with pleasure'. Although scarred by childhood smallpox, Mrs Manley's 'imperfect beauty' was crowned by an abundant mane of hair, the colour of pale ash.

In her *New Atalantis*, Mrs Manley offered an exposé of the 'secret' lives of rich and powerful peers and politicians; in doing so she slandered many public figures and as a result spent most of the following winter in jail. Swift said of her work that it seemed 'as if she had about two thousand epithets and fine words packed up in a bag, and that she pulled them out by handfuls, and strewed them on her paper, where about once in five hundred times they happened to be right'.[5] Mrs Manley's motives for all this badmouthing may have lain in her unhappy early life. She married her cousin ('that heartless ruffian') who abandoned her when she fell pregnant. She never recovered from this downfall. 'Men were afraid of her wit,' wrote one mid-Victorian scholar, 'and ladies talked of, at, and against her, behind their fans, as a dreadfully intriguing hussy who ruined the men out of revenge for the outrage by which one man had embittered her whole life.'[6]

Later, Mrs Manley moved in with Swift's good friend, the printer Alderman John Barber, and lived with him as his mistress. Barber printed Swift's *Examiner*, one of the earliest journals of political essays, and when Swift resigned as editor in June 1711, it was Mrs Manley who slipped into the editorial chair. She lasted only a few weeks, but she did the job in a revolutionary way, as an informer, newsmonger and purveyor of political gossip. She was the first woman editor to realize that, through print, 'private intelligence' could be public political currency. According to one modern commentator: 'As a woman whose reputation was irreparably damaged by the circulation of scandal, Manley recognised the profound power of anonymous talk.'[7]

She had already harnessed this power in *New Atalantis*, which was laden with coded information about who in public life was doing what to whom in private. When the Whig MP Arthur Maynwaring reported on the *New Atalantis* to Sarah Churchill, Duchess of Marlborough, he tried to set her mind at rest about 'this vile book' in which the Duchess was one of the main targets of Mrs Manley's satirical pen. (At first, Maynwaring made the mistake of letting slip that he rather enjoyed the book, describing one aspect as 'delightful' and describing a particular scene, in which the Duchess is set upon by the 'rabble', as one 'which I think you could hardly help laughing at'.) Recovering his composure, Maynwaring assured the Duchess that Mrs Manley's printed gossip was 'all old and incredible stuff of extortion and affairs' of which nothing related to the Duchess herself. Commenting on the growing power of the political press, and the problems of controlling Manley's brand of anonymous gossip, Maynwaring wrote: 'The licence of the press is too great, and I hope some proper way be found to restrain it this winter; but I would not have the rise taken out of this trifling book, which, as you observe truly, would only make it spread more... Yet I am afraid it will be very difficult quite to cure the mischief; for as long as people will buy such books, there will always be vile printers ready to publish them: and low indigent writers will never be wanting for such a work.'[8]

History pays few tributes to Della Manley. Her scribblings earned her a harpy's reputation. G. M. Trevelyan dismissed her as 'a woman of no character'.[9] Winston Churchill described her writings as 'the lying inventions of a prurient and filthy underworld served up to those who relish them and paid for by party interest and political malice'.[10] A modern biographer agrees that Mrs Manley suffered for her political views, being a Tory and therefore not best beloved by the Whigs. And like the targets of twentieth-century gossip writers like William Hickey and Hedda Hopper, 'those who had suffered at the end of her pen squealed very loud.'[11] These days, she is perhaps best remembered for a line from one of her plays: 'No time like the present.'[12]

The first magazine specifically by and for women, the *Female Spectator*, was launched by another infamous woman novelist, Eliza Haywood, in 1744. Although following in the tradition of *Tatler* and the prestigious *Gentleman's Magazine*, it differed from both. It was exclusively concerned with women's affairs, which were written about in a light but morally serious tone and were observed through the eyes of a supposed circle of four women, each in different stages of life: a beautiful unmarried female, a happily married sophisticate-about-town, a wise widow of quality and the Female Spectator herself, the most mature of the four, who 'never was a Beauty' and who is now 'very far from being young', two aspects of Eliza Haywood's own character. Although Mrs Haywood had packed her novels with Mrs Manley-style scandals involving the leaders of contemporary society, scarcely veiled, she drew back from the scandal pit when formatting her magazine. The

Female Spectator had no gossip column, Mrs Haywood insisting that she intended no 'gratifying a vicious Propensity of propagating Scandal!'[13] Alexander Pope was so appalled by Mrs Haywood's 'most scandalous' novels that he heaped abuse on her in some of the bitterest and coarsest lines in his *Dunciad*, adding a note describing her as one of those 'shameless scribblers...who, in libellous memoirs and novels, reveals the faults or misfortunes of both sexes, to the ruin of public fame or disturbance of private happiness'.[14] Pope's attack was repeated by his friends. Swift rounded on Mrs Haywood, calling her a 'stupid, infamous, scribbling woman'.[15]

Mrs Haywood may have scribbled but she was not stupid. In order 'to secure an eternal Fund of Intelligence' she had installed spies throughout London and the fashionables provincial spa towns, as well as in France, Italy and Germany 'so that nothing curious or worthy of Remark can escape me'. If this sounded suspiciously like the gossip-gathering she had repudiated, Mrs Haywood reassured her readers that scandal had no place in her design. 'Whoever sits down to read me with this View, will find themselves mistaken,' she explained, adding that whilst she planned to deal in 'real Facts', names would be changed, 'my Intention being only to expose the Vice, not the Person'.

Mrs Haywood also excluded most other features of modern women's magazines: there were no recipes, no household hints or dress and knitting patterns, and no advice on child care. But she did develop Mrs Manley's idea of an agony column, dispensing advice to desperate lovers, distraught mothers and unhappy daughters, who may or may not have been genuine correspondents. Her pungent replies are liberally spiced with instructive anecdotes to illustrate a point. Having enjoyed what Mrs Haywood concedes was 'an Education more liberal than is ordinarily allowed to Persons of my Sex', she often calls for a more enlightened attitude to education than was normally accorded to women in the early eighteenth century. There is an improving tone throughout, not unlike that of the 'courtesy' or conduct books that had been in fashion for some time and that offered practical, down-to-earth advice to both men and women on various topics. Haywood's magazine ran for two years.

Hers was an age in which the British first forged a national culture. The Duke of Marlborough triumphed over the French, Britannia ruled the waves and the Industrial Revolution had created in Britain the workshop of the world. With the death of Charles II in 1685, the high priests of culture had descended from the royal and aristocratic circles of the court to the everyday commercial streets of the capital, with its coffee-houses, theatres, clubs, galleries and concert halls. Between the Restoration and the accession of George III, London spawned a host of cultural producers of whom journalists and Grub Street hacks were among the first rank. The media were being born – that 'furious Itch of Novelty' as one critic disparagingly called the developing press – and culture was transforming itself from an instrument of patronage to a booming business serving the people at large.

The cockpit for this new public culture was the coffee-house; by 1739 there were well over five hundred of them. Together with taverns, they served the capital as places of pleasure and of commerce, catering to customers from all walks of life. Women were welcome. Newspapers were devoured, critics were invented, while sexual scandal and political rumours were hotly debated. 'He that comes often,' remarked one pamphleteer, 'saves two pence a week in Gazettes, and has his news and his coffee for the same charge.'[16] But many readers were irritated at the trifling nature of much of what appeared in the papers. 'A Man of any Distinction cannot steal out of Town for a Day or two,' complained a contributor to the *Gentleman's Magazine*, 'but the Secret is immediately made known to the World.' On the other hand, the same correspondent called for more candour, suggesting that the papers should 'tell us when his Grace, or his Lordship, went to Bed to his Lady – When he broke his Custom, and kept his Word with his Tradesmen or Dependants – When they said a witty Thing – or did a Wise one – These Articles would be News, and we should thank them for our Surprizes.'[17] Book sales fell in the 1740s, a victim of the growing news industry. 'Nobody at present reads anything but news-papers,' lamented the novelist Henry Fielding, who confessed himself staggered at the profusion of news-writers. Fielding consoled himself with the thought of their many imperfections. Writing in his anti-Jacobite journal, the *True Patriot*, he grumbled:

> there is scarce a syllable of truth in any of them... no sense... in reality, nothing in them at all.

And this also must be allowed by their readers, if paragraphs which contain neither wit nor humour, nor sense, nor the least importance, may be properly said to contain nothing. Such are the arrival of my lord — with a great equipage, the marriage of Miss— of great beauty and merit, and the death of Mr— who was never heard of in his life, &c.&c.[18]

Nevertheless, the coffee-house customers were hungry for such gossip. As they also chewed over the greater issues of the day, including European and world affairs, such establishments quickly became popular with journalists and politicians as a source of news and opinions. Lord Arlington, when he was secretary of state, sent agents into the London coffee-houses to collect political gossip. Henry Coventry, another holder of that office, admitted that 'we are without news, but what the coffee houses make'.[19] Lorenzo Magolotti, a Florentine nobleman at the court of Charles II, observed groups of gossip-grubbing journalists at work in the gloomy corners of coffee-houses. The gossip gleaned by these news-gatherers was duly forwarded to the owners of various journals for publication. Not everyone applauded the use of rumour as a source of copy, and one high-minded paper attacked those others 'whose only excellencies consist in their propagating, and improving, with art and subtlety, every factious story, and idle rumour, they can glean up in coffee-houses, and other places of public resort'.[20]

Political invective became an art form. News-writers were hired by both government and opposition and were paid good money to write squibs about their enemies in the public prints. By 1740, the government's 'hireling scribes' were being characterized as 'reptiles', an insult that still attaches to journalists today. In the 1730s, the French philosopher Montesquieu, visiting England as he fought against failing eyesight, was struck by the proliferation of London newspapers, and also by their licentiousness. Moreover, the readership was changing. For the first time, printed news was reaching the working man. 'The very slaters had the newspapers brought on to the roof that they might read them,' he observed.[21] What they read, as they clung to the chimney stacks, was gossip and scandal. Grub Street was in its heyday, and the *Grub Street Journal* was the preferred reading matter of many. Brimming with scurrility, it was written by a crew of drinking, dissolute hacks who served the needs of the expanding newspaper public whose interests extended far beyond the court circles that had so mesmerized the previous generation. The *Journal* and its hacks operated from a garret in the real Grub Street, a noisome thoroughfare in Cripplegate Ward Without, long since swallowed up by the Barbican development on the fringe of the City. Freed from old controls, and nurtured by the coffee-house culture, the hacks abandoned their inhibitions and wrote what the readers wanted to read. The result was a new kind of journalism, vivid, spicy, often salacious and shocking, but seldom dull. The paper had announced itself in 1730 to be chiefly concerned with literature, a subject to which it apparently planned to bring a humorous and ironical approach. That soon changed. Gossip and scandal was the name of the game. As one historian observed, 'The new paper prized beyond all others the virtue of the gadfly, and . . . revelled in personalities set down in gall.'[22]

The intellectual force behind the *Grub Street Journal* was the poet and critic, Alexander Pope, the so-called 'Wasp of Twickenham' and a pre-eminent figure in the London literary establishment. His vindictive lampoon, the *Dunciad*, in which he ridiculed contemporary writers, had made him many enemies. He had recruited his influential friends, including Gay and Swift, into his Scriblerus Club, which pilloried literary incompetence. Pope's links with the *Grub Street Journal* are hard to define, but the paper was always friendly towards him and his circle, and correspondingly hostile to Pope's Dunces and other adversaries. Pope's hired assassin in the editorial chair at the *Journal* was Richard Russel, the diminutive son of a clergyman and himself a one-time vicar who had lost his living because he refused to swear an oath of allegiance to the new monarchs, William and Mary, at the end of the seventeenth century. He had been forced to turn to literary hackwork to eke out a living. When the *Journal* was launched in 1730, with Russel as principal editor, he disguised his identity by writing under the pseudonyms 'Mr Bavius' and his assistant 'Mr Maevius'. He quickly earned a reputation as the scourge of the rival newspapers, which he scorned for their stupidity and viciousness, their threadbare coverage of news and the irresponsibility of their news-writers. 'To furnish materials for the Dayly Papers,' he recalled, 'Collectors are sent all over the City, suburbs and neighbouring villages, to pick up articles of News; who being payed according to the length and number of them, it is no wonder that so few of them are true.'[23] The *Journal* printed no political news, but plunged headlong into the controversies of the day and developed a propensity for personal attack. It also contained articles on a huge range of topics, from love and marriage to how to converse with servants, happiness, swearing, chastity and curiosity. This weekly four-page mix soon caught on. Meanwhile its daily rivals continued to serve up the thinnest of gruel. Most of the 'news' consisted of accounts of murders, suicides and crimes of violence, reported in unflinching detail, alongside the activities of the great and the good. In the summer of 1733, Russel offered his readers this piece of analysis:

> First, it is said, come the doings of the royal family, whether they are dining at home or abroad, whether they walk, ride, or go on the water. Such news is valuable since it informs the public that the royal family is in health, and also since it gives entertainment to those of low station. Second comes the activities of the nobility; their entertainments, births, deaths and comings to town. At first glance such matter may not seem important, but it is very useful to tradesmen, who thus know the proper time to solicit custom or the payment of bills. In the third place, (and with the most sarcasm) one finds preferments in church and state. Thus the public sees how well the younger sons of gentry and nobility are provided for, as well as the dependents of some few great men, and learns of the elevation of men of great parts, never heard of before.[24]

Across the spectrum of London newspapers in the early eighteenth century, however, news coverage was patchy. Many news items were recycled, appearing in one paper one day and others the next, and to the modern reader there appears to have been little attempt to separate wheat from chaff. In the debut issue of the *Weekly Miscellany* at the end of 1732, readers were warned that those looking for gossip would be disappointed, since the paper's policy was 'to insert such Things principally as may deserve the Perusal of an intelligent Reader, avoiding as much as possible, such trifling Particulars as are unworthy of the Attention of a Person of Sense'.[25] The following year, Eustace Budgell, launching his new weekly magazine the *Bee*, rubbished the domestic news agenda of the London papers as being preoccupied with crime, accidents and trivia about 'the Nobility, Gentry and Clergy, and of the Days when some of the Royal Family go to the Play House, or take the Air.'[26] Budgell's lofty tone did him no good; the *Bee*, a hotchpotch of material from other magazines, was accused by its rivals of 'nothing more than a direct Pyracy' and soon failed. (Budgell was unhinged by the experience, but kept his Grub Street enemies at bay for four years before scribbling his will, stuffing his pockets with stones and throwing himself into the Thames.)

Some years later, in 1766, a writer to the *Gentleman's Magazine* echoed the general despair felt in exalted circles at the newspapers' preoccupation with the trifles and banalities of daily life, 'pages of unconnected occurrences, consisting of politics, religion, picking of pockets, puffs, casualties, deaths, marriages, bankruptcies, preferments, resignations, executions, lottery tickets, India bonds, Scotch pebbles, Canada bills, French chicken gloves, auctioneers and quack doctors ... Not a syllable of news'.[27] In the late eighteenth and early nineteenth centuries, people shed the cold formality of the classical age and emerged as people in the round: human, individual, eccentric, sentimental, fiery, emotional. They were sufficiently peculiar to be perceived as personalities. They were, as the writer T. H. White has pointed out, the first people in English literature to be real enough for gossip.

This age of scandal – White coined the phrase – was also an age of intimacy in which the aristocratic writers of the day such as Thomas Creevey, who hobnobbed with royalty, gossiped deliciously in their diaries. 'They moved in the tight world of the Drawing-rooms and of the Birthdays, knew each other as well as the boys at a public school in England might know each other today, chatted about the latest scandal, and, because they had learned to be literate, they wrote it down.'[28] It was a rare moment of calm in Britain's history, this age of aristocracy, liberty and cultural creative vigour. After the turmoil and transition of the early part of the eighteenth century, there emerged a cultural elite. G. M. Trevelyan described it as 'a generation of men wholly characteristic of the Eighteenth Century ethos, a society with a mental outlook of its own, self-poised, self-judged, and self-approved, freed from the disturbing passions of the past, and not yet troubled with anxieties about a very different future which was soon to be brought upon the scene by the Industrial and the French Revolutions'.[29] This elite was educated and well read, although for every noble-born person who could quote the Latin poets and spout Greek in Parliament, there was another steeped in ignorance. 'Their literature,' according to White, 'was one of personalities. Great thoughts on large political or on moral issues were absent, leaving only the trivialities of life and the anecdotes about character which are nowadays the bane of serious historians.'[30] People wanted to read of nothing more taxing than the kind of 'bootikins' Horace Walpole wore for his gout, or what Dr Johnson used to do with his dried orange-peel.

Women's interests were increasingly catered for, with material about manners, morals, romance, marriage and family life growing in importance as an ingredient in newspaper content. This lighter, more entertaining approach encouraged editors to sprinkle their papers with social chit-chat and gossip, often by way of fillers. Even so, newspapers continued to look plain. They were laid out on a standard design, with such hard news as there was being mainly political, and the reporting was derivative, anonymous and impersonal. Many stories were lifted wholesale from other papers, usually without acknowledgement, and there was little for the 'journalist' to do but to retail the rumour and conjecture that flourished in a semi-closed, political society. As a result, many items were inaccurate, unchecked and speculative. The emphasis was on events, with scanty analysis and the background only lightly sketched in. Most items were brief, with neither explanation nor introduction. But by the 1780s, newspapers brgan to print more non-political news, especially items describing social habits or fashions. The papers were chasing the readers who had become accustomed to this fare in their weekly and monthly magazines: news of the theatre and the arts in particular began to appear, and sports news, largely ignored in the first half of the century, was now included with reports on horse racing, boxing, cockfighting and cricket. But while the press set about enlarging the public world of Hanoverian Britain, its influence remained limited. Most people did not read a newspaper, and most of those who could read appear not to have bothered to do so. And the papers themselves were out of tune with the times. 'The press was more part of polite culture than of its popular counterpart,' observes newspaper historian Dr Jeremy Black in a study of the eighteenth-century British press.[31]

For two years in the early 1750s, the two-page *London Advertiser, and*

Literary Gazette (later the *London Daily Advertiser*) ran a feature of scurrilous news and gossip, which Isaac D'Israeli (father of the future prime minister) later characterized as 'a light scandalous chronicle'. The writer, Dr James Hill, promised to report on 'the Polite World, and their Entertainments...which have never yet appeared as Part of the Intelligence of the Day: These we shall search after among the Assemblies of the Great, and the Amusement of the Gay; at Routs and Assemblies, at Masquerades and Ridottoes, at Operas and at the Playhouses'.[32] Hill, a rakish figure in his early thirties, criss-crossed fashionable London in a magnificent chariot, picking up paragraphs and sowing mischief in his daily column, which he signed 'The Inspector'. He made many enemies along the way, and his column was so littered with retractions and apologies for earlier falsehoods that one wag was moved to versify:

> What Hill does one day say, he the next does deny,
> And candidly tells you, – 'tis all a damned lie:
> Dear Doctor, – this candour from you is not wanted,
> For why should you own it? – 'tis taken for granted.[33]

Hill can claim to have been England's first personality columnist, in that he was the first writer of a regular signed newspaper feature. He soon discovered the hazards of his calling. One victim of Hill's vicious pen physically attacked him at a social gathering and drew his sword before Hill was rescued by officers of the law. Sometimes his targets were the celebrities of the day, among them the novelist Henry Fielding and the poet Christopher Smart, with whom he tangled in lengthy and public arguments. Hill also crossed one of the darlings of the London scene, David Garrick. Hill had written a farce, which Garrick's theatre management had presented at Covent Garden; it was so bad that the audience had hissed it off the stage. Hill raged at Garrick in his column, but the famous actor–manager retorted with acid brevity:

> For physic and farces, his equal there scarce is;
> His farces are physic, his physic a farce is.[34]

Hill made good money from his vitriolic squibs as 'The Inspector'. His salary from the *Advertiser*, together with his other earnings as an author, were said to amount to a staggering £1,500 a year, an income that afforded him two lavish London houses. But in 1753 he threw up his column to concentrate on other things, including the writing of some seventy books and a long and unavailing attempt to be elected a Fellow of the Royal Society. Hill went on to devote himself to his most ambitious work, a twenty-six-volume botanical study titled *The Vegetable System*, complete with 1,600 copperplate engravings illustrating 26,000 different plants. This massive undertaking occupied Hill from 1759 to 1775, but it brought with it the (unconfirmed) offer of the post of superintendent of the Royal Botanical Gardens at Kew and the patronage of various foreign dignitaries. In 1774, Hill styled himself Sir John, on the strength of an honour bestowed by the King of Sweden. In later life, Hill became a prolific herbal quack, cultivating at his country house in Bayswater such specimens as waterdock and valerian from which he produced large and profitable quantities of bottled remedies. One of his nostrums was tincture of bardana, which Hill claimed to be an invaluable treatment for gout. When Hill himself succumbed to this painful affliction in 1775, at the age of fifty-nine, one of his enemies from the old Grub Street days provided his epitaph:

'Poor Doctor Hill is dead! Good lack!'
'Of what disorder?' 'An attack
Of gout.' 'Indeed! I thought that he
Had found a wondrous remedy.'
'Why, so he had, and when he tried,
He found it true – the doctor died!'[35]

In an age of scurrility, Captain Philip Thicknesse was ranked among the most scurrilous. He came to journalism late – he was in his forties when his first piece appeared – and (after some success with articles on gardens and gardening) he turned to gossip-writing in the mid-1760s. As a young man, Captain Thicknesse had lived abroad and published books of travel, which were much read and admired. But he was a perennial picker of quarrels and managed to fall out with a host of English notables, among them actors, dramatists, physicians and surgeons, the brothers Wesley and the Archbishop of Canterbury. One of Thicknesse's targets, the Irish peer Lord Mountgarret, described him as 'a boisterous ruffian, a poor, crafty, super-annuated lunatic...by no means a real gentleman'.[36] Unsurprisingly, when he took up his gossiping pen, Thicknesse cloaked himself in anonymity. He masqueraded as 'A Wanderer' in the *St James's Chronicle*. In the *Gentleman's Magazine* his paragraphs appeared above the pen-name 'Polyxena'. His many enemies called him 'Dr Viper'.

It was partly to ventilate his private quarrels in public that Philip Thicknesse became a gossip writer. He also badly needed money. Not only did he take payment for his paragraphs, but he was widely believed to be a blackmailer. The Revd Henry Bate, then editing the *Morning Herald*, denounced Thicknesse as a social pest and warned his readers against this 'hoary offender [who] has long escaped the cudgel of resentment and sword of exasperated rage. He has menaced public men into liberal contributions, and has held numerous families in apprehension and terror. It will not be necessary to put P. T. under this infamous but faithful picture.'[37] In fact, there would have been no need. In his private correspondence, Thicknesse cheerfully admitted to blackmail, and in his *Memoirs* boasted: 'I can at any time muster up ten or a dozen knaves or fools who will put a hundred pounds or two into my pocket merely for holding them up to public scorn.'[38]

One of Captain Thicknesse's most fruitful sources of gossip was Snobdon, the Herefordshire seat of Lord Bateman. Thicknesse was a regular guest there for many years and counted Bateman as one of his few friends. At Snobdon, Thicknesse picked up stories of high jinks among the landed gentry, which he duly inserted into his columns. In doing so, he strained the patience of his host who, although fast friends with Thicknesse, disliked journalists as a breed. Invited to meet a colleague of Thicknesse in 1771, Bateman declined on the ground that he 'abhors News Paper writers, and has not the least desire to be acquainted with one'.[39]

Thicknesse bought a house in Bath. With its fashionable Pump Room, parade and promenade, gossip bubbled up with the waters, and Thicknesse was on hand to catch the juicier drops and bottle them for the public fancy. What he didn't send to the London prints, he wrote up in his travel books. He had no compunction about including his own circle in his gossiping. One member was the celebrated Irish actor James Quin. Eclipsed by Garrick, Quin had retired to Bath where, one evening in the Pump Room lobby, Thicknesse came across his friend the worse for wear:

> It was after dinner. Quin was what he would call in another man, sack-mellow. At the time I was in conversation with a Wiltshire Esquire (now living), to whom Quin walked as steadily up he could, when putting his heels upon the Esquire's toes, made them crash again! and then, without saying another word, walked off. Whether pain, surprise or timidity overcame the Esquire's upper-works I cannot say, but as soon as he could speak he asked me whether I had observed Quin's conduct, and whether I thought it was an accident, or done with design to affront him? I replied that Quin had been drinking and probably did not know what he was about. But the next morning, meeting him on the parade, I asked him why he treated a good-natured man with the whole weight of his body corporate? D—n him, replied the comedian putting on one of his most contunding looks, the fellow invited me to his house in Wiltshire, laid me in damp sheets; and seduced my servant; fed me with red veal and white bacon; ram mutton and bull beef, adding, and as to his liquor, by my soul it was every drop sour except his vinegar, and yet the scrub had the impertinence to serve it upon dirty plate.[40]

No one, however exalted, could escape the gossiper's pen. *The Secret Memoirs of the Connexion existing between the D— of R— and Mrs C—* was the title of a typical scandal sheet hawked in the days of George III, but such publications were not intended for polite society. James Boswell, Johnson's biographer, on the other hand, dragged personal gossip out of the shadows of Georgian London and into the glare of public gaze in his column for the *London Magazine*, written under the pseudonym 'The Hypochondriack'. Some seventy monthly columns appeared in unbroken succession between 1777 and 1783, covering such topics as drinking, diaries and hypochondria, for Boswell, a manic depressive ('I was born with a melancholy temperament'), was a hypochondriac himself, being a lifelong martyr to gonorrhoea. Among his columns are accounts of the public execution at Tyburn of a forger named Gibson and a highwayman called Benjamin Payne, the first such reportage by a named London journalist.[41]

Boswell, with his overwhelming love of life, was greedy for human detail. He scoffed at his critics, who accused him of recording private conversations and listening 'beyond civility'. 'No one had a greater passion for the inside story,' declared the American scholar Margery Bailey, who edited Boswell's columns for publication, 'but he wore his rosemary with a difference. By temperament and training an honest man, he had no interest in the gossips' hints and half truths; he wanted the whole truth, and every scrap of it. By instinct a humanist, he saw no reason why anything worth human consideration should be secret.'[42] Boswell's columns, like modern gossip paragraphs, are brief and chatty, making no claim to weightiness or thorough journalistic probings. They were often dashed off at great speed, against a deadline, or thrown together from scraps of things he had read. He was interested in ideas and oddities alike. His flashes of acquaintance delivered astonishingly vivid cameos of everyday eighteenth-century life: the old laird who grumbles about separate soup plates merely making a man sup his broth twice; the anatomist who reflects that even in a beauty, muscles are no better than blubber; the country clergyman who quotes wife and servants at every third sentence; and the elderly squire who suits his glasses to the capacities of his guests, so keeping them 'drinking fair' together.

Boswell's columns read like information being delivered first-hand, as though Boswell himself, glass in hand, had met the reader at a party packed with his acquaintances. As well as the sparkling glimpses of the London whirl and his travels in Europe, Boswell also offers more reflective vistas, composed at a more leisurely pace. The arrangement of tingling detail hints at the master journalist, most strikingly, perhaps, in the terrible quiet of the forger Gibson, sucking his orange while the hangman's knot is adjusted beneath his ear.

3

A Scandalous Profession

When Noel Gallagher of Oasis called the *Mirror*'s 3 a.m. girls 'mingers' in front of 80,000 people at Wembley Stadium,[1] he was sharing a widely held public perception of the gossiping trade. In the pantheon of the professions, the journalist has historically ranked low, 'somewhere,' as E. S, Turner puts it, 'between apothecary and cat-skinner'.[2] Ned Ward, the rumbustious hack of the 1690s, admitted to following 'a scandalous profession' and likened it to whoring, in that 'the unhappy circumstances of a Narrow Fortune, hath forc'd us to do that for our Subsistance, which we are much asham'd of'.[3] Hack-writers for the early eighteenth-century newspapers were a despised class; journalists and reporters were spoken of mainly in tones of contempt, whose calling was regarded as one of last resort for literary starvelings. A century later, little had happened to dignify the reputation of journalists. Sir Walter Scott believed that 'nothing but a thorough-going blackguard ought to attempt the daily Press'[4] whilst Henry Brougham, the Lord Chancellor of Scott's day, described newspaper-writing as 'dirty work'.

During the Georgian era, the *Morning Post* under Henry Bate, its infamous parson–editor, enjoyed a rakehell's reputation. When Bate libelled the Duke of Richmond, John Baker, the Duke's legal adviser, pointed out that this was at least true to type; for at least two years the paper had run 'many scurrilous paragraphs...about Lady Derby, Duchess of Devonshire, and Duke and Duchess of Gordon, and many others'.[5] With its raffish preoccupations it became known as the 'West End Sheet', packed with fashionable trivia. It certainly made a lively read. One eighteenth-century editor of the *Morning Post* believed that most of those who figured in its society paragraphs had only themselves to blame if they didn't like it. 'It may be said,' declared John Taylor, 'that Bate was too personal in his strictures in general and in his allusions to many characters of his time, but it may also be said that they were generally characters of either sex who had rendered themselves conspicuous for folly, vice, or some prominent absurdity by which they became proper objects for satirical animadversion.'[6] Bate's successor as editor was another clergyman who was even more disreputable. Among the several eccentricities of the Revd William Jackson was his disconcerting habit of scribbling his scurrilous paragraphs 'in a very large hand upon very large sheets of paper, which appeared like maps or atlases spread over the table'.[7] This so upset the paper's owner that when he stumbled on Jackson writing in full flow, he retreated in dismay and called for the editor's dismissal, lest he should ruin the *Post* by the vast amount of paper he used up.

Jackson was said to be the inspiration for Snake, the Grub Street fixer in Sheridan's *The School for Scandal*, since he appears in the play dressed in clerical black. Certainly, his reputation as a vicious assassin of reputations – like Philip Thicknesse, he was known as 'Dr Viper' – made Jackson a fearsome figure. A journalist contemporary, Peter Stuart, reported that his squibs were 'like the darts of the savage, barbed and poisoned with the most refined art and rankest venom'.[8] Under Jackson and the paper's new owner, John Benjafield, the *Post* recovered its fortunes, largely thanks to Benjafield instituting a system of extortion whereby the targets of the paper's scandalmongers were forced to pay to have material suppressed.

It was an age of extraordinary excesses, of gluttony and gambling, of sexual misdemeanour, all of which were grist to the journalistic gossip mill. Beneath an outer shell of elegance and style, life for the ruling classes during the Regency was exciting, dramatic, earthy and robust. Leading the *haut ton* was the Prince of Wales, pleasure-seeker, drunkard and lecher, who gathered around him a brilliant motley circle of politicians, gamblers, courtesans and society hostesses. From the Prince's mansion off Pall Mall in London, the 'Carlton House Set' dictated the morals and manners of society. As he languished in enforced idleness, awaiting his royal destiny, Prinny's extravagant antics as 'the overweight, overdressed and oversexed buffoon' transfixed the British public.

The *Morning Post* blackmailed the Prince of Wales when he secretly contracted a 'marriage' with Mrs Fitzherbert, a widow older than he was and a Roman Catholic to boot. In February 1786, the *Post* ran a harmless paragraph skitting Mrs Fitzherbert for grandly renting an expensive box at the opera. Ten days later, the *Post* moved in for the kill: 'It is confidently reported that a certain marriage has been solemnized by a Romish Priest, who immediately quitted the kingdom.'[9] Desperate to avoid a political crisis, the Prince promptly paid up.

A couple of years later, during the Regency crisis, he was blackmailed again, this time by the *World and Fashionable Advertiser*, a self-appointed authority on manners, taste and fashion run by a flamboyant Old Etonian, Captain Edward Topham. Topham drove around London in a curricle built to his own design and drawn by four black horses 'splendidly caparaisoned', followed by a pair of liveried grooms. In September 1788 Captain Topham set this paragraph afloat:

MRS F—TZH—T
To the Remembrance of one
Who was — —, Wife and no Wife, Princess
and no Princess, sought, yet shunn'd,
courted, yet disclaimed; the Queen of all
Parties, yet the Grace of none...

This time, the Prince offered Topham £4,000 in cash and a lifetime annuity of £400 to buy his paper outright. Topham refused, but he did accept a subsidy.

According to the critic William Gifford, Topham's *World*, written in a strange, jargon-ridden style, was 'perfectly unintelligible, and therefore much read', particularly the 'unqualified and audacious attacks on all private character, which the town first smiled at for their quaintness, then tolerated for their absurdity'.[10] Nevertheless, the *World* did well at first. The blue-stocking feminist Hannah More confessed to Horace Walpole in 1787 that she read it 'feasting upon elopements, divorces and suicides, tricked out in all the elegancies of Mr Topham's phraseology'.[11] The paper was tricked out, too, in the latest typographical fig, and is said to have been the first to abandon the long letter 's'. But in content, the *World* failed to move with the times; flippancy was going out of style.

Political reporting was then a fledgling art. For most of the eighteenth century, it was illegal to report debates in the House of Commons, and most accounts were second-, third- or fourth-hand, invariably collected, according to the playwright Oliver Goldsmith, 'from the oracle of some coffee-house, which oracle has himself gathered them the night before from a beau at a gaming-table, who has pillaged his knowledge from a great man's porter, who had his information from the great man's gentleman, who has invented the whole story for his own amusement'.[12] But times were changing. In 1795, the MP William Windham dismissed journalists as a bunch of 'bankrupts, lottery-office keepers, footmen and decayed tradesmen',[13] but this was no longer an accurate judgment. The press was becoming better informed and more responsible in its reporting of political debate.

But gossip and scandal continued to preoccupy the educated classes, who traded in and laughed at the foibles and follies of society. It was a preoccupation often born of idleness. Benjamin Franklin satirizes a typical gossiping woman as Alice Addertongue, in her mid-thirties, living with her mother, who, having 'no care upon my head of getting a living', feels it necessary to exercise her talent at censure. 'By industry and application, I have made myself the centre of all the scandal in the province,' she boasts.[14] In the spring of 1777, every Alice Addertongue in London flocked to Sheridan's new play, *The School for Scandal*, inspired by the young playwright eavesdropping on the gossiping tongues of the ladies of Bath.

Lady Sneerwell and her Grub Street contact Snake are discovered drinking chocolate. 'The paragraphs, you say, Mr Snake, were all inserted?' asks Lady Sneerwell.

'They were, madam,' the scoundrel Snake replies, 'and as I copied them myself in a feigned hand, there can be no suspicion whence they came.'

Sheridan was gripped by the whirl of scandal and intrigue. He may well have had the notorious *Morning Post* in mind as he wrote his masterpiece; a contemporary reviewer for the *London Magazine* believed the play reflects on a 'certain modern daily publication' and ought 'to crimson with blushes every cheek which has encouraged such a butchery of male and female reputations'.[15]

Jackson also penned a series of more discursive general attacks on public figures of the day, signing himself 'Curtius'. These imitated the infamous 'Junius' letters, which appeared in the *Public Advertiser*. In November 1778 Jackson wrote anonymously to the famous actor–manager David Garrick, threatening him with exposure by Curtius and warning him that his reputation would be 'humbled in the dust'. Although Garrick sought to appease his tormentor, in the event Jackson was thwarted by Garrick's death in January 1779. After leaving the *Morning Post,* Jackson led a shadowy life as a sort of secret government agent, and in 1795 he was convicted of treason, a capital offence. He cheated the hangman by taking poison in the condemned cell. The paper, too, languished. A libel on 'a lady of quality', accused by the *Post* of criminal intercourse with an army officer, turned out to be the most expensive of the eighteenth century. She was awarded £4,000 damages, an enormous sum at the time, in a case that marked the lowest point in the paper's fortunes. With money short and circulation at an all-time low of a mere 350 copies a day, the owners sold out for just £600.

The new owner, a remarkable young Scot called Daniel Stuart, found the paper 'despised even by the few readers whom it supplied with more scurrilous and scandalous gossip than was given in any other paper of the day'.[16] He changed the full title from the *Morning Post and Fashionable World* to the *Morning Post and Gazetteer* and, while keeping the paper's 'Fashionable World' column, determined to fill it with other than scandalous matter. Stuart gave the paper a literary flavour, hired the poet Coleridge to write for him, and aimed 'with poetry and light paragraphs...to make the Paper cheerfully entertaining, not entirely filled with ferocious politics'.[17] Under Stuart, the *Morning Post* prospered once more; within two years, circulation was 1,000 copies a day and, within three, double that. Advertising poured in. The young Charles Lamb was also taken on, and at twenty-five found himself the paper's society reporter, going down to Margate to gather news of the 'fashionable arrivals' eager to join the novel craze for sea-bathing. 'The chat of the day, scandal – but above all, dress – furnished the material,' Lamb reported.[18] He was moonlighting as a paragraphist, rising at 5 a.m. to turn out half a dozen or so witty squibs at sixpence a piece before leaving home at eight for his day's work as a clerk at East India House.

Daniel Stuart's golden age reached its height in 1803, but did not last. The falling-off was swift and profound. When Lamb and others left, the paper lost its literary distinction and compromised its independence by so many entanglements with the Prince Regent, later George IV, that it came to be mocked as the 'Fawning Post'. The paper had been anxiously scrutinizing his love life ever since 1788, when it discovered his attachment to Mrs Fitzherbert while he was still Prince of Wales. The Prince had, indeed, taken a share in the paper under the terms of a libel settlement. But once he became Regent, the *Post* and its writers simply wallowed in sycophantic adulation and extravagant flattery. When he finally became king in 1820, the *Post* duly backed him in the parliamentary proceedings to dissolve his marriage to Caroline of Brunswick and strip her of her royal title, vilifying 'the Queen and her three Bs – the Baron – the bath – and the bottle' as 'A hag of fifty-two!'

The *Post* gossiped on, even as the paper turned more of its attention to political matters. Its fashionable reputation wore on well into Victoria's reign, and the paper was particularly popular with women, 'imparting just as much of private affairs as the public ought to know and no more'.[19] The *Post*'s gossip-gatherers were unstinting, one commentator observing how 'the *Morning Post* has its fashionable friend buzzing about Gunter's [patisserie] to hear of fashionable routs, or about Banting's to learn full particulars of a fashionable funeral.'[20] In 1838 Disraeli, who was then a well-known novelist and a rising MP, was mentioned in the paper, signalling his social standing. 'The Londonderrys gave the most magnificent banquet,' he reported. 'Fanny was faithful and asked me, and I figure in the *Morning Post* accordingly.'[21] The paper became an early Victorian byword for snobbish pretension.

The newly launched *Punch* magazine led the attacks on the *Post* in 'The Yellowplush Correspondence', initiated by the humorist Douglas Jerrold (who satirized English snobbery before Thackeray did) and then by Thackeray himself. In *Punch*, Jerrold and Thackeray guyed the *Morning Post*'s social obsessions by creating Jenkins, the toady, and Lickspittleoff, his 'Russian editor'. In this weekly invention, Jenkins, flunkey of flunkeys, lived on herrings in a rickety garret and daydreamed about high society. Occasionally he would iron his single shirt-front and venture forth to collect a few backstairs crumbs of gossip – one *Post* reporter did, in fact, get into Apsley House in the livery of a footman – but usually he relied entirely on his imagination. The Jenkins caper became such a fixture in *Punch* that a real footman called Nathaniel Jenkins wrote in pointing out, rather crossly, that he had no connection with his namesake of the *Morning Post*. *Punch* persisted with the joke, nevertheless. The fictitious Jenkins was modelled on a *Morning*

Post reporter by the name of Rumsey Forster, whose job was to note down names as people entered receptions at various fashionable London venues. Forster once took revenge on Thackeray by omitting his name from a list of guests at Lansdowne House. This annoyed Thackeray, who accosted Forster at the next reception and announced in a loud voice: 'I am Mr Thackeray.'

'And I, sir,' replied Forster, 'am Jenkins.'

The *Post* was usually deferential to royalty, adopting a tone towards court and society 'hardly in keeping with modern ideas of manly independence'.[22] But it took a violently anti-establishment line early in Victoria's reign when it covered the case of Lady Flora Hastings. She was thirty-two and unmarried, a lady-in-waiting to the Queen, who disliked her. Lady Flora was cut by the court when the symptoms of an enlarged liver prompted the Queen to suspect a pregnancy. The *Post* supported Lady Flora in what the diarist Charles Greville described as 'violent and libellous articles'.[23] When she died, shortly afterwards, the paper announced 'The Death of the Lady Flora Hastings', an 'unfortunate victim of Court vice and intrigue',[24] framing the report in the black borders usually reserved for the death of royalty.

Fashionable intelligence had always been the *Morning Post's* speciality, but Daniel Stuart changed the paragraphing policy by banning scurrilous jokes and vicious tittle-tattle. His writers laboured, not in grubby back rooms, but in opulent offices in the Strand in 'a handsome apartment with rosewood desks and silver inkstands'.[25]

Theodore Hook launched *John Bull* as a Sunday paper in 1820. His was the first of three scandal sheets of the Georgian era peddling squibs, gossip and scandal to middle- and upper-class readers. It was followed by the *Age* (1825), edited by Charles Molloy Westmacott, and finally the *Satirist* (1831), run by Barnard Gregory. All three reeked of gossip and abuse about, or aimed at, famous people of the day. As the nineteenth century came of age, so did the journalism of personality, although as early as 1811 the lawyer and politician Henry Brougham was complaining about licentious journals, which satisfied prurient curiosity by identifying 'for the indulgence of that propensity individuals retiring into the privacy of domestic life, to hunt them down, and drag them forth as a laughing-stock to the vulgar'.[26] Brougham knew what he was talking about, being a frequent target of printed gossip himself. But despite his protestations, the genre spawned many offspring, including the *Palladium* (1825–6), *Paul Pry* (1830–31), the *New Satirist* (1841) and the *Crim-Con Gazette* (1838–40; later renamed the *Bon-Ton Gazette*). All purveyed a weekly offering of scurrilous gossip designed not only to upset the likes of Henry Brougham, who might have sued for libel, but others who took direct action, turning up at their offices and threatening to throttle the editor, or worse. (Hook had his own way of dealing with these depredations, but Gregory and Westmacott employed, at a guinea or so a week, a man of Herculean proportions armed with a cudgel, who appeared with it under his arm whenever someone arrived demanding to see the editor, announcing – invariably in an Irish brogue that inspired still greater terror – that *he* was the editor.) But of all these papers the extraordinarily successful *John Bull* was a paradigm in its revelations about what public people got up to in private.

In fact, most of what was in *John Bull* was mere milk and water: news from home and abroad, legal and parliamentary reports, reviews and columns and columns of advertisements. The paper supported the recently installed George IV, who had got into a tangle over his ill-starred marriage to Queen Caroline, and the *Bull* quickly became known for its fierce attacks on Caroline's circle of friends. Hook aimed his heaviest bombardment at the ladies who buzzed around Caroline, flattering and fawning; he picked these women apart, week by week, mercilessly exposing their private lives and foibles in the squibs and paragraphs tumbling out of the pages of the *Bull.* It meant that many great Whig ladies ceased to visit Caroline's court, afraid that they might be next for public humiliation. Of Henry Brougham's wife, it noted that 'the advertisement of her marriage and that of the birth of her child followed one another much more closely than has been usual in "well-regulated families".'[27] Brougham himself had calumnies heaped upon him, for he had successfully defended Caroline in a parliamentary inquiry into her private life. The *Bull* fired off a salvo of embarrassing questions: did you not offer to abandon the Queen if the government would 'bestow on you a silk gown or patent of preference?' 'Did you not in a letter to a friend remark that in your attendance on one of the queen's public appearances, "I had great difficulty to Bring Her to the Post Sober"?'[28]

Hook and his writers on *John Bull* knew how to scandalize and to shock; they also grasped that publicity can be dangerous as well as damaging. When a jury returned manslaughter verdicts against some soldiers who had killed two people in the riots on the day of Caroline's funeral in 1821, Hook published all the names, addresses and trades of the jurors, so that 'their customers may at their discretion reward the activity and talent they have severally displayed in the attainment of truth and the cause of justice'.[29]

One of the main reasons for the extraordinary success of the *Bull* was that Theodore Hook's editorship of it was one of the best-kept secrets in London. No one knew, which meant that the larger-than-life Hook, a tireless gossip, gadabout and socializer, could keep tabs on the world he knew and wrote about without fear or favour. When Lady Jersey protested that no one connected to 'that detestable weekly' should be received in her house, it was in vain. The next number contained a rejoinder in which the anonymous editor made it clear that he was one of her closest acquaintances, having pressed her hand only two days previously at her own mansion. The Duke of Wellington's friend Harriet Arbuthnot, a fan of *Bull* ('a most ably written paper'), was flummoxed too. 'They cannot find out who the editor is,' she recorded in her diary at Easter 1821, noting that its circulation had soared to 9,000, 'more than any other paper that ever was known'.[30]

'It seems that our paper is in a very extraordinary state,' teased the *Bull* in an editorial in 1822. 'Every body praises us – every body reads us; but, as to writing us, every body disowns us.'[31] In fact, Hook wrote every word of every eight-page paper every week.

John Bull was published every Saturday afternoon, in time to catch the post for Sunday, priced at sevenpence (3p) a copy. Hook's printer was William Shackell, with whom he had collaborated in 1820 in the production of *Tentamen*, a pamphlet supporting the new king, George IV. The dissolute former Prince Regent had long been separated from his wife Caroline, but she continued to claim her right to become Queen. The question divided the British people and the two main political parties. The Whigs backed Caroline, the Tories were for the King. With Hook in financial straits, Shackell put up the money, leaving Hook to supply the content. The ownership deal was 50:50. They employed a third man, Henry Fox Cooper, to correct the proofs and act as libel-catcher for three guineas (£3.15) a week. Like the creature that inhabited Westmacott's lair at the *Age*, part of Cooper's job was deterrence. One account describes him greeting outraged visitors to the paper's offices off Fleet Street in a broad Irish brogue: '"Oi'm th'idditer, Sur".'[32]

Launched a week before Christmas 1820, *John Bull* was an instant success. On the question of 'this sickening woman,' Queen Caroline, the paper was unsparing. Hook pulled off a stunning journalistic coup, printing the names of all the ladies who had signed Caroline's visitors' book at Brandenburgh House and attaching a scandalous, rude or indiscreet fact about each. 'As these ladies come forward to vouch for the Queen's purity,' *Bull* explained, 'it seems just and natural to enquire into the value of their evidence.' So, for example, the Hon. Mrs Damer was pilloried as a lesbian ('strangely susceptible to the charms of her own sex'), whilst Lady Tankerville stood accused of being 'mixed up with a disgraceful and criminal affection for a menial servant'.[33] The readers lapped it up. By the end of January 1821, *John Bull* was selling 10,000 copies a week.

Hook's sources for gossip and dirt-dishing on Caroline were to be found both above and below stairs. In a confidential letter to his friend John Wilson Croker, a junior member of the Tory government, Hook describes making contact with an informant named Lesswich. Lesswich was a Fleet Street confectioner who employed a servant who had once attended the wretched Caroline 'and saw more than anybody has yet said they have seen'. This unnamed servant could be persuaded to talk, according to Hook. 'I do not know if the man actually is in the employ of Mr Lesswich at this moment,' Hook explained, 'but from the way in which the thing was told me I am inclined to think he might be easily forthcoming.'[34]

Hook was Pickwickian in the time of Pickwick, the model for Thackeray's journalist Mr Wagg in *Vanity Fair* and *Pendennis*, with his 'white waistcoat spread out . . . with profuse brilliancy; his burly red face shone resplendent over it, lighted up with the thoughts of a good joke and a good dinner. He liked to make his entrée into a drawing-room with a laugh, and, when he went away at night, to leave a joke exploding behind him.'[35]

Hook was indeed a wag, devilishly droll, a dazzling deviser of practical jokes. His best was the gigantic Berners Street hoax of 1809, when the whole street was thrown into uproar for a whole day as hundreds of people, servants, tradesmen, professional men, even princes and potentates, all made their way there at Hook's bidding. He had sent out 4,000 letters, all (under various pretences) inviting the recipients to call on a certain day at the house of a wealthy Mrs Tottenham at 54 Berners Street. Dawn had scarcely broken when dozens of heavy coal wagons came rumbling up the street from both directions, blocking it completely. There were cooks carrying massive wedding-cakes, tailors, bootmakers, undertakers with coffins, draymen with beer-barrels, all swarming towards the dismayed Mrs Tottenham's door. An eye-witness takes up the story:

> Medical men with instruments for the amputation of limbs, attorneys prepared to cut off entails; clergymen summoned to minister to the mind; and artists engaged to portray the features of the body, unable to draw near in vehicles, plunged manfully into the mob. Noon came, and with it about forty fishmongers, bearing forty 'cod and lobsters'; as many butchers, with an equal number of legs of mutton; and as the confusion reached its height, and the uproar became terrific, and the consternation of the poor old lady grew to be bordering on temporary insanity, up drove the great Lord Mayor himself – state carriage, cocked hats, silk stockings, bag wigs and all, to the intense gratification of Hook and his two associates, who, snugly ensconced in an apartment opposite, were witnesses to the triumph of their scheme.[36]

In the street below, people were rolling about, incontinent with laughter.

But the cream of the hoax was still to come. Hook had put out a tale about a complicated fraud being perpetrated in various high places, a story so terrifying in its implications and yet so thoroughly believable that such personages as the governor of the Bank of England and the chairman of the East India Company were lured to Berners Street, only to be swept into the mêlée. Finally, the Duke of Gloucester, complete with liveried entourage, believing himself summoned to receive a message from a dying woman who was formerly a confidential attendant to his mother, found himself floundering in the boiling mob of shouting tradespeople and men of business, jammed together in a hopeless, impotent rage. Hook was immediately suspected as the architect of the hoax, but he had taken care to cover his tracks. No charges were brought, and Hook grew more famous as a consequence.

Hook's dazzling reputation as practical joker, raconteur, punster and party-goer – he was an habitué of every fashionable Mayfair salon and boudoir – had drawn him to the attention of the Prince Regent in the year 1812, when Hook was only twenty-four. Learning that his new favourite had neither income nor position, the Regent found him the job of accountant-general and treasurer to the colony of Mauritius, at a salary amounting, with allowances, to nearly £2,000 a year. At a stroke, Hook found himself out of debt and out of London, bound for a sunny Indian Ocean paradise, sumptuous free accommodation and a magnificent government job, an office shorn of both cares and responsibilities by the happy fact that his boss, the governor of the colony, was a distant relative by marriage. As one of Hook's biographers, A. J. A. Symons, has pointed out, life for the lucky ones in Mauritius was an idyll, 'an alternation of operas in the winter and races in the summer, with a background of balls, bathing, lounging, love-making, and claret at tenpence [4p] a bottle'.[37]

Hook indulged in all of these, but not for long. The governor fell ill and was replaced. Within two months, Hook had been denounced to this new official by a clerk who accused him of embezzlement. Hook denied responsibility for what was an alarmingly large deficit, running into many thousands of pounds. Nevertheless he was arrested, and all his property seized and sold. Repatriated to England under military guard, he arrived at Portsmouth to learn that the attorney-general could find no grounds for a criminal charge, and Hook was released from custody. From Mauritius came word that Hook's accuser had slit his own throat. Although it seems almost certain that it was the clerk himself who had siphoned off the government's money, Hook found himself still mired in suspicion and the subject of unpleasant interrogations by the Board of Colonial Audit, which lasted a further three years. Insofar as he could, Hook went to ground, living anonymously in north London and directing his undiminished restless energy towards journalism.

John Bull was the result. Hook's half-share in the paper restored his fortunes. Circulation soared, Hook recovered his £2,000 a year, and his happiness should have been complete. Unfortunately, however, the ruminative Board of Colonial Audit suddenly announced that it had concluded its deliberations over the deficit in Mauritius and gave judgment against Hook for a ruinous £13,000, seized his goods and chattels (again) and threw him into debtors' prison where he languished for two years. On his release, he turned to writing novels, still dining out, feasting and roistering all over London until his liver gave out and he died, not quite fifty-three, in 1841.

John Bull and its ilk put no great gloss on the profession of journalism. On the contrary, the governing classes (who tended to be the ones most written-about in the gossip columns of the early nineteenth century) were always sneering at the scribbling tribe. Hook's old adversary Henry Brougham described newspaper writing as 'dirty work, like most works of necessity, and one which nothing but the absolute impossibility of finding others who will do it, could ever reconcile me to'.[38] It is not difficult to find reasons for this kind of public execration. The country was governed chiefly by aristocrats, so it was hardly surprising that journalists, especially the scandalmongering kind who whipped up the prejudices of the ordinary people, should be viewed with suspicion and hostility. Their social status was miserable, largely because they had become early masters of the black arts of manipulation, and people despised them for it. As the *London Review* observed in 1835: 'Society treats the gentlemen of the Press much as folks used to behave to witches. It dreads their secret malice and irresistible power, and pays them off for great injuries by petty spite and contemptuous exclusion.'[39]

As *Bull* grew in confidence, it widened its field of fire. Soon, not only were ladies in Caroline's circle lampooned, but any prominent Whig who strayed into Theodore Hook's sights. One was the MP Sir Robert Wilson, who, suspecting that Hook was in fact the paper's editor, accosted him in the street about a rumour that he was next:

'Hook, I am to be traduced and slandered in the *John Bull* next Sunday.'
Hook expressed surprise and abhorrence.

'Yes,' continued Wilson, 'and if I am, I mean to horsewhip you the first time you come in my way. Now stop! I know you have nothing to do with that newspaper, you have told me so a score of times. Nevertheless, if the article, which is purely of a private nature, appears let the consequences be what they may, I will horsewhip you.'[40]

Hook suppressed the intended article, but pilloried Wilson incessantly in *John Bull* for years. Wilson clearly knew that Hook was his tormentor, and many shared his suspicions that he was the editor of that notorious sheet. As public curiosity grew, Hook and his associates took steps to preserve their anonymity, arranging to meet at different coffee-houses for their editorial conferences, which they numbered privately among themselves from one to ten. Nevertheless, word started to spread. '[F]or you see,' Emily Cowper wrote to her brother, 'it is not written by a common hack, but by some man who knows society. Theodore Hook denies it, but is strongly suspected.'[41] Hook tried to throw sand in the public's eyes, even printing a letter to himself as editor, denying that he was the editor. Business boomed, so that a Monday edition joined its Sunday stablemate. After Caroline's death and the loss of Hook's principal target, the *Bull* began to leaven its scurrility with serious journalistic campaigns, notably backing moves to outlaw the practice of sending women to the treadmill.

Although imitators sprang up, Hook's *John Bull* preserved its pre-eminence in the scandalizing business, a distinction remarked on by *The Times* when it described the *Bull* as having been established for the express purpose of libelling private character.[42] With Hook imprisoned and others in charge, the *Bull* lost its dangerous edge, eclipsed by Westmacott's Tory *Age* and Gregory's Whiggish *Satirist*. Both papers were awash with gossip about their political enemies. The rebarbative *Age* guyed William Hazlitt as 'an old weather-beaten, pimple-snouted, gin-smelling man, like a Pimlico tailor, with ink-dyed hands, a corrugated forehead, and a spiritous nose.'[43] Politicians suspected of straying from the path of virtue were written up and dispatched, sometimes in rhyme as in the case of Lord John Russell, a minister in Earl Grey's government who helped draft the first Reform Bill:

> I brought the Bylle in Parliament,
> And after that was donne,
> I used to go to Jermyne Strete
> To have a bytte of funne...
> Oh, lette them talk about 'Reforme',
> Yn whyche I take such pryde,
> I'd rather clasp my Cora's forme,
> Than all the world's besyde![44]

Grubby and cramped, the *Satirist* was no less intrusive, turning its lantern beam on the Irish Chartist Feargus O'Connor and remarking that while his intentions were all very well, 'We think, on the whole, he was just as well engaged making love to Mrs Nisbett.'[45] A popular feature was a series called 'Bastardy', in which the *Satirist's* writers unearthed the illegitimate forebears of titled politicians and printed the details.

Unlike *John Bull,* what these journals did was to publish scandalous gossip about people not in the public eye, and who, living private lives as private individuals, might have expected to be free from the prurient attentions of scandalmongers. 'Is Miss Baynton aware that Vaughan is a married man?' asked the *Satirist* in a typically menacing tone. 'Surely she could not be or she would not expose herself in the way she does.'[46] Like all such publications, the *Satirist* relied heavily on tip-offs from readers for copy. Sometimes, it openly appealed for help: 'If a Reader of the Satirist will furnish us with evidence of the "publication" on the part of the "Gin-and-Water Curate residing in the neighbourhood of Dorset Square," we will make the reverend tippler repeat it.'[47]

The motive to betray foes, friends and sometimes even family to the likes of the *Satirist* was invariably financial; then, as in our own tabloid age, such papers paid well for freshly minted gossip and scandal. But it was a two-way process. Throughout the eighteenth century and well into the nineteenth, papers raked in a regular income by charging fees for suppression and contradiction. So the intended target would be warned that his or her name would shortly be featuring in a squib or mischievous paragraph, unless, of course, he or she paid hush-money. In the event of no reply, the item would be printed and a copy sent to the person concerned, together with a suggestion that if he or she paid a 'contradiction' fee, a statement from him or her on the subject of the paragraph would be published. In this way, newspaper owners earned as much from gossip suppressed as from gossip printed and then gainsaid.

The founder of *The Times,* the first John Walter, became a wealthy man in this way. His own newspaper also prospered from suppression fees. When Mrs Fitzherbert, the Prince Regent's morganatic wife, took exception to some paragraphs she sent her brother to threaten John Walter at his office. The story comes from Mrs Sumbel, the one-time mistress of Captain Topham, founder of the *World* scandal-sheet. She also claimed that her own husband ordered the editor of *The Times,*

William Finey, to call at the Sumbel house to complain about stories in the paper concerning his wife.

'Will that be enough?' cried Mr Sumbel, producing some banknotes from his escritoire.

'Give me a few more,' Finey replied, 'and by St Patrick I will knock out the brains of anyone in our office who dare ever *whisper* your name.'[48]

The Times's first foreign staff correspondent, Henry Crabb Robinson ('Old Crabby'), railed against his 'dishonest and worthless' employer, whilst William Combe, the Treasury writer, declared that Walter had never done an honest act in his life and 'became rich by the vilest arts.'[49]

John Walter had a deal with the government, promising editorial support from *The Times* in return for a subvention of £300 a year, plus the prestigious and lucrative job of printer to HM Customs. Specifically, Walter agreed to insert in his paper certain paragraphs supplied on paper bearing a distinguishing mark, the signature of authenticity. In February 1789, Walter duly inserted two such paragraphs, supplied by Mr Steele, Secretary of the Treasury, and 'signed with his private Mark'. They concerned the mental state of George III who, amid scenes of public jubilation, had just been officially declared sane and restored to health:

> The Royal Dukes, and leaders of opposition in general, affect to join with the friends of our amiable Sovereign, in rejoicing on account of His Majesty's recovery. But the insincerity of their joy is visible. Their late unfeeling conduct will forever tell against them; and contradict all artful professions they may think it prudent to make.
>
> It argues infinite wisdom in certain persons, to have prevented the Duke of York from rushing to the King's apartment on Wednesday. The rashness, the Germanic severity, and the insensibility of this young man, might have proved ruinous to the hopes and joys of a whole nation.[50]

The Prince of Wales was criticized in a similar paragraph that appeared a few days later. Both princes sued for libel, in a case that has set a precedent ever since, for it turned on the question of who bears responsibility for what appears in newspapers. Walter was prosecuted in his capacity as a bookseller. He pleaded guilty but argued in extenuation that as owner he could not control every single detail in his paper. He also, famously, refused to disclose his sources, a journalistic tradition that has survived down the centuries. Walter's defiance cost him dear: on the first libel he was fined £50, imprisoned in Newgate for a year, sentenced to stand in the pillory at Charing Cross for an hour (this was later respited), and ordered to guarantee his good behaviour for seven years. As soon as he had served his time, he began a second twelve-month sentence for libelling the Prince of Wales.

Not everyone admired John Walter for his hard-faced attitude to hard-knock paragraphs. When the radical William Cobbett's daily paper *Porcupine* failed in 1801 after just a year, Cobbett blamed himself. 'It was not, I found, an affair of talent but of trick,' he confessed. 'I could not sell paragraphs. I could not throw out hints against a man's or a woman's reputation in order to bring the party forward to pay me for silence. I could do none of those mean and infamous things by which the daily Press, for the far greater part, was supported and which enabled the proprietors to ride in chariots, while their underlings were actually vending lies by the line and inch.'[51] Cobbett had in mind the kind of smeary stuff that appeared during the low-water days of the *Morning Post*, which targeted the lecherous 1st Duke of Queensberry, known as 'Old Q', in 1789:

> Strayed from his stall in Piccadilly, THE PARISH BULL, commonly called Q, in the corner. He was seen to take the Dover road, and is supposed to have gone in pursuit of a favourite cow. It is a little old beast with only one eye, and a thin grey curl on each side of his head. He has been seen roaring about the streets for some time past. Whoever will bring him to the Wine Vault in Piccadilly shall be properly rewarded. N.B. He has a star on his left flank.[52]
>
> The Duke of Queensberry's sudden retreat from the gayer circles has occasioned various speculations. Some imagine that he has buried himself in his study, to contemplate on political subjects... Others knowing his juvenile powers and gallant propensities think that he has retired with some tender female to indulge in the delights of love and sentiment.[53]

This smutty tittle-tattle smacks of the servants' hall, a fruitful source of gossip for Georgian newspaper editors who would not have enjoyed social contact with dukes. By the time of the Regency, twenty years later, editors were upwardly mobile, mixing freely, if not with nobility, at least with the raffish crowd who flitted around them. In his memoirs, Charles Knight, one-time owner of the *Windsor and Eton Express*, described how Mrs Lane, wife of the editor of the *British Press* newspaper, held court in her drawing room every morning as authors, actors, artists and MPs called to impart the gossip of the day.[54] Always on the lookout for juicy scraps of news, the distinguished Thomas Barnes of *The Times* regularly entertained the great and the good at his house, although oddly he seemed ill at ease in such exalted company. Henry Brougham's principal secretary, Le Marchant, a guest at Barnes's dinner table in 1833, records how 'our host was embarrassed by his company', possibly because Mrs Barnes was 'vulgarity personified'.[55] Aware of their recent social advancement, journalists, even eminent ones like Barnes, struggled to mix with gentlemen without, as Le Marchant put it, showing signs of conscious inferiority.

Blackmailing editors like Gregory and Westmacott were in a baser league than the men from *The Times*, of course, and their methods were cruder and coarser. *The Times* disdained mention of anyone not in public or political life, whereas both Westmacott's *Age* and Gregory's *Satirist* delighted in scandalizing the smallest social fry in order to make money. The gossip that spilled out over their columns concerned, for the most part, total nonentities. It didn't seem to matter to the readers, who feasted on the stories anyway, apparently on the basis that even scandal about people of no consequence is better than no scandal at all. These scurrilous sheets traded on the fact that everyone has something to hide, some personal flaw in their background, some private vice or folly that they are anxious to conceal. Gregory and Westmacott had recognized a journalistic truth, which remains at the heart of the bargain that the modern downmarket tabloids strike with their readers: sex-obsessed tittle-tattle about celebrities and would-be celebrities in return for an apparently insatiable appetite for the astoundingly uninteresting. Both sides feel guilty about such material, the journalists for writing it, the readers for devouring it. But neither stops. In his study of early Victorian scandalous journalism, Donald J. Gray points out that the pleasure of reading such scandal about the well known and the unknown must have been a guilty one. 'It was at least naughty to enjoy this traffic in scandalous knowledge, and while they were indulging their guilty pleasure in the imperfections of others, readers were acknowledging themselves to be gladly at home in this imperfect world.'[56]

Then, as now, the tone of gossip columns was a knowing one: that of a gentleman at ease with the London social round. In both the *Age* and the *Satirist*, this identity found its voice in the running jibes about the lowly social origins of prominent people. Jokes about them and their scandalous behaviour appeared in columns headed 'Chit Chat' or 'Facetiae', full of smutty anecdotes and bawdy puns. The effect of such gossip is akin to being let into a confidence by a man of the world who knows that a lot of life is sordid and trivial, particularly within the magnetic fields of the rich and powerful. 'The knowing response of writer and reader,' Gray remarks, 'is amused imperturbability, and the scandalous pleasure of this response is the wicked affectation of not being shocked by what is deliberately calculated to be shocking.'[57]

Not everything in the *Age* and the *Satirist* was so calculated; most of the editorial space was filled with advertisements and the kind of political, social, financial and other news that appeared everywhere else. But a subtext ran throughout: that whatever public figures might do as they strutted their hour amid the events of the day, what was really interesting was the gossip revealed exclusively by this or that journal, about what these people got up to in private. The implication was that these peccadilloes, inconsequential enough in themselves, were symptomatic of some kind of bigger institutional malaise, a corruption within the Church or the City, the law or the military, medicine, politics or the penal system. But neither Westmacott nor Gregory dwelt for long on these loftier concerns. Knowing that their bread and butter lay in providing scandalous gossip and gags, they ensured that their journals preserved a murky mystique, with a promise to shine a searchlight into the darkness of the wicked world and to expose its scandalous goings-on behind closed doors. For the young journalist Charles Dickens, making his way in Fleet Street, it was a lightweight promise. 'The *Age* and the *Satirist*, though infamous indeed,' he wrote, 'were mere weekly scandal-sheets of no influence or political import.'[58]

Following in their blackmailing tradition, the *Town*, a weekly society paper dealing with 'flash life', appeared for three years at the end of the

1830s. Its popularity stemmed from its intrusion into the private lives of insignificant figures and, because it was unstamped, it could sell at twopence, thereby appealing to a downmarket readership for whom a stamped newspaper at sixpence (2½p) was too expensive. 'We are proud to be considered the organ of the working, or, as they are sometimes called, the lower classes,' one *Town* editorial proclaimed.[59] The paper was edited by Renton Nicholson, who wrote several gossip columns, one of which was called 'Facts and Rumours':

> It is a fact that Joe Millward, the grocer's porter of Queens-row, Pimlico, is an amorous description of an individual...
>
> It is a fact that Nicholls, the Bromley omnibus conductor, is perpetually railing against his mistress.
>
> It is a fact that a certain gentlemanly lawyer's clerk, residing not a hundred miles from Stockbridge, is very frequently engaged in pleading at a certain bar in that town, in the cause of Cupid versus the landlady's friend.
>
> It is a fact that Dick Rider, the butcher of Bond-street, has a vast idea of his own powers of lady-killing politeness.[60]

It went on to cover the doings of a tailor; the ballet-master at Covent Garden; a shopkeeper; a former dealer in marine stores who was giving himself airs; a penny baker; a piano teacher being pursued by a 'lecherous toad' in the Admiralty; a prize fighter; and an ex-carpenter, tiring of matrimony because his new wife made him dress every evening in 'a fustian jacket and ditto unmentionables'. Being unstamped meant that, unlike its rivals, the *Town* couldn't publish the general news that padded out *John Bull*, the *Age* and the *Satirist*. It attracted a unique readership, consisting largely of the uneducated, the incurious and the politically unaware. As a result, Nicholson cut back on the gossip he printed in favour of material that was more easily understood, such as fiction, news of fraud, quackery and double-dealing, jokes and quasi-pornography. Certainly the *Town* was bawdier than its rivals, and brighter to look at. And while its gossip paragraphs mainly concerned the likes of Joe Millward and bus conductor Nicholls, they occasionally did feature more lustrous folk. 'Lord Chesterfield...rode a favourite pleasure mare, at Doncaster, called Laura Honey [an actress]. His beautiful filly...has cut him in consequence...Oh, my lord, if your grandfather were alive, what would he say to your want of taste and discretion, to say nothing of your immorality.'[61]

Town tilted at royals too, sometimes coarsely, as when the young Queen Victoria reportedly bribed a beautiful dancer to leave Britain because Albert was winking at her: '"Is not one thing at a time enough for you, you dirty German prig," said Victoria, in a rage. "By gar, if I may not hab one ting, you shall not hab de oder," responded the Prince; and so saying, his sulky Highness locked his German self and his German sausage in the cabinet all night.'[62]

Disregarding the journalistic tradition of dog not eating dog, Renton Nicholson and Barnard Gregory waged a war of words on each other in their journals throughout the late 1830s. It was mostly hot air, the kind of vituperation designed more to boost circulation than to land any painful blows. Nicholson called Gregory a 'common extortioner, gaming-house keeper, pimp and brothel spongee'[63] and derided Mother Parlby, in whose brothel Gregory reportedly sponged, as 'the antiquated Cyprian of whom you make use in every way'.[64] But Nicholson in turn was sometimes forced to defend himself in the *Town* against adopting Gregory's gossip-gathering tactics, countering claims that someone purporting to represent it had resorted to blackmail. What gossip did get into the *Town* was comparatively meagre fare. Nicholson was more interested in titillation, and such tittle-tattle as was printed was usually preoccupied with sex. The *Town* paved the way for the saucy Sundays, printing reports of celebrated sex trials, trumpeting such tempting features as 'Sketches of courtezans', 'Brothels and brothel keepers' and 'Female Sinners, aged and middle-aged'. It also became tiresomely obsessed with coarse word-play (Albert's German sausage was a recurring wheeze).

By 1843 and the launch of the *News of the World*, the *Town* was extinct and the *Age* and *Satirist* were faltering. Closing the *Town* a year earlier, Nicholson apologized with typical chutzpah for his editorial 'neglect unparalleled in the history of periodical literature, and unmatched in the records of designed inattention'.[65] *John Bull*, during the previous twenty years, had transmuted itself from scourge of the rich and powerful to required weekly reading for conservative clerics; the *Age*, too, sloughed off its scandalous past and was relaunched as a conventional Tory newspaper named the *English Gentleman*.

The *Satirist* ran until 1849, finally ruined by the cost of libel suits. By then, Barnard Gregory had married a rich woman and retired into comfortable obscurity. For nearly twenty years, he had been almost continually mired in litigation, occasionally imprisoned, and castigated by the courts; he was once described by Lord Denman as 'a trafficker in character'.[66] His career as an editor collapsed when he libelled the man who printed Renton Nicholson's rival paper, the *Town*. Nicholson responded with a series of articles exposing Gregory's blackmailing activities, and although he persevered with the *Satirist* he was finally overwhelmed by hostile public opinion, which was bolstered in the courts and supported by the Duke of Brunswick, with whom Gregory had been waging a losing battle.

The *Crim-Con Gazette* flourished for a much shorter time. Each Saturday from the summer of 1838 to the beginning of 1840, it doled out soup-plate-sized dollops of sexual excess, notwithstanding its pledge at launch not to become an obscene publication ('Trials not fit to meet the public eye rigidly excluded'), but to stay true to its declared intention of arresting the progress of aristocratic vice and debauchery. 'Crim-Con' (criminal conversation) was code for adultery, and at the dawn of the Victorian age there was plenty about, from the lowest-born to the most exalted. The first issue delivered a lengthy, almost verbatim, report of a case involving Lord Melbourne, then Home Secretary, involving another man's wife and featuring at length the evidence of servants. Reputations were scrutinized and swiftly torn apart in a series spotlighting 'Box-Lobby Loungers' of whom the first, a Mr Cornelius Rivers, was assailed as 'a lump of senseless clay – the leavings of a soul – who cast aspersions on his mother's virtue and wondered whether his real father was a sportsman or a dustman'.[67] With its 'Columns of the Cuckolded', features on 'Libertines of the Day' and the 'Amours of a Clergyman', its premature demise went largely unlamented, leaving any readers who felt a sense of loss to ponder the *Gazette's* own dictum, printed over every crim. con. trial report: 'Oh shame, where is thy blush?'

4

Blackmail and Lady Blessington

Barnard Gregory's *Satirist* finally folded at the end of the 1840s. Blackmail and extortion were profitable rackets, but even when Gregory and his contemporary Westmacott were reputed to be making £5,000 or £6,000 a year, costs – particularly legal costs and libel awards – were heavy. Neither Gregory nor Renton Nicholson of the *Town* were prudent men, and scandal sheets were a risky business, so when sales began to decline in the 1840s, their profit margins shrank accordingly. The fall-off was largely due to changing journalistic trends. The mainstream papers, and their readers, were moving with the times, replacing the fear and bitterness of the Georgian era with a more sophisticated and cosmopolitan tone.

The 1830s had proved an age of disillusion, dashing the high hopes of the Great Reform Bill with its promise of popular enfranchisement. The streets swarmed with the ragged poor; the ruling Whigs proved to be overweening, aristocratic and indifferent rather than the friends of the people. Beneath the established press ran a ranker tide of gutter titles, near-pornographic and hysterically abusive periodicals that divided savagely along party lines or prosecuted private feuds in their pages. James Grant, a Victorian newspaper historian writing in 1837, found Gregory's *Satirist* 'full of personalities, but there is generally something so amusing, blended with good-nature in the manner in which its paragraphs are written, that even those parties at whose excesses the laugh is raised, can hardly be angry with it'.[1] But there was an undeniable coarseness to the *Satirist* and its virulent contemporaries, and while the principal papers assumed a more subdued tone and employed calmer language in their commentaries and discourse, that old coarseness was picked up and echoed by a fresh rash of newspaper nasties that broke out in the 1830s and lasted for another thirty years.

Oozing scandal and gossip of the most vicious kind, these shoddy imitations of Nicholson's *Town*, with titles such as *Sam Sly*, *Paul Pry*, *Fast Life*, *Cheap John* and *Peeping Tom*, proclaimed their provenance from the masthead and plumbed the depths of cheap and obnoxious journalism. They appeared suddenly, and disappeared without notice. Sometimes their staffs overlapped.[2] With them came a slew of comic papers, launched – like the scandal sheets – half for fun and half in the hope of turning a profit. A historian of *Punch* magazine described the 'embittered raffishness' from whence these publications sprang, '[s]cribbled on greasy table-tops in chop-houses, on bar-counters, in college rooms, in the wings of theatres, at smoky sing-songs in dubious cellars, in sponging-houses and Debtors' Prisons.'[3] No one knows the circulation of these 'low, low papers', one of which ruined the reputation of Lady Dorothy Neville with a single paragraph, but they were all so scurrilous that even the most liberal champions of popular taste were unable to defend them. A disgusted Thackeray scooped up half-a-crown's worth of these scandal sheets in Paternoster Row in 1838. He wrote:

> The main point of these papers seems to be a wish to familiarize every man in London who can afford a penny with the doings of the gin-shops, the gambling-houses, and [whore]-houses more infamous still. The popularity of the journals, and their contents, are dismal indications indeed of the social conditions of the purchasers, who are to be found among all the lower classes in London. Thanks to the enlightened spirit of the age, no man scarcely is so ill-educated as not to be able to read them; and blessings on cheap literature! No man is too poor to buy them.[4]

Such pre-Dickensian journalistic stews were doomed. Peel's new-look Tories heralded a more benign mood, which eventually suppressed the harsh, derisive voice of the streets. Life seemed sweeter all round. Chartism finally fizzled out as the Hungry 1840s gave way to the more prosperous 1850s, in which the bohemian stirrings of modern journalism were first felt, redolent of Thackeray's smoke-filled 'land of chambers, billiard-rooms, supper-rooms, oysters... where soda-water flows freely in the morning; a land of tin-dish covers from taverns, and frothing porter.'[5] Journalistic excrescences like *Paul Pry*, *Sam Sly* and

Peeping Tom, in which scandal and gossip became entangled in a mire of pornography, failed and folded in this fresher atmosphere, and others that managed furtively to keep going were outlawed by the Obscene Publications Act of 1857.

Charles Molloy Westmacott, editor of the Tory scandal sheet, the *Age*, levied blackmail without mercy. His most celebrated trophy was Lady Blessington, queen of Regency London's glitterati, about whom he published a string of damaging and defamatory allegations, linking her with her brother-in-law, the dashing, dandified Count d'Orsay. The recently widowed Marguerite, 'the most gorgeous Lady Blessington' in the estimation of the elderly classical scholar Dr Samuel Parr, was the daughter of a handsome Irish spendthrift. After a chaotic early life and a whirlwind succession of unsuitable husbands and lovers, she had been sold, according to rumour, for £10,000 to a wealthy Irish peer, Lord Mountjoy, who was subsequently created Earl of Blessington. Such a delinquent career for an Irish girl of common stock placed her firmly beyond the social pale. Marital irregularity was tolerated among the *haut ton*, but only if the parties concerned put on an outward show of conformity. Lady Blessington had broken the rules and therefore was deemed ineligible to receive visits from society ladies. And while her colourful history proved to be the making of her, it also provided red meat for the gossipmongers of the Regency.

By 1831, when she opened her salon, Marguerite Blessington had been twice widowed. She was forty-two, but still magnetically beautiful, in the words of one admirer, 'with eyes as quick as lightning... [with] the keenness of an Irishwoman in relishing fun and repartee, strange turns of language, bright touches of character'.[6] The complimentary Dr Parr had predicted that 'with her shrewd and masculine mind, she would be even more impressive in middle age than while in the lovely splendour of her youth'[7] and he was right. At Seamore Place, off Park Lane, and later at Gore House in Kensington, she created the ideal relaxed atmosphere for a glittering circle of guests who, by and large, were judged as rich, intelligent and charming as she was. Because of Lady Blessington's mongrel past, those paying court were mostly men.

Men worshipped Marguerite Blessington. She was not only beautiful, but a natural hostess whose parties attracted the finest brains; writers, artists, journalists and politicians brought to her salon a raffish glamour that eluded some of the more 'respectable' drawing rooms. Statesmen including Castlereagh, Canning, Brougham and Earl Grey mingled with the stars of literary London, novelists, historians and poets. Byron, on meeting Lady Blessington in Genoa, had approved of her at once – 'very literary – and very pretty, even of a morning'[8] – and her friendship with the cantankerous writer Walter Savage Landor sealed her preference for literary figures.

But Lady Blessington's bohemian bent had already marked her out as gossip-column fodder. Although her behaviour since marrying Lord Blessington had been above reproach, a new arrival at their door in 1821 caused a certain frisson. He was a French nobleman, Count Alfred d'Orsay was attractive, clever, charming and, at only twenty, some twelve years younger than Marguerite Blessington. What attachment (if any) developed between them can only be surmised, but it seems that Lord Blessington took a shine to his French visitor, inviting d'Orsay to accompany him and his wife on an extensive cultural tour of the Continent. The threesome remained abroad for the next eight years, finally alighting in Paris where Lord Blessington, a wine-bibber of prodigious appetites, died of a stroke. Matters were further complicated by the fact that during this European tour, Count d'Orsay had married Lord Blessington's fifteen-year-old daughter, Lady Harriet Gardiner. The terms of Blessington's will were such that Lady Blessington, his beloved wife, was left perilously insecure while d'Orsay inherited the bulk of his father-in-law's estate. Lady Blessington, to spare her stepdaughter the trauma of her own experience, had insisted that Harriet's marriage to d'Orsay should remain unconsummated for four years, arousing suspicions that this was in order to allow Marguerite an excuse for flinging her ringlets at the 'gorgeous dragon-fly' Count herself.

In August 1829, while tongues were furiously wagging in Paris and in London, the scandalmonger Westmacott got wind of these whispers and decided to share them with readers of the *Age*, stirring into his sulphurous mix the added ingredient of d'Orsay's sister, the Duchesse de Guiche. 'The Count d'Orsay, who a short time since married a daughter of the late Lord Blessinton [*sic*] continues to reside with his wife and noble mother-in-law, but for some reason or other their only visitant of rank is the Duchesse de Guiche – more it were not polite of us to tell.'[9]

A month later, Westmacott's *Age* printed an anonymous letter commenting flippantly on various society men and women, including Count d'Orsay: 'Alfred D'Orsay, with his pretty pink-and-white face, drives about à la Petersham with a cocked-up hat and a long-tailed, cream-coloured horse. He says he will have seventeen thousand a year to spend; others say seventeen hundred; he and my Lady go on as usual. The Duchesse de Guiche visits there in solitary womanhood; indeed she says it is a great bore and she can stand it no longer.'[10] The writer signed himself 'Otiosus'. It would have been Westmacott's practice at this point to issue a demand for money, in order to suppress any further scurrilous speculation in his grimy columns. But if he did, his offer to sell his paper's silence was either rejected or ignored.

Two weeks later, 'Otiosus' wrote again from Paris. His tone had changed from insinuation to insolence: 'What a ménage is that of Lady Blessington! It would create strange sensations were it not for one fair flower that still blooms under the shade of the Upas. Can it be conceived in England that M. Alfred D'Orsay has publicly detailed to what degree he has carried his apathy for his pretty, interesting wife, and has boasted of his continence? This young gentleman, Lady Blessington, and the virgin wife of sweet sixteen all live together.'[11] This insult was instantly the talk of fashionable London. Hearing of it in Paris, the shocked Lady Blessington instructed her solicitor to issue proceedings against the paper. But he advised her to treat the allegations with contempt by ignoring them. In a flurry, Lady Blessington (acting on something she had heard) rounded on a man she knew and accused him of writing these libels. This acquaintance strenuously denied it, and it was only when another of Westmacott's victims managed to secure from him a fragment of the letter from Paris containing the aspersions on Lady Blessington that the matter was settled: the writing was definitely not that of the accused man.

'I have never seen a single number of the *Age*,' wrote Lady Blessington to a friend, 'do not know a single person who takes it in, and never hear it named, so that I am in total ignorance as to the attacks it contains.'[12] In fact, if her friends did read these printed scandals, they took no notice. In any case, although d'Orsay remained a close confidant of Lady Blessington, even after the break-up of his marriage to Harriet, she was not interested in him sexually, since he was almost certainly homosexual and a lifelong narcissist.

Lady Blessington never obtained redress against the wretched Westmacott. However, he got his comeuppance the following year, when Charles Kemble left the stage at Covent Garden and thrashed him in a box at the theatre in retaliation for him having libelled his daughter, the actress Fanny Kemble. Westmacott eventually went to live in Paris, where he died in 1868. He belonged, in the estimation of one late Victorian observer, 'to a "rowdy" class of editors which may now be pronounced obsolete. In his days an organ of defamation was necessary to both political parties alike. The Tories had the *Age*; the Liberals the *Satirist*; two scandalous prints long since gone to their unhonoured graves.'[13] Lady Blessington suffered at the hands of both: in 1831, nearly two years after her vilification in the *Age*, newspaper scandal broke out afresh, but this time in the *Satirist*, which published this 'Riddle by Lord Glengall':

My first the reverse of a curse
My second a very great weight is
My whole neither better nor worse
Than a dame from the land of potatoes.
Of her daughter-in-law
She makes a cat's-paw
(Ask the fair virgin bride
By Count d'Orsay's side.)[14]

Lord Glengall's jingle may have been inelegant, but it was indubitably authentic. Lady Blessington's most protective modern biographer, Michael Sadleir,[15] believed that she would not have been troubled by it had Glengall not belonged to a tiny but influential circle of aristocratic trendsetters who 'found a delightful coincidence between the yellow press idea of society news and their own idea of self-advertisement. This clique, despite its bad-mannered presumption, stood for "ton".'[16] It could make or break a career in society, and in Lady Blessington's case, the campaign of gossip at which her enemies connived proved socially catastrophic. Her old vivacity was gone, the laughter trailed away. Thanks to her whispering adversaries, she was permanently tainted and had moved even further beyond the pale. A few years later, another scurrilous rag, the *Crim-Con Gazette*, commenting on her dignified retirement, noted that 'few if any persons have been subjected to so many libels'[17] but added that she had countered them so spiritedly that her critics had generally come off worse.

Marguerite Blessington took up a new career as a writer, publishing a record of her encounters with Lord Byron in Italy together with travel books and several novels. These were well received, but her expenses outstripped her income and she had to turn to journalism to make ends meet. In January 1846, when she was seriously short of money, her friend Charles Dickens hired her as a gossip writer for his newly launched *Daily News* at a salary of £250 for a six month's trial. The rising young novelist had been introduced to Lady Blessington some years before, and the pair were on cordial terms. Dickens's gossip-column brief was a generously wide one: she was to contribute (in the strictest confidence) 'any sort of intelligence you may like to communicate, of the sayings, doings, rumours, and movements in that World which you know all about'.[18] Her contributions would be billed in the paper as 'Exclusive Intelligence'. There was some embarrassment over terms; Dickens had invited her to name her price ('tell me how many Hundreds a Year the Paper may pay you') and she had done just that, asking for £800, a figure that was quickly reduced to £500 by the paper's money-manager.

Nevertheless, Fleet Street's first titled gossip writer was soon scribbling her paragraphs, to Dickens's apparent satisfaction. 'They are very good indeed,' he assured her at the end of January. 'I wonder how you make so much of such a dull time.'[19] Dickens's rapture quickly turned to irritation. 'An unexpected botheration at the last moment'[20] led to her column being killed on press night; in fact, it was not her fault, and the paragraphs were printed after a couple of days. But a week later, two of Blessington's *bonnes bouches* had to be pulled. One was about the Queen's consort, the other concerned Louis Napoleon. Dickens, as editor, had to explain. 'The Paragraph about Prince Albert is very curious and quite new to me,' he wrote to her, 'but I am afraid to insert it. You have no idea how many people would take offence at it, if it appeared in a New Paper.'[21] The copy has long since been lost, so we have no way of knowing its content. As for the item about Prince Louis Napoleon, Dickens explained that his aide Crowe had objected to it. Scholars believe the offending paragraph was a comment on the

French government's refusal to allow Louis Napoleon to visit his dying father in Florence. Dickens told Lady Blessington that while Crowe went along with the sentiment expressed, '[he] thought it unwise, with reference to our French Relations, to put it in'.[22] Since 'French Relations' came within Crowe's field of responsibility, Dickens had no choice but to agree.

Within a few weeks, Dickens had resigned from the *Daily News*, and when a new editor arrived, he decided not to renew Lady Blessington's contract as 'Society Correspondent'. It was the start of a long and painful financial decline. The jointure paid under the terms of her husband's will ceased as a result of the Irish potato famine, and although she managed to recover part of her income, she had to pawn her jewels. She and d'Orsay (who had moved into her residence, Gore House, having impoverished himself through a life of unbridled extravagance) found themselves besieged by bailiffs. The contents of her sumptuous Kensington home were put up for auction and the couple fled back to Paris. Lady Blessington died of a seizure there in the summer of 1849. The first titled writer to put her name to columns of society intelligence, she was also the first woman who, having been badly bitten by the blackmailers of the scandalous press, had bitten back, albeit in the strictest confidence.

With the 1860s came a new breed of gossipmongers, the society journals that inherited the mantle of Westmacott, Gregory and Nicholson. Like the bad old scandal sheets, journals like Edmund Yates's *World* and Henry Labouchere's *Truth* combined a worldly knowingness with defining pointers on the whole business of being 'in society'; advice on dress, manners, how to entertain, even what to talk about, jostled for attention among the gossip paragraphs and squibs. What Edmund Yates achieved with his *World* in the 1870s was a form of cleansing in which his gossip smelt and tasted better. His secret was a matter of tone. Today, it might be called 'light'n'easy', gossip that satisfies without wounding or denigrating its subject. The change reflected improving public manners, as raw, mud-slinging, blackmailing invective yielded to a new sense of dignity and decorum. Not that these newcomers flinched or lacked bite. Much of the fodder each week at the news-stands continued to cock disrespectful snooks at distinguished figures in the public eye, with what Donald Gray called this 'steady impertinence'[23] reflecting the decline of deference in society at large.

Yates is credited with inventing society journalism, describing his formula for the success of his *World* as a confection of 'all the light and gossipy news of the day', plus 'good political and social articles written in a bolder, freer and less turgid style'[24] than had been served up to earlier Victorians. The *World* sprang directly from the scarlet of Westmacott's *Age*, Gregory's *Satirist* and Hook's *John Bull*, but while the newcomer might have mended its manners, it nevertheless identified the British public's unquenchable thirst for juicy gossip. Yates, as one Victorian commentator observed, persuaded himself that the public's supposed horror of 'personal journalism' was a sham and, 'provided it was not vulgar or scurrilous, not too redundant of feminine chit-chat and free from rowdyism, that it was certain to be acceptable' because of 'the insatiable demand for details, however minute, of those in authority, in affluence, or in peril'.[25]

5

Yates and his *World*

He has been called the first Nigel Dempster,[1] and certainly Edmund Yates was, in his Victorian heyday, Britain's best-known gossip writer. He invented what became known as 'society' or 'personal' journalism, Americanized the British press by introducing personal interviews, and pioneered the trend towards short, snappy paragraphs and titbits. With his weekly paper, the *World*, Yates made gossip essential reading and forced it to compete with other features vying for the attention of his readers. Yates's idea for the *World* descends directly from Defoe's Scandal Club and its imitators. Gossip, tittle-tattle and personal abuse – invariably entertaining but also personally wounding to the people who were pilloried – were the staples of many eighteenth-century newspapers, the *Morning Post* in particular. But in the mid-1850s, Yates (describing himself as 'a recorder of the floating light gossip of the day'[2]) had been the first journalist to recognize the potential of the harmless personal paragraph. Kennedy Jones, who helped launch the *Daily Mail* in 1896, believed that Yates was the man who purged such paragraphs of malice and spite. In 1855, while still in his early twenties, Yates had started a weekly column called 'The Lounger at the Clubs' in the *Illustrated Times*, a flourishing offshoot of the *Illustrated London News*. It satisfied the tastes of the time, but Yates entertained no illusions about such columns. He spoke of gossiping paragraphs as 'flippant nonsense', and while proprietor of the *World* he referred to himself as a tradesman, the paper as his shop and his paragraphs as his wares.

Yates appreciated that, far from originating in the servants' hall, most of these paragraphs were contributed privately by someone with a direct interest in their content. Newspapers had been fed gossipy items from the royal court for years because courtiers recognized the value of personal publicity. A former maid of honour, for example, recorded how in 1854 'a lot of reporters travelled down in the special train with [the royal family to Balmoral], among others one who had on his card, "Mr—, Fashionable Department of the *Morning Post.*" [3] Yates fed the mid-Victorian public's appetite for paragraphs that were 'personal in the inoffensive sense of the word ... neither vulgar, scurrilous, malignant, nor vindictive; above all ... amusing'. This was something new; very little humour found its way into the mainstream press of the day. As Yates himself observed, it was a quality that, to most owners and editors, 'was stamped with the mark of the Beast. With their readers it was different,' Yates added; 'to them the tiniest thread-like rivulet of fancy in the midst of a dreary desert of fact was acceptable, and eagerly seized upon.' [4]

In the *World*, launched in July 1874, Yates pioneered a new genre of newspaper that assembled gossipy reports of upper-class life, speckled with intimate trivia and the odd indiscreet revelation that became known as 'personal journalism'. He spotted a gap in the market, and filled it at a time when, *The Times* recalled, 'there were great numbers of highly respectable persons who looked with an avid, but the most part futile, curiosity on the gilded and brilliant existence of those who formed the world of pleasure and leisure, of high politics and high birth.' [5] Some attributed his success to a lack of imagination: the roistering bohemian journalist Joseph Knight apparently thought that Yates was morally and intellectually colour-blind, and in the judgment of another Victorian editor, he just missed being a really great man. [6] But he was shrewd enough, in the wake of the celebrated horsewhipping of Grenville Murray by Lord Carrington on the Conservative Club steps, to spot a trend. He saw that the public's appetite for society journalism had been whetted and, taking Murray into his confidence as a collaborator, packed the *World* with frothy gossip about the great and the good. The Prince of Wales was a particular obsession in the late 1870s. Every issue of the paper contained royal snippets from the backstairs at Marlborough House, which were crowned – using a technique imported from America – by an informal *Hello!*-style interview with HRH himself, conducted for the magazine's 'Celebrities at Home' feature by the flamboyant *Daily News* war correspondent, Archibald Forbes. (Yates gave the Prince, and everyone else interviewed in the *World*, copy approval, 'full liberty, if they wished it, to inspect the article in proof before it was published',[7] prefiguring the sweetheart deals struck with celebrities today.)

It was Yates's style to innovate. But it was also his good fortune to flourish at a time of great change in the British press, which was the result of technological advances and the loosening of political controls. Before 1855, when the last penny was removed from newspaper duty, most Fleet Street titles had artificially high cover prices and comparatively small readerships. Within a few years, everything changed. Titles that before had attracted only a particular type of reader now broadened their appeal; they aimed less and less for readers from a particular social class, and sought a wider audience. Yates grasped this and, believing good journalism to comprise 'all the light and gossipy news of the day, properly winnowed and attractively set forth',[8] made it his business to deliver just that to an increasingly literate and sophisticated readership.

He also understood that these homogenized readers wanted something different. They had tired of the old newspaper fare, mixing scurrility with heavy politics, and craved something lighter and more 'respectable'; they frowned on sexual innuendo and expected their papers and magazines to be fit for all the family to read. Harmless gossip, of the kind Edmund Yates pioneered, was quite acceptable, provided that it steered clear of the sort of personal abuse that filled the old-style scandal sheets. With bohemian gusto and boundless self-confidence, Yates plunged ahead, never afraid to experiment with his journalism in order to satisfy his many 'tax-paying, church-going and society-fearing obligations'.[9] Money drove him; he wanted to enjoy life, unfettered by political, moral or ideological constraints, and gossip was the key that would unlock his ambition.

It was his 'Lounger' column in Henry Vizetelly's twopenny *Illustrated Times* that made Yates's name as a gossip writer. Between 1855 and 1863, it became the best-known gossip column in Britain, the foundation, as one contemporary observed, of an entire 'school of public journalistic gossip'.[10] In it, he introduced the personal voice that has characterized so many gossip columns ever since, sharing confidences with his readers, like a well-informed friend dropping a word in one's ear. Phrases like 'I hear', 'I understand' and 'I learn' – familiar gossip currency even today – were all coined by Yates as 'The

Lounger' and were instantly imitated by his contemporaries. His sharp eyes and ears picked up snippets of what he called 'semi-private gossip, those pleasant rumours which originate in cliques, and coteries, and flit from smoking-room to smoking-room'.[11] He ranged widely, writing on topics as diverse as financial chicanery in public life and the domestic hypocrisies of the Victorian *bourgeoisie*. But in retrospect, the actual content of Yates's column is unimportant; it is his tone that establishes it as a journalistic milestone. As one observer of Victorian Fleet Street put it, Yates's 'Lounger', 'with its slightly impertinent and intimate asides',[12] was something quite new and it took London by storm.

Sex seldom surfaced. Neither did 'The Lounger' resort to the kind of coarse language used by the likes of Westmacott, Nicholson or Theodore Hook. This urbanity was also the tone taken by Yates's new column in the *World*, 'What the World Says', which was launched, in his own words, as 'an amusing chronicle of current history, divested of the nonsense which has hitherto stuck like treacle to public business'.[13] He left others to deal with scandals in high finance and political analysis. What interested Yates was life's small change, the flecks and straws in the wind. He combed the papers voraciously, talked to people in the street, dined out at his clubs, all in pursuit of gossip. But his was not exclusively a one-man show. He relied heavily on a network of anonymous informants, who sold him information and stories, and on other members of his *World* staff. Sometimes things went wrong. Yates liked to hire women reporters, and in 1883 it was a stray paragraph by one of them that pitched him into jail. He served seven weeks of a four months' sentence for publishing a true, albeit malicious, anecdote about the sexual delinquency of Lord Lonsdale who, although not named, issued a writ for criminal libel. Although he despised slovenliness in his subordinates, Yates gallantly protected his female writer, took the blame and served the sentence at Holloway on her behalf, refusing to name his sources.

The case provoked a fierce public debate about newspaper gossip. The more staid papers assailed Yates and his *World* for debasing the character of English journalism, with the *Manchester Guardian* hoping that his imprisonment would 'administer a wholesome corrective to habitual abuses of the privileges of the press'.[14] The *Morning Advertiser* pointed out that Yates and his contributors were by no means the only sinners, but insisted that details of the private lives of public men should be 'excluded from a paper which professes to supply the public with news'.[15] At the head of the countercharge came the crusading W. T. Stead, with a leading article in his *Pall Mall Gazette* headed 'A Plea For Tittle-Tattle' in which he railed against the 'wholesale anathema upon society journalism'. Many people of all classes shared a natural desire for such stories. 'Everyone delights in a Boswell,' Stead added, 'and what is the society journal but the Boswell to an innumerable number of personages ... known to the man in the street?'[16]

Yates had come to the *World* with a dash of notoriety. Sixteen years earlier, in 1858, as a young contributor to the penny paper, *Town Talk*, Yates had been rude about the novelist Thackeray, accusing him of undue obsequiousness towards the nobility. This had so incensed the author of *Vanity Fair* that he had Yates thrown out of his cherished Garrick Club. Yates campaigned unsuccessfully for reinstatement, helped by Charles Dickens who, while in the throes of an embarrassingly public separation from his wife, had heard that Thackeray had tittle-tattled about his affair with the actress Ellen Ternan. The row, which divided the London literary world, led to a breach between the two best-selling novelists of mid-Victorian England that was only partially healed shortly before Thackeray's premature death five years later in 1863.

The *World's* best-ranking contemporary for gossip and society news was *Truth*, launched in 1877 by a swashbuckling chancer called Henry Labouchere. Detested by Queen Victoria (who called him 'that horrible lying Labouchere') and feared by his political enemies, he was a gambler, diplomat, reformer, politician and gossip-gleaner – and as a result a leading figure in the comic conscience of the Victorian age. Labouchere was one of Yates's original recruits. As the *World's* city editor, he lambasted company promoters, newspaper share puffers and moneylenders in a series of exposés unprecedented in British journalism. The *World's* circulation boomed, and boomed still more when a disgruntled stockbroker named Abbott attacked Labouchere in the street and threatened to horsewhip him. A crowd gathered to watch the two top-hatted tusslers, and their subsequent brawl landed Labouchere's assailant in court.

Small, puckish, debonair, hand in pocket, head tilted to one side, monocled and chain-smoking, Labouchere seemed to stroll through life always managing to make the best of circumstances. The grandson of a French clerk who made good, at sixteen young Henry was removed from Eton to be taught by tutors. He was subsquently thrown out of Cambridge – accused, apparently unjustly, of cheating in exams – with racing debts of £6,000. To steer him clear of London's gaming haunts and brothels, his puritan father packed him off to Europe and later America and Mexico, where he joined a travelling circus. On his return he went into the diplomatic service and was posted from embassy to embassy, making scant progress on the career ladder but learning much about the ways of the wider world. Having proved himself a thorn in many an ambassadorial side, he turned to journalism and to Radical politics, becoming an MP in the mid-1860s. When, in 1869, Labouchere inherited a quarter of a million pounds from his uncle, Lord Taunton, he suddenly found himself with the means to realize his idea for a weekly magazine that mixed exposure of wrong-doings with urbane society gossip. The result was *Truth*.

The gossip in *Truth*'s 'Entre Nous' column was harsher than the corresponding feature in Yates's *World*, being less concerned with the fashions of society and more bitingly satirical and censorious. 'Labby' (as everyone called him) mixed social chit-chat with personal scorn, spicing it all with dashes of his own outspoken brand of political radicalism. He cared nothing for the sensibilities of his fellow writers. 'An outcry of literary men is raised against sensationalism,' he once complained. 'It is the business of a newspaper to create a sensation.'[17] *Truth* was bright, impertinent, personal, its gossip (according to a contemporary) 'fresh, careless, well-informed, and fearless'.[18]

Labouchere helped himself to many of Edmund Yates's ideas, among them his series of 'Anecdotal Photographs', profiles of well-known public figures in the mould of Yates's 'Celebrities at Home', whose sole purpose was to feed the Victorians' fascination with public figures. 'Celebrities at Home' provided an eye-to-the-keyhole peep into the private lives of the famous, and virtually coined the modern use of the world 'celebrity'. By submitting to a personal interview, luminaries like Gladstone, Disraeli and Tennyson allowed readers to venture into hitherto private areas of their lives. It was a technique that Yates had imported from America, where he had lived for a year before returning to London to launch the *World*. It sounds absurd today, but such newfangled ideas became the cause of divided consternation in Fleet Street.

'What are we coming to?' complained one crusty old clubman to another, overheard by Labouchere. 'Interviews in the *Pall Mall Gazette*!'

'Yes,' replied the other, 'and not only interviews, but pictures!'[19]

Labby himself twitted the *PMG*'s editor W. T. Stead for 'degrading the dignity of the press' by introducing interviewers, and nearly a decade later, when printed interviews had become part of the journalistic scenery, one prominent journalist was still complaining about dumbing-down, 'a lessening of the call upon the mental powers, and ... a gratification of the idle curiosity of the reader'. He blamed such 'lapses of taste' on the excesses of America, where 'the interviewer forces himself upon unwilling subjects, and so constitutes himself a bore and a nuisance'.[20] At the same time, the American-born novelist Henry James, one of the leading writers of the day and himself a former journalist, had come to loathe the daily press for being at the root of most infelicities of late-Victorian life. He blamed the British newspapers of the 1890s ('a really squalid crew')[21] for aping the American scandal sheets by reducing knowledge and understanding to the level of personal gossip.

Nevertheless, 'Celebrities at Home' continued to rank among the star attractions of the *World*. Although the portraits of the great and the good that emerged were often rather anodyne – as well as granting copy approval, Yates always avoided any overt criticism of his subjects – they were not exclusively flattering. He probably stretched his friendship with Wilkie Collins to its limits in describing him as 'a rapid inventor and a slow producer'; it was perhaps this kind of unexpected barb that put some star Victorians on their guard and caused others, like Anthony Trollope, Yates's arch-enemy who disapproved of 'society journalism',[22] to refuse to take part.

But Yates was a consummate master of trifles. He was superficial, and he knew it, but he was also enough of a journalistic magician to know how to lend his gossip an improving tone, leaving his less-educated readers with what one commentator called 'an agreeable sensation as of a clever and not too exacting appeal to their intellectual perceptions'.[23] Even at the unexalted level of the gossip-gleaner, Yates made his mark as one of the pioneers of the New Journalism in Britain, who passed on the flame to giants such as Harmsworth, founder of the *Daily Mail*, which was launched two years after Yates's death in 1894. Yates knew his limitations, admitting to nothing more than an abiding interest in 'news, scandal, tittle-tattle, truth, lies, and *gobemoucheries*[24] alike'.[25] He satisfied a late-Victorian appetite in the newspaper-reading public for 'mental food...in minces and snippets, not in chops and joints'[26] but, more importantly, he made gossip a crucial ingredient in the mainstream British press of the 1880s and 1890s. 'The world has been considerably transformed in recent years,' remarked T. P. O'Connor, the Irish MP-turned-journalist and another great gossip promoter. 'No one's life is now private: the private dinner party, the intimate conversation, all are told.'[27] And, he might have added, you can blame the Americans.

6

Not for Babes, Prudes, Idiots or Dudes

The man who first served America with bumper scoops of newspaper gossip was a squint-eyed Scot who knew what his readers wanted and ladled it out to them hot and heavy. James Gordon Bennett may not have invented the popular cheap mass-circulation newspaper but he was a pioneer; his editorial innovations, pandering unashamedly to taste at its basest, ensured that his *New York Herald* became the most successful paper in mid-nineteenth-century America. Gossip, scandal, rumour and hearsay, reported in a jaunty read-me style, made up the breezy Bennett mix, for his concept of news stretched across the whole of human endeavour and experience, embracing sex, society and crime as well as life's more uplifting and cultural aspects. As an ex-society reporter himself, Bennett knew where to find the stories his readers wanted; he kept a reporter posted at Saratoga Springs for the summer season to chronicle the comings and goings of the elite of New York. 'The visiting season is now at its height,' reported the local *Saratoga Sentinel* in August 1845, giving Bennett his cue to send the *Herald*'s man up the River Hudson to cover the tide of 'full four thousand strangers' who had washed up at this most fashionable of spa resorts.

American journalism was still a fledgling thing. Weekly newspapers had been established by the early eighteenth century in almost all the principal towns, but they were in the main parochial and dull. The kind of gossipy controversies that held the attention of the British reading public rarely surfaced; indeed, some of the early printer–editors tried to outlaw it altogether. In Boston, Thomas Fleet of the *Weekly Rehearsal* resolved 'never to publish anything wherein the character or interest of any particular Person is concerned or pointed at',[1] but he resolved in vain; the cult of personality took hold and by mid-century another Boston editor, Richard Draper of the *News-Letter*, was promising 'Pieces of Speculation that may be entertaining to the Reader' whenever there was a shortage of hard news.[2] The religious eccentric Samuel Keimer disdained to stoop to such trifles, however, and confessed in the launch number of his *Pennsylvania Gazette*:

> We have little News of Consequence at present, the English Prints being generally stufft with Robberies, Cheats, Fires, Murders, Bankruptcies, Promotions of some, and Hanging of others; nor can we expect much better till Vessels arrive in the Spring... In the mean Time we hope our Readers will be content for the present, with what we can give 'em, which if it does 'em no Good, shall do 'em no Hurt. 'Tis the best we have, and so take it.[3]

The best Keimer had to offer was an extract from an encyclopedia.

In the 1840s Bennett inaugurated a gossip column in his *New York Herald* to prove that American upper-class life was just as dazzling as that of the European aristocracy.[4] Bennett's scurrying reporters ransacked the city for gossip, pestering the rich and fashionable for personal information, the 'floating gossip, scandal and folly'[5] of the day. New York's penny press had hitherto furnished depressingly familiar fare, grubby news for the millions: lurid crime stories, reports of prize fights, political and sexual shenanigans, and sensational trials. But Bennett, seeking to carve for his *Herald* a share of the penny market, had the vision to identify a new area of interest and realized that society – that is, the thick cream of Society with a capital S – offered succulent pickings. So alongside the daily chronicles of low life, Bennett began running stories about playboys and society matrons, snippets of gossip about New York's great and good whose doings (and misdoings) astonished and quickly enthralled the *Herald's* rapidly multiplying readership.

In Britain, Fleet Street noted Bennett's success but seemed reluctant to follow suit. Gossip stayed confined to weekly periodicals like Edmund Yates's sixpenny *World* and Henry Labouchere's *Truth*, with the British daily press uncertain about the proprieties of printing society snippets in an age of deference and rigid hierarchy. It wasn't until two generations later that Fleet Street was finally galvanized into following the American pattern. When T. P. O'Connor launched his Radical paper, the halfpenny evening *Star*, in London in January 1888, he revived the old Georgian tradition and slapped gossip right on to the front page. In Victorian London it was a seismic shock, an innovation to match the arrival of Page Three girls nearly a century later, and it attracted considerable flak from his rivals. There were dark mutterings about the pernicious influence of American practice on British culture. O'Connor called his gossip column 'Mainly about People', and it became one of the paper's most famous and popular features. Suddenly gossip became a nightly fixture, following Bennett's pioneering approach. 'The *Star*,' trumpeted O'Connor's henchman H. W. Massingham, who briefly succeeded him as editor, 'represents the most complete adaptation to this country of the method which gives the American press its vast circulation and immense popularity.'[6] The *Star*'s circulation duly soared. Readers loved the mix of brief paragraphs broken up by such offbeat items as Gladstone becoming stuck in a snowdrift. O'Connor's populist approach even earned the approval of the cerebral George Bernard Shaw, who wrote the *Star*'s leaders. Until the *Star* came along, such a thing as a gossip column in a halfpenny paper devoted to 'putting two lumps of sugar in the washerwoman's teacup instead of one'[7] (O'Connor's version of Swift's famous two grains of wheat) was unheard of, Shaw recalled. For a time, until their marriage failed, 'Mainly about People' was written by O'Connor's attractive American wife.

So successful was the column that when he left the *Star* O'Connor developed it into a fully fledged periodical, also named *Mainly about People* but known popularly as *M A P*. Although a committed Irish Nationalist (Edmund Yates called him 'Tay Pay' and the name stuck), O'Connor recognized the danger of boring his readers with too much politics, and from the outset made his *Star* twinkle in a bright and breezy way. He rushed to embrace the New Journalism, breaking with the old traditions and making journalism, as his rival W. T. Stead acknowledged, 'a living thing, palpitating with actuality, in touch with life at all points'.[8] His interest in human stories and personalities marked him as a pioneer in the development of Britain's nascent popular press. But O'Connor quickly ran out of steam, hampered, Shaw believed, by an outdated political view rooted in the Ireland of the 1860s, which poisoned him against the English. In 1891, with the *Star* a sparkling success, he sold his stake in it for £17,000 and only revived his interest in gossip some years later, with *T P's Weekly*, *P T O* (Please Turn Over) and, of course, *M A P*. Launched in June 1898, this gave him the big canvas he wanted. 'In journalism as in life,' he had once declared, 'it is the personal that interests mankind.'[9]

It was a sentiment shared by Stead, who, perhaps even more than O'Connor, championed American influence on the British press. In the great cultural debate of the late 1880s it was Stead who squared up to Matthew Arnold, the poet and critic, who deplored and feared the corrupting Philistine influences sweeping in from across the Atlantic. Arnold had coined the expression 'the New Journalism' in 1887, criticized it as 'featherbrained' and credited its invention (without actually naming him) to Stead. Not all Stead's Fleet Street compatriots swarmed to support him. 'By the New Journalism,' wrote Evelyn March Phillipps in 1895, 'I take it we mean that easy personal style, that trick of bright colloquial language, that wealth of intimate and picturesque detail, and that determination to arrest, amuse or startle, which has transformed the press during the last fifteen years.' But there were flaws too. Miss Phillipps welcomed gossip of the trivial kind, but deplored the sensational, especially 'an impertinent, prying curiosity [and] heartless intrusion' visited on public figures, and the prominent people in private life who 'can scarce endure the constant spying and badgering of the society papers'.[10] Stead was not blamed for this, but many thought that it was the baleful influence of America, rather than the home-grown tradition of Georgian and Victorian scandal sheets, that had sensationalized the British press, including Stead's own *Pall Mall Gazette*, which one contributor, Andrew Lang, deplored as 'an Americanised sensational product',[11] no better than the fare that eventually came to be called the tabloids.

And yet this was hardly a new debate. Half a century before, British travellers had returned from the United States with horror stories of a brutalized popular American press, filled with the rankest slander. In 1842, Charles Dickens had complained in his *American Notes* about this 'monster of depravity', declaring that he had 'neither space nor inclination to convey an adequate idea of this frightful engine in America'.[12] Dickens's friend and biographer, John Forster, took up the cry in his *Foreign Quarterly Review*, attacking in particular James Gordon Bennett's saucy *New York Herald* as a 'broadsheet of lies and filth'. Such criticism drew outrage from several New York papers and a volley of abuse from the *Herald* itself, which, as its defenders swiftly pointed out, was actually 'freer from gross obscenities and ribald jests' than either the *Age* or the *Satirist*, then still appearing in London. As for its propensity for gossip and scandal, Forster noted that the *Herald*, 'by means of course of its evil gains', could afford a comprehensive network of stringers in every chief city of the union, describing them as 'such reckless libellers of everything decent and such impudent dealers in everything vile' whose cue from Bennett was: 'Spare no one. Thrust yourselves into whatever house you can get, and everywhere leave your slime.'[13] A few years later, in 1851, when the famous editor of the lofty New York *Tribune*, Horace Greeley, testified before a committee of British Members of Parliament on the state of the American press, things were much the same. 'We call the New York *Herald* a very bad paper',[14] said Greeley, adding that for all its faults it was an improvement on various scandal-rags with such titles as the *Scorpion* and the *Flash*, blackmailing sheets that lived only short trembling lives.

All this was taking place against the background of newspaper revolution. As the nineteenth century progressed, millions of ordinary people who had never done so before were now reading newspapers. Cheap, visual and, by Victorian standards, sensational, dailies for the first time in their history were setting out to entertain as well as to educate and inform, and gossip was central to that aim. The late nineteenth century was a speeded-up age, and the press reflected this new, more hectic and unbuttoned world with crisper coverage, more vivid descriptions, striking headlines and arresting illustrations. The popular Fleet Street papers borrowed several key elements of newspaper culture in New York: the news-gathering process was vastly accelerated; newspaper offices became much more informal (in London, some reporters and editors were still wearing frock coats and top hats as late as 1900); and there was a seismic shift in the definition of news, which now became story-led and suffused with human interest – the stirrings of modern tabloid instincts. As John Bogart, city editor of the New York *Sun*, put it: 'When a dog bites a man, that is not news; but when a man bites a dog, that is news.'[15] And it was another American, Charles Tatum, the fictitious reporter in Billy Wilder's film *Ace in the Hole*, who pushed the definition to its logical limit: 'If there's no news,' says Tatum, 'I'll go out and bite a dog.'[16]

Gossip was now a crucial element in a successful newspaper. Whilst in Britain it tended to flit at the edges of public discourse, in the United States it received star billing. This was due partly to a fuzzier line in America between what is public and what is private; partly to more liberal libel laws; and partly to a greater degree of social curiosity, which helped broaden the definition of what counts as legitimate news. Bennett's *New York Herald* made the early running, with its vast web of nosy reporters sniffing at the affairs of the nouveaux riches and that newly defined breed that later became known as 'celebrities'. Bennett had set a trend by inventing the interview technique as early as 1836, when his *Herald* ran a lengthy 'interrogation-interview' with the landlady of the house in the Robinson–Jewett murder case where the prostitute victim lived. Although by the 1860s, it had become a commonplace device in American journalism, the interview remained untried in Britain until Edmund Yates took the idea home to London in the mid-1870s. Interviewing broke through as a form of entertainment in Joseph Pulitzer's New York *World* a decade later, creating the fashion for 'celebrity journalism' that survives today. Pulitzer held that public people are public property, and urged his reporters to conduct aggressive interviews with such figures, to give 'a striking, vivid pen sketch of the subject ... to bring him more clearly home to the average reader',[17] whether by invitation or not. So his reporters were to be found importuning some unsuspecting individuals, including a startled Queen Victoria in the churchyard at Crathie, who murmured, as the *World* man approached: 'He is as audacious as the rest of his nation.'[18]

In America, old James Gordon Bennett passed his tabloid instincts to his son, James Gordon Bennett Jr, whose many intuitive skills included star-spotting. In 1882, when the Prince of Wales's discarded mistress Lillie Langtry sailed to America, Bennett Jr assigned a reporter to follow her twenty-four hours a day and to report her every doing in the *New York Herald*. Lillie's acting tour took her to Chicago, where reporters staked out her hotel, and to St Louis, where a morally outraged editor of the *Globe-Democrat*, finding her breakfasting *déshabillée* in her boudoir with her fabulously rich new beau, Fred Gebhard, challenged him to a duel.[19] All this served to boost the Jersey Lily's profile, although Lillie herself professed not to read personal tittle-tattle in the press.

According to Mark Twain, who met her several times, far from being a beautiful airhead, she was a voracious book-reader with an opinion on everything. 'She also reads the newspapers,' Twain confirmed, 'and doesn't bother with the trivia.'[20]

At first the socialites were affronted by the Bennett clan's appetite for gossip and they threw the newshounds out of their gatherings because, as one socialite complained, 'to submit to this kind of surveillance is getting to be intolerable'.[21] For the rest of the nineteenth century, this stand-off soured relations between the press and the smart set, resulting in a tendency simultaneously to jeer and fawn.[22] 'That's nobody's business!' snapped Commodore Elbridge T. Gerry to a young *New York Tribune* reporter who had asked for details of a party he was throwing.[23] A century later, the same sort of party had become everybody's business.

Change was signalled in the late nineteenth century when Mrs John Jacob Astor asked one of America's social lions, Ward McAllister, to compile a list of eligibles for a ball she was planning. McAllister agreed. 'After all,' he pointed out, 'there are only four hundred of us.' With this casual remark, he coined a whole new currency for America's emerging media. Soon, enterprising newspapers were printing the names of the four hundred elect. Editors quickly realized that naming the members of New York's charmed circle had caught the public's interest. Circulations rose. The Sunday papers in particular focused on this superior social set, expanded their number beyond McAllister's remit and chronicled their doings. The *Tribune's* social editor was the Englishman Philip Cunliffe-Owen, son of the head of Kensington Museum (later the Victoria & Albert). Owen's column of intimate gossip about European nobility seems unlikely fare for an American readership, but it was widely syndicated. In 1913, when Howard White succeeded Owen, the *Tribune's* Sunday society section consisted of a single page. Under White, it expanded by the early 1930s to as many as twenty-two pages a week. Wire service reports from all the fashionable American resorts followed, a method pioneered almost a hundred years before by the resourceful Bennett to launch his mass-circulation *New York Herald*.

Bennett's penchant for society news spawned a number of urban weeklies. The earliest appeared in Boston, a city that before the

American civil war was the nation's financial capital and home to a large leisured class. Educated, worldly and rich, this group had ample time to graze on the tittle-tattle served up by the likes of the *Boston Home Journal* and the *Saturday Evening Herald*. These titles soon extended themselves beyond solely chronicling society events and developed first-rate coverage of the arts, mixing book and music reviews with items on travel and art. But the overall effect remained staid; in New York, where high society was less coherent and was taken less seriously, magazines were at first frivolous and fun, but soon became risqué and scandalous. A ten-cent magazine called *Truth* paved the way. But the best-known and most notorious was *Town Topics*, a blackmailing monthly with a legendary relish for spiciness and titillation.

It was the brainchild of Colonel William D'Alton Mann, a dashingly bewhiskered young millionaire who had made the honest part of his fortune by designing and building the world's finest railway sleeping car, patents for which were later bought by the Pullman company. His scheme for trading gossip for dollars took root in the late 1870s in London, where he had met and admired Edmund Yates, the pioneer of British society journalism with his weekly *World* magazine, and Henry Labouchere of its much ranker offspring *Truth*, which was laden with gossipy snippets of upper-class life, spiced up with intimate trivia and indiscretions. Nearly twenty years later, back in New York, Colonel Mann made his move, buying *Town Topics* from his younger brother and boosting its profitability by extorting money from members of the New York upper crust whose peccadilloes he threatened to expose. While he considered himself one of their number, he assumed the mantle of a crusader. 'My ambition,' Colonel Mann once explained, 'is to reform the Four Hundred by making them too deeply disgusted with themselves to continue their silly, empty way of life. I am also teaching the great American public not to pay any attention to these silly fools. If I didn't publish *Town Topics*, someone else without moral responsibility would do so. I am really doing it for the sake of the country.'[24]

In pursuit of this lofty ambition, Colonel Mann installed himself in a lavishly carpeted office and invited his network of informants, drawn from people who served or had dealings with the rich and powerful, to drop by and dish dirt. Personal and household staff, tradespeople, coachmen and cooks beat a path to the colonel's door, where they were warmly welcomed, offered a bone-crushing handshake and an expensive Havana cigar. Rumour and hearsay below stairs, letters stolen or steamed open, the spiteful surmises of the discharged or the merely disgruntled, all were grist to Colonel Mann's money-spinning mill. Most of these grubby titbits were rewarded with a few nickels and dimes, but the colonel (who even in early middle age resembled a massive, scary version of Santa Claus) reportedly kept a hoard of silver dollars to press on any nubile young informants from whom he managed to extract a kiss by way of a seal to their treachery.

It wasn't only servants that he enlisted. Colonel Mann employed rat-like cunning to widen his circle of whisperers. He recruited the chief night telegraph operator of the Western Union at Newport, Rhode Island, to the *Town Topics* cause, bribing him to blow the whistle on any adulterous billets-doux humming across the wires, especially at night when cabling rates were cheaper and the lovebirds chirped for longer. Such was his charm and savoir faire that the cunning colonel often persuaded his wealthy friends and acquaintances to dish the dirt on themselves, to snitch on their nearest and dearest, often in the expectation that by so doing they would insure themselves against the colonel's displeasure. Another tactic was to lunch at a fashionable restaurant – Delmonico's was a favourite haunt – and to wedge himself at a table to which he had arranged for galley proofs of the next issue of *Town Topics* to be delivered, the ink barely dry. Pointing out an embarrassing or inconvenient paragraph to a mortified fellow diner, he would offer to kill it on the spot, a favour he would unhesitatingly call in later by asking the person concerned for a trifling loan ('Shall we say five thousand dollars?'), which would seldom be repaid. 'I believe that the possession of great wealth, the presence of continual luxury and an existence of sybaritic ease are sufficient to lead voluptuous natures into a system of sensual gratification more intensely and ingeniously base than is found in humbler walks of life,' Colonel Mann declared in the guise of 'The Saunterer' in *Town Topics*. 'The Four Hundred of New York,' he added, returning to his grand obsession, 'is an element so shallow and unhealthy that it deserves to be derided almost incessantly.'[25]

And so it was, with few punches pulled. 'Miss van Alen suffers from some kind of throat trouble – she cannot go more than half an hour without a drink,' was a typical 'Saunterer' squib. 'Mr Henry Sloane has been looked upon as a complaisant husband who wore his horns too publicly,' was another. Often, of course, names were withheld, but the copy was sprinkled with enough clues to enable do-it-yourself readers to break the code and to identify the bride of the season with illegitimate twins, the cotillion leader with a dose of syphilis, or the prominent matron from Philadelphia being sued for divorce because of her affair with a woman librarian. As historian Egon Larsen has pointed out, America's smart set, viewed through the distorting lens of *Town Topics*, was infested with adulterers, nymphomaniacs, cuckolds, homosexuals, tricksters and drunks.

> What puzzled many readers, however, was that the 'Saunterer's' kicks often turned, from one issue of *Town Topics* to the next, into friendly pats on the back; or that people whose notorious conduct seemed to be just the stuff for a whole series of paragraphs were never mentioned; or that what appeared to be only the beginning of a campaign against some society personality suddenly stopped, never to be resumed. What had happened behind the scenes in such cases was, of course, that the victims had paid up.[26]

Not that the gentlemanly colonel ever stooped to talk of something as crude as blackmail. One of his favourite ruses was to 'invite' subscriptions to a new transatlantic version of *Who's Who*, a vanity volume to be called *America's Smart Set*. Almost the entire panoply of American bluebloods 'subscribed' or 'invested': William K. Vanderbilt ($25,000); the financier J. Pierpont Morgan ($2,500); Charles M. Schwab of United States Steel ($10,000); John Gates, the barbed-wire tycoon ($20,000). There was scarcely anyone in the smart set prepared to hazard their reputation by not paying up; to most of these plutocrats, Colonel Mann's 'subscriptions' were a trifling investment to buy off 'The Saunterer' and his nosy network of correspondents and informants. For the colonel, the seemingly fireproof arrangement guaranteed a fat income from those who paid, and an endless supply of scandalous stories about those who did not. It was with a certain entrepreneurial flourish that 'The Saunterer' proclaimed his column 'an *olla podrida* of gossip . . . not for babes, prudes, idiots or dudes'.[27]

Such heady whiffs of cordite from a low scandal sheet proved irresistible, and circulation soared twelvefold in the late 1880s.[28] Even society swells subscribed, although not all of them would have left it lying on their drawing-room tables. (Scurrilous it may have been, but it looked swanky enough: a handsome black-and-white quarto with a cover showing two pretty women whispering some secret.) One blueblood recalled that the magazine 'found its way into almost every cottage in Tuxedo Park, as it did into the cottages, villas and mansions at Newport. It was read upstairs, downstairs, and backstairs.'[29] Part of its allure was the inescapable fact that for all its venality, *Town Topics* was seldom wrong. Gossip was checked and double-checked. 'Above all,' Mann's one-time managing editor testified, 'the Colonel insists upon accuracy.'[30] It was Colonel Mann's boast that for the first fourteen years of his editorship, he had never been sued for libel. But his luck didn't hold. Oddly, though, Colonel Mann's nemesis roared in not from the gilded ranks of society but from his own inky trade.

In the autumn of 1904, Robert Collier, the 28-year-old publisher of *Collier's Weekly*, was scandalized to read in *Town Topics* an unseemly gossip item about President Theodore Roosevelt's daughter Alice. According to 'The Saunterer', the 20-year-old miss, while staying out at fashionable Newport, Rhode Island, had engaged in conduct unbecoming a well-connected young woman:

> from wearing costly lingerie to indulging in fancy dances for the edification of men was only a step. And then came a second step – indulging freely in stimulants. Flying all around Newport without a chaperone was another thing that greatly concerned Mrs Grundy...If the young woman knew some of the tales that were told at the clubs at Newport, she would be more careful in the future...I was really surprised to hear her name mentioned openly there in connection with...certain doings that gentle people are not supposed to discuss.[31]

(As an old woman, Alice Roosevelt Longworth smiled at the memory of her Newport debut. 'When I danced the hootchy-kootchy on Grace Vanderbilt's roof,' she told the high-society historian Cleveland Amory, 'you would have thought the world was coming to an end.')[32] Robert Collier was so affronted by this insult that in the next issue of *Collier's*

Weekly he denounced the story and the colonel as no better than 'an ordinary forger, horse-thief or second-story man'.[33] Collier's words signalled the start of a rancorous exchange of insults between the two magazines, culminating in Colonel Mann announcing that he would sue Collier for criminal libel, along with his editor Norman Hapgood. But before the case completed its run through the courts, the tale took another twist. Colonel Mann's agent, Charles Ahle, was arrested and charged with extortion.

It had all the elements of a classic sting. Ahle had arranged to meet the New York stockbroker Edwin Post, husband of the popular novelist Emily Post, in the men's washroom of a Manhattan hotel. When Post handed Ahle an envelope containing five $100 bills, a detective stepped out of one of the cubicles, seized the money and arrested Ahle. In court, Post testified that *Town Topics* had blackmailed him over a proposed paragraph about himself and 'a fair charmer' with whom he shared 'a little white studio' and who had a racy yen for 'white shoes with red heels and patent leather tips'. Post claimed that the magazine's price for dropping the story was $500, a sum that would at the same time guarantee a favourable mention in *America's Smart Set*. After consulting his lawyer and then his estranged wife, Post told the District Attorney's office that he would be prepared to act as live bait in a trap set for Colonel Mann's agent, Charles Ahle. The trap was duly sprung.

The Collier libel trial turned out to be a trap too, with Colonel Mann the quarry. He found himself in the anomalous position of being the principal source of forensic and public opprobrium, even though he was only a witness for the prosecution. (A technicality meant that a colleague appeared as the plaintiff rather than Mann himself.) The colonel's unhappiness became evident on the fourth day of the trial, when he was called to testify. One reporter who heard his cross-examination likened the hapless colonel to 'Andromeda chained to the rock in the act of being devoured by the dragon';[34] he could not remember this incident, had forgotten all about that incident. It was time for the defence counsel to refresh his memory. Had not one of 'The Saunterer's' victims been pilloried in no fewer than fifty abusive paragraphs after refusing to pay the Colonel's tribute? Mann's old self-assurance and ebullience now deserted him, and he could only stutter his replies in croaks and whispers. He was asked how he had found the courage to approach the most unapproachable of millionaires, J. Pierpont Morgan, with a demand for a $2,500 loan. 'I went to Mr Morgan the same as I did to other men of prominence,' replied Colonel Mann, 'because I felt they were of such standing that if they accommodated me there would be no occasion for me to criticize them.' The case ended with a Not Guilty verdict, Colonel Mann unmasked as a hypocritical liar and uproar in the court.

Robert Collier crowed that he and his magazine had dealt 'a death blow' to the blackmailing business of *Town Topics*. In fact, Colonel Mann and his column sauntered on. But the kind of gossip dished up in his notorious magazine turned to milk and water compared with the old sulphurous brew. With *Town Topics* on the wane, *Collier's* (the name had been abbreviated at the time of the Mann case) enjoyed a crescent prosperity. Colonel Mann remained in harness for a dozen more years until his death, at eighty-one, in 1920. One of his staff bought *Town Topics* and soldiered on with the magazine, until it, too, faltered in the early 1930s. When the journal finally closed during the Depression, it transpired that its advertising salesmen had pressured prospective investors into buying stock by threatening to disclose 'uncomplimentary' information that the magazine had collected on cards. New York State's attorney-general ordered *Town Topics* to burn all 500 of its cards in the furnace of the State Office Building – an incineration described by the *New York Times* with smug satisfaction as 'ceremonious'.[35]

It all sounds sordid, but in its heyday Colonel Mann's handsome magazine was much more than a low scandal sheet. 'The Saunterer's' gossip took up less than half the magazine; it also published well-written fiction, light verse and reviews, and ran crusades on assorted social issues of the day, 'crisp, varied, sensible, humorous and good-humoured'.[36] But because of its gossipmongering reputation, *Town Topics* was dominated by journalistic riff-raff, writers who were not without ability but who also carried a baggage of problems (drink, drugs, women) that made them unemployable on so-called respectable magazines. 'Literary flotsam,' as one junior editor described them at the height of the notoriety of *Town Topics* in the 1890s; 'we had all slunk on to the magazine from limbo, usually of our own creation.'[37] If some of these literary misfits bore a grudge against society, and saw their chance to spit in the eye of its upper crust, *Town Topics* was a hazardous berth. 'What's Reading is Worth Printing' may have been the rubric beneath the magazine's masthead, but not every socialite saw it that way. When any outraged reader burst through the office door threatening to horsewhip the man responsible for a particular gossip paragraph, staff were instructed to explain: 'You can't – he died yesterday. Those were the last words he ever wrote,' and to burst into tears. As Colonel Mann's brother, a shrewd judge of human nature, noted: 'Nobody ever licked a weeping man'.[38]

To make amends for these unpleasant exigencies of life at *Town Topics* (or unwittingly, perhaps, to add to them) the colonel enforced an iron rule that every member of his staff should dine with him at home at least once a week. From April to November, all his editors were required to weekend – every weekend – at the colonel's country home, Saunterer's Rest, on his private island on Lake George. The colonel himself was unabashed by the buffets of fate. 'I made society the talk of the town,' he once boasted in one of his 'Saunterings' columns.[39]

Indeed he had. But what was it that eventually set the spark to the revolution in society journalism and rid American society papers of the old-style chroniclings, stately and discreet, during the 1880s and 1890s? Unlike the old-money nobs, who fought shy of personal publicity, the vulgar and ill-bred nouveaux riches, who now thronged resorts like Newport and Palm Beach, relished it. They posed in public, while the masses got a good look at them for the first time. Within two turbulent decades, America forged itself a celebrity culture. In the 1870s, the best-known New Yorkers were philanthropists, politicians, merchants, artistic and cultural figures. But by the 1890s, these titans had been swept aside in the public consciousness by a new elite, people celebrated not for their accomplishments but for their gossip value. The papers had learned what the American humorist James L. Ford called the 'trick of feeding a vulgar public fancy' by making 'a monkey who can do nothing but grin through a horse-collar a personage of far greater interest and importance...than the President of Harvard University'.[40] It was a crucial turning point for the American gossip business.

As the twentieth century loomed, and the New York circulation war between Pulitzer and Hearst grew fiercer, brief reports of society happenings – the teas, dinners, balls and weddings of the fabulously wealthy – mushroomed into full-blown society pages and eventually spilled over into special Sunday supplements aimed at people who perhaps couldn't read but just wanted to look at pictures. Society news became a forerunner of soap opera, a counterpoint to the daily round of murder, rape, doom and disaster that constituted the average American newspaper. Society figures, with their glittering parties and balls, had become the new gods, worshipped, in the words of James L. Ford, like a 'brazen calf', a graven image replacing the Biblical Israelites' golden calf as the most inspiring symbol of wealth and worldly power. Gossip from this fantasy world offered plain folk a goal to strive for, a portable community of familiar figures, as historian Richard Schickel put it, 'containing representations of good values, interesting traits, a certain amount of within-bounds attractiveness, glamour, even deviltry'.[41] Especially deviltry. Sin and sex. That old black magic. That's what sold papers. But in strait-laced New York, it took all the wizardry of a Humpty-Dumpty society reporter called Maury Paul to charm his way through the social barricades and, for the first time, to hoist the gossip he heard there to the Olympian heights of news.

Maury Henry Biddle Paul (he claimed kinship with the socially prominent Biddles) was very short and very fat, with hands like stout starfish, and steel-blue eyes set in a bland, triple-chinned, moony face. His secretary, Eve Brown, recalled a chain-smoking dandy, 'an ink-stained exquisite' who pinned a fresh carnation in his lapel each morning, worshipped his widowed mother and kept a personal valet. From his bare, draughty office (where he entertained a string of elegantly frail young men) he telephoned all day to his upper-crust contacts, fly zipper open 'to relieve pressure', his personal jewellery flashing as he typed up his stories on his personal smooth yellow copy paper. His gossipy paragraphs appeared in Hearst's New York *American* in a column headed 'Cholly Knickerbocker', an ancient society byline owned and copyrighted by Hearst, 'Cholly' being a Preston Sturges-style play on the way upper-class Americans pronounced 'Charlie'.[42] As well as masquerading as Cholly, Maury Paul also wrote as 'Polly Stuyvesant', in a syndicated column as 'Billy Benedick' in the *Evening Journal,* and as 'Dolly Madison' in the *Evening Mail.* It was in this incarnation, it was said, that Hearst's mistress, Marion Davies, first drew the great man's attention to this gossiping dynamo. When Hearst finally signed Paul to an exclusive contract at $250 a week in 1922, he became the world's highest-paid society editor, renowned for his formidable inside knowledge of who was doing what to whom in American society, and equally celebrated for his extraordinary purple style. In his column, people didn't fall in love, they 'succumbed to the darts of the greatest of sharpshooters, Dan Cupid'. On sunny days 'Old Sol Reigned Supreme' over both the lovely ('Sweetie Sweets') and unlovely ('Soury Sours') people. Girls, never merely beautiful, were 'beauteous'; those with black hair 'raven-tressed'; those getting married 'embraced holy matrimony'; while the upwardly mobile socialite 'donned her Annette Kellermans' for a 'dip in the turbulent social seas'. Dollars, Maury Paul's abiding obsession as 'Cholly Knickerbocker', were '$$$$$'.

Money always seized Paul's attention, 'oodles of ducats' as he called it, and he carefully kept count of New York millionaires' millions. Walter Winchell wrote admiringly that Paul was 'not only a good newspaper reporter, but a good book-keeper'.[43] He was the first gossip writer to recognize people's curiosity about the wealth of the wealthy, and to report shamelessly on a subject that had hitherto been taboo. He was shameless too when it came to payola and kickbacks: Woolworth heiress Barbara Hutton reportedly sent him ruby and diamond cufflinks; hotels showered him with cases of liquor; and there were private gifts of gold cigarette boxes, lighters, silver ornaments, personal jewellery, Aubusson rugs – even (one Christmas in Connecticut) a Cellophane-wrapped station wagon and (another Christmas) enough dollar bills to pay off his mortgage. He took extended holidays with his lover, the illustrator Carl Haslam, and bathed other, casual, boyfriends in bathtubs of champagne.

His feuds were legendary. One of the bitterest was with Lady Mendl, the woman with the ever-changing hair who, as Elsie de Wolfe, became one of America's top interior designers, setting the trend for light, airy decor in place of heavy Victoriana. Before her marriage to the British diplomat Sir Charles Mendl in the 1920s, she ran one of New York's most fashionable salons at which Paul was a frequent guest, networking for paragraphs among the rich and famous. What soured the relationship is unclear, but in the early 1930s Paul suddenly bitched about her in a column that began: 'Is over seventy, but still stands on her head and turns handsprings.' Paul declared that she owed everything to her friend, Elisabeth Marbury; that she was vain and opinionated, loved pomp and luxury, and spoke sloppy French; that she wasn't as rich as everyone thought; that she indulged in silly fads, had tinted her 'fast-thinning tresses' every colour from blue to green, wore gloves while eating to mask her ageing hands and was a 'prima-donna about her press clippings'.[44] The resulting stand-off lasted for the rest of Paul's life. On New Year's Eve 1942, he and Lady Mendl were invited to a huge party at a swanky Fifth Avenue apartment, and found themselves seated at the same table with the hostess, Mrs James P. Donahue. White-faced with rage, Lady Mendl, seeing her least-favourite gossip writer weaving through the throng, stood up, declared she would *not* sit at the same table as Maury Paul, called for her wrap and flounced out. Pandemonium ensued. Paul, of course, wrote it all up, railing in his column at that 'silly old lady' who didn't know the meaning of the phrase 'grow old gracefully'. Shortly after Paul's death the following summer, Elsie Mendl invited his long-time secretary Eve Brown to tea. 'We had no weapon against him,' Lady Mendl reflected. 'His column was his dagger to stab us in the back. We had no such dagger to fight back.'[45]

Maury Paul chiselled social history with a first draft. On a bitter, sleeting night in February 1919, he stumbled on an unprecedented scene: a group of Newport socialites dining out with another group from New Jersey in the swish Ritz-Carlton in midtown Manhattan. Realizing that society wasn't staying home to entertain any longer, next morning he sat at his typewriter, inserted a sheet of yellow copy paper and made history by coining a phrase: café society. It became a household term, as familiar as Winchell's 'blessed event', as casual an addition to the freshly minted vernacular of the age as 'glamour girl' (another Maury Paul original). His was the first gossip column to use pictures of revellers in nightclubs – daring stuff in the age of Prohibition. He was always getting scoops and prophesied with accuracy, sometimes to prove a negative. 'Don't you believe for one minute – no suh! Not for even a second – that Mrs Graham Fair Vanderbilt has any intention of marrying Frank Rediker,' he once trumpeted. 'I am willing to bet anyone a nice juicy cream-puff against an equally juicy chocolate éclair that Mrs Vanderbilt NEVER will become Mrs Rediker. Or Mrs Anyone Else – for that matter. And that's that.'[46]

After Maury Paul's death in 1942, the mantle of 'Cholly Knickerbockers' passed to Igor Cassini, an Italian with Fascist links. A few years earlier, Cassini had survived a kidnapping by five young society blades at a country club in Virginia. Displeased with what Cassini had written about them in his column, they lured him away from a dance, drove him to a deserted spot ten miles away, stripped him naked, and tarred and feathered him. Three of the five, whom Cassini had managed to identify, were subsequently convicted of assault and battery, fined and given suspended jail sentences. Cassini's supporters in this unpleasant business included Maury Paul himself. 'Until you find a bomb every night in your car,' Paul counselled, 'until you be chased from every club, and are the fear of every hostess, you will not be a newspaperman.'[47]

Igor Cassini's finest hour came twenty years later during the Kennedy years when, as he recalled, '[t]he world was my oyster'.[48] Like Maury Paul, Cassini was a phrase-maker and he coined the expression 'jet set'. When President Kennedy was elected to the White House in 1960, Cassini was already one of America's most popular gossip columnists with an estimated 20 million readers. Despite his unsavoury political leanings in early life, Cassini had become close to the Kennedy clan. Not only was he the favourite gossip writer of America's First Lady, Jackie Kennedy, but his brother Oleg was her dress designer. Leaving much of the spadework for his 'Cholly Knickerbocker' column to his Texan assistant, Liz Smith, Cassini whooped it up, launching an exclusive nightclub and starring in his own television show. No one knew more Kennedy secrets than Igor Cassini, but he couldn't keep them to himself. The President whinged to Oleg Cassini about his 'damned brother', but Igor could only shrug, saying that 'private lives were my stock in trade...I always wrote everything I knew. It got me into trouble.' Kennedy couldn't conceal his exasperation. 'He's basically a newspaperman,' the President complained. 'He can't keep a secret'.[49]

7

Lillie Langtry and *Vanity Fair*

People who broker gossip and scandal are not there to bottle up secrets; they are instead supposed to uncork them. 'What is more dull than a discreet diary?' wondered the gossipy twentieth-century London socialite Sir Henry 'Chips' Channon. 'One might as well have a discreet soul.'[1] In Victorian times, discretion was generally reckoned a public and a private virtue to be breached at one's peril, and a scandalous career invariably meant social ostracism. Yet, if ever a woman carved herself a role as gossip-column fodder in the late nineteenth century, it was the stunningly beautiful and sensual adventuress Lillie Langtry, the first 'official' mistress of the Prince of Wales, whose antics titillated polite society and the vulgar mob alike, and who became Fleet Street's first sex goddess.

Victorian high society kept itself entertained with an annual cycle of pleasures in season: the days and nights of the idle rich followed an unchanging pattern of drives, dinners and parties, a round so drearily predictable that to stave off boredom they sought sensation. So one craze followed another; in the summer of 1877 Lillie Langtry, posing wide-eyed for photographer and painter alike in the cheap little black dress that became her trademark, created the nineteenth century's first personality cult. Soon that dress was ditched in favour of a succession of shimmering gowns, and she was pictured in every rig and pose imaginable, her portraits festooning the windows of all the fashionable shops in London, usually alongside or (by way of a sexual innuendo) surmounted by pictures of the Prince. She was mobbed in the streets. Lillie's husband, the shy and unprepossessing Ned, was reluctantly pressed into service, first as her chaperon and then as her bodyguard. 'I never wanted this publicity,' Lillie complained towards the end of her life. 'I was shocked and bewildered when it came.'[2]

As newfangled photography flourished in mid-Victorian London, Lillie Langtry was one of the first to pose for the camera as a 'PB', a Professional Beauty, whose image adorned thousands of postcards sold in tobacconists' shops all over Britain. She was not in exalted company; most Professional Beauties lived by their looks; many were prostitutes, and sepia prints of them in assorted poses often found their way into gentlemen's wallets or, if especially daring, locked desk drawers. At twenty-three Lillie, an aspiring actress and model – still young, apparently untainted and clearly uncorseted – stood in direct line to the Page Three girls teetering on their heels a hundred years in the future. Looking back on her debut in London society, Lillie apologized for 'chronicling the curious whim of the public', explaining that in the comparatively cosmopolitan 1920s 'the excitement caused by my advent could never be repeated'.[3]

In June 1877, Lillie met the Prince of Wales at a small private dinner party in London. Princess Alix was conveniently abroad, and their affair began almost at once. By the year's end, the Prince was so besotted that he was building her a house at Bournemouth (the twentieth-century tabloids would have called it 'a love-nest'), where he could relax with Lillie without the constant drunken surveillance of vigilant Ned. By the following summer, when Lillie was presented at court to the unsmiling Queen and to a resigned and accepting Princess, the affair was public knowledge, due in no small measure to the paragraphs appearing in the smartest magazine of the day, *Vanity Fair*, and *Town Talk*, one of the scruffiest.

For a weekly shilling (5p), *Vanity Fair* offered twenty-two large, creamy pages of 'political, social and literary wares' with features on entertainments, books, a social calendar and lots of gossip. 'The Social Week' was a column of tittle-tattle signed 'Rasper', while the smoother-sounding 'Ruffler' contributed paragraphs on the latest society engagements and society anecdotes in a column headed 'Vanities'. In 1877, the year of Lillie Langtry's first society appearance, 'Ruffler' examined the price of a party, declaring 'it is now almost impossible for anybody having less than £10,000 a year to give any Party, still less any Ball, that will not be looked upon with contempt'.[4] ('Ruffler' had done his sums with great precision. An evening party for 400 at one of London's great houses, thrown by 'a hostess of high rank', would cost

£386 11s 2d. A ball for 600 would set the host back £498 1s 9d, while a Concert for 250 would come in at exactly £601.)

The germ of *Vanity Fair* came from a wayward genius called Grenville Murray, who perfected the art of teasing inside information from the world of society. Murray was reputedly the son of the 2nd Duke of Chandos, but any fortune that he might have inherited was frittered away by the Duke's monumental extravagances, leaving young Murray to shift for himself. He made a hesitant start in journalism; then the Foreign Secretary Palmerston fixed him up with a job at the British Embassy in Vienna, on the (secret) understanding that he would be allowed to contribute society tittle-tattle to the *Post*. Unfortunately, his surreptitious paragraphing was discovered. Rashly, Murray used to send his copy back to London in the diplomatic bag; when, by some misadventure, one of his contributions fell into the hands of Lord Westmoreland, the British ambassador at Vienna, the balloon went up. Palmerston moved him to Persia, a posting in which Murray was able to continue his correspondency, now sending his 'Roaming Englishman' letters to *Household Words*. This, too, got him into trouble. Murray's copy caricatured the British ambassador in Persia, and he had to be moved a third time, to Odessa, where he made himself unpopular with the other British expatriates while continuing his literary antics unchecked.

'When in the humour,' wrote *Truth* magazine of Murray,

> he was a brilliant conversationalist – humorous, caustic and full of anecdote. In person he was slim, and rather below medium height, with well-cut features, exceedingly bright eyes, and with a face that lighted up when he was animated; but few of those who may have seen him in an old felt hat and a still older shooting-jacket, strolling along the boulevards or in the alleys of the Bois de Boulogne, would have imagined they were in the presence of the ablest journalist of the century.[5]

Back in England, ten years later, Murray embraced journalism full time, and in 1868 persuaded Thomas Gibson Bowles to launch *Vanity Fair*, the prototype society journal.

Vanity Fair's gossip columns were always on the edge. Sometimes, actual names were used; other paragraphs concealed the true identities of people, although few 'society' devotees would have had trouble in breaking the code. Curiously, the more outrageous paragraphs were those in which real names were used. Tommy Bowles was an inveterate ruffler of Victorian feathers – is that why he signed a gossip column so? – but no matter how rude or indiscreet he was in print, he always seemed able to smooth things over afterwards. Even royalty was not safe from his weekly lashings. He attacked the Prince of Wales for permitting himself to be installed as Grand Master of the Freemasons, protesting that 'a Prince who will one day be called upon to reign over this Empire would do well to hold himself aloof from such vanities'.[6] Items of news from the court often found their way into *Vanity Fair*'s gossip columns, thanks to Bowles's network of well-placed tipsters within the royal households.

But Bowles's informants relied on his total discretion, and when Henry Labouchere began his rival magazine *Truth* in 1877, one of Bowles's sources at court, Lady Seymour, wrote to him anxiously about her 'little contributions'. Her husband Sir Francis Seymour, the Queen's Master of the Ceremonies, was responsible for receiving foreign ambassadors with full canonicals, and Lady Seymour was no doubt keen for him to remain so. 'Dear Mr Bowles,' she wrote from her apartment at Kensington Palace:

A report has reached me which caused my husband and myself a good deal of annoyance, and I think it best to write at once to enquire into the truth of the matter. I was informed that you told Mr Labouchere lately that you had entered into an arrangement to pay me 10 guineas a week, in return for which I was to supply *Vanity Fair* with Society news, and that this had been repeated by him and various persons (I do not know him personally). Now I cannot believe you to have said this, as of course no such arrangement was ever made between us, and also because you yourself cautioned me to be careful not to mention that I ever wrote anything for your paper.

I am afraid that my husband will not consent to me sending any more little contributions now, as he is a good deal annoyed at what I have told you. Can you in any way explain it?[7]

Although Bowles's reply has not survived, he appears to have mollified the Seymours, because later that same year *Vanity Fair* published a cartoon of Sir Francis, with a caption proclaiming that his discretion was 'much relied on' by the Queen, and that he had been entrusted by the royal family with 'many missions of a delicate nature'. Whether this persuaded Sir Francis to lift his ban on his wife's activities as court gossipmonger is not documented, but Tommy Bowles kept all his corners covered and had other, if less exalted, sources too.

An item of staff news from the Prince of Wales's kitchen at Clarence House, for example, appeared in *Vanity Fair* on 5 May 1877: 'The Prince of Wales has discharged his Indian cook, and sent him back to his native land. No ladies will henceforth have to smile approval while the roof of their mouth is being burnt off by the devilish arts of the heathen.' This inconsequential piece of intelligence – which by all accounts appears to have been perfectly true – upset the Prince so much that he took steps against Bowles and his magazine. The royal swipe was not aimed directly at Bowles himself but at one of his contributors, Lord Ronald Gower, brother of the Duchess of Westminster, who was immediately snubbed by the Prince on the grounds that he wrote for *Vanity Fair*. The fact that Gower's contributions weren't actually gossip paragraphs at all but items of harmless fiction and personal reminiscences left Bowles doubly vexed. When the Prince refused to meet him to discuss the matter face to face, Bowles wrote accusing him of showing 'a feeling of personal animosity towards me for which I am at a loss to account'[8] that went back four years. Whether that was true or not, within a year the matter seems to have been forgotten. In July 1878, Bowles included a complimentary paragraph about the Prince which was apparently genuine, and relations between *Vanity Fair* and Marlborough House were further improved the following autumn when Bowles pulled an item from publication concerning the Prince's friend Christopher Sykes. However, the rapprochement was not to last.

The Viceroy of India's personal habits were lambasted, and the Liberal leader was pilloried mercilessly:

Mr Gladstone goes about in a very cowed and tail-between-the legs manner ever since the Duke of Sutherland called him a Russian agent. Any ordinary man who said this of him would have been smothered with post-cards and demonstrated to be ignorant, malicious and false; but a Duke is a being whom Mr Gladstone has never dared to face like an ordinary mortal, and a rebuke from one of so exalted a position leaves him miserable and penitent, instead of rendering him aggressive and pugnacious. Yet some people were surprised when years ago it was pointed out in these columns that Mr Gladstone had never been considered a gentleman by Society.[9]

Even the Prime Minister came in for censure: 'The cutlers of Sheffield have, I hear, presented Lord Beaconsfield with a pair of carvers. "Peace with Honour" is engraven on the handles. It is only natural to suppose that the gift is an expression of admiration by the donors for his Lordship's artistic vivisection of Turkey.'[10]

As for the Russian ambassador, Count Schouvaloff, *Vanity Fair* was ready with a lecture on the social graces: 'His manner and tone of conversation towards ladies might now, without any damage to the cause of his august Master, be slightly improved. It might have been necessary for him some time ago to mark his contempt, and that of his august Master, for the English Royal Family by telling coarse stories in public to an English Princess, and by exulting to others over the blushes he had raised; but that necessity can surely no longer exist.'[11]

In April 1879, *Vanity Fair* was once again in bad odour with the royals, this time because of a paragraph concerning Sir Robert Peel, eldest son of the great Victorian statesman, whose 'recent speech in the House of Commons has, very naturally, given great offence in high quarters in consequence of his disrespectful allusion to George IV, and his personal remarks upon the Queen. Several members of the Royal family have declared their intention never to take any notice of Sir Robert for the future.'[12] Peel fired off a complaint to Bowles as soon as he had read this, and followed with another a week later, in response to a further paragraph about him. This second letter was so abusive that Bowles at first refused to publish it and declined to discuss any inferences Peel may have drawn from the offending lines 'until he shall have mended his manner and his language'.[13] In the meantime, the Prince of Wales had weighed in again, complaining that the original paragraph (quoted above) was inaccurate, and telling Peel that it 'was inserted neither by his Royal Highness's authority nor with his knowledge'.[14] Bowles pointed out that he had never claimed such authority, and in the following week's *Vanity Fair* printed the long and angry letter from Peel that he had earlier withheld. Copies were in such demand that they changed hands for as much as ten shillings (50p) each.

It seems likely that the Prince was already vexed with *Vanity Fair* over its thinly veiled references to his affair with the siren Lillie Langtry. The magazine had shadowed her for several months, dropping the odd paragraph here and there about 'the little Jersey beauty' who had so captured the heart of the heir apparent. But by the summer of 1878, the rapture had already started to wane, and Lillie launched a parallel affair with Arthur Jones, a childhood friend from Jersey. On top of this, she was dallying with London's favourite American painter, James McNeill Whistler, and casting a bewitching, if unlikely, spell on Oscar Wilde. If the Prince caught any whisper of these infidelities, he held his tongue. But shortly before Christmas Ned Langtry's patience snapped and he lashed out at his wayward wife in a drunken fit: 'A lady well-known in society,' reported *Vanity Fair*, 'is said to have been seen with two black eyes, not the result of self-embellishment. The question asked is, who, or rather which, gave them?'[15] Ned was dogged by debt, drink and depression, exacerbated by his wife's wanton ways. His threats to divorce Lillie sent Fleet Street into a frenzy; *Vanity Fair* led the pack with a sarcastic disclaimer of the rumours, but in January 1879 its mischievous downmarket rival *Town Talk* waded in with a paragraph from the pen of its radical owner–editor, Adolphus Rosenberg: 'I wonder how the husbands of the "beauties of Society" like their wives to be shown about in a "visitors-are-requested-not-to-touch" sort of way. I don't believe they are husbands at all – only dummies. Some of the beauties, I'm afraid, have too many husbands.'[16]

Within a matter of weeks, Rosenberg had realized he was on to a terrific story, with society and royal connections. In February, he wondered if the rumours were really true; that London was about to be rocked by a sensational divorce case involving a famous beauty and an eminent society figure. A month or so later, *Town Talk* had its answer:

> About the warmest divorce case which ever came before a judge may shortly be expected to come off. The respondent was a reigning beauty not many centuries ago, and the co-respondents – and they are numerous – are big 'pots'. The poor husband is almost frantic. 'Darn this country,' he says, 'nothing belongs to a fellow here. Even his wife is everybody's property.' Oh

that woman! I myself loved her. I bought her portrait – oh, years and years ago – in thirty-five different positions, and wept over it in the silent hours of the night. And I am not even a co-respondent.[17]

When Ned Langtry read this he exploded in rage, threatening to sue *Town Talk* for libel even though he knew the story was largely true. Lillie, meanwhile, was appalled at the prospect of 'being dragged before the public' in a divorce case. Even the paper's editor, Adolphus Rosenberg, may have harboured private misgivings, recalling the result of Greville Murray's attack on Lord Carrington in 1869, and its consequences. For all his republican zeal, Rosenberg, at twenty-seven, was no hothead; he lived a blameless suburban life with his wife and two children on Brixton Hill, and cared there for his elderly Jewish parents. But *Town Talk* did not relent. On the contrary, on the last day of May Rosenberg finally named names: 'I am informed that Mr Langtry has announced his intention of breaking my neck. Now, if the brave gentleman wants to go into neck-breaking, surely he can find plenty of his friends (?) who have injured him more than I have.'[18] A week later, Rosenberg cheerfully printed a retraction, the result, no doubt, of threats from Ned Langtry's lawyer. He knew, however, that it would merely stir the bubbling pot: 'There has been lately a rumour that Mrs Langtry was about to appear in a divorce court, with more than one illustrious correspondent. The rumour is, like many others, without the least foundation.'[19]

By now the Prince of Wales's roving eye had fastened on Sarah Bernhardt, the notorious actress newly arrived in London from Paris with the Comédie Française. Gossip about a possible Langtry divorce drove him deeper into her bosom; although, like Lillie, Bernhardt was fêted for her beauty, unlike Lillie she had no husband and carried little emotional baggage. By the end of August, with London empty at the end of the season, *Town Talk* was taunting again, but this time with the unmistakable ring of authority: 'A petition has been filed in the Divorce Court by Mr Langtry. HRH the Prince of Wales, and two other gentlemen, whose names...we have not been able to learn, are mentioned as co-respondents.'[20]

In the same issue Rosenberg followed with a personal attack on Lillie, accusing her of insatiable vanity and criticizing her for constantly posing for photographs in 'suggestive attitudes, to leer and wink and simulate smiles that can only be ranked one degree beneath lewdness'. Rosenberg couldn't resist a sexual jibe, which he scarcely troubled to disguise. Since Lillie's pictures were displayed 'in conjunction with representations of well-known harlots...the question arises "Who is Mrs Langtry?"....There was something not very pleasing to the loyal mind to see, in a dozen shop windows, Mrs Langtry side by side or else beneath the Prince of Wales.' As a peroration, *Town Talk* drew itself up to its loftiest height of scornfulness: 'To be exposed in the windows of shops with her name attached to the picture, to have her points criticized as if she were a horse for sale, to give 'Arry and Hedward an opportunity of passing indecent remarks about her, and to disgust all respectable thinking women at the public exhibition she makes of her charms.'[21]

With no response to his tirade, Rosenberg felt confident enough to crow: 'No attempt has been made to contradict the statement published in these columns last week as to the Langtry divorce case, and my readers may be assured that it was no invention. I now learn that a few weeks ago an application was made that the case be tried *in camera* and I believe the learned judge acceded to the request.'[22]

But Rosenberg had crowed too soon. Ned Langtry withdrew his divorce petition and the case was disposed of. In October, Rosenberg took a swipe at his rivals, who were cock-a-hoop at *Town Talk's* loss of face: 'It is useless for the sixpenny twaddlers to deny that Mr Langtry ever filed a petition. He did, and as I have said before, an application was made to Sir James Hannen to hear it privately, and he consented.'[23]

Tommy Bowles and *Vanity Fair* continued to attract trouble. In the 1880s he landed in court as the result of a paragraph he published about the scandalous case of a Mrs Trevelyan. Lord Marcus Beresford, who was mentioned unfavourably in the piece, ambushed Bowles outside his office in Tavistock Street with the intention of giving him a sound thrashing. But as *Truth* magazine reported, Beresford got as good as he gave. 'This must always be the case where the would-be thrasher and the thrashee are equally matched,'[24] *Truth* explained. The two men were eventually pulled apart, but by the time the police arrived Beresford had jumped into a cab and decamped. Bowles issued a summons against him for assault and battery, but the evidence was confused and conflicting, and the issue was finally settled by a full-scale jury trial at which Beresford was acquitted.

Another, less violent spat the same year had a happier outcome for Bowles. He upset Lord Randolph Churchill, father of the then young Winston, with a paragraph declaring that Churchill and the Prince of Wales, who had fallen out some years before over 'private matters', had been reconciled. 'It is understood, however,' the paragraph added, 'that while Lord Randolph feels much satisfaction at being again on friendly terms with the Heir-Apparent, he does not propose to become intimate with all the Prince's friends.'[25]

'My dear Bowles,' wrote Lord Randolph from the Carlton Club on 14 March, 'I thought you were my friend. I find you are my enemy. No one except of the latter character could have inserted such a mischievous paragraph as you have done this week in *Vanity Fair* about HRH the P of W and myself. In future we must be entire strangers.'[26] Bowles wrote back by return, regretting the publication of the offending item and explaining that until receiving Churchill's angry letter, 'it did not I confess occur to me that the paragraph could do you any sort of injury'.[27] Bowles's apology appears to have mollified Churchill, who wrote back on 18 March admitting to having been 'terribly vexed' by the piece, and asking that any future references in *Vanity Fair* should be signalled to him first. 'This is not asking too much,' added Churchill. 'Let us forget the incident.'[28]

There was more to *Vanity Fair* than gossip, of course. Two features endeared it to readers. One was its weekly cartoon of a prominent personality, first by the Italian Carlo Pellgrini, later by Leslie Ward, using the pseudonyms 'Ape' and 'Spy' respectively. From 1874, there was also the regular editorial feature headed 'Hard Cases', the precursor to the 'Dear Mary' column in the modern *Spectator*. This presented readers with 'some case of social law which imperatively requires decision, and which yet presents difficulties rendering it no easy matter to come to a decision at once proper and prudent'. The first of the series gave a flavour: 'Miss A is engaged to marry Mr B, but suddenly discovers that she prefers his friend Mr C. What should A do?' Complications set in the following week: 'Mr C marries Miss D. What should A do?' Further twists follow: 'B informs A that C has warned him not to marry her, on the ground that she is inconstant in her affections. What should

A do?' And so on. Readers responded with their suggestions and solutions in their hundreds. These 'Hard Cases' were supposedly hypothetical, although some suspected Tommy Bowles of borrowing heavily from life, especially since correspondents often complained that they saw themselves mirrored in these social and moral conundrums.

Although 'Hard Cases' was one of *Vanity Fair*'s most popular features, not everyone appreciated the column. The journalist Robert Buchanan, who hated *Vanity Fair* and every other society journal, spluttered over 'Hard Cases', calling the feature 'a literary system of indecent exposure' that filled anyone with any common delicacy with 'abomination and loathing'. As for his general opinion on the magazine, he was nothing if not succinct: 'a more or less hideous caricature, a little tenth-rate fiction, a few notes on passing events, one or two flashy articles and a large sugar plum of indecent suggestion and pitiable scandal'.[29]

Bowles turned his attention to the *Lady* magazine in 1885, but as proprietor and not as editor. He continued to edit *Vanity Fair* and wrote the 'In Society' column, which, like all its gossip features, mixed the authentic with the apocryphal. Bowles was regularly ahead of the field, especially when it came to royal gossip. In July 1887 he twitted the editors of the daily papers for ignoring *Vanity Fair*'s exclusives, such as the news that the Prince of Wales had decided not to give his annual party at Marlborough House to mark the end of the London season. Bowles was right – again – but *The Times*, the *Morning Post*, the *Standard* and other dailies foolishly continued to preview the party until the day came – and went – with no party in sight. Bowles couldn't resist a little low-key crowing: 'I do trust this will be a warning to the daily papers not to admit into their columns anything inconsistent with what has been previously stated in *Vanity Fair*.'[30]

The same issue recorded an investiture at Windsor Castle at which a man 'of Brobdingnagian proportions' was kneeling before the Queen to be knighted, but on being told to rise 'he was quite unable to obey the Royal command, and in his confusion he literally rolled over before the Queen and her courtiers.'

A month later, Bowles was sniping at the court again:

If there is a class of Her Majesty's Household who have my sympathy above another, it is the ladies who attend to the personal wants of the Queen for the small sum of £300 per annum. During the three months when they are at the Castle their lives are hardly their own from the rising of the sun unto the going down thereof. When Her Majesty rings for the morning cocoa, they must be on the spot, ready at any moment for an hour or an hour and a half to assist her in rising. Later in the morning she has a dozen commands for them, reading, writing, running; and then, when they have had their luncheon, there is the inevitable drive, from which they only escape once or twice during the week. In the evening they must join the Royal circle, and look solemn for a couple of hours in the drawing room; then only are they free. These ladies clearly earn their £300 a year.[31]

In October of the same year, Bowles took a jaundiced view of a newfangled invention destined to revolutionize home entertainment: 'Somebody ought to tie Mr Edison up permanently with his own wires. He is becoming the greatest nuisance of the century, and in fact of all time. The development which he has just announced of the phonograph offers a conclusive reply to those who are always anxiously enquiring whether life is worth living. Life is not worth living if every word one utters is to be crystallized, held in suspense for years, and then launched upon one's head again.'[32]

But Bowles was flagging. His wife had died that summer, aged only thirty-five, leaving him with four young children. The following summer he bought a schooner and announced he was taking an extended holiday, taking the children on a long Mediterranean cruise with a crew of eight, a governess and a nurse. On his return, Bowles reviewed his commitments, decided he had too many, sold *Vanity Fair* for £20,000 and went into Parliament. He was an MP for over twenty years, first as a Tory, then as a Liberal. Losing his seat in 1910, he cast around for something new to do, even though he was then in his seventies. Eventually, in February 1914 he launched a quarterly magazine, the *Candid Review*, which was modelled on the *Edinburgh Review*. It covered political, social, scientific and literary topics, but was conspicuously light on gossip. But Tommy Bowles was older and more tired than he knew and he folded the magazine after only twelve issues. He died in 1918.

Grenville Murray, meanwhile, having in some mysterious way involved himself in the launch of *Vanity Fair* back in 1868, had quickly struck out on his own. Seeking what one critic described as 'a bolder channel for his spite', he started the *Queen's Messenger* in January 1869. It lived only an insect's life. In June, Murray published an offensive article about the first Lord Carrington for which he was soundly horsewhipped on the steps of the Conservative Club in St James's Street by the second Lord Carrington, son of the first. The two men ended up in front of the magistrate at Marlborough Street. Carrington was sent for trial, charged with assault. Murray denied authorship of the article, 'Bob Coachington, Lord Jarvey', and was accused of perjury. But he jumped his bail, fled to France and never returned to England. the *Queen's Messenger* ceased publication, but the Carrington–Murray affair had the effect of boosting sales of *Vanity Fair* by increasing public interest in personality journalism. At the same time, other 'society journals' began to spring up to meet the demand for gossip and scurrility.

As for Lillie Langtry, it was fitting that once her fleeting moment of fame had passed, the woman who had been so greedily gossiped about toyed with the idea of becoming a gossip writer herself. The artist Sir John Millais, one of her many bohemian friends, suggested to Heinrich Felberman, editor of *Life* magazine, that he give her a job as a social columnist.[33] But Lillie wanted 800 guineas (£840) a year, and although Felberman was prepared to haggle over terms it came to nothing. Instead she launched her career on the stage. According to her biographer James Brough, Lillie 'bore a deep rooted resentment of the newspaper people who had contributed so eagerly towards making both her money and her reputation'.[34] In America, when asked by one of 'these ghastly women reporters' if she was not very much impressed by the people she had met at a party, Lillie could only marvel at the journalist's earnest naivety. 'My good woman,' she replied, 'you forget I'm in the impressing business myself.'[35] In old age, she wrote her monumentally unrevealing memoirs, posthumously vindicating the judgment of Lord Northcliffe, who had been offered serial rights on her reminiscences for the *Sunday Dispatch* a year before he died. Northcliffe argued that, forty years on, Lillie Langtry was definitely a back-number, whose story would not only not attract new readers but might even lose existing ones.[36] He turned her down, and he was right to do so; her autobiography, when it finally appeared in 1925,[37] was remarkable only for its blandness. Taxed about it, the Jersey Lily merely smiled wanly. 'You don't really think I would ever do such a thing as to write my *real* reminiscences, do you?'[38]

8

The Bracing Sea of Sex

The Langtry affair, like most gossip, eventually boiled down to a question of who was bedding whom, 'a matter of perfectly reasonable public curiosity', according to the journalist Auberon Waugh (one of gossip's greatest twentieth-century exponents), 'where public figures are concerned'.[1] But the British tabloids have always taken a lubricious and panoramic view of illicit sex, seldom scrupling to differentiate between public and private practitioners, and enjoy nothing more than feasting on the most intimate and embarrassing details of fornication and adultery. 'The [Daily] Mirror wanted Sex,' reporter Harry Procter recalled of his arrival at the paper in the 1930s. 'It was not hypocritical about its needs – it was perfectly honest to both its employees, its readers, and its advertisers. Sex, the Mirror discovered, sold papers – papers – papers by the million.'[2]

One of the most time-honoured and fruitful sources of sexual hanky-panky has been the divorce court. Throughout the nineteenth century and into the first quarter of the twentieth with the rise of the modern press, divorce suits were reported extensively and sometimes even verbatim, particularly in the cheekier papers, which ran the most painfully private evidence over many columns for the lip-licking delectation of their readers. When reporting divorce evidence was outlawed in the 1920s, it marked a shift in approach from the dowsers of dirt in Fleet Street: stories of sexual high jinks, now unreportable from the divorce court, began to surface instead in the gossip columns, which, in turn, started to smack of an extra piquancy, a new sauciness.

The press first began to take a serious interest in such shenanigans in the late eighteenth century, with a boom in trials for 'criminal conversation', popularly known as 'crim. con.' – adultery by another name, technically the seduction of a man's wife by her lover. It coincided with a massive explosion of newspapers, books and pamphlets. Publishers were casting around for interesting copy, and there was no shortage of sharp-eyed reporters to tap into this juicy vein of sexual material flowing through the courts. Caricaturists, too, battened on to these crim. con. actions, and started to produce great quantities of satirical prints, illustrating some of the more lurid and sexually explicit cases. But, crucially, with this emergence of illicit sex into the public domain came a fundamental change in the attitudes of the ruling elite. Extramarital sex was no longer viewed as sinful and shameful, but as an interesting and amusing aspect of life. Even the vocabulary grew less harsh: 'adultery' softened up to become an act of 'gallantry', a 'love affair' an 'intrigue'. Improved techniques in shorthand writing led to a proliferation of stenographic trial records. When these appeared in the newspapers, editors fanned the human interest angle and highlighted any detailed evidence of adultery gleaned from peeping through keyholes, listening to creaking beds and inspecting linen. Everyone, it seemed, was agog for sexual titillation, but none more so than the upper classes, including idlers like Horace Walpole, hungry for gossip about the sex lives of people they knew.

The most infamous source of scurrility at the time was *Town and Country Magazine* because of its monthly feature profiling a prominent public figure. For most of its twenty-one years, the barefaced 'Tête-à-Tête' feature was written by Stephen Beaufort. Each month, Beaufort's contribution was a *chronique scandaleuse* in which he openly discussed the irregular love life of the person – or personality – whose life he had subjected to his merciless gaze. The invariably accurate text was accompanied by two crudely engraved portraits, one of the man, the other of his mistress, with the identity of both thinly disguised by initials or pseudonyms. Sir Bullface Doublefee, Tom Tilbury and Sir Simony Scruple, for example, were recognizable as Sir Fletcher Norton, the Earl of Northington and the Revd Martin Madan respectively, while the Hostile Scribe and the Stable Yard Messalina were none other than William, 2nd Viscount Barrington and Lady Harrington. It was not difficult to penetrate the disguises, because Beaufort littered his text with clues and the illustrations were based on actual portraits. Cabinet ministers, noblemen, libertines, clergymen and infamous rakes all took their place in this unique gallery of cuckoldry. Nobody, not even royalty, escaped its attention. Yet curiously, not one of those whose profiles appeared in *Town and Country Magazine* between 1769 and 1790 ever sued or sought legal redress. After Beaufort's death in 1786, the feature continued for a further four years, but whoever the unknown author was he appears to have been just as well informed. The column was required reading among the aristocracy, and it was the principal reason for the enormous success of *Town and Country Magazine.*

The stories that unfolded in its pages were an early form of soap opera. As well as the splashes of sexual titilation, readers were riveted by the human drama. They enjoyed weighing the evidence for themselves, comparing the courtroom performance of the lawyers involved, and speculating about the likely level of crim. con. damages the jury might award. People were already reading novels that dealt with similar themes (love, marriage, sex and money) and showed a keener appetite for sensationalism, which newspapers were now exploiting. In 1786, *Town and Country Magazine* reported that one sex-soaked trial 'is at present the topic of conversation in all the polite circles'.[3] By 1820, at the climax of the sensational trial of Queen Caroline for adultery, the poet and essayist Leigh Hunt complained to his friend Shelley: 'You may look upon the British public, at present, as constantly occupied in reading trials for adultery.'[4]

All this publicity meant that more people began to understand how to get divorced, but these scandalous stories from the courts were also deterring couples from seeking a remedy in law for their marital woes. The prospect of sensational coverage in the press of a crim. con. action threatened reputations all round: husbands exposed as cuckolds, wives branded as whores and lovers often unmasked as treacherous friends. In 1700, Congreve rang a warning bell in his comedy, *The Way of the World.* Lady Wishfort, contemplating a crim. con. action, is advised that not only would she have 'her name prostituted in a public court' but also that 'it must after this be consigned by the short-hand writers to the public press; and from thence be transferred to the hands, nay into the throats and lungs of the hawkers... And this you must hear 'till you are stunn'd; nay you must hear nothing else for some days.'[5] When crim. con. actions were finally abolished, with the first British divorce act of 1857, the effect of newspaper publicity was one of the factors that weighed against such trials, in the course of which the 'foulest of French novelists might have learned something from the innuendoes gratuitously thrown out on either side'.[6] But the new legislation still allowed the newspapers to print extensively the sordid details of divorce proceedings, and this so outraged Queen Victoria that she protested to the Lord Chancellor, asking for a curb on publishing items 'of so scandalous a character that it makes it almost impossible for a paper to be trusted in the hands of a young lady or boy. None of the worst French novels,' she added, 'can be as bad as what is daily brought and laid upon the breakfast-table of every educated family in England, and its effect must be most pernicious to the public morals of the country.'[7] But the Queen complained in vain; so did the attorney-general, who spluttered about how 'crowds congregate [in court] for the purpose of hearing details which would give gratification to depraved and diseased minds'.[8] A proposal to silence the press and to conduct divorce court hearings in private was heavily defeated in the House of Lords.

So mass-market Sunday papers like the *News of the World*, the *Umpire* and the *People* continued to thrive on sensational divorce cases well into the twentieth century. The detailed evidence, often personal and invariably sexual, that was adduced in the course of these hearings commended itself to the editors and their millions of readers as much as the great capital murder trials of the day. But while the working classes feasted on sex-sodden cases, the governing elite tried to bring forward proposals to curb the 'evil' divorce reports so as 'to prevent injury to public morals': in other words, to come the killjoy. Until the divorce court was set up in 1857, reports of matrimonial cases reached only those who could both afford and read a newspaper – the upper classes. The huge literacy boom that followed the 1870 Education Act, and the flood of cheap, popular papers from the mid-1890s onwards, meant that Jack as well as his master was doled a daily dose of detail from the divorce court. The Establishment had always resented this. In 1859, the attorney-general, Sir Richard Bethell, had complained about the low-life crowds who thronged the divorce courts to soak up the salacious details for their own entertainment and gratification. In reality, very little of what appeared in the newspapers was actually obscene. 'Even the *News of the World* is said to have somewhat bowdlerised its reports,' declared the journalist W. T. Stead, in evidence to the Royal Commission on Divorce, 'and obscene reporting in the daily press is practically unknown.'[9]

The result was that well into the twentieth century, the papers were allowed to publish details of adultery cases. 'I think they are spicy reading,' Sir George H. Lewis, a divorce court judge, admitted in evidence to the Royal Commission on Divorce in 1912. '[A] great many people take up the paper and the first thing they do is to turn up and read about the Divorce Court.'[10] Figures produced in evidence to the commission showed that in 1909 Edwardian England was indeed mesmerized by such scandalous fare: respectable papers like *The Times*, *Daily Telegraph* and *Daily Mail* devoted up to 126 columns a year to divorce cases, while one Sunday paper, the *Umpire*, ran no fewer than 238, an average of more than four and a half lurid columns a week. It would take a single extraordinary case to force a change in the law, to take the reporting of salacious detail out of divorce cases and divert them into the gossip columns. One eminent legal historian hailed the so-called Russell Baby case as 'perhaps the greatest *cause célèbre* of its kind since the creation of the Divorce Court'.[11] In the course of two trials and two appeals, the evidence was so scabrous that Parliament rushed through legislation to ban the reporting of such details in England and Wales.

A week before Christmas 1920, the Hon. John Russell, twenty-four, gangling son and heir of Lord Ampthill, shared a bed with his wife. The consequences had silken lawyers lost for words and Britain agog for weeks. For when, nine months later, Christabel Russell duly gave birth to a baby boy, the Hon. John disclaimed paternity, insisting that she must have committed adultery, not at Oakley House, the Russell family's country seat in Bedfordshire, but at one of the various flats and hotels at which Christabel admitted spending nights with – in her husband's words – 'a string of detestable young men'.

Lady Ampthill, Christabel's starchy mother-in-law, was appalled. The two women had never got on. Christabel, tall and striking at twenty-five, lived fast and loose in a world of dancing partners, nightclubs and post-war gaiety. The dignified mistress of Oakley House was a Victorian throwback, a Lady of the Bedchamber to Queen Mary, who thought her son had married beneath him. Neither Lord nor Lady Ampthill attended the wedding of their son in October 1918. On the day before the ceremony, Christabel made her husband-to-be promise that they would not have children 'for at least a year or two'. During this time, they would not live as man and wife. In fact, both agreed in the course of the subsequent divorce case that the marriage was never fully consummated. The newly-weds spent part of their honeymoon at Oakley House, a late-seventeenth-century manor with lawns sweeping down to the River Ouse.

Christabel found life on the sprawling 250-acre estate of parkland very much to her taste. Two years into the marriage, such connections as had taken place were, in the words of Christabel's lawyer, 'of a very incomplete character'. According to John Russell, the couple had had no sex at all after August 1920. At Oakley, they were usually assigned separate rooms. But when they returned there for the nights of 18 and 19 December 1920, Lady Ampthill put them in a guest room with a double bed.

Whilst Christabel claimed that incomplete intercourse had taken place, John denied this.

She discussed the physiological details on which the case hinged with such composure that her husband's barrister, Sir John Simon KC, seemed flummoxed. The editor of the *Sunday Express*, James Douglas, saluted Christabel as the typical modern girl who could now 'swim in the bracing sea of sex without being drowned'.[12] The image was apt. Christabel's description of 'Hunnish scenes' in the connubial bed at Oakley was no less startling than the theory, canvassed in court, that she had become pregnant while soaking herself in a bath recently vacated by her husband. As a result of these disclosures, Christabel's baby boy Geoffrey, born in October 1921, became known variously as the 'Sponge Baby' or 'The Baby in the Bath'.

The Russell divorce was only the start of Christabel's long fight to prove that her son was not illegitimate. She denied having sex with two named co-respondents, and it was established that she was indeed technically a virgin at the time of the baby's birth. There were two trials. The first was inconclusive on the paternity question. But at the second, Christabel was found guilty of adultery with an unknown man and the Hon. John got his divorce. Although her appeal was unsuccessful, it was subsequently allowed by the House of Lords and the divorce was rescinded. The implication was that Christabel Russell was no adulteress and that her son Geoffrey was legitimate after all.

As the extraordinary Russell baby case unfolded to general astonishment across Britain's breakfast-tables, no one was more vexed than the King himself who professed himself 'disgusted at the gross, scandalous details'. As George V ran his beady eye down the columns of his carefully ironed *Times*, he found himself unable to recall such shocking material, violating, as he believed, the unwritten code of British decency which had always placed 'such an exposure of those intimate relations between man and woman... out of range of public eye or ear. The pages of the most extravagant French novel,' he went on, 'would hesitate to describe what has now been placed at the disposal of every boy or girl reader of the daily newspapers.'[13] The King, like his grandmother before him, wanted such cases heard in public no longer. He was told that in the past it had been possible to rely on the discretion of newspapers and their editors to leave out 'repulsive details', but the King let it be known that he considered such material an evil that coarsened public morals and lowered public taste, and he declared that something would have to be done. It was. The case of *Russell* v *Russell* led to the Judicial Proceedings Act of 1926, when, after several years of dither and delay, the Conservative government under Prime Minister Stanley Baldwin finally changed the law and it became illegal in Britain to report details about a divorce.

Much later, in 1973, when John, by then Lord Ampthill, died, the vexed question arose of who should succeed him: Geoffrey or the son he had fathered in 1950, in the course of his third marriage. The question was settled in 1976 when a House of Lords committee confirmed Christabel's son, Geoffrey Russell, as lawful heir and the 4th Lord Ampthill. After a career as a theatrical impresario, he became a deputy speaker of the House of Lords. Christabel never lived to hear the Lords' judgment on her son's succession. The wayward virgin had died aged eighty a few weeks earlier.

The Russell baby case planted a marker in Fleet Street's moral landscape. In the mid-1920s came one of the biggest serendipitous boosts to the British gossiping trade, in the wake of two particularly sensational society sex cases. The 1926 Act had had the immediate effect of driving sex off the news pages. But the law that banned the press from reporting details of divorces forced the papers to look elsewhere. Robert Graves and Alan Hodge recalled that the press became 'cleaner and cleaner' as the decade advanced, and as Fleet Street's sex obsession waned.[14] But in the event, by damming the tide of sexual titillation from the courts, the papers built up a towering head of frustrated curiosity, which years later burst through and overwhelmed the gossip columns like a freak wave. No one seems to have foreseen this wholly unexpected outcome. Yet had the nation's legislators not tinkered with the law, the papers might have handled sex and sexuality very differently in the years ahead.

Itchy-fingered moral guardians have always wanted to clamp down on what newspaper readers can and cannot read. In the mid-Victorian era, when Parliament established the first modern divorce courts, there was a move to conduct the proceedings in secret. It failed. The fact that evidence of sexual shenanigans could and did get into the papers didn't seem to matter much at first: newspaper circulations were low by modern standards, and hardly any of the vulgar masses read them anyway, so the governing class wasn't worried about any risk of moral corruption. What soon became apparent, however, was that the aspiring middling orders were being exposed to it instead, and this alarmed the very highest in the land. When Queen Victoria complained to her Lord Chancellor, Lord Campbell, in 1859 about divorce reports, he could only shrug, explaining that he was 'helpless to prevent the evil'. But in spite of contemporary buttoned-up sensibilities, these reports, often spectacularly detailed, have left us with an unrivalled perspective on the nineteenth-century marriage bed. Along with the gas-lit criminal courtrooms of the age, the Victorian divorce court offers one of the best vantage points from which to spy out the social landscape of the day, and it also holds the key to its sexual secrets.

The mid-Victorian desperation to avoid publicity at all costs was nowhere more clear than in the Aylesford case. Although the principal parties in the affair succeeded in stoppering any public leakage, the details soon circulated in society. The story struck terror into many a noble heart; much anxious consternation was excited in particular by the prospect of a public airing of all the juicy details – adultery, illicit passion, compromising letters and a royal connection. In a way, it was a variation on the Victorian double standard, which held that while husbands were allowed, or even expected, to indulge in extramarital affairs, wives were expected to remain above reproach. What was really at stake was not so much a question of morality as the fear of the newspapers exposing the sexual delinquencies of the ruling classes to the prurient scrutiny of the gaping mob. 'It is only by trying to understand the horror and fear attached to publicity rather than to sexual misdemeanour itself that one can see why [this] intended divorce caused such a hubbub,' one account explains. 'A divorce meant the Divorce Court, and the Divorce Court meant publicity. The Prince of Wales felt particularly strongly on the subject because he had been dragged into court himself in the Mordaunt divorce case of 1870. Though quite innocent, he had been strongly censured. Scandal must be avoided at all costs.'[15]

At the centre of the Aylesford affair stood the adulterous and mercurial Lord Blandford, at thirty-two the eldest son of the Duke of Marlborough, and his mistress Edith, wife of Lord Aylesford, a jolly young chum of the Prince of Wales, who was popularly known as 'Sporting Joe'. Aylesford was accompanying the Prince on an official tour of India early in 1876 when Edith's hysterical screed arrived at the royal encampment, announcing her impending elopement with Blandford. Although Aylesford and the Prince probably already knew of the affair (Blandford being a close friend of both), they were nevertheless shocked and appalled at the prospect of an open scandal, the Prince denouncing Blenheim's heir as 'the greatest blackguard alive'. With his reputation still smoking from the Mordaunt affair, his royal displeasure was acute. A public eruption might seriously threaten the established social order, and Albert Edward himself (a casual acquaintance of the lady in the case) could barely conceal his horror at the prospect of being toppled from his princely pinnacle by lurid headlines. Aylesford immediately returned to England, where he loud-mouthed the Prince's dim view of Blandford into every corner of society and announced his own intention of divorcing his wife.

In such aristocratic Victorian circles, divorce was nothing short of a catastrophe. It ruined public men like Dilke and Parnell, whilst women appearing as the guilty party faced not only social ostracism but the loss of their children. Edith Aylesford reflected on this, and (beseeched by her family) changed her mind about marrying Blandford. She also appealed to her husband to withdraw his threat of divorce. But Sporting Joe, in no mood to back off, flatly refused. Beside himself with rage, he threatened to challenge Blandford to a duel, and was only dissuaded with difficulty. The stage seemed set for a painfully public showdown in the divorce court, with the papers poised to print every morsel that bubbled up in the evidence. What saved the day was an unexpected intervention from Blandford's younger brother, Lord Randolph Churchill. Randolph had got it into his head that the Prince of Wales had deliberately taken Lord Aylesford on his Indian jaunt so that the lovers could canoodle undisturbed. When he wired the Prince, begging him to intervene in Aylesford's plans to divorce Edith, and received a dusty royal refusal, Randolph raised the stakes by threatening blackmail.

It seems that the Prince and Edith Aylesford had a history. It was a harmless flirtation by all accounts, but one recorded in a series of indiscreet letters that the Prince had written 'in a strain of undue familiarity and containing many foolish and somewhat stupid expressions'. Edith had kept the Prince's billets-doux, which in a flap she now passed to Blandford, who in turn handed them to Randolph. By threatening to publish them, Randolph now possessed the means of bringing the Prince to heel and forcing him to persuade Aylesford to drop his divorce action. Randolph bragged openly about these letters, and boasted that he 'held the crown of England in his pocket'. But now it was Randolph's turn to make a mistake. He foolishly dragged the Prince's wife, Princess Alexandra, into the affair by calling at Marlborough House and telling her that he held letters of 'a most compromising character' (not true), and proclaiming that if they were ever published, 'His Royal Highness would never sit upon the throne of England.' If the case came to court, he said, the Prince would be forced to appear as a witness, the letters quoted in evidence and his dalliance with Edith Aylesford exposed in the papers to public glare.

When Queen Victoria heard of this, she clucked her disapproval in the manner of any mother-in-law, complaining to her prime minister Disraeli 'that the Princess of Wales's name should be mixed up in this, she being so young'.[16] The Prince, informed of Randolph's interview with Alexandra, was less measured. He was in Cairo, returning to England from his tour of India, and this attempt to bully his wife so vexed him that he dispatched Lord Charles Beresford ahead of him to London to challenge Randolph to a duel. It was an empty challenge; duelling had almost completely ceased, and in any case its code of honour forbade a confrontation between a subject and his future king. When Beresford invited Randolph to name his seconds for a duel with pistols, Randolph replied with a curt and discourteous letter implying that the Prince was a coward who had issued a challenge knowing that it could not be accepted.

Queen Victoria, loyal to her son throughout this 'dreadful disgraceful business',[17] accepted his protestations of innocence over the letters to Edith Aylesford. Nevertheless, she was acutely conscious of the damage a public scandal might do, and warned, through her private secretary Ponsonby, that should the letters be quoted in court, 'a colouring might be easily given and injurious inferences deduced from hasty expression'. Some courtiers advised the Prince to remain abroad until tempers cooled, but with the press still silent on the matter, the Queen thought that the moment of greatest risk had passed. Even so, Ponsonby added, 'had there been any probability of a public scandal into which his name could be dragged by these villains she would have agreed to thinking it advisable that he should not return until a frank explanation had been publicly made.'[18]

When the Prince did return to London, he heard that Aylesford had finally dropped his insistence on a divorce 'in order to avoid a great public mischief'.[19] But if the threat of public scandal had receded, the animus with Churchill continued unabated. The Prince demanded an apology for his insolence, but Randolph demurred, forcing the heir to the throne to blacklist any house where the Randolph Churchills were received as guests, a gesture tantamount to social ostracism. Eventually Churchill did apologize, a gesture grudgingly made that was never acknowledged, but the Prince refused to lift his ban and it was only when Disraeli suggested making the Duke of Marlborough viceroy of Ireland that the impasse was broken. Randolph followed his parents to Dublin, where he worked as unpaid private secretary to his father and nursed a poisonous hatred of society and its princely leader. It was several years before the Churchills were rehabilitated into royal social circles, thanks to Randolph's stunning young American wife, Jennie Jerome, on whom the Prince fixed a glad eye. By then, the Aylesford affair had frozen over, and whilst it had certainly generated much excitable gossip in society, a public scandal had been avoided, to the enormous relief of the participants. But several lives were ruined. The roistering Aylesford went ranching in Texas and died of drink aged only thirty-six, while his wife Edith, after briefly living abroad with Blandford, found herself 'out of society for ever',[20] her name stricken from guest lists and studiedly 'cut' in public. Blandford himself continued to womanize and became entangled in several prominent society sensations, most spectacularly six years later with Lady Colin Campbell, yet another titled lady with whom he was (erroneously) reported to have eloped.

In the autumn of 1882, one of Lady Colin's society acquaintances, the Hon. Mark Bouverie, spotted her travelling by train from London to a hotel at Purfleet, where she and Blandford spent the weekend. Bouverie floated a rumour that the couple had run away together, and tipped off a gossip writer for a widely read society newspaper, who promptly passed the story on to his readers. There was no elopement, but there was certainly an affair, and the Campbell family were obliged to assemble in the biggest box they could find at a London theatre to demonstrate in public that Lady Colin had not run away. The gesture was hollow. With her husband ailing, Lady Colin threw herself into what today's tabloids would have billed as steamy sex sessions at her London townhouse, causing such a stir that when the papers did finally ladle out the details, thousands milled in the street for a glimpse of the woman scorned as 'a lady with utter contempt for the commonest laws of decency'.[21]

For eighteen wintry days in 1886, Britain's longest divorce case held the country spellbound. For newspaper readers, *Campbell* v *Campbell* had become a national obsession. Born Gertrude Blood, the daughter of an Irish landowner, Lady Colin was possessed, as one reporter spluttered, of 'the unbridled lust of Messalina and the indelicate readiness of a common harlot'.[22] Her husband, in his mid-thirties when the scandal broke, was the youngest son of the 8th Duke of Argyll. Lord Colin's birthright had secured him a seat in Parliament, but he was not a wealthy man. Furthermore, he had contracted syphilis, which was one of the reasons Lady Colin entertained other men.

After the wedding in July 1881, the Campbell marriage remained unconsummated for several weeks until the couple journeyed to Scotland to stay with the Argylls at the castle of Inverary. There, Lady Colin lost her virginity and caught her husband's 'loathsome disease' –

her father's words – before returning to London. At Lady Colin's home in Cadogan Place, Lord Blandford was her most frequent visitor, calling on average twice a week, ringing the bell where others usually knocked.

Another favoured visitor was the dashing chief of the Metropolitan Fire Brigade, Captain Shaw. He began calling at Cadogan Place before the Campbells had even moved in. Lord Colin testified to calling unexpectedly at his home-to-be and finding his wife in the empty drawing room with Captain Shaw. James O'Neill's predecessor as butler, Albert de Roche, explained that Lady Colin had instructed him on what to do when certain visitors called. 'She said I was not to announce Captain Shaw or Lord Blandford in his lordship's hearing.' De Roche also testified to finding Blandford and Lady Colin together on the drawing-room sofa. Blandford's arm was round her waist and her dress was disarranged. O'Neill had a similar experience while taking up a tray of tea. With Lord Colin ill in bed, Lady Colin was again alone on the drawing-room sofa with Blandford. 'I noticed that her dress was disordered,' said O'Neill, 'and her face was flushed.' Blandford, who had become the 8th Duke of Marlborough by the time of the divorce case, explained that his friendship with Lady Colin was due to their common interest in literature. There were not many good books at Cadogan Place, he explained, and he had loaned her several improving volumes.

In July 1882, butler O'Neill again caught her ladyship *in flagrante*, this time through the dining-room keyhole with the London fire chief. 'I saw Lady Colin lying down with Captain Shaw on the carpet,' he told a shocked court.

'Did you see her bust?'

'I certainly saw more than that.'[23]

O'Neill went on to describe the couple's exact position, but all the newspapers suppressed his testimony, saying the material was 'unfit for publication'.

Lady Colin also dallied with Tom Bird, a surgeon attending her husband. A servant at Cadogan Place noticed the pair smoking cigarettes together in the drawing room, and a cabman caught them canoodling in his hansom on the way back from a concert. In June 1883, Lord Colin, 'displeased because he [Bird] sat so long in my wife's bedroom', banned him from 79 Cadogan Place. In 1884, Lady Colin convinced the courts that her husband had infected her with syphilis and was granted a decree of separation. Her solicitor, hearing the sad story of her marriage, urged her to sue for divorce. Lady Colin's enraged husband – whose family motto was 'Forget Not' – swore revenge. The result was a painfully public exchange of sexual misconduct claims at Cadogan Place. Lady Colin accused her husband of adultery with a housemaid. He cross-petitioned on the grounds of his wife's adultery with the four named co-respondents. In the end, the jury found none of the adultery allegations proved and the couple, while judicially separated, remained man and wife. Lord Colin died in 1895 from syphilis. Lady Colin moved into a first-floor flat near Victoria and earned her living as a journalist and writer. Shunned by Edwardian society as a *déclassée*, she ended her days in a wheelchair and was dead at fifty-three, another victim of her husband's 'loathsome disease'.

The Campbell case might never have surfaced in public had it not been for Lord Colin's intransigence. Lady Colin's solicitor offered him a deal that would have kept the case out of the courts, but this was angrily rejected, despite her lawyer pointing out 'how essential it may be for your own interests that [Lord Colin's syphilis] may not become public'.[24] He would have been better advised to ponder the prospect of such a lurid case spilling into the public domain. Ever since the days when marriages were ended in the old Court of Arches, the threat of publicity cooled the ardour of many a litigant; one victim, writing in 1733, warned bitterly that anyone appealing a matrimonial case there 'must expect to have as much filth as a scavenger's cart will hold emptied upon him'.[25] In the Georgian age, the scandalous press so blew up reports of actions for crim. con. that one Franco-American visitor to London remarked that 'all the details and proofs of the intrigue . . . are highly indelicate and scandalous. The testimony, for instance, of servants, of young chambermaids, who are brought into open court to tell, in the face of the public, all they have seen, heard or guessed at, is another sort of prostitution more indecent than the first.'[26]

Throughout the seventeenth century, husbands had haggled with their wives' lovers for money rather than submitting to the process of an ecclesiastical court, where punishment for sin was meted out. 'So psychologically wounding was the publicity of those shame punishments,' says historian Lawrence Stone, 'that most lovers were willing to compound with the husband to buy his silence'.[27] By the early eighteenth century, many potential plaintiffs were still ashamed of washing their dirty linen in public and exposing their cuckoldry to the world. But crim. con. trials were attracting increasing press attention: reporting techniques were improving, thanks mainly to the use of shorthand by professional law reporters, and by mid-century an explosion in the number of news outlets was delivering a much bigger readership. Crucially, the Georgians – unlike their forebears who regarded sex as sinful – grinned and gaped in idle amusement. The Prime Minister, Lord North, while sympathizing with calls for curbing the popular press, believed that the habit of reading the papers arose not from any worthy desire for self-improvement but from idle and foolish curiosity.[28] According to William Cobbett, it encouraged drunkenness: 'What,' he asked, 'was so likely as a newspaper to lead a man to the ale-house?'[29] As religion began to be replaced by a general secularization of thought, pornography, such as John Cleland's breathlessly best-selling *Fanny Hill*, appeared, fuelling demand for full transcripts of detailed evidence produced in trials for crim. con.[30]

The eighteenth century saw a general boom in the reporting of legal cases, but also a move away from stressing the sensational aspects in accounts of criminal trials, to be replaced by the legal and moral ones. Even so, readers devoured them like real-life novels. One publisher promised that 'these little stories will afford the curious not only instruction but an agreeable amusement... They may be considered as a collection of dramatic pieces.'[31] By the 1770s, the trickle had become a flood. In 1780 a seven-volume collection, *Trials for Adultery ... at Doctors' Commons,* featured verbatim evidence 'taken in shorthand by a civilian [i.e. civil lawyer]'.[32]

As well as reports intended for the legal community, crim. con. actions also generated a small number of articles written or paid for by one of the parties involved. These either appeared in newspapers or were issued as privately printed pamphlets as a way of moulding public opinion in favour of the author. Lawrence Stone quotes a case from 1793 in which Yorkshire landowner William Middleton and his family planted a racy description of his wife Clara's adultery with the family groom in the *Bon Ton Magazine* under the heading 'The Wanton Wife, or the Lady in the Straw'. The piece was immediately suppressed by an injunction from the puritanical Lord Chief Justice following a formal protest by the defence. The magazine nevertheless teased its readers with the promise of even juicier copy as the case unfolded;[33] the author of the offending tale was apparently a man called Simons, a member of the household of William Middleton's mother, 'where he was employed to read plays'. After Mr Middleton's victory in his crim. con. case, his family paid for a stenographic record of the trial published in pamphlet form. The scandal was the talk of London. Having won the battle, the Middletons used the press to publicize their victory as widely as possible. Although these tracts were printed in very small numbers, they gained a bigger circulation because the London newspapers picked them up and they were also distributed to the London clubs for perusal by their members.

In the 1850s, when Parliament was debating a new divorce bill, Emily, the former Lady Westmeath, published at her own expense a 200-page pamphlet regurgitating the story of her own failed marriage. In the words of her ex-husband, it 'had been placed on the tables of the clubs, with a view to vilifying my character'.[34] He complained in the House of Lords that the pamphlet had been followed up by an article in 'a most respectable newspaper'[35] (an article planted, he assumed, by his ex-wife) which, like the pamphlet, brimmed with 'the grossest perversions of . . . fact' and 'the most unjustifiable untruths', all intended to blacken his reputation and make the world think that 'I was a villain'.[36] According to Stone, the various lawsuits between the Westmeaths in the 1820s and early 1830s were 'probably the longest, the most expensive, the most complicated, and most famous war over marital separation of all time,'[37] and they paved the way for the divorce reforms of 1857.

By far the biggest category of crim. con. publications was the shorthand reports of the trials, which stressed the human interest element. They contained detailed evidence of adultery supplied by witnesses who testified about keyhole glimpses, the noise of creaking bedsprings, soiled bedlinen and so on. Again, these appeared both in pamphlet form and as reports in the papers. The more sensational cases were gathered together and published in book form, some running to multiple volumes, which were hawked in the streets and sold by specialist book-dealers.

If nothing else, all this publicity certainly educated an increasingly curious public about the ins and outs of matrimonial law. It also made the names (and the fortunes) of some of the era's greatest lawyers. After the widely reported case of *Cibber* v *Sloper* in 1738, the brilliant young defence counsel William Murray, later Lord Mansfield, reported that 'henceforth business poured in upon me from all quarters' and that his annual income rose 'from hundreds to thousands'.[38] Crim. con. suits also hugely enriched Thomas Erskine, another distinguished advocate who later became Lord Chancellor. But while one effect of scandalous press reports was to stimulate litigation, another was to discourage it. As early as 1688, Lord Halifax had warned his daughter against having her modesty scrutinized in open court, and the kind of roaring publicity given to crim. con. suits a century later persuaded many an unhappily married couple to seek a private rather than a public separation. By the early twentieth century, little had changed. In 1910, in the first flush of modern popular journalism, most of the witnesses giving evidence before the Royal Commission on Divorce testified that fear of newspaper publicity still put off many potential divorce litigants. One former London editor echoed the view widely held by journalists of the day that restricting reports of divorce cases would be against the public interest 'since the real punishment for matrimonial offences is the exposure in the newspapers'.[39] One distinguished judge, on the other hand, while insisting that divorce reports had no deterrent effect, pointed to an unexpected side-effect, that of blackmail. Worried that friends and family would 'read all these details', Sir George Lewis said that litigants were sometimes willing to pay to keep painful reports out of the papers, 'painful to themselves, painful to their children, and painful to their relations'.[40]

When the Victorians established the divorce court in 1857, they didn't anticipate the huge newspaper boom that lay ahead. Evidence in divorce cases was given in public, in open court, and was reported, often at length. The details, as the Edwardians acknowledged, were 'more suggestive than actually indecent',[41] but the question of banning publication was one of the hottest topics when they came to consider reforming the law in 1910. The Lord Chief Justice, Lord Alverstone, was plainly vexed by 'the mischief done by...certain low-class papers', in particular those (mainly the cheap Sunday papers like the *News of the World*, the *People* and the *Weekly Dispatch*) that headlined 'the lady's maid's evidence' and 'the housemaid's evidence'.[42] What the editors of those papers themselves thought about the matter remained a mystery, since they refused to testify to the commission. The Victorian sunset years of the 'Naughty Nineties' produced a slew of scandalous cases, most notably the trials of Oscar Wilde, in which the evidence was judged so 'extremely repulsive' by one editor that he banned the case from his pages altogether, announcing the fact in his list of contents. Sidney Low, then editing the evening *St James's Gazette*, was able to ignore normal commercial considerations, since his paper, while influential, had a tiny circulation, and he boasted that he was one of the very few to volunteer self-censorship. 'A sensational or painful divorce suit or criminal trial,' he agreed, 'will send up the circulation of some newspapers by tens of thousands of copies daily.'[43] A year earlier, one such society suit created such a hullabaloo and so affronted the sensibilities of the day that it very nearly led to an immediate ban on reporting any evidence from a divorce court. The editor of the *Manchester Guardian*, C. P. Scott, considered that the Stirling case threw an extraordinary light on upper-class morality, and that press coverage was 'a moral document of extraordinary interest – the spectacle of these people who had every luxury that wealth could produce and never did a day's work for themselves or anybody...I think it is an appalling thing,'[44] he concluded, sinking back in his chair at the end of his evidence to the Royal Commission on Divorce.

Although the Stirling case created an Edwardian sensation with its glimpses of raffish and adulterous behaviour among the ruling classes, it offered nothing in the way of raw sex beyond a catalogue of furtive assignations, stolen kisses and intercepted letters, set against a background of a dappled, sunlit world of swanky hotels and restaurants and the excited social ferment of the Henley regatta. Nevertheless, press coverage was unprecedented, with the *Daily Telegraph* running an astonishing sixty-nine solid columns of evidence in a single week, the equivalent of a hundred columns in the downmarket *Umpire*, which vied with the *News of the World* for saturation coverage on Sundays. These so-called gutter papers had the market to themselves in an age that continued to observe the Victorian Sabbath. 'The Sunday newspaper,' as Sir Charles Petrie noted, 'was unknown in any respectable household.'[45] But on the six remaining days, even *The Times*, recently acquired by the populist genius Alfred Harmsworth, featured the Stirling case at length as a way of increasing circulation. 'I wish to give the devil his due,' observed C. P. Scott of the *Manchester Guardian* drily, 'and I think the weekly papers are not the chief offenders.'[46] The case lifted a corner on the *Upstairs Downstairs* swirl of London society and focused not on the traditional love triangle but a young and attractive foursome: on the one side, a Scottish laird and his wife (a former actress); and on the other, an impoverished minor aristocrat and a notorious divorcee. Reviewing the evidence from his bench in the Court of Session in Edinburgh, Lord Guthrie remarked that it amounted to no more than 'petty incidents in selfish, idle lives, containing nothing that is romantic, not much that is even mock-heroic and little that is legitimately interesting'.[47] Yet for fifteen days, millions of readers across Britain and her still-intact empire were not merely interested but totally riveted.

It was, in fact, two actions clamped together, an arrangement prompting one weary lawyer to grumble (in spite of its now-faded glittery theatrical origins) about 'this interminable case and its twin'. Clara Stirling, twenty-four (who, when less plump, had hoofed it as one of the 'Cosy Corner Girls' in the hit West End show, *The Earl and the Girls,* at the Adelphi Theatre), sued her 28-year-old stockbroker husband Jack for divorce on the grounds of his adultery (then called misconduct) with his mistress, Mrs Mabel Atherton, a striking divorcee ten years older than he was and known to her friends as Nancy. Jack Stirling counter-petitioned his wife for adultery with his schoolfriend and fellow Guards officer, Lord 'Fatty' Northland, twenty-seven, eldest son of the Earl of Ranfurly and currently secretary to a large insurance company. They were all, in their way, glamorous but deeply unattractive people. Nancy Atherton was already a divorced woman and had sued her lover for breach of promise when, instead of marrying her, he ran off with a pretty young actress. The judge Lord Guthrie (best recalled by posterity as the man who, a year earlier, had sentenced Oscar Slater to hang for murder, a case still regarded as one of Scotland's gravest miscarriages of justice) could scarcely contain himself in the scorching glare of Nancy Atherton's considerable charms, endowed as she was 'with a kind of beauty which a man like Mr Stirling admires'. As Mrs Atherton nodded appreciatively, the gigantic white aigrette adorning her toque of sable fur bobbed and waved at the scribbling reporters. She was a lady, his lordship drooled, with 'tact, perfect control of temper and gracious manners, the sort of fascination which captivates man; indeed,' he added, peering at her admiringly over his glasses, 'apart from past history... she is fitted to grace any society'.[48]

First to counter these judicial effusions was Nancy Atherton's French maid, Thérèse Dagorne. In the broken English of a stage soubrette, she told the court how she frequently found her mistress with dashing Jack Stirling on the sitting-room couch in the flat Nancy rented at the Cadogan Hotel, a scandalous address still redolent of sexual misdemeanour nearly fifteen years after Oscar Wilde's arrest there for committing indecent acts. At Amberley Cottage, Nancy's verandahed house on the Thames at Maidenhead, the servant testified to finding one of Jack's monogrammed handkerchiefs under Nancy's pillow. At a hotel on the Isle of Wight, it was 'Jackie, dear' and 'Nancy, darling', a glimpse of Nancy in a kimono wrap, her intentions betrayed by a trail of dull gold hairpins scattered in Jack's bedroom. Stirling, tall and slim with a quick manner, hands thrust in pockets in the witness box, swatted aside questions about an affair, throwing his head back and glancing at the ceiling before answering, and dismissing the maid's talk of endearments as 'mostly a fabrication of the servants'. Not only did he deny a romance with Nancy Atherton, but he accused his wife Clara of throwing herself at 'Fatty' Northland when the foursome swanned over to Paris for the Grand Prix at Longchamps in June 1908. A few weeks later, Stirling announced that he was sending her to America for two months to break up the affair. In fact, Clara pre-empted her husband by moving her belongings out of the marital home in Chesham Street and leaving him a note. 'My dear Jack,' she wrote. 'I think it best to get the whole thing over, so I am leaving today for good.'

The problem, Stirling explained in cross-examination, was that after marrying Clara – in secret, because his family disapproved of actresses – she had decided to stick with her old theatrical friends. 'We lived to an extent a bohemian life,' he added. He agreed that Nancy was a woman with a reputation. 'But I don't love *her*,' he snapped, glaring at Clara. 'Never have, and never will.' At this, Clara turned pale, almost fainted and had to be helped from the court by her American mother. For the first time in the case, Nancy Atherton flushed like a peony. Titters and giggles filled the air. That night Lord Guthrie busied himself with some behind-the-scenes fixing and next morning he moved to a smaller court to exclude what one reporter called the 'idlers and curiosity-mongers' who, at the least provocation, had given vent to loud and raucous laughter. This was not a wholly successful manoeuvre; before the case was over, the judge had to interrupt the proceedings again to order a dozen sniggering ladies to leave the court.

This foursome, punting by moonlight on the Thames during regatta week at Henley, flitting furtively in and out of restaurants while arranging nightly surveillance of bedroom toings and froings, danced inevitably towards their own destruction. To the delight of the public, the papers framed increasingly vivid vignettes: Nancy finding Clara sitting in Northland's lap in a sitting room at the Hanover Restaurant; Clara in such an emotional state that they had had to unscrew the telephone from her wall; the night that Jack Stirling returned home to find the front door on the chain and 'Fatty' Northland inside with Clara – these and other incidents were repeated in bars and taprooms, and even found their way into music-hall gags. The night porter at the Cadogan Hotel testified to admitting titled gentlemen at all hours of the night to visit 'ladies' staying there. No wonder that an entire row of junior counsel were reportedly briefed to watch the case on behalf of various interested, but unidentified, noblemen.

When, towards the end of the proceedings, Clara Stirling admitted buying a revolver with a view to shooting herself and her lover, she buried her tear-stained face in her muff and clutched at a bottle of smelling salts. Well she might. When what the *News of the World* billed as this 'squalid drama of the smart set' drew to a close, her action was dismissed and it was her husband Jack who won his divorce, together with custody of the couple's two-year-old son Patrick. Much agonizing ensued over why the case had attracted so much coverage, with the *Spectator* noting huffily that in some papers, reports on the case had taken up far more space than an important parliamentary debate, and identifying a new demand from readers of the cheaper prints.[49] Whether such saturation coverage had the sort of salutary effect on errant spouses that some supposed – the Victorian Prime Minister Gladstone changed his mind on the subject when the president of the divorce court spoke of 'the hideous glare of this publicity'[50] acting as a considerable deterrent

– became a crucial point the following year, when the idea of banning such reports was considered at enormous length by the Royal Commission on Divorce. In essence, the nobs appointed to examine the question of divorce reports were anxious to keep the lid on the nation's high life tightly screwed down, and seemed affronted that the sexual peccadilloes of their class should be considered worthy of scrutiny by everyone else. 'Would you just tell us,' boomed the chairman, Lord Gorell, to one national newspaper editor giving evidence to the commission, 'what advantage there was to the public in the publication of one word of [the Stirling] case?'[51] Although the commission recommended an absolute ban on reporting divorce case evidence, Parliament proposed instead a system of voluntary self-regulation by the papers. Not for the last time did the press find itself drinking in the last-chance saloon.

After the Russell baby case the press seemed less sure of its ground. In what the foremost critic and scholar, Professor George Saintsbury, described as 'an age of tabloids',[52] Fleet Street pondered the way forward, given the unceasing craving for details of sordid and sensational cases. Before going down on the *Titanic* in 1912, W. T. Stead, inventor of the New Journalism, had argued passionately for more rather than less reporting and had likened the divorce court to a modern Day of Judgment, thanks to newspaper publicity – 'the greatest security we have for justice'. Beset by adultery, fornication and other sins, the old crusader regretted that 'we should put our head in a bandbox, as it were, to hide ourselves from the facts, and I think the daily papers go very wrong in not reporting them enough'.[53] But most voices within the mainstream press were urging restraint, scenting statutory controls in the absence of self-regulation. 'So marked has been the desire to pander to the morbid taste of a certain section of the public,' noted one anonymous commentator in 1923, 'that the advisability of hearing unsavoury cases *in camera* has been seriously considered.'[54] In the event, within two short years the notorious Dennistoun case swamped all the papers with details of such unbridled sexual excesses that the King once again thundered to the government 'his feelings of disgust and shame at the daily published discreditable and nauseating evidence'[55] that spilled across his morning papers, finally tipping the balance in favour of an outright ban on reporting evidence that has applied to divorce cases ever since.

When Dorothy Dennistoun divorced her husband in 1921, she did so quietly in Paris, hoping that the bizarre story of her marriage would remain safely out of the sensation-hungry British papers. The union had lasted nearly eleven years, a remarkable span considering that for most of that time the Dennistouns had abandoned all pretence of marital bliss and had, by mutual consent, entered into the most unconventional of arrangements. Ian Onslow Dennistoun, an undistinguished officer in the Grenadier Guards during World War I, had obtained preferment, rising to the rank of lieutenant colonel, by selling his wife to one of the most important men in the British Army, General Sir John Cowans. Dennistoun's defenders called this an 'astonishing' act of sacrifice, but it was naked prostitution: Dorothy's sexual favours were bestowed in exchange for her husband's military advancement on the nod of General Cowans. Dorothy had known Cowans since her girlhood. Their affair, if that's what it could be called, seems to have begun before the war, in 1912, when Cowans secured Captain Dennistoun (as he then was) a post as secretary to the governor of Jamaica. During the war, Cowans promoted Dennistoun to the rank of colonel and gave him cushy jobs in Gibraltar and France, plus a seat on the Supreme War Council.

As a senior soldier, Cowans must have realized that this was a high-risk strategy. He was one of the best-known men in the British Army, not for any gallant feats of derring-do but for his outstanding talents as an administrator; as quartermaster-general to the forces throughout the Great War, he fed and clothed millions of British troops from Flanders to Mesopotamia, his admirers hailing him as 'the greatest quartermaster-general since Moses'. But women were his weakness. In December 1916, when he was already bedding Dorothy Dennistoun, his name featured in a sensational inquiry into irregularities surrounding the transfer of a junior officer and involving Shelagh Cornwallis-West, the estranged wife of the Duke of Westminster. The government expressed its 'displeasure' with Cowans, but allowed him to keep his job. Cowans always survived such scrapes. As well as being a womanizer, he was also a spendthrift; after his death in 1921, his fortune of £8,500 was swallowed up by debts, his orders and decorations were sold, and his widow was left with a pension of only £225 a year. Dorothy Dennistoun remained devoted to him. 'He was a very charming man,' she recalled, 'and a wonderful personality.'[56]

It was money that finally dragged the Dennistoun affair into the open. In March 1925 Mrs Dennistoun launched an action against her ex-husband for various sums, including £336 that she had loaned him during the marriage, and another £616 she claimed to have borrowed at his request to pay his debts. She also sought an order against him to activate an agreement under which, she said, he promised to provide for her (in lieu of alimony) as soon as he had the means. By now, Colonel Dennistoun was a wealthy man, having married the Countess of Carnarvon, the widow of the man who discovered Tutenkhamen's tomb, so quite why he didn't simply pay up remains a mystery. Instead, he denied his ex-wife's claims and raised the curtain on a sordid legal squabble on an unprecedented scale that ran for three weeks at the High Court. Even Lord Burnham, owner of the *Daily Telegraph*, was shocked at the level of muckraking. During the case, 'I happened to call for proofs of the proceedings,' he explained, 'and the editor had cancelled a remark by Lady Carnarvon in her evidence which was not calculated to hurt public morals but was, to say the least of it, in bad taste; at the same time it could hardly, in my opinion, be called indecent ... [Later] I went out to dinner [with some government ministers] and the very thing that we had omitted was being discussed.'[57]

Dennistoun, the court heard, knew that his promotion was due to his wife's friendship with General Cowans, a friendship which, as Dorothy Dennistoun was said to have told her husband, was burgeoning into affection and could culminate in only one thing. As her counsel, the leading divorce lawyer of the day, Sir Ellis Hume-Williams KC, put it: 'Colonel Dennistoun was prepared to accept from his wife that she should pass into a condition of adultery with the General – a relation from which he proposed to profit, as he had done.' From letters in the case, it was plain that not only was Dennistoun egging his wife on in this affair, but he was offering both protection and advice. 'Darling heart,' he wrote at one point, 'take great care of yourself; you seem sometimes such a tiny, small, brown mouse ... Don't go further than you want ... great big kiss. Tiger.' In 1916 Dennistoun met his wife at the Ritz in Paris, knowing that Cowans was coming over to see her and even inspecting the suite he knew they would share. It was at this point that Dennistoun was promoted to colonel and sent to Gibraltar, crowning his career in 1917 as acting adjutant and quartermaster-general at Versailles, in the post of Cowans's second in command. When the sensational Dennistoun allegations burst over the gothic spires of the Law Courts, people could only wonder at the nature of a War Office in which top generals could fix top jobs as payment for their sexual indiscretions.

Once again, a squalid sex case had panicked the British Establishment. The Home Secretary, Sir William Joynson-Hicks (an unloved puritan busybody known to headline-writers as 'Jix'), called a secret meeting of newspaper owners and appealed to them 'to try to stop some of the filth ... in press reports of indecent cases'. The *Telegraph*'s Lord Burnham agreed that the well-to-do were badly prejudiced by having 'the misdoings and the moral offences of their members held up as if they constituted a test of their average conduct'. The *News of the World* chairman, Lord Riddell, scoffed at this and accused the government of providing toffs with a fig-leaf in the shape of its new bill banning divorce reporting because 'the governing classes don't like their doings to be made public.'[58] Yet it was the governing classes, or at least their wives ('stylishly-dressed', as one reporter noted, 'some well-known in society'),[59] who daily sat in court to hear the case that, in Mr Justice McCardie's words, 'scarcely has a parallel in the annals of British law'.

What *Punch* sniffily called 'The Dustbin Case' made the reputation of one of Colonel Dennistoun's lawyers, the young silk Norman Birkett KC, who, without notice, had to step in to compose and deliver the defence's closing speech to the jury because of the illness of his leader, the great Sir Edward Marshall Hall. The outcome was complex, but on balance, judgment was in favour of Colonel Dennistoun. Neither side, however, gained a single farthing. So much dirty linen had been publicly washed that Mr Justice McCardie observed that such cases 'do not in any way represent the general way of life of well-to-do people in England. They give a wholly false impression of English social and family life.'[60] Within a matter of months, Parliament had passed a new law, banning 'the evil' of indecent and obscene reports, and restricting accounts of divorce and other matrimonial cases to the barest minimum of information.

9

Daddy's Girls and Boys

With adulterous sex effectively banned from the newspapers, Fleet Street summoned wealth and glamour to fill the void. But sources of gossip about the wealthy and glamorous were in short supply; journalists were considered below the salt, and grubby reporters trying to cover private parties at London's grand houses seldom made it past the first footman at the door.

(Today it is the reverse: most British modern gossip columnists are toffs, snappy dressers with upper-class accents, Old Etonians, Harrovians and Wykehamists to the fore. The *Mail*'s Nigel Dempster went to Sherborne; Ross Benson of the *Express*, known enviously as the James Bond of Fleet Street, was a contemporary of Prince Charles at Gordonstoun.)

Back in the 1920s, Beverley Nichols (who gleaned gossip himself for the *Weekly Dispatch*) portrayed a flyblown world of a gossip writer on six guineas (£6.30) a week, rubbing talcum powder (or even white bread) on his only dress-shirt (to make it 'do' another time) and patching his shoe soles with rubber solution. While the public saw such shabby figures as mean and slightly comic, Nichols considered the gossip writer as one of the world's great tragic figures, and in his novel *Crazy Pavements* confessed himself 'sick at heart for these lingerers in the outer courts of Society, with their brave gentility, their ears pricked for some wearisome trifle about some wearisome woman'.[1] But at least such trifles were gleaned at one remove. Until the late 1920s, gossip columnists were considered social pariahs, obedient to the Nichols dictum: 'No gossip writer should ever meet his victims in the flesh.'[2] That changed almost overnight.

By the late 1920s Fleet Street was sharpening up, and newspapers were recruiting a slew of minor and obscure aristocrats to contribute gossip paragraphs, on the basis that, unlike most hacks, they might actually know some of the people they were expected to write about. Most were men, but among the women was one of the famous Mitford girls. The Hon. Nancy Mitford, the rebellious, beautiful and exceptionally tall eldest daughter of the eccentric Lord and Lady Redesdale, earned pin money by supplying anonymous gossip to various papers. 'I'm making such a lot of money with articles,' she twittered to one of her admirers, Mark Ogilvie-Grant.[3] Nancy had her hair shingled at the age of twenty, applied lipstick, wore trousers, played the ukulele and smoked. Ogilvie-Grant belonged to a set of young bloods – Hearties and Arties – who, at weekends (according to her sister Jessica), 'would swoop down from Oxford or London in merry hordes, to be greeted with solid disapproval by my mother and furious glares from my father'.[4] One of the Arties, the aesthete Harold Acton, recalled that as a debutante Nancy enjoyed a conventional succession of seasons during that hectic period, immortalized by Evelyn Waugh, when Nöel Coward represented the younger generation of gatecrashers and jazz was in the air.[5] She was still living at home when she published her first novel, *Highland Fling*, in which members of her family, barely disguised, were portrayed with the sharp, acid wit that she inherited from her maternal grandfather, Thomas Gibson Bowles, founder of the sensational Victorian weekly *Vanity Fair* and the *Lady*. It was thanks to this family connection that early in 1930 Nancy was offered a contract to write a gossiping weekly article for the *Lady*, 'a sort of running commentary of current events', she explained, 'starting with the all England croquet championship at Brighton'.[6] It was a freeloader's dream. 'They're sending me to everything free,' she reported, 'the Opera, the Shakespeare festival at Stratford...'[7] Such was Nancy's delight at finding that her gossip-grubbing life at five guineas a week [£5.25] had become 'one huge whirl of gaiety'[8] that she treated herself to 'a divine coral tiara – the family think I've gone mad'.[9] With *Highland Fling* selling well, Nancy's stock as a writer was rising; barely a year later she was able to command £30 from *Harper's* for a short story and had become 'so rich I go 1st class everywhere and take taxis'.[10] At the age of twenty-seven, she turned down an offer from *The Tatler* to write gossip for £10 a week.[11] By then she had outgrown the paragraphing trade and embraced discretion, never to gossip in print again. When Nancy much later moved to France, the *Sunday Times* offered her a contract as 'a kind of Paris William Hickey',[12] but she refused and gave up her regular column in the paper.

'Whenever I see the words "Peer's Daughter" in a headline,' her mother Lady Redesdale once commented ruefully, 'I know it's going to be something about one of you children.'[13] When the *Daily Express* muddled two of them up and splashed a story about the wrong one having vanished on a visit abroad in 1937, it cost the paper £1,000 in libel damages. The other papers, meanwhile, had a field day at the *Express*'s expense. 'You were the first one in the family to be on posters,' Nancy told the real runaway, her sister Jessica.[14]

The unlikeliest people were taken on as gossip-gleaners. In the late 1920s, Lady Eleanor Smith, the feisty and unconventional daughter of Lloyd George's Lord Chancellor, Lord Birkenhead, was hired to write a twice-weekly column of 'Women's Gossip' in Beaverbrook's *Evening Standard*. The circumstances were lurid. The roistering Birkenhead, one of Beaverbrook's closest confidants, was having an affair with Mona Dunn, a beautiful young blonde and the daughter of wealthy financier Sir James Dunn, another of Beaverbrook's cronies. To complicate matters further, Mona and Eleanor Smith were also fast friends, being the same age and having attended the same Paris finishing school as seventeen-year-olds in 1919. Eleanor was furious when Beaverbrook furnished her father with opportunities to canoodle with Mona at a house he owned in Fulham. Beaverbrook's offer of a column effectively bought her silence.

Eleanor was highly talented and not entirely untutored in the writing trade. By the age of seventeen she had completed her third unpublished novel. As a skittish figure in London 'society' in the mid-1920s, she and two sisters, her old school friends Theresa ('Baby') and Zita Jungman, had posed as women reporters from non-existent newspapers, pulling off some remarkable interviews with visiting Hollywood film stars. 'They wore shapeless old tweeds, glasses, and in cold weather would ride on top of the old open omnibuses before an interview, in order to reduce their noses to what they considered an appropriate shade of blue,' Eleanor's brother Freddie Furneaux[15] recalled.[16] Eleanor had a special business card printed:

MISS BABINGTON GOOCH
Amalgamated
Provincial Press

Although occasionally rumbled – Lilian Gish saw through them at once – the trio met with surprising success. John Barrymore demanded to examine their notebooks, but Mae Murray cheerfully submitted, 'titupping eagerly down the corridor to her room to prepare for her interview'.[17] They hoodwinked the actor Tom Mix, whom they interviewed in a 'wonderful room, full of smoke and men', and managed to talk to film stars George Arliss and Alice Joyce, who was so charming at the Embassy Club that the three impostors revealed their true identities. As a reward, they were driven to the studios where they proceeded to interview the likes of Clive Brook, Colleen Moore, Alma Taylor and Norma Talmadge. 'If one is inclined to wonder at the gullibility of the stars,' Eleanor's brother observed, 'we must remember that these girls were remarkable actresses and totally devoid of any form of self-consciousness.'[18]

At the *Evening Standard*, Eleanor Smith drew a weekly wage of £3 while pursuing doggedly for six months what her brother mocked as 'this grim calling'. Then a young journalist friend, Charles Graves, fixed her up with a job on the *Sunday Dispatch*, writing a column of society news under the lumbering title 'From My Window in Vanity Fair'. Although Graves encouraged her to believe that she could make a success of it, Eleanor was an unlikely choice for such a column. 'She detested Society,' brother Freddie explained, 'despised gossip writers and refused to attend parties, so that an odder appointment could scarcely have been made, and had her million or so readers only realized, they were obtaining their glimpse into High Life by extremely remote control.'[19]

Green she may have been, but Lady Eleanor buckled down to the task with determination. Her social position and family ties meant that she was resented by some of the other journalists, who scarcely troubled to conceal their feelings. Eleanor herself hated the work but recognized that turning in a weekly column was a valuable discipline, even if, as she admitted herself, she must have been the worst journalist ever wished on Fleet Street. 'At least I learned to write briefly and I learned to write fast,' she recalled. 'These are valuable lessons for any writer. A journalist cannot afford to be temperamental – there are too many others queuing up on the pavement outside the office.'[20] She soon identified gossipdom's fascination with the rich:

Mrs Corey, Mabelle Gillman that was, the famous American hostess, is supporting the [Russian] ballet magnificently. Do you know that she has taken a box and four stalls for every single night of the season? And that, if you work it out, costs her something like ten pounds a day.

Still, she can afford it.

Mrs Corey is great fun; I am sure you would like her.

It adds piquancy to her conversation that she invariably pronounces people's names wrongly.

For instance, my father is always referred to by Mrs Corey as Lord Beaconsfield.[21]

Lord Birkenhead sneered at his paragraphing daughter because he felt that she was trading on her position. In one moment of irritation, he told her: 'If I died tomorrow, you would never get another job. That's why I find your tomfoolery exasperating.'[22] Miraculously Eleanor clung to her berth at the *Sunday Dispatch* on a rising salary for three dreary years. After twelve months, she also took on the mantle of film critic for another weekly paper, a job she relished at the expense of her gossip column. She once libelled Tallulah Bankhead by mistake, calling her an Anglophobe when she meant an Anglophile; the actress sued, but withdrew her claim on a promise that her name would never be mentioned in any Rothermere paper again.[23] Eleanor was eventually sacked, leaving her to 'only marvel that I had been retained so long. Every year, for instance, I was supposed to write about Ascot; I paid various persons I knew to give me a story. I could not bring myself to go there, and I never went.'[24] Those 'various persons', Eleanor revealed in her autobiography, included the Duchess of Westminster and Lady Dufferin. Eleanor left newspapers to write a series of successful romantic novels, sustained in part by an allowance from Beaverbrook of £325 a year. This arrangement was reached in September 1930, when Lord

Birkenhead, enfeebled by years of hard drinking, died aged only fifty-nine, leaving a trail of debts. Eleanor had come to detest journalism, but acknowledged that it had given her a comfortable income. What she really hated was the 'insufferable' business of gossip-writing. 'It still seems to me somewhat depressing,' she reflected some years later. 'By publicising a loathsome clique of advertising nit-wits, I felt that I was making myself as bad as these people. I ate because they ignobly revolved in the limelight, and this knowledge made me very bitter.'[25]

The gruesome *galère* revolving in the limelight of the 1920s largely eluded scrutiny. Beverley Nichols's thinly drawn disguises in *Crazy Pavements* dropped plenty of hints, and there was a good deal of speculation in society circles about the real identities of characters, and even rumours of legal action, which boosted the book's sales. His doppelgänger Brian Elme, the gay gossip writer drawn dangerously into society's web, finds that, close up, the familiar names who crowd his columns have feet of clay after all. But Nichols and his like were forced, by the legal and moral constraints of their time, 'to fawn and smirk and lie and prate,' as Elme puts it, 'about the great ones whose littleness he knew so well! To pretend a lackeyed respect for those whom he knew to be contemptible and obscene! Oh, God! – if he could but tell the truth! If instead of his specious platitudes he could take up his pen and dip it in bitter aloes, and give to the world a few of the facts which seemed to have shrivelled his own heart. That would be worthwhile indeed!'[26]

Anyone who has laughed at Evelyn Waugh's 1930 society satire *Vile Bodies* will recognize the same brittle milieu. Waugh's novel features two young journalists who scarcely bother to compete with each other to file the details of the latest society party to their respective newspapers. Reflecting real-life trends, these two gossip-gatherers are both aristocrats. So it is that at Archie Schwert's party, the 15th Marquess of Vanburgh, Baron Brendon, Lord of the Five Isles and Hereditary Grand Falconer to the Kingdom of Connaught, is comparing notes with his rival, the 8th Earl of Balcairn, Viscount Erdinge, Baron Cairn of Balcairn, Red Knight of Lancaster, Count of the Holy Roman Empire and Chenonceaux Herald to the Duchy of Aquitaine. Waugh's caricatures only barely concealed the real-life Valentine, Viscount Castlerosse and 6th Earl of Kenmare, and the Hon. Patrick Balfour, 2nd Lord Kinross.

1. Thomas Nashe, first English journalist, one of 'the riffe-raffe of the scribling rascality'.

2. Daniel Defoe, 'the fellow who was pilloried', sneered Swift, but no 'base Inck-dropper', rather the creator of the prototype gossip column.

3. Sir Henry Bate Dudley, 'the fighting parson' who edited the scandalous eighteenth-century *Morning Post*.

4. Theodore Hook, drollest of Georgian gossip writers and dazzling deviser of practical jokes.

5. Lady Blessington, Fleet Street's first titled gossip writer, hired by Dickens for his *Daily News*.

6. Edmund Yates, a Victorian Nigel Dempster who invented 'society' or 'personal' journalism.

7. Henry Labouchere of *Truth*, whose 'Entre Nous' column mixed social chitchat with personal scorn.

8. Lady Colin Campbell, Victorian sex goddess, painted by Boldini, 'possessed of
the unbridled lust of Messalina and the indelicate readiness of a common harlot'.

GROSS OUTRAGE;

OR, PAUL PRY IN THE HIGHLANDS, MAKING A SKETCH OF THE ROYAL CHEST OF
DRAWERS THROUGH THE KEYHOLE.

9. Gross Outrage: Victorian keyhole-peeper, as observed by *Punch* in 1848.

10. Steamy stuff: *Tomahawk* magazine views the divorce scandal of the day in March 1870.

JUSTICE PROFANED; OR, WHAT WE ARE COMING TO.

11. Justice Profaned: how *Punch* saw the notorious Dennistoun divorce case in 1925.

12. Lord Castlerosse, gossip writer for the *Sunday Express*, and his wife, the former Doris Delavigne, on the town in 1929.

13. Patrick Balfour (with cocktail shaker, centre) hosts a bright young party in 1930 in search of paragraphs for his column in the *Weekly Dispatch*. In the foreground, Miss Rosemary Hope-Vere refuses a cocktail from the designer Oliver Messel, while other guests and gossip writers (pictured L to R) are Mr and Mrs Philip Kindersley, Lord Donegall, Sir Anthony Weldon, Lady Seafield, Lord Rosse, Lady Eleanor Smith, Miss Baby Jungman and Mr Eddie Tatham, with the Hon. Hugh Lygon leaning over the banister.

14. Tinsel trawl: Marquess of Donegall, Thirties gossip-gleaner, visiting Hollywood in 1937, meets Carole Lombard and Fredric March during the filming of David O. Selznick's *Nothing Sacred*.

15. Walter Winchell at his *New York Mirror* desk in the early 1930s, in characteristic hard-bitten, fast-talking, chain-smoking pose.

16. Marquess of Donegall gets the low-down on royalty in exile from the Duchess of Windsor, the former Mrs Wallis Simpson.

Castlerosse was a rotund Irishman, who invariably swathed himself in fur-collared overcoat and silk waistcoat, with a specially tailored pocket enclosing an enormous hip flask. He smoked an 8s 6d cigar 'like a jackass's penis'[27] and his 'Londoner's Log', launched in 1926, was a star feature in Beaverbrook's *Sunday Express*. He was one of the Killarney Brownes (guardians of 'the lakes of Killarney, the water and fish therein contained, and the bottom thereof'), and claimed to be descended from a Catholic bishop who moonlighted as a highwayman; his grandmother's ancestors included the Marquess of Bath. This was the era of the Bright Young People, about whose drink-fuelled antics both Castlerosse and Balfour scribbled relentlessly. The 1920s chroniclers John Collier and Iain Lang detected a whiff of *nostalgie de la boue*; when the peerage was no longer written about, it wrote. '[W]hen, Sunday by Sunday, Viscount Castlerosse discussed the affairs of his celebrated acquaintances, the man or woman who had paid twopence for the revelation felt assured that the subjects were actually his lordship's acquaintances, though they might not in future be his warmest friends.'[28] His problem, according to the American diarist and MP Chips Channon, was that he had created two precedents: one was choosing to write gossip, and the other was becoming a journalist 'in the days when it was still thought extraordinary and in bad taste to be either'.[29]

Castlerosse was the first to step outside the charmed circle of his own glittering friends and start gossiping about them in print. This put a strain on old friendships. Once, provoked by Churchill's glamorous son Randolph, Castlerosse hurled a glass of champagne at him.[30] Young Churchill admired Castlerosse's stunningly beautiful wife, the former Doris Delavigne, a fact that gravelled him and prompted a piece in the *Daily Express* headed 'Pity These Great Men's Sons', in which Castlerosse piqued young Churchill's vanity. 'He is a charming youth,' boomed Castlerosse, '[but H]istory proves almost indisputably that major fathers as a rule breed minor sons, so our little London peacocks had better tone down their fine feathers and start trying to make a name of their own.'[31] Randolph flew into a rage, telephoning Beaverbrook to complain bitterly. Beaverbrook suggested he compose a reply. This appeared in the *Express* a few days later, in which Churchill accused Castlerosse of jealousy. 'The years have passed him by,' wrote Churchill.

'He can only ease the smart of his own failure by jejune attacks upon young men half his own age.' As for Castlerosse's calling, Churchill was withering: '[T]he function of the gossip writer is not among those which commend themselves most highly to my generation.'[32] Curiously, before the decade was out, Randolph Churchill was in the trade himself, working as one of the best-paid gossip columnists in Fleet Street.

The Hon. Patrick Balfour helped to modernize the craft of gossip-writing. A strikingly tall, louche figure (his looks put John Betjeman's daughter in mind of a mosquito), he moved and mixed easily among gossip-laden London circles. But this versatile writer had once famously sat on the step at the Duke of Windsor's one-time residence at Fort Belvedere, sharing a flask of tea with the abdicated King. Balfour covered 'culture' for the 'Londoner's Diary' of the *Evening Standard*, attending art shows and the ballet, hobnobbing with friends like Evelyn Waugh, John Betjeman, Beverley Nichols and Somerset Maugham, even turning up at publishers' cocktail parties, the gossip-writing equivalent (as Malcolm Muggeridge wryly observed) of slumming. It was Balfour who claimed to have coined the phrase 'The Roaring Twenties', only admitting some thirty years later to having plundered it from its true inventor, Maurice Bowra.[33]

After Oxford, Balfour enrolled at the Sorbonne, ostensibly to study French. But at twenty-one, finding that he preferred gay company at the Ritz, he swanned around Paris with Michael Arlen (who was not homosexual but, as Hugh David has pointed out, 'in the climate of the time…*gay*'),[34] Somerset Maugham and Earl Beauchamp[35] and he blew most of his money. An attentive Beverley Nichols advised him to try journalism. 'He says that what really pays is writing gossip,' Balfour told his mother, Lady Kinross, 'which is quite easy to believe because of course [newspapers] haven't many reporters who move in the sort of world to collect good gossip.'[36] Nichols boasted that after the success of his memoirs, *Twenty-Five*, the *Daily Sketch* paid him ten guineas (£10.50) for a weekly article of celebrity gossip, an arrangement that Nichols told Balfour would be indefinite, 'as he can always find enough celebrities to write about'.[37] Back home in Scotland, Balfour's champagne tastes were tempered by an apprenticeship on the *Glasgow Herald*, during which he supplemented his wages by sending social titbits to the London papers, 'paragraphs about people I did not know'.[38] When the Dean of Balliol heard of Balfour's departure for London, he remarked: 'That's that. He'll become a butterfly.'[39] He was right. Before long, it became clear that the gossip column was Patrick Balfour's natural canvas.

Starting on the *Sunday Dispatch*, Balfour helped Lady Eleanor Smith on her 'Window in Vanity Fair' ('an easy life – too easy, probably – but can't be permanent'),[40] at the same time establishing a home for himself in an Italianate studio flat at 26a Yeoman's Row, a backwater not far from Harrods that soon became a magnet for those Bright Young Things. 'Parties all the time, all day, all night',[41] he reported to his mother in 1928. At the end of that year he moved to the downmarket *Daily Sketch* as 'Mr Gossip'. Balfour's circle was small if brightly coloured. Even his doting mother, back in Edinburgh, noticed the same names coming round again. Balfour excused this lapse, pointing out that 'at this time of year ... there are so few parties [that] one has to write about restaurants, and the number of people who constantly frequent restaurants is comparatively limited. I think, as a matter of fact, that I offend less than a good many other papers in writing always about the same people.'[42] At Yeoman's Row, he was photographed for *Vogue* seated at a refectory table with Cyril Connolly, who shared the house with him. Balfour warned Connolly that his job as a gossip writer would mean he would be out a lot at night and might be 'slightly society'. Balfour also laid down some ground rules: 'no apologies for our guests ... no mutual resentments if we lead fairly independent lives'. Many years later, Connolly recalled these raffish days and nights as a time when 'we didn't know where the next meal was coming from, nor whom to ask to it'.[43] Connolly was followed as Balfour's house-mate by John Betjeman, whose biographer Bevis Hillier records that 'the Yeo', as Betjeman called it, 'became on a modest scale what the Prince of Wales's Carlton House had been during George III's reign: a place of refuge and a headquarters of disaffection'.[44]

Unlike the sober-suited woman-chaser Connolly, Balfour affected a high-camp style, bedizened in plus-four suits of green or orange tweed with matching ties and stockings. Fancy-dress parties, fancy-undress parties, wild parties, bath parties, bottle parties, pyjama-and-bottle parties, even chloroform parties, all featuring prodigious amounts of drink, drugs and sex: these were Balfour's social scene. Despite appearances, Balfour still struggled financially, and sponged off his family and wealthy friends to pay for this lifestyle. One of his house guests, Mary Lutyens, daughter of the architect, recalled friends charging him £10 for titbits of gossip for his column on the *Daily Sketch*. They suspected that he obtained much of his information by other means, even prying into Connolly's diary.

Unlike Cyril Connolly, Betjeman lived with Balfour rent-free and, his host recalled, 'did not seem to notice my social proclivities'.[45] Betjeman enjoyed teasing the overtly gay Balfour about his own homosexual leanings, but by the time he arrived at 'the Yeo', Betjeman had become increasingly interested in women. Balfour, meanwhile, aspired to belong to the Bright Young People, 'even becoming one evening so bright', he reminisced, 'as to be received by Miss Tallulah Bankhead in her bath'.[46] As well as gay icons, he sought the company of young black people, although few of their social rounds seem to have been recorded in his gossip columns. Balfour wrote that the gossiping trade opened some doors to him and closed others; when he took it up again in the 1950s after a career as a travel writer, he discovered that it had risen in public esteem. Where in the 1920s he had withered under the frosty glares of society's mightiest, he now incurred 'no cold looks, but the compliments of dowagers, the gratitude of debutantes, and even the benevolence of courtiers'.[47] When he joined the *Evening Standard* in the early 1930s, Balfour was moving effortlessly in the capital's homosexual circles, drawing flak from his lawyer father in Edinburgh about his 'unsuitable friends', exasperation about 'the futility of your mis-spent life in London over the last 3-4 years' and mystification about 'why you sometimes write the stuff you do'.[48] When Balfour spent a New Year with Earl Beauchamp at Madresfield Court, his lawyerly father had to send him £5 to tip the staff. Within weeks, he was warning his son about his 'endless' debts and complaining that 'it will take me four years to pay off your obligations'.[49]

Patrick Balfour was deaf to these effusions. He continued his spendthrift ways, slipping abroad from time to time to flee from his creditors. On his first visit to the South of France, he cashed a worthless cheque aboard the Blue Train. In Monte Carlo an uncle took him to lunch with Oscar Wilde's old lover, Lord Alfred Douglas, Balfour's second cousin once removed. Fearing that Bosie would have a corrupting influence on his son, Lord Kinross had forbidden them to meet, but the uncle overrode him and Balfour found Bosie to be a lively and apparently respectable middle-aged gentleman 'with bright restless eyes and a shrill boyish voice',[50] taking an evident pride in his son, who was the other guest present. Later, Balfour battened on to Somerset Maugham at his villa at Cap Ferrat.

Balfour's career as a columnist was by this time waning. He had been on the *Standard* for two years when Beaverbrook summoned him to Stornoway House, praising him for the style and content of a feature that Balfour was writing single-handedly every Saturday. To Balfour's astonishment, Beaverbrook then announced that he would in future write it 'in a style of his choice and to his own dictation'. Beaverbook 'telephoned in my presence several lady friends of his, repeated to each what the other had said of her, disclosed to me what he himself knew of each, and proposed that all this material, put forward as my own personal view of these ladies, should be the topic for my next Saturday column'.[51] In a fit of high-minded pique, Balfour stood his ground and refused. The column was abolished on the spot.

Balfour's incursions into London's best houses and hotels in pursuit of gossip not only provided him with free food and drink but also with material for a book. In *Society Racket*, published in 1933, he expounded his views on the British class system. 'Society is "news",' he wrote, 'because of that little germ of snobbery that lies hid in everyone.'[52] Balfour had first discovered the pleasures of snobbery while at Oxford, 'a place quite unsnobbish', he explained in middle age, 'but nevertheless peopled by young gentlemen of breeding, who behaved towards lesser men as though they were just like themselves'.[53] Balfour pointed out that gossip writers were no longer beyond society's pale but fully paid-up members of it. 'People who lead public lives are fair game for social columns. Unless they are secretive about their private affairs they must pay the penalty of publicity.'[54] The web was woven and spread ever wider, drawing in the multitude as well as the mighty. 'If these people can be charming,' went one popular song of 1927, commenting ironically on the title of one of Michael Arlen's best-sellers, 'then we can be charming too.'[55] But such an aspiration affronted many moral guardians of the day. As Mrs Orraway-Smith, the Tory committee woman in *Vile Bodies,* observes, gossip revelations were 'such a terrible example to the lower classes, *apart from* everything'. 'That's what I mean,' agrees Mrs Ithewaite. 'There's our Agnes, now. How can I stop her having young men in the kitchen when she knows that Sir James Brown has parties like that at all hours of the night...'[56]

By 1930, gossip columns presented society as a metropolitan and glamorous upper crust that couldn't be found anywhere else in Europe. Weimarian Germans lionized their cultural elite and the French their political one, but neither had the London mix of aristocrats, sporting figures and theatricals, which mesmerized the popular newspapers. Behind them, pressing buttons and pulling levers, were the great hostesses of the day: Americans like Lady Astor and Lady Cunard, and the intelligent, cultivated Lady Colefax, who probably knew more smart people than anyone else in London. 'I would so like to ask someone to meet you,' novelist E. M. Forster wrote to her in 1934, 'whom you don't know, but whom do I know whom you don't know? I don't know.'[57] However loudly they might have denied it, the hostesses of society courted publicity, indeed craved it; their offspring even more so, especially Lady Cunard's daughter Nancy. For the press created a cult of youth and, having wrought it, promoted it tirelessly. The absurd antics of the Bright Young Things, so sparklingly drawn in Waugh's *Vile Bodies*, were as much for public consumption as private delectation and, indeed, would not have happened at all but for the gossiping papers, orchestrated by Patrick Balfour and his feather-wit friends:

> People rush from one party or restaurant to another, to a third and fourth in the course of one evening, and finish up with an early morning bathing-party, transported at 60mph to the swimming-pools of Eton through the dawn. On the river, a languid evening on a punt is not enough. There must be dancing as well, at Datchet or at Bray, and a breakneck race down the Great West Road afterwards.
>
> The next day there is no question of resting in preparation for the evening's exertions. Appointments all the morning, with hairdressers or commission agents or committees; cocktails at the Ritz before lunch, luncheon parties; tennis afterwards or golf at Swinley, or bridge; charity rehearsal teas, then cocktail parties, a rush home to change for an early dinner and the theatre or ballet, after which the whole cycle begins again.
>
> Once the week-ends were a rest from all this feverish activity; but now

they are more strenuous than the week itself – all its pleasures crammed together into a third of the time, with large, riotous, bright young house parties, a dozen people motoring down for the day on Sunday, everyone rushing round the countryside in fast cars, and at night bridge and backgammon and truth games and practical jokes till all hours of the morning.[58]

Then, as now, film and sports stars drove the press frenzy even harder. Society embraced popular musicians (even black ones), long-distance aviators and speed aces such as the Mollisons and Sir Malcolm Campbell, the fleeting heroes of the age. As the world became faster and faster, so did society's butterfly-dance, until one frame followed the last one so quickly that life viewed through Fleet Street's unblinking lens seemed a jerky continuum of the shiny and the sleek. While it entranced the multitude, it troubled not a few; 'the vile social columns of the *Mail* and *Mirror* and *Express* describe day by day the extravagance and vulgarities of the smart London set – a positive disgrace,' complained the 27th Earl of Crawford early in 1932. 'And it is all ascribed to fashionable society whereas the heroes and heroines of this tittle-tattle from the cocktail parties and night clubs are all second-rate people.'[59]

Crawford, a Tory MP and minor courtier, a patrician with a social conscience who had succeeded to the premier earldom of Scotland, divided his time between Westminster and Haigh Hall in Wigan, where his Victorian predecessors had amassed a fortune from coal. He fretted over the Lancashire miners, to whom he owed his privileged way of life and who were suffering the severe effects of an economic slump. In his diary, he railed against the popular press and the men who ran it, denouncing Beaverbook ('dishonest'), his *Express* ('a vile newspaper'), the *News of the World* ('infamous') and Rothermere (a 'scoundrel' and a 'traitor'), while rounding especially on 'the boastful record printed week by week by *déclassés* like Donegall and Castlerosse . . . The Sunday papers describing the doings and witticisms of the smart set provide the Socialists with their most telling arguments when they denounce the idle rich and contrast this pursuit of costly pleasure with the grinding poverty of the unemployed.'[60]

Even a lifetime ago, the popular press recognized the symbiosis between rich and poor and fixed upon it. The *Mail* and its imitators saw society news as social glue, plugging the gaps left by its strident rants against enemies abroad ('It must have a hate on,' noted one German expatriate)[61] and – at home – murders, sporting records, socialist plots and business scandals. Gossipy information about the lives of the great and the good proposed an intimacy between them and the newspaper reader that contained an astonishing untruth at its core: that they are exactly like us after all. 'The reader is intended to get the feeling of being on intimate terms with earls, dukes and Princes of the Blood,' explained the social historian, Paul Cohen-Portheim. '[H]e knows all about their private lives, and you may be sure they correspond to his idea of them, according to which all these grand people know no higher ambition than to live and think exactly like Mr and Mrs Smith and the children in their suburban villa.'[62]

Valentine Castlerosse understood this rapport between his readers and the people he wrote about. He was, in every sense, the biggest of the Fleet Street gossip writers between the wars; physically big, and big in his expenditure, his vanity, his loves and hates. 'His temperament was mercurial, his appetite gargantuan, and his thirst prodigious,'[63] recalled Robert Bruce Lockhart, who edited the *Evening Standard*'s 'Londoner's Diary' when Castlerosse presided over his 'Londoner's Log' in the *Sunday Express*. Castlerosse drank champagne in pint tankards that he emptied in one gulp, and in his frequent fits of depression would weep like a child and bite the carpet. Women were his weakness. But for the last quarter-century of his life, his most emotionally intense relationship was with Lord Beaverbrook, his mentor, friend and employer. It was a form of love, and it was fully reciprocated. Beaverbrook believed him to a journalistic genius, paid him a potentate's salary of £3,000 a year plus expenses, settled his bills and flattered his enormous ego. Less than a year after launching the 'Londoner's Log' in the *Sunday Express*, Beaverbrook was predicting that Castlerosse would have 'the most brilliant journalistic career of our age. Already he has reaped his first striking successes – already his fingers have "touched with golden bowl".'[64] Physically elephantine, Castlerosse was journalistically nimble, an iconoclast who pioneered the twentieth-century Fleet Street ritual of building up figures in popular culture only to destroy them. Typically, Charlie Chaplin would be rubbished in his column, and Gary Cooper exalted in his place. Such fickleness accorded with Beaverbrook's own capricious mood swings, while hoisting the circulation of the *Sunday Express* to record levels. Castlerosse was contentedly baffled by his own success. 'I am finding the only way I can express myself is in journalism,' he offered. 'There is nothing that enthralls me quite so much as the written word – particularly at the bottom of a cheque.'[65] Money and popular acclaim flowed in, and Fleet Street's plum pudding became its unlikeliest pin-up. But while women all over Britain bombarded him with sexually explicit propositions, in 1928 Valentine Castlerosse himself fell in love with Doris Delavigne, the most arrogant, temperamental, foul-mouthed and ecstatically beautiful woman in London. He determined to marry her. But in doing so, he incurred the wrath of Beaverbrook, who felt that Castlerosse had betrayed him as sure as any faithless lover and who knew instinctively that the marriage was doomed. Famously promiscuous, Doris continued to entertain other men, even after becoming Lady Castlerosse, and when Beaverbrook intervened she bit back. 'Max,' she purred, 'I would have you know that an Englishwoman's bed is her castle.'[66]

One of Doris's admirers was another impoverished Irish peer who had been recruited the year before by Lord Reading to write gossip for his paper, the *Sunday News*.[67] Edward Arthur Donald St George Hamilton Chichester, Earl of Belfast, Baron Fisherwick of Fisherwick (in the County of Stafford), Hereditary Lord High Admiral of Lough Neagh, Governor of Carrickfergus Castle and the 6th Marquess of Donegall, preferred to be known as Don Donegall while networking in London society. When he too fell beneath Doris's spell, he contented himself with the occasional hilarious evening sitting on her bed at her little house in Deanery Street while Doris munched caviar on toast, opened a bottle of Cliquot and told scandalous stories about her latest tycoon suitor. Donegall noted that after her marriage to Castlerosse, Doris had a viscountess's coronet woven into her crêpe de Chine sheets, which she sent to Paris to be laundered. Doris and his other friends called him 'The Don', acknowledging his aristocratic background, but while he cut a slight, pale and earnest figure in nightclub, restaurant or ballroom, his reputation as a recorder of society gossip quickly grew. With a self-confessed weakness for blondes, Donegall's quick temper and charm, tempered by a 'coolly erratic and calmly cruel' disposition, reminded his contemporary Charles Graves of 'any French Dauphin, just as Lord

Castlerosse is evidently a reincarnation of Henry VIII'.[68] Like Castlerosse, Donegall was instantly frozen out by his family who, he noted, 'turned up their noses with that degree of 105% wordless contempt that only the British landed gentry can achieve'. On the other hand there were his new colleagues, horny-handed hacks 'who would obviously look on me as a phoney muscling in' and who, on finding this Old Etonian of twenty-four drawing a salary of £1,000 a year, resolved to be as 'coldly civil and unhelpful as possible'.

Donegall's first move was to join the National Union of Journalists. 'I had a suspicion,' he recalled, 'that I would get the worst of both worlds (except for the lovely lolly).'[69] On arrival, he found his desk located in a hovel, which he shared with his friend Pat Dixon, the paper's film critic. The editor Williams, a Northcountryman, was profoundly ignorant of the goings-on of the kind of people Donegall had been hired to write about. The paper's drama critic, Percy Cudlipp, also turned in a weekly page of feeble puns beneath the unavailing title 'Keep Smiling'. It was Cudlipp who suggested a title for Donegall's page: 'Confidentially Yours'.

'Trite!' declared Pat Dixon. 'In Confidence – how about that?'

'Bit deceptive,' said Donegall. 'It isn't quite, is it?'

Then, all three in unison: 'Almost in Confidence.' The title stuck.

Donegall shot envious glances across Fleet Street at Valentine Castlerosse who, as a badly wounded war veteran, could fill his gossip page by drawing on a hugely greater experience of life. A few weeks after the debut of 'Almost in Confidence', Castlerosse invited Donegall to lunch at the Guards' Club.

'D'you write your own stuff?'

'Of course. Why do you ask?'

'It isn't "Of course",' snorted Castlerosse. 'Most of these so-called journalists don't.'

He drew on his fat cigar. 'How much are you getting? Got a contract?'

'A thousand a year,' said Donegall. 'No contract yet.'

'I'm fed up with my "Londoner's Log",' Castlerosse said. 'You can have two thousand a year and a three-year contract on the *Sunday Express* to take it over. And I'll help you with it at the start.'

Donegall said nothing for several moments. 'Sorry,' he muttered presently, 'I'd love to, but I just can't do it. They've spent quite a bit of money advertising the feature, and I simply can't play the dirty on them.'

'Pity,' said Castlerosse, helping himself to another brandy. 'You must be the last man in Fleet Street with a conscience. However,' he added, 'it's not fatal. You'll grow out of it.'

Back at the *Weekly Dispatch*, editor Williams happened to wander into Donegall's poky office. Donegall told him about his lunch with the great Castlerosse. Twenty minutes later, Williams appeared again, placing before him a contract for three years at £2,000 a year. Donegall signed.

Castlerosse and Donegall became friends, but weren't intimate. Their weekly pages lasted throughout the 1930s and defined a new journalistic function, that of 'columnist'. They both provided what poet and novelist Robert Graves recognized as 'a critical and authoritative commentary on life in general rather than humble gossip about the private lives of his social betters'.[70] Donegall, while concerned principally with social froth, charted the rise of Hitler ('the man of the moment',[71] he affirmed in March 1933), and covered world economics, the deteriorating international situation, as well as miscellaneous reflections on topics ranging from Nietzsche ('Germany's tin god')[72] to his own agnosticism. In Dublin and Manchester, Donegall reported, 'I met people who do not care any more whether Lady Bloggins looks sweet in purple moiré or tartan taffeta. "Do confine yourself to people who do things!" they said. I will.'

And by and large he did.

10

Talk of the Town

Lord Beaverbrook, unlike most newspaper proprietors, regarded the nightly diary page in the *Evening Standard* as his own private fiefdom. He saw the 'Londoner's Diary' as an armoury from which he could seize a weapon at will; bludgeon, cudgel and rapier lay at his disposal as he sought to fight his way to even greater heights of power and influence in between-the-wars Britain. Brian Inglis, a one-time gossip writer, later editor of the *Spectator*, likened Beaverbrook to the journalistic Messalina of his day 'with his newspaper brothels, his editors as madams, and with his reporters as streetwalkers'.[1]

Britain between the wars was dominated by a rich, decadent, selfish clique who knew nothing of the blighted lives of ordinary people and cared still less. By the early 1930s the *Standard* had become flabby and effete, 'the house-journal of the exclusive London West End',[2] as Michael Foot put it. The diary editor, Robert Bruce Lockhart, had a weakness for the high life and led a life of drunkenness, debauchery and debt; he worried constantly about money. 'He made himself at home in the fast set which passed for Society,' one acquaintance remarked, 'with a vulgar snobbishness and no sense of discrimination.'[3] Personally and professionally, as Anne Chisholm and Michael Davie point out in their monumental biography of Beaverbrook, Lockhart was in thrall to his patron 'in a way that he recognized but could not easily break'.[4] As a result, Lockhart's position lay 'somewhere between that of a courtesan and a call girl, churning out articles and Londoner's Diary paragraphs to suit his employer's grotesque fancies and cruel whims'.[5] After World War II, when newsprint shortages eased, Beaverbook was the first Fleet Street mogul to understand that the kind of froth that bubbled in and around the entertainment industry – especially from Hollywood – would sell more newspapers than any amount of hard news coverage or political acumen. He set particular store by glittery gossip and regarded it as a critical performance indicator. 'The first page to which [Beaverbook] turned in any of his papers, delivered to him daily where ever he happened to be in the world, was the gossip column,' recalled 'Londoner's Diary' writer, Douglas Sutherland. 'Should anything displease him, retribution was swift and dire.'[6]

Not all Beaverbook's caprices were diabolical, and even his bitterest critics admitted that he had an unerring eye for talent. He spotted good gossip writers and hired them, sometimes on a whim. For example, he brought in Howard Spring to write for the diary of his *Evening Standard* on the strength of a single phrase. In 1931, Spring was forty-two and working in Manchester as a reporter at the *Manchester Guardian.* That autumn Britain left the Gold Standard and was, as Spring put it, 'up to the eyes in hell-broth';[7] politicians were on the stump in the 'doctor's mandate' general election campaign. Spring, assigned to cover a speech by Beaverbrook at an Empire Free Trade meeting at Darwen in Lancashire, arrived with an hour to spare. 'It was a Saturday night,' he recalled,

> and the weekly market was being held in the big square of the town. I lingered there, looking at the flaring naphtha lamps, the hucksters shouting their wares, the gay ephemeral traffic of the cheapjacks' lies and promises. Adjoining the fair-ground was the hall where Lord Beaverbrook was to speak; and I began to see his meeting and this chaffering tumult as all part of one thing: the pedlars of promises without, the pedlar of dreams within.[8]

Spring had actually described Beaverbrook as 'a pedlar of nightmares', but, according to Malcolm Muggeridge, this had been changed at the office, and Spring's report duly appeared under the heading 'The Pedlar of Dreams'. This image struck Beaverbook who immediately sent Percy Cudlipp, the *Standard's* assistant editor, to Manchester to recruit Howard Spring to the Beaverbook press.

Malcolm Muggeridge also transferred from the *Manchester Guardian* to Shoe Lane. He had been working as the *Guardian's* correspondent in Calcutta for two years when, as he later wrote, 'salvation came in the shape of a telegram out of the blue from Percy Cudlipp, [by then] editor of the *Evening Standard*, offering me a job on the Londoner's Diary at twenty pounds a week.'⁹ But life on the diary wasn't what Muggeridge imagined. The paper was produced in a single, large clangorous room, likened by Rebecca West to 'a wild, wild garden',¹⁰ with the diary corralled in one corner. Muggeridge was shocked at the un-*Guardian*-like ambience. Working for its editor–proprietor C. P. Scott had been 'like waltzing with some sedate old dowager at a mayoral reception in Manchester; for Beaverbook, like taking the floor in a night-club in the early hours of the morning, when everyone is more or less drunk'.¹¹ Bruce Lockhart, the diary editor, struck Muggeridge as 'a cheerful, amiable Scot',¹² he was in fact Britain's first spy in Moscow, who had been caught and swapped for a Russian, but who remained on cordial terms with the Soviet Embassy in London, from whom he received an annual gift of caviar.

Lockhart joked that Muggeridge's paragraphs in the 'Londoner's Diary' had led to the discontinuance of this largesse. Like Castlerosse, another Beaverbook confidant, Lockhart was often broke and Beaverbrook would bale him out; Muggeridge thought this was his way of keeping friends, 'a kind of Devil's sacrament – "This is my money…" '¹³ Lockhart and Castlerosse repaid him in kind, 'the two wild ones, *avec peur et avec reproche*, in Beaverbrook's little court, who brought to it a flavour of high living and society gossip; as Aneurin Bevan and Michael Foot did of Radical thinking and political gossip, enabling Beaverbrook to enjoy vicariously the sensation of being a rake and a rebel without jeopardizing either his social or financial standing'.¹⁴

Unlike Howard Spring, Muggeridge was not summoned to Beaverbrook's house to be briefed on a piece to be written on the instant. Rather, he settled into a routine of drudgery, hurrying along Fleet Street or to and from the cuttings library, tortured by 'the old loathing, disgust'¹⁵ and fighting his repulsion for work that was not only pointless but exhausting. Beaverbrook's dictim, unspoken but implied, was to dumb up. 'The basic policy,' Muggeridge explained, 'was to write always on the assumption that our readers were a notch or two higher in the social scale than was actually the case.'¹⁶ So in the mind's eye, Beaverbrook's diary readers had all been to public schools, played rugby rather than soccer, changed for dinner, attending private showings at the Royal Academy and galas at Covent Garden, read the novels of Evelyn Waugh, enjoyed the plays of Shaw and Coward, went horse racing, skiing and motoring, and knew their way around the Riviera and the Rue de Rivoli. Some might even hunt, it was assumed, but this was probably an ambition too far and was more likely to have been included in the mix out of deference to 'Captain' Mike Wardell, Beaverbrook's lieutenant at the *Standard*, who, as the result of a hunting accident, wore a piratical patch over one eye.

Diary assignments were divided among the writers according to their inclinations. So Lockhart dealt with diplomats and diplomacy, and had first pick of the honours' list. He had a good nose for a diary item; he was an inveterate networker at parties and spotted stories hidden in the morning papers that everyone else had missed. Once, the personal column of *The Times* announced that a dog had been lost near Churt. Could it be Lloyd George's? wondered Lockhart. It was, and he led that day's diary with the story of how the little terrier, which had once disgraced itself by biting the Italian Prime Minister at Rapallo, was now at large in Surrey. Muggeridge's own role, as the new boy, was to handle unconsidered trifles. But he was also regarded as resident expert on the Labour Party's alternative Establishment, which was then taking shape, with figures from the worlds of politics, the universities, Church, armed services, law and literature beginning to loom large. Names like Shaw, Wells and Bertrand Russell began to appear, as well as those of members of the Bloomsbury Group. 'Well might an old-timer like George Lansbury rub his eyes over so gilt-edged a recruitment,' Muggeridge mused, 'but from a gossip-writer's point of view, it was gravy.'[17]

Grim and futile though he found the work of diary writing, Muggeridge conceded that the hours were short. The staff came in at 10 a.m. and the diary went to press at 12.30 p.m. with few changes between editions. With a dozen journalists at work, each needed to produce two, maybe three, paragraphs a day; often, though, Muggeridge managed none at all. Each Friday the diary writers were paid in cash, in Muggeridge's case four white, crinkly five-pound notes. 'It was, on any showing, good money for very little work.'[18]

Muggeridge coasted. Where others roamed London making contacts, attending parties, receptions, first nights, he merely sloped off to the library, preferring to rely on the cuttings and his own inventiveness. He found that no one complained about what appeared in his paragraphs, as long as it pandered to the subject's self-esteem. Muggeridge's precedent was Dr Johnson, who produced reports of parliamentary debates without ever going near the Houses of Parliament; realizing that his fictitious speeches attributed to peers and MPs were actually believed, he resigned. It never occurred to Muggeridge to feel any qualms when his own imaginary conversations passed unchallenged.

Sometimes Lockhart would push across the desk a paragraph marked 'must', signifying that it had come from Lord Beaverbook himself. Muggeridge remembered one garbled quotation about many aspiring but few succeeding. Beaverbrook wanted this to be applied to an item observing that politicians who moved from Westminster to the City were seldom successful. 'The point,' wrote Muggeridge, 'was clear enough; Beaverbrook had acquired a huge fortune, but been a relative failure in politics, and so wanted to read in the Londoner's Diary – a favourite feature – that making money was a more difficult pursuit than politics.'[19] Another 'must' paragraph concerned Sir James Barrie, dying of a bronchial complaint, which Beaverbrook pointed out was known as 'old man's friend' because it was so painless. Again, Muggeridge realized the reason for Beaverbook's interest: as an asthmatic, he expected to die of a similar complaint, and wanted to be assured of an easy death by reading it in his own newspaper's diary. Muggeridge duly made the point, despite failing to find confirmation in Harley Street, merely to keep his little old Canadian reader happy.

After only a few months of this, Muggeridge resigned. Weary of sucking up to his proprietor and his 'wayward fancies and malign purposes',[20] Muggeridge also found himself exposed to 'a steady and insidious process of corruption'[21] which he could not handle. Gossip-writing might be chasing so much chaff, but he sensed something more insidious at work. 'Underneath all the buffoonery,' he wrote years afterwards, 'I detected a whiff of sulphur; a transposing of values, whereby whatever was most base was elevated, and the only acceptable measure of anyone and anything was money, the only pursuit worth considering, worldly success.'[22] He decided to move to Sussex to write a novel.

Whatever Muggeridge's feelings about the column's shortcomings, the 1930s represented a golden age on the 'Londoner's Diary', thanks largely to the inspired editorship of Bruce Lockhart. Just weeks after taking over in September 1928, Lockhart had landed an exclusive interview with Kaiser Wilhelm II, who had not spoken to a British journalist since the Great War. Beaverbook was so impressed that he redefined Lockhart's role, allowing him to continue to contribute to the diary, but harnessing him up as a liaison man with the *Daily Express*, a leader writer for the *Sunday Express* and a permanent sidekick for himself, not unlike the role Beaverbrook had ordained for Castlerosse. Looking for someone to take his place as diary editor, Lockhart turned to Harold Nicolson, an old aristocratic friend from the Foreign Office who had combined a diplomatic career with that of a successful biographer and novelist.

Despite some reservations, Nicolson started work at New Year 1930 on £3,000 a year. By only his second day, he had devised a routine of scanning all the morning papers in the train in search of a good paragraph. He wrote to his wife, Vita Sackville-West, that he supposed he would 'get into the way of finding these paragraphs leaping ready-armed to the mind. At present they are rather a bother to think of, rather a bother to write, and terribly feeble when written. But I shall settle down in time.'[23] He did. 'I have found my feet,' Nicolson reflected a year later, 'and Beaverbrook likes me.'[24] But all was not well. Like Muggeridge, Nicolson at forty-two entertained loftier literary ambitions than grubbing for paragraphs. 'I was not made to be a journalist,' Nicolson admitted, 'and I do not want to go on being one. It is a mere expense of spirit in a waste of shame. A constant hurried triviality which is bad for the mind.'[25] Lockhart was having doubts about Nicolson, feeling that the column had become too highbrow under his stewardship. When Mike Wardell took Lockhart to lunch at the Savoy in April 1931, Lockhart warned him against making 'a grave mistake' by leaving Nicolson in charge of the diary. 'Harold's tastes are not the public's tastes,' Lockhart explained. 'He is altogether too precious.'[26] But Beaverbrook took no heed of his lieutenant and insisted on the changes. 'Nicolson is not only to sub-edit and "give a Nicolson twist" to all paragraphs,' recorded Lockhart gloomily, 'but is actually to select the paragraphs for the diary...Harold Nicolson is Beaverbrook's star.'[27] Lockhart's humiliation was complete when in June Beaverbrook offered Nicolson the editorship of the *Standard* itself. But Nicolson not only turned down the offer, he left the paper altogether. 'My last day,' he rejoiced in August. Like Muggeridge, Nicolson was acutely conscious not just of the frittering nature of the paragraphing trade but also of the pernicious effect of shallowness, 'the supreme evil'. 'I have learned that rapidity, hustle and rush are the allies of superficiality,' he added. 'My fastidiousness has been increased and with it a loathing of the uneducated. I have come to believe that the gulf between the educated and the uneducated is wider than that between the classes and more galling to the opposite side.'[28] Knowing that he had not been popular in the office, Nicolson made perfunctory farewells. Walking out into the street, he shook his shoes symbolically. Despite repeated requests from Beaverbrook's henchman Wardell to return, he never did.

Lockhart too harboured misgivings. 'Fleet Street is no place for me,' he confided. 'The Londoner's Diary' was languishing and 'goes from bad to worse'.[29] By 1934, Lockhart was forced to admit that the *Daily Telegraph*'s 'Peterborough' column had now overtaken it in terms of quality. Whilst the hours were short, Lockhart nevertheless complained that he was 'nailed to my desk' for much of the day, writing an estimated 400,000 words a year for Beaverbrook's papers. 'Much of the night,' points out Kenneth Young, who edited Lockhart's diaries for publication, 'he dissipated in the mushroom *bôites*, ill-lit and sordid, of the West End of London; sordid yet lures, lairs of the still-rich sprigs of the aristocracy, and the ex-officer would-be aristocracy.'[30] Lockhart himself was neither; he was a 'personality', mainly on the strength of his exploits in Russia, and he became, as Kenneth Young recalls, 'a remarked-upon figure in London society'.[31] In pursuit of paragraphs, he was a frequent guest of London's best-known hostesses, Lady Colefax, Lady Cunard and their ilk, and was lionized by the frivolous rich gossips of the day. Nevertheless he was a reluctant reporter, with a scant and unhappy home life; he felt the strain of working in Fleet Street all day and (when not gathering gossip) writing books at night, until his health faltered and he left the toils of daily journalism ('I hope for ever')[32] in 1937.

The diary page was by this stage perking up. Another Beaverbrook pal, the young Randolph Churchill, son of Winston, at twenty-six blond, good-looking and self-obsessed, took over the column as soon as Lockhart left. Malcolm Muggeridge, who had returned to the 'nightmare...grubby and unhappy and hysterical[33]...[of the] Beaverbrook circus'[34] for financial reasons, recorded the 'considerable awe' in which the diary staff held the new man. His contacts were impeccable. He could telephone almost anyone without fear of rebuff. Muggeridge caught the tone: 'That you, Bobbity? Duff? Fruity? Bob? Rab?'[35] 'Talks nineteen to the dozen,' noted Lockhart, 'and is a kind of gramophone to his father.'[36] The father himself, a handy conduit to those in power, doted on his only son. Like his godfather Lord Birkenhead, Randolph drank too much, encouraged in his youth by Churchill *père*. During the 1930s, Randolph led a glamorous life; girls swarmed to him, and his prodigious memory meant that he could quote reams of poetry, a delicate counterpoint to his thunderflash tempers. In October 1937, as if to seal his appointment as the 'Londoner's Diary' editor, he pulled off a world scoop by interviewing the exiled Duke and Duchess of Windsor in Paris.

Gossip writers attract invitations, and in London no first-night party or book launch, no opening of a new nightclub, bar, hotel or restaurant, would be complete without a journalist from the 'Londoner's Diary' burrowing for a paragraph. But because of its distinctive metropolitan cachet and ritzier contacts, the column has always been able to infiltrate more than its share of private parties too. Douglas Sutherland, who worked on the column in the 1950s, recalled that it was not uncommon to be invited to a party on a personal basis and be given some spicy gossip on the strict understanding that it was unattributable. 'It was considered in the very worst possible taste if, when giving any sort of private party, you invited anyone from the Press along,'[37] Sutherland noted in his memoirs, unlike today when publicity-hungry guests would only show up at a party with a guarantee that a journalist from one of the top gossip columns would be there too.

In Beaverbrook's day, the *Standard* had a distinctive tone and agenda, giving prominence to domestic stories, society divorces, financial scandals and murders. But the 'Londoner's Diary' was always the central feature of the paper, a touch of class in something of a workaday wilderness. Its reputation for attracting some unusual talents was enhanced in the late 1950s, when Beaverbrook promoted Nicholas Tomalin from the 'Hickey' column on the *Express* to edit 'Londoner's Diary'. He is by far the best candidate for the job, Beaverbrook told the *Standard* editor, Charles Wintour, 'and particularly gifted in diary work'.[38] When Tomalin, then only twenty-seven, was formally appointed, Beaverbrook predicted 'a great success for that young man

Tomalin',[39] and as usual Beaverbrook was right. The diary page was Tomalin's natural habitat; he was dynamic and energetic, and he injected a sense of fun. His team of bright and amusing young gossip writers reflected the excitement of the post-war London ferment with its vibrant cultural scene and flamboyant new personalities, setting the trends in clothes and music. He seemed to know every interesting person in London, and had a knack of turning up at all the best parties. When he eventually left to edit Michael Heseltine's glossy new *Town* magazine, the diary page was already prefiguring the swoops and swirls of Swinging London.

For nearly ninety years, 'Londoner's Diary' has entertained, amused and enlightened generations of strap-hanging commuters with its eclectic mix of trend-spotting, cultural bon-bons, political squibs and trivial fluff. There have been downs as well as ups: by the end of World War II, the column was weary and, in the view of one of Beaverbrook's henchmen, 'inclined to unnecessary dullness'.[40] After its resurgence in the 1950s and 1960s, the pendulum had swung again, and by 1980 Jeremy Deedes, then running 'Londoner's Diary', was being ordered to recapture the greatness of the past. 'I want it to go back to what it was in Beaverbrook's days,' declared Lou Kirby, the *Standard*'s new editor, urging Deedes and his team to deliver 'really interesting disclosures about big business, publishing, politics and the arts'.[41]

Despite the occasional *longueurs*, Londoner's Diary remains one of the most distinctive and best-known gossip pages in Britain. Its readers have always included both the humble and the mighty, for the *Standard* circulates widely through the corridors of power. Bruce Lockhart, interviewing Winston Churchill about his latest book, was startled to discover that his reputation as a gossip writer had caught the great man's attention. Lockhart had recently run a paragraph criticizing Churchill for an indifferent speech. 'Oh,' snorted Churchill, 'you're the villain who wrote the other day that I was the worst-dressed man in London and that I was tired when I made my speech. What awful rot you journalists write sometimes.'[42]

11

Like Socrates, a Gadfly

For over half a century, the 'William Hickey' column was the most celebrated and eagerly read newspaper feature in Britain. The name Hickey came to define the glossiest in gossip, yet the column was fashioned by a wayward left-wing journalist who detested personal tittle-tattle in print, and despised the wealthy social butterflies whose deeds and misdeeds he did his best to ignore. Although Tom Driberg, the first William Hickey – hungrily homosexual, politically perverse – became in his day the most famous, and subsequently infamous, British gossip columnist, he considered the description an insult. In private, however, he was an inveterate, unstinting gossip, a High Churchman in whom, as one newspaper contemporary put it, 'the urge to unbutton was overwhelming'.[1] A fund of scandalous stories in his unsparing and indiscreet memoirs, published after his death in the 1970s, threatened the public and private reputations of many of Britain's great and good, living and dead. In print, he conducted a dazzling daily discourse, an intensely personal record of the 1930s that chronicled Britain's slide into war. He created something new: an urbane, cultured and witty diary column, in which he single-handedly chronicled the delights, doubts and dangers punctuating life in what his Oxford friend, W. H. Auden, called that 'low, dishonest decade'.[2] The column's breezily rhapsodic form disguised a baroque inner discipline: Driberg as Hickey was a fastidious stylist who, as another contemporary noted, 'could be as punctilious about ecclesiastical ritual or a semi-colon as he was obsessional in his trawl of the "cottages" of Britain'.[3]

Expelled for homosexuality from Lancing, the public school in Sussex where Evelyn Waugh was two years his senior, Driberg was almost as precocious in his politics as he was sexually. He seduced a younger boy at the age of twelve, and by fifteen had joined the Communist Party. At

Oxford he wrote poetry, mingled with aesthetes, flirted with journalism and, after slumping into a drunken stupor during his Schools exam, left 'completely disgraced' and without a degree. Driberg drifted back to Sussex and his widowed mother. But he hankered after London, after Soho in particular, 'and most of all,' he reflected in his memoirs, 'I craved a certain deep and dark doorway in Rupert Street, in which I had stood for hours at a time enjoying the quick embraces and gropings of other young layabouts.'[4] He scraped a living as a film extra and by sponging off friends, enough to cover the rent on his narrow top-floor room in Frith Street. He took a job as a waiter in a disreputable café in Romilly Street for five shillings (25p) a week all found, sharing a chaste bed with the Irish chef and successfully rebuffing the advances of the good-looking young boss. Downstairs, the café's villainous clientele muttered about thievery; upstairs, fat prostitutes plied their trade, catering to various fetishes. In his spare time, Driberg dabbled as a poet; when he mentioned his circumstances to the eccentric Edith Sitwell, she immediately arranged an interview for her youthful acquaintance with Beverley Baxter, then managing editor of the *Daily Express.*

When he joined the *Express* in 1928, Tom Driberg worked as a general reporter until, a few months later, he transferred to the paper's 'Talk of London' column. This was a daily ragbag of the doings of the idle rich, chronicled by the melancholy Colonel Percy Sewell, whose unhappiness, Driberg heard, stemmed from his unrequited love for a lesbian. Driberg began introducing items about his friends from Lancing and Oxford; he wrote up some of the parties thrown by the Bright Young People, to which (unlike coarser hacks) he had actually been invited, and for which he invariably arrived in white tie and tails. He contributed frivolous articles about the coming literary figures of the late 1920s, including Evelyn Waugh, Nancy Mitford and John Betjeman, people who, unlike the titled nonentities favoured by Sewell, were intrinsically interesting.

Driberg strove to infiltrate a subversive tone into the column, which, 'as far as I could influence it, became more and more satirical. I described in detail the absurdities and extravagances of the ruling class, in a way calculated to enrage any working-class or unemployed people who might chance to read the column; at a time of mass unemployment I felt that I was doing something not without value to the Communist Party, to which I was still attached.'[5] What the working classes and unemployed made of the Driberg *galère* of Bright Young Things is unknowable, but throughout the late 1920s and early 1930s he was the enthusiastic chronicler of their tiresome japes and ridiculous parties. He reported their eccentricities of style: a scion of the Tennant family attended one party clad in 'pink vest and long blue trousers' and another in 'football jersey and earrings', arriving, as he invariably did while living in London, in an Edwardian electric brougham. ('He says it is like riding in a bow window.')[6]

But alongside these frivolities, Driberg struck a more serious note, especially when Sewell was away, leaving his young assistant in charge. As his confidence grew, he slipped in references to capital punishment and radical new developments in the arts. In 1932, Sewell retired, and Driberg took over the running of the column, retaining the archaic nom de plume 'The Dragoman' with which Sewell had signed the column throughout the 1920s. (A dragoman was an Oriental interpreter or guide.) Although the *Express* granted him virtually a free hand in deciding what to include in his column, Driberg felt imprisoned in a journalistic straitjacket. He hated having to turn out newspaper gossip for a living; the notion of becoming a serious poet, rather than a daily columnist in a popular paper, gnawed at him. When Robert Bruce Lockhart, editor of the *Evening Standard's* 'Londoner's Diary', bumped into him at the notorious '43' drinking club in Soho in April 1932, Driberg admitted he was 'very unhappy' in his work. 'He writes poetry,' Lockhart recorded in his diary. 'He said that if he died now and I had to write his obituary would I ring up Edith Sitwell and she would tell me all about him. He said he *must* get away, go round the world as a steward in a ship – anything. But has he – have any of us? – the courage? I doubt it.'[7] In the event, Driberg was spared the agony of deciding what to do. Just over a year later, in May 1933, Beaverbrook decided to abolish the 'Talk of London' and its social gossip altogether.

'His onslaught was characteristically ruthless and total,' Driberg recalled.

> He knew (or rather, he felt, for Beaverbrook was essentially an intuitive impresario) that no half-measures or 'tapering-off' would do. They had been tried before. 'Goddammit,' he had snarled at his gossip-writers, 'write about people who do things – who do real work – not about these worthless social parasites and butterflies...' The response was a piece in praise of two ravishing

debutantes who had embarked on real work – in a Mayfair flower-shop. So the time came to make a clear break with the past. 'William Hickey' was born.[8]

The birth was painful and prolonged. Beaverbrook wanted a column modelled on a feature in *Time* magazine headed 'People', and the rubric: 'Names make news: last week these names made news.' So he launched his new *Express* column as 'These Names Make News', instructing Driberg to imitate *Time's* distinctive machine-gun-style prose. 'A staccato telegraphese emerged,' Driberg remembered,

> which was certainly not English: it had few verbs, and no definite or indefinite articles; it consisted almost entirely of adjectives – often elaborately quaint and neologistic – and such gruesome portmanteaux as 'cinemagnate'. It was shock treatment, but it worked: there was no more social gossip in the *Express* – no more 'Lady X, who is, of course, Lord X's third wife, was charming in blue'; no more, 'The Aga Khan, looking bronzed and fit' … After several weeks of uncertainty, Beaverbrook decided that it should be signed, pseudonymously, William Hickey, thus reviving the memory of a great diarist of the late eighteenth century who had, says the *Oxford Companion to English Literature*, 'a weakness for women and claret' (which I should have thought were two separate weaknesses, if indeed weakness is the word).[9]

Driberg announced the dawn of the Hickey revolution by printing a 'statement of policy' in the paper:

> Discerning readers of this column will have noticed, during the last few weeks, a distinct change in its character.
>
> It has ceased to be a diary of events, a causerie, or even (except implicitly) a commentary. All of those things it has tended to be in the past.
>
> It is most emphatically not a social gossip-column (not that it ever has been in the ordinarily accepted sense of the phrase).
>
> It has become an intimate biographical column – giving day by day anecdotal character studies about men and women who happen to be prominently in the news.
>
> Men and women who work. Men and women who matter. Artists, statesmen, airmen, writers, financiers, explorers, stage people sometimes, dictators, revolutionaries, fighters …

Mayfair may find this new departure boring – but not half so boring as the rest of the world finds Mayfair.

Social chatter about the eccentricities of gilded half-wits is dead.

Occasionally I may ornament my page with the photograph of some lovely but idle debutante. This will be for decorative purposes only.

In general, any woman who is 'in Society' and has no other justification for her existence, will be out of this column.

I believe that this experiment is on the right lines.[10]

While his contemporaries such as Castlerosse, Donegall and Balfour were serving up large helpings of society news, Driberg fashioned a column of dazzling eclecticism, covering politics, foreign affairs, sport, the arts; indeed, just about the entire range of human endeavour. 'A columnist,' he once explained, 'must be interested in a large variety of special subjects. *The real secret is not to appeal to the majority but to appeal to as large a number of minorities as possible.* This will in effect get you a majority readership.' He believed in putting forward 'a strong, coherent, philosophic view of life … irreverent, sceptical, pungent: like Socrates, a gadfly'.[11] He was a ragpicker, an alchemist, who trawled through specialist magazines on subjects like bee-keeping, philately and architecture, all of which, he discovered, were 'astonishingly quotable'.

It was not that Driberg ignored personal gossip completely, however, especially if it involved the rising stars in the artistic and literary circles in which he moved. The love life of Evelyn Waugh, for example, a friend from Lancing and Oxford, and a not-quite-contemporary on the *Express*, was of abiding interest, mainly because of Waugh's fame as a successful young man of letters. But Waugh's conversion to Roman Catholicism in 1930, a result of his unhappy first marriage, also magnified his newsworthiness, and this was duly reported – exclusively, if in a somewhat offhand way – by Driberg in his 'Hickey' column. Driberg, a High Anglican, was perplexed to find himself invited to be the sole witness at the service, but according to Waugh's biographer, Christopher Sykes, it was part of a cunning ruse. 'If Evelyn's conversion was reported in the widest-selling newspaper in the country,' Sykes noted, 'then he would be spared the labour of writing numerous letters.'[12] It seems to have worked to both men's satisfaction, because thereafter, as Francis Wheen observes, Waugh often used the *Express* as a tribal noticeboard.

Waugh was a skilled manipulator of journalists, having picked up some tips during his time as an *Express* reporter and later as a war correspondent for the *Daily Mail.* Knowing how newspapers work, he prevailed upon Driberg to get him out of a small difficulty when, in 1936, he prepared to marry for a second time. Waugh's first wife having deserted him, he obtained an annulment from the Vatican and became engaged to Laura Herbert. For various reasons, Waugh wanted the news of the engagement to be held back, which is why 'it is not to be announced until after Xmas', Waugh explained to Lady Mary Lygon in a letter written that summer. 'So you must not tell people I am engaged,' he warned, 'or Driberg will put it in the papers. And don't tell pauper,' he added (a reference to Patrick Balfour, another Oxford friend, writing as 'Mr Gossip' in the *Daily Sketch*), 'as he will spread foul lies about Miss H. in his unchivalrous way.'[13] Lady Mary duly kept quiet for several months, but in January 1937, as soon as Waugh wanted the news of his engagement announced, he sent Driberg a note, proposing a deal:

My Dear Tom,

I have got engaged to be married & shall be announcing the fact early next week. I don't imagine the story will be of great news value but if you care to publish it you can have it a day ahead of *The Times.* In return could you oblige me in one particular? I think that by now most people have forgotten or have never known that I was married before. That marriage has been annulled by the papal courts and it would be very painful to me & my young lady to have it referred to. (1) because in ecclesiastical circles they get embarrassed if annulments are given publicity (2) because my future wife is a near relative of my former wife's and there are numerous mutual aunts who would be upset. So may I rely on you not to bring the topic up?

Apart from that you can have all the details you need. She is named Laura Herbert, 20 years old, student at Academy of Dramatic Art, in my opinion a great beauty. Youngest daughter of (late) Aubrey Herbert who was a famous chap in his day. I can give you a photograph of her if you want one for Tuesdays [sic] paper – announcement Wednesday ...

Kindest regards

Yours

Evelyn (Waugh)[14]

It was a deal. Waugh was able to tell all his friends about his engagement for nothing in the *Express*, and Hickey had his scoop a day ahead of *The Times*.

Having to gather up such bits of social fluff, essential gossip column fare, was a source of acute embarrassment to the urbane and sophisticated Driberg, who preferred to discourse on cultural topics such as books or the ballet. It was one thing dropping the names of his Oxford friends like Waugh into his column, but Beaverbrook couldn't resist scattering the names of his own cronies into the Hickey mix too. Thus, as Driberg remembered, 'I was occasionally favoured with items dictated by his lordship himself, and these, rather more often than I liked, were about some worthy but boring businessman from New Brunswick.'[15] In private, Beaverbrook was one of nature's inveterate gossips, a fund of countless anecdotes and scraps of tittle-tattle about the rich and powerful with whom he mixed. His fondness for such indiscretions was reflected in the ideas he offered for inclusion in two of his newspapers' most enduring columns, 'Hickey' of the *Express* and the 'Londoner's Diary' in the *Evening Standard*. But although Beaverbrook may have claimed to have introduced the modern gossip column to Britain, his papers never dabbled in the private lives of public figures. John Junor, who edited the wildly successful *Sunday Express*, once summarized Beaverbrook's pithy view on sex in gossip columns. 'All fucking is private,' Junor whispered to a startled new reporter. 'Always remember that.'[16]

With his bishop-like bearing, cultivated bent and faintly satanic countenance (Waugh had him down as 'that sinister character'),[17] Driberg appeared to have stepped straight out of mankind's 'priestly' caste, to which he believed all columnists should belong. He thought that the Hickeys of the world should be undomesticated, make regular and lengthy journeys abroad, and develop highly sensitive antennae, 'not only the positive news-sense which all good journalists have,' he explained, 'but a sense which warns him that a particular news-item or anecdote is unreliable or dangerous (in that it may involve him in a libel), or is merely "publicity" for some person or interest'.[18] But Driberg's Socratic inclusiveness, his irreverence, scepticism and pungency, not to mention his avoidance of puffery, were attributes that took several years to perfect to his own satisfaction. He disliked much of his early Hickey work in the mid-1930s and did not refer to it in his memoirs. His own selection of columns, published after World War II, only included material from 1937 onwards. But as the years slipped by, Driberg increased the propaganda count, inserting more and more Communistic views into his Hickey paragraphs and always appearing to get away with it. (His trick, he revealed, was to submit one outrageously biased paragraph that he knew would be struck out by the editor, leaving the rest untouched.)[19] By the time another Beaverbrook journalist, Michael Foot (later leader of the Labour Party), encountered Driberg in his heyday as Hickey, the column had become 'a genuine social criticism of the 1930s Establishment', written, Foot added, with Driberg's 'gift from the gods…a splendid love and mastery of the English language'.[20]

When King George VI and Queen Elizabeth visited Scotland in May 1938, Hickey reported how the royal couple saw 'busy factories, well-soaped children in community centres, folk-dancing, housing schemes'. But Driberg slipped away from the royal progress to visit some overcrowded Clydeside tenements, reporting his findings in a column headed: 'Where the King Did Not Go':

Four housewives, cheerful and free from bitterness, though they said it was a scandal that they could get nowhere to live but the 14-roomed tenement which they share with 44 other people, said I'd better call on a Mrs McIlveney round the corner.

We knocked. Husband McIlveney let me in. This family have what is known as room-and-kitchen. Mostly they live in the kitchen. The 'room' is a small space in which husband and sons sleep.

In the kitchen sleep wife and 3 daughters. The bed is fairly big, but the wall by it is usually damp, which is bad for Mrs McIlveney's sciatica. They also eat there. On the floor, among discarded shirts, were some stale slices of bread. On the radio set stood a shaving-brush, a comb, a bowl containing one gold-fish, a crucifix with a dusty palm-cross stuck in it, a picture postcard of some priests.

This kitchen-bedroom-living-room's proportions are not bad. It is fairly lofty. It is about the size of, say, one of the older bathrooms at Claridge's; but has only one tap, above the sink by the window.

The lavatory is outside. In the yard also is a dark, ill-ventilated washhouse which has to do for 12 families; so that each of them gets at it about once a fortnight.

McIlveney is not in work. A 20-year-old son works at John Brown's as a heater. They pay £1 10s [£1.50] a month rent.

'You're an old soldier,' says doctor. 'You'd do better in a tent.'

McIlveney wishes he could find one.[21]

Tom Driberg's biographer Francis Wheen has pointed out that, like George Orwell, Driberg had a somewhat romanticized vision of the working class, and especially of working-class men. In Driberg's case, says Wheen, 'it was both political and homo-erotic: those sinewy thighs and rough hands, that heroic nobility in adversity, the sweat of labour...'[22] While discovering that many working-class households were forced to exist on the breadline, Driberg himself was an unashamed bon viveur who loved and understood good food and wine, the sort of high-living revolutionary dismissed by his admiring, if baleful, employer Lord Beaverbrook as a 'café Communist'. He certainly revelled in the fleshpots of London, going to fashionable parties and swanky nightclubs; he was a familiar figure at the Embassy or the Café de Paris where he would be seen with the likes of Margaret Whigham, the most celebrated debutante of her day who later became the notorious Duchess of Argyll. He also drank at raffish dives in Soho and clubs where most of the staff and customers were black.

Although he was well paid as Hickey (by the outbreak of war, he was earning thirty-eight guineas (£39.90) a week, plus another twelve guineas (£12.60) expenses), Driberg was a hopeless spendthrift who lived beyond his means. He leased a small mews house in Kensington, hired a manservant-cum-chauffeur, ate out every day, not always on expenses, and ran up a lifelong overdraft. Like Lord Castlerosse, Driberg frequently accepted handouts of money from Beaverbrook, either to settle debts or, as in 1940, to prevent his imminent bankruptcy. Having begged for a loan, Driberg's heart sank when the office manager sent for him and explained that such advances were strictly against company rules. 'But,' added the manager, 'Lord Beaverbrook has instructed me to make you a free gift of £1,000. Here is a cheque.' Little wonder that Castlerosse had crowned Beaverbrook 'my never-ending lord of appeal'.[23]

It was Beaverbrook who single-handedly silenced Fleet Street in November 1935, rescuing Tom Driberg's reputation by ensuring that no paper reported the *Express* columnist's sensational trial for indecent assault. 'In theory and in principle,' Driberg insisted, 'I deplore such suppression of news, if what is kept out is newsworthy (which my trial perhaps, just marginally, was); but I am bound to admit that when it is something which concerns one personally, the suppression is jolly welcome.'[24] Driberg had been accosted in the West End late one night by two unemployed Scottish miners, asking if he knew where they might find a bed. Seeing that they were reasonably young and not unattractive, Driberg asked them back to his house, where all three slept in Driberg's bed. Next morning, the miners complained to the police. 'It was buggery, you know,'[25] Beaverbrook growled. (This seems unlikely, given Driberg's self-confessed proclivity for fellatio.) Driberg told the editor, Christiansen, about the miners' allegations and pleaded with Beaverbrook to kill the story. Beaverbrook obliged, contacting every other newspaper proprietor in Fleet Street, ensuring that not a line appeared anywhere, either about the case or the trial itself at the Old Bailey. Furthermore, Beaverbook gave Driberg 500 guineas (£525) to hire a top-ranking defence barrister, J. D. Cassels, who called two character witnesses of such upstanding demeanour and silky reassurance that Driberg was cleared by the jury.

The dam of silence held. The only whispered comment in print came in the journalists' trade paper, the *World's Press News*. 'That was a curious case that Fleet Street was talking about last week,' the item ran. 'Not all names make news.' Driberg was so relieved that he didn't mind the joke. 'What I did rather mind,' he reminisced, 'was having to go back to the office, on bail, each afternoon when the Court rose and write a light-hearted Hickey column.'[26]

In May 1937 he outraged hundreds of *Express* readers with his description of George VI's coronation at Westminster Abbey, observed from a seat high in the triforium, measuring, he complained, just 1'7" × 2'1". Deliberately avoiding any sense of hushed awe, he overturned the conventions of generations of royal reporters: 'St Augustine and St Gregory, in Victorian stained glass, looked rather yellow; but Mrs Tate [a Tory MP] looked extremely well ... resting her chin on her white-gloved arm ... Lloyd George folded his arms, looked bored. Ribbentrop appeared to go to sleep.'[27] There was nothing overtly republican or libellous, but readers objected to the tone of Driberg's report. 'My offence seemed to be that, by watching a coronation in the way in which a dramatic critic might watch a stage show, and by treating those taking part as a moving, breathing human beings and as performers, I had in some way robbed the ceremony of its glamour and the monarchy of its mystique.'[28]

Driberg wrote as Hickey for a full ten years, and became a famous journalist. In the pre-television era, few of his readers would have recognized his face in the street, and while millions knew the name William Hickey, almost no one would have known that he was really Tom Driberg. Driberg enjoyed the cachet bestowed by the Hickey name, and the influence it brought him. Women wrote to him admiringly, unaware of Driberg's private predilections.

In the late 1930s, he heard that a young man was trying to pass himself off as Hickey, boasting about being the writer of the column while standing drinks in the bar of a music hall in south London, apparently to impress one of the show's pretty chorus girls. Accompanied by two friends, and a private detective who lurked in the background, Driberg joined the impostor's circle of admirers, lobbing him fatuous questions: 'What an interesting life you must have ... What a lot of interesting people you must meet.'

Then Driberg set his trap. 'How do you *get* such a job?' he asked. 'What are the qualifications?'

'Oh, you just have to have a flair, old boy,' said the bogus Hickey. 'The screw's jolly good,' he added. 'But it's a hell of a life. Most of the money goes to the brewers in the end anyway ...'

Driberg felt sorry for the make-believe Hickey, with his shabby coat, floppy felt hat, weak chin, nicotine-stained fingers and, he noted with a twinge in his groin, his rather pleasant face. 'I think this has gone on long enough,' Driberg snapped. 'Will you tell me why you are passing yourself off as Hickey?'

The denouement was low key. 'I don't know what you mean,' said the young man, taking Driberg aside and explaining, *sotto voce*, that he had done it to impress the girl. 'I wanted to *be* somebody,' he added.

Later, Driberg and the young man went up the West End for a drink, finally shaking off the witnessing friends and private detective before repairing to the columnist's flat where, as Driberg put it, 'a more intimate identification occurred'.[29]

As Hickey, Driberg travelled extensively, reporting from the Middle East, Spain, Prague and the Sudetenland in 1938, and from Rome the following year on a papal coronation. But he was based mainly in London, from where he watched Hitler's shadow lengthen ominously across Europe. Occasionally, he allowed himself a little tease:

> Hitler, accommodatingly, has put his telephone number in this year's English *Who's Who*.
>
> He gives it as Berlin 11 6191.
>
> Taking this as an invitation and feeling that he might be in a mood of exhilaration after dealing with Schact, we put in a call to this number last night.
>
> Maybe the whole thing's just a Teuton prank, but it's a wrong number. We asked for Hitler. A voice said: Oh you want Berlin 12 6481.
>
> We got that number. A woman said: Reichschancellery Berlin speaking.
>
> We asked for Hitler, Herr Adolf Hitler.
>
> Woman: One moment please.
>
> Man: Who is it you want?
>
> We: Herr Adolf Hitler.
>
> 2nd man: One moment please.
>
> Woman: Who is it you want?
>
> We: Herr Adolf Hitler.
>
> Woman: One moment please.
>
> 3rd man: Herr Hitler? I am afraid it is not possible. Unfortunately it cannot be allowed. Goodbye.
>
> Then why put a number in the book?[30]

When war finally came, Driberg declared in his Hickey column, 'We are all in it,'[31] a remark that earned him a rebuke from the Communist Party, followed a couple of years later by expulsion, with neither explanation nor appeal. Driberg toured the provinces during the Blitz ('Coventry seemed the most cataclysmic; then Manchester shook me'),[32] filing on-the-spot descriptions that have became classics of war reporting. 'Blitz habits vary considerably in different places,' Driberg reported from Bristol in March 1941. 'In Liverpool ... the bouncing, red-headed girls, the sailors, the wizened Mersey weasels in furtive caps or raffish bowlers really do stroll and sing along Lime Street while bits and pieces are flying, guns banging. In Bristol, they take raids more seriously.'[33] The worst night of all was back in London. Driberg was working late at the *Express* office when word came of a direct hit on the BBC's headquarters at Broadcasting House. He hurried to the scene. In fact, it had been a near miss, but two firewatchers on the roof had been killed.

A hundred or more yards from it the air smelt charred; drifts of dark smoke began to obscure the tiaras of flame that hovered above us, as in some hellish pantomime or firework pageant.

As usual, all the burglar alarms had been set ringing; nothing would stop them for the rest of the night. Scores of shops were wrecked; as I got near the incident I had to step over doors and window frames that had been hurled bodily into the road.

Wading at last through an ankle-deep porridge of glass and water, I looked at the slagheap that had, an hour earlier, been a block of – fortunately – empty offices. Less fortunately, one corner of it had been a pub; 'there was usually 20 or 30 of 'em in there about that time,' said a copper.

I was glad of living human company – glad when the ARP people stopped me, took me to see their Incident Officer. Half-sheltering in a ruined shop that his office-for-the-moment (two blue lamps and a wooden flag mark it), he was a shadowy, lean, quickly-moving figure under a white tin hat. Henry, they called him. He used to make Savile Row suits.

Decision and a clear head are needed. Henry had them. In this half-light of flame and smoke there were even forms to be filled up and signed. A man came up with a form. 'CD driver,' he announced himself. 'Mortuary. Got any particulars about this body over here? Approximate time of death? Time when found? Sex?'

'Female, what's left of her,' said Henry.[34]

After the Japanese attack on Pearl Harbor, Driberg reported from Washington: 'a fantastic hub-hub of traffic jams, armed guards, cordons... The astonishment felt by ordinary Americans...seems merged today in a mood of exhilaration... They are moving in and with history.'[35] He then moved to the west coast, staying with Alfred Hitchcock at his house in Hollywood. On his return to Britain, Driberg heard on the radio of the death of the MP for the Essex constituency containing Bradwell, the village where he was born. On the carpet in front of the gas fire was stretched out, naked, the slender, rangy form of a Canadian soldier, Driberg's pick-up for the night. 'I must have betrayed some interest at the brief news item,' Driberg recalled, '[and] I must even have said something to the effect that I might stand for Parliament myself.'[36] He did, and within three months was MP (Independent) for Maldon.

But Driberg's political triumph was tempered with professional doubts. For a year, he led a double life, going to the Commons and then on to Fleet Street in the evening to write as Hickey. Beaverbrook turned an admiring but increasingly suspicious eye on the column, saw that it was becoming more and more political, and warned the editor, Arthur Christiansen, not to let Driberg 'get away with all this left-wing propaganda'.[37] In June 1943, a reporter on the *Express* mentioned a rumour that Churchill's minister of supply, Sir Andrew Duncan, planned to give up politics and return to private industry. When Driberg checked, he discovered that, far from being a rumour, it was Duncan's firm intention. In Driberg's view this was a scandalous state of affairs, which he proceeded to denounce in a widely reported speech in his constituency. Christiansen called Driberg into his office two days later and sacked him on the spot, a decision he instantly regretted.

Driberg refused all entreaties to return. Hickey limped on, with various *Express* journalists trying their hand, but none had Driberg's flair and range, and the column that had become one of the most distinctive features of the paper floundered through the 1940s, trying to find a new direction. After his retirement in 1957, Christiansen recalled ruefully that he had tried no fewer than twenty-three Hickeys in his time, of whom only two were any good at all. The problem, Christiansen explained, was that Driberg 'set such a standard that it was a heart-breaking job trying to find a successor for him'.[38]

Unfrocked as Hickey, Tom Driberg MP became a weekly columnist on the left-wing *Reynolds News*, from where he continued to aim mischievous darts at Establishment targets. In 1946, along with Michael Foot, he persuaded the government to set up a Royal Commission on the Press to investigate the power and influence of newspaper owners like Lord Beaverbrook, who had run the *Express* 'purely for propaganda, and with no other purpose'[39] since 1918. In his evidence to the commission, he annoyed his former employer by publicly revealing the existence of the 'white list' of people whose names were banned from Beaverbrook's papers for various, often malign, reasons. The 'white list' was, in reality, a blacklist of individuals who, for various reasons, had offended or upset Beaverbrook. The names were constantly changing, but among the permanent fixtures from the entertainment world were Charlie Chaplin (on the grounds of his Communist sympathies), Noël Coward (because of his homosexuality) and Paul Robeson (because, as another Beaverbrook columnist, Douglas Sutherland, explained, 'he was a bit of both and black into the bargain').[40]

Driberg claimed to have been issued with his copy of the 'white list' shortly after joining the *Express* as a young reporter. As Hickey, he had been forbidden to write about G. K. Chesterton because his name headed the list and it stayed there until his death in 1935. The commission was astonished to learn that even Stanley Baldwin had been briefly added to the list, following his stinging 'prerogative of the harlot'[41] remarks about the press in March 1931, although, as Driberg explained, since Baldwin was Prime Minister at the time 'it was impossible to keep him permanently on the list'. In any case, Driberg added, it was not a blanket ban for obvious reasons, but Baldwin was 'not to be publicised unduly or not to be publicised without personal reference to the editor, or something of that sort'.[42] Beaverbrook swatted away the criticism, saying that the 'white lists' amounted to little more than advice. He evidently convinced the commission, which concluded that the lists were mostly 'a tangible expression of the risks of a libel action', to which gossip writers were every bit as vulnerable as news reporters.

After the war Driberg was voted on to Labour's national executive committee – thanks to what Ian Mikardo described as the star columnist's 'celebrity factor' – and in 1957 Fleet Street's first William Hickey became the first former gossip writer to be promoted to the office of party chairman. Unquestionably, his election to this important-sounding but largely back-room post improved Driberg's standing in the Labour Party. But after his sudden death in 1976, biographers, obituarists and commentators began to speculate about the influence his burgeoning political career might have had with Britain's Cold War enemies in 1950s Moscow. In 1992, Vasili Mitrokhin, a former archivist for the Russian secret service, the KGB, arrived in London with thousands of smuggled documents copied from original papers. Among other things, the so-called Mitrokhin archive purported to show that, at the height of the Cold War, two Labour MPs with pro-Soviet sympathies were working as KGB spies. One was Raymond Fletcher, the other Tom Driberg. According to Mitrokhin, Driberg's recruitment dated from 1956, when he had propositioned a KGB agent while 'cottaging' in a public underground urinal behind the Metropole Hotel in Moscow. Driberg's pro-Stalin views were already well known, and his impressive contacts as a gossip writer and politician, particularly at Westminster, would have commended him to Soviet spymasters almost as highly as his susceptibility to blackmail as a promiscuous homosexual. During Mitrokhin's debriefing by MI5 and MI6, the Russian revealed that Driberg had been known to the KGB by the code-name Lepage. He had spied for the Russians for twelve years.[43]

According to Francis Wheen, Driberg's descent into the gloomy underworld of spies and counter-spies seems to have begun in his days as 'The Dragoman' on the *Express* in the early 1930s, when he got to know Dennis Wheatley, writer of best-selling thrillers on Satanism and the occult. Wheatley belonged to a club called the Paternosters, a group of writers, journalists and critics who met each month at the Cheshire Cheese in Fleet Street. When Wheatley was elected chairman in 1934, in an effort to broaden the membership, he invited several gossip writers to join, including Don Donegall and Tom Driberg. Wheatley's motive was plainly stated: 'for every person who reads literary criticism in their papers,' he pointed out, 'ten read the gossip column; so mentions of new books in such columns are of great value to an author.'[44]

At one of the Paternoster gatherings, Driberg was introduced to Captain Maxwell Knight, another new member, who happened to be head of MI5's counter-subversion section. Although ostensibly anti-gay, Knight was really an active homosexual with a penchant, like Driberg, for rough trade. But he seems to have made an exception for his sophisticated new gossip writer friend, with whom he quickly became sexually obsessed. While visiting Driberg at home or lunching with him at smart restaurants, Knight pumped him for snippets of information, knowing that he was a Communist Party member and an inveterate gossip. Whether he actually recruited Driberg as a British agent is a moot point. Another Labour MP, Leo Abse, thought it possible. Moreover, even though Driberg was expelled from the Communist Party in 1941, Abse thought it perfectly feasible that his colleague might have become a double agent, working for MI5 as well as the Soviets. 'Driberg walked all his life on a tightrope and gained his thrills in public and private by a never ending series of adventures, courageously and foolhardily oscillating from one role to another almost every day of his life,' Abse reflected. 'The spy is a man of identities and each day he must act many parts. Driberg could have played the part of the spy with superb skill, and if the officers of MI5 were indeed inept enough to have attempted to recruit him, then, in turn, Tom Driberg would have gained especial pleasure in fooling and betraying them.'[45]

But what use would Driberg have been to Moscow? As a talented journalist, and even as a left-wing Labour politician, he would not have known any great secrets of state. Even so, either side in the Cold War may have overlooked Driberg's notorious unreliability in their desperation to recruit anyone operating near the centre of power, which Driberg certainly was. If Mitrokhin was right, he was only confirming a story published nearly twenty years before by Chapman Pincher, dating Driberg's treachery from his sunset days as Hickey in 1942, the year in which he was first elected to Parliament. He was indeed, said Pincher, a double agent, working for the KGB and MI5, reporting on the personal and political activities of his friends and colleagues in Parliament to both agencies. 'Both MI5 and the KGB had no illusions about the fact that he was working for the other side,' added Pincher, 'and both sought to use him for their own purposes.'[46]

Long after his ten-year stint as William Hickey, gossip continued to furnish Tom Driberg with a living of sorts. As he flitted between Westminster and the gay clubs and 'straight' restaurants of Soho, he noted and retailed a steady stream of indiscretions about the rich, famous and powerful, telephoning paragraphs to *Private Eye* or, more lucratively, the 'Londoner's Diary' page of the *Evening Standard*. He needed the money, for he lived his entire life beyond his means, forcing him in the 1950s to open his beautiful Essex mansion, Bradwell Lodge, to the public twice a week and charging an entrance fee. Triumphs like his world exclusive interview with the Soviet spy Guy Burgess in 1956 (sold to the *Daily Mail* for a whopping £5,000) were spiked by financial tangles and disasters, books commissioned but unwritten and the advances spent. Somehow he muddled through, contracting a *mariage blanc* with a woman called Ena and, a year before he died, accepting a life peerage, for which he chose the style and title of Lord Bradwell. In May 1975, he eyed the guests at his seventieth birthday party and counted with satisfaction one duke, two dukes' daughters, assorted lords, a bishop in full episcopal purple and a poet laureate. 'Not bad for an old left-wing MP, eh?' he chuckled. And not bad for an old gossip-grubber either.

But perhaps his greatest gossiping triumph was accomplished from beyond the grave. A year after Driberg's death, his autobiography *Ruling Passions* appeared, trumpeted as 'one of the most sensational and scandalous political memoirs ever'.[47] It did not disappoint. 'It is a devastating, stomach-turning document,' pronounced the *Sun*'s political editor Walter Terry. 'Probably the biggest outpouring of literary dung a public figure has ever flung into print.'[48] The book chronicled Driberg's astonishing career as a promiscuous 'cottager', and included the seamier side of his life as Hickey, in which he had seduced several men about whom he had either written or proposed to write. Then there was the encounter, in blacked-out wartime Edinburgh, with a 'flaxen-haired and smilingly attractive' Norwegian sailor. A young police constable who disturbed them in a deserted air-raid shelter could scarcely believe his eyes. 'Och, ye bastards,' he cried out, 'ye dirty pair of whoors.' Caught *in flagrante* in the beam of the officer's torch, Driberg managed to keep his head. He flashed a card proclaiming his identity as Tom Driberg MP, also known as William Hickey of the *Daily Express*. '*William Hickey!*' exclaimed the officer. 'Good God, man, *I've read ye all of my life!* Every morning!' Ordering the Norwegian to leave ('Get awa' oot of it, ye bugger!'), PC George Crowford, far from arresting Driberg, sat down and talked enthusiastically about the 'Hickey' column and the pleasure it gave him every morning. The two men parted amicably, Driberg judging 'that it would be going too far, in the circumstances, to make a pass'.[49] Instead, he sent Crowford a book of poems and six guineas' worth (£6.30) of book tokens.

Tom Driberg's memoirs may have shocked and scandalized, but they also disclosed a lonely figure whose talents as a columnist were overshadowed by the excesses of his private life. To his friends, he remained (as one of them observed shortly after his death) an unravellable tangle of contradictions.[50] As a journalist, he rescued gossip from the tired litanies of 'society' figures and made it sparkle with a virtuoso use of language and a defining new style; having ground down what he admitted was the 'angular barbarism' of his early 'Hickey' columns, Driberg was left with 'a certain residue of tautness and crispness'[51] that still marks out good newspaper writing today. To his millions of readers of the *Express* in its pre-war heyday, Tom Driberg was unmistakably the original, and arguably the greatest, William Hickey.

12

Sprinkled with Stardust

It was a difficult act to follow. As Hickey, Tom Driberg had created not just a unique persona but a distinctive landscape of the world. His sure grasp of history, as it unfolded beneath his critical eye, gave him an Olympian pre-eminence in an otherwise humdrum gossiping trade. Various replacements were tried. Derek Tangye, an experienced Fleet Street gossip writer, held the record for the shortest tenure as Hickey: on his first day, when Christiansen ordered a complete rewrite of his debut column, Tangye crumpled. 'I'll never be any good as Hickey,' he moaned. 'I'd better quit now.'[1] He had lasted just three hours. More successful was Simon Wardell, son of one of Beaverbrook's henchmen, who, Christiansen recalled, had the Driberg knack – 'and doing a passable imitation of Driberg's prose style was a knack'[2] – but who soon got bored and emigrated to the West Indies.

During the 1940s, as the *Daily Express*'s once-mighty Hickey page languished for want of a new Driberg, its sister paper the *Sunday Express* showered glitter into the wartime gloom from the pen of failed actor-turned-columnist Godfrey Winn. Shortly before the war, Beaverbrook had impishly tossed him into a weekly cat-fight with the star writer on the rival *Sunday Chronicle*, Beverley Nichols. Both specialized in gossip dressed up as sentimental gush, which while derided by its detractors as 'sob-sister stuff' nevertheless appealed hugely to women readers. As well as sycophantic paragraphs about stage and screen celebrities, Winn and Nichols tried to out-treacle each other in breaking stories about 'real life, real people' over Britain's Sunday breakfast tables.

Godfrey Winn had joined the *Mirror* in the mid-1930s when it was relaunched as an American-style tabloid. Hugh Cudlipp, the paper's dynamic young assistant features editor, wanted him to imitate Beverley Nichols's page in the *Chronicle*; Cudlipp had seen a column that Winn had written for the *Sunday Referee* and was impressed because, as Winn himself remembered, 'it wasn't the usual kind of society chit-chat, which he abhorred, and was determined to banish forever from the pages of *The Mirror*'.[3] When Cudlipp took him to lunch, Godfrey Winn found himself staring into 'the deep set Celtic eyes of a visionary turned fanatic who gave me the impression at sight that if anyone touched him, electric sparks would shoot out in every direction'.[4] Cudlipp explained that he was about to kill the *Mirror*'s moribund gossip page, and to replace it with a page about 'real people'. The job was Winn's, Cudlipp added, starting with a month's trial at £20 a week. Winn took it, despite the fact that Bill Connor, the *Mirror*'s previous gossip columnist, was still there, though in a different capacity: Connor had been given his own daily column under the pseudonym 'Cassandra'. Cudlipp had promised to make Winn a star, and he was as good as his word. Within weeks, Winn recalled, it was as though every bus in London was plastered with the same invitation: READ GODFREY WINN'S PERSONALITY PARADE IN THE DAILY MIRROR.

Winn's page about 'real people' attracted the attention of John Gordon, editor of the *Sunday Express*. Over lunch at the Savoy Grill, Gordon offered Winn his own page in the paper as an antidote to Lord Castlerosse's page of social comment. Like Beverley Nichols on the *Sunday Chronicle*, Winn would enjoy complete freedom and choice of subject. Gordon marched the bewildered young man into the hotel lobby, sat down at a writing-table and drew towards him a sheet of Savoy stationery. 'This constitutes a contract,' Gordon announced in his decisive Dundee accent after scribbling down several short, sharp paragraphs. 'We would never go back on it. You need nothing more in writing from us.'

Winn never got it. What he did get was a brutal brief from Beaverbrook, who summoned him to dinner and told him to 'go out and speak for the inarticulate and the submerged'. 'Y'see,' drawled Beaverbrook when Winn had left the room, 'he shakes hands with people's hearts.'[5]

Thanks to Beaverbrook's patronage, Winn was able to claim that he was the highest-paid journalist in Fleet Street. He was also the most fireproof, appealing to Beaverbrook for protection when John Gordon, a rabid homophobe, started making waves for his star columnist. ('My, my,' murmured Tom Driberg, when he spotted Winn trotting in Gordon's wake into the El Vino wine bar in Fleet Street. 'I see that there are fairies at the bottom of our Gordon!')[6] As a young Fleet Street writer, Winn had idolized Beverley Nichols and had copied his style. They knew each other through a gay coterie headed by Lord Lathom, the wealthiest homosexual in London. But something had soured their relationship, and by the time Winn was poached by the *Sunday Express*, Nichols was the man he hated most in the world.

In the late 1920s, while still a coming novelist and journalist, Nichols had spent a disastrous few months in New York as editor of a low-circulation 'society' magazine, *American Sketch*. The American publisher George Doran offered him the job over a lavish dinner at the Savoy, in the belief that Nichols could match the success of the *New Yorker* and could beat it on its own terms. Doran paid for Nichols to take himself, his furniture and his outrageously camp manservant, Gaskin, to Manhattan. Once installed in his East Side apartment, Nichols sold his (mostly bad French) furniture and replaced it with much Victorian mahogany, to reinforce Doran's pre-launch publicity hype about Nichols being the personification of Britishness. Introduced to the American press at a cocktail party, Nichols effortlessly loosed off a fusillade of epigrams and bons mots, which earned him many column inches and stoked American expectations of a snappy Mayfair-style gossip sheet to outpace the sophisticated brittleness of the *New Yorker*. But when it launched in December 1928, the new *American Sketch* glowed only with dullness; true, it contained some wit, irony and queenly bitchery, but remnants of the magazine's dreary antecedents, including endless dog advertisements, still afflicted its pages. Nichols did make improvements, but within a couple of months Doran told him that the title was being sold following company reorganization, and that he was redundant. Nichols sailed for England, leaving behind a young New Yorker with whom he had started an affair, but bringing with him a $12,000 profit from his brief but highly successful dabblings on the Wall Street stock market. On rueful reflection, Nichols felt it was inevitable that 'only stark failure could attend any attempt to match my Oxford-cum-Fleet-Street brand of humour, which was in the old British tradition of leisurely under-statement, against the machine-gun fire of American wit.'[7]

Nichols, an Oxford prodigy, first appeared in Fleet Street in 1921 as a cub reporter on Northcliffe's *Sunday Dispatch*, working 'on space' without a salary. 'Little by little,' he recalled in one of his several autobiographies, 'I acquired the reporter's technique and – which was more important – learned the twists and turns of that strange mass of prejudice, superstition, tradition and, above all, snobbery, which made up the Fleet Street mentality.'[8] News stories paid at the rate of three guineas (£3.15) a column, features at four guineas (£4.20); on Saturday nights, he totted up his weekly earnings with a tape-measure. His working week began with the Tuesday morning conference in the luxuriously appointed office of the editor, Bernard Falk, a horn-rimmed Lancastrian who nervously stroked his enormous nose with one hand while plucking his jacket lapel with the other.

Falk gave Nichols his own column in 1922 following his spectacular coup at the end of the Bywaters–Thompson murder trial. Edith Thompson and her lover Freddy Bywaters had been sentenced to death for the murder of Mrs Thompson's husband, Percy. Young Beverley (he was only twenty-four) signed up the parents of the doomed Edith Thompson for the rights to her life story, in the teeth of ferocious Fleet Street competition. He saw the family every day, heard their stories and shared their grief. Between the verdict and the hangings, Nichols had to persuade various celebrities to pontificate on the case in articles that he ghosted for them. Falk was delighted when, by a subterfuge, Nichols managed to doorstep the prima donna Dame Nellie Melba for a piece headed 'We Women and Edith Thompson'. But Nichols remained sunk in gloom at Mrs Thompson's fate and was distressed at the incomprehension of her parents, the Graydons. 'He felt their misery deeply,' reported Nichols's biographer Bryan Connon, 'but the journalist in him was never far away; when Mr Graydon cried out in pain: "That this should happen to people like us!" Beverley knew he had the line which would make the story echo round the world.'[9]

Away from his desk at the *Sunday Dispatch*, Beverley Nichols was forging his reputation as a talented dandy. Discreetly homosexual, he moved in the decadent circles of London society inhabited by the likes of Lady Emerald Cunard, Cecil Beaton and the most notorious gay icon of the day, the bisexual Tallulah Bankhead. With three published novels to his credit and his journalistic career in bloom, he became a founding member of the Bright Young People and shot to stardom as the author of *Twenty-Five*, his first book of memoirs, which assured him even greater social success. His triumph was sealed early in 1927 when his novel about gossip-writing, *Crazy Pavements*, appeared to critical acclaim. As Bryan Connon observed, it satirized not only the newspaper-reading public's fathomless appetite for gossip but also contemporary Mayfair society with its cast of people who, if not as young as they tried to be, were certainly startlingly bright.

Crazy Pavements sold well, helped by stories about the real identities of the book's characters and by rumours of legal action. The novel's gossip-writer hero Brian Elme was based on Nichols, while the degenerate Lord William Motley was inspired partly by gay Lord Lathom (whom Nichols adored) and partly by another socialite (whom he detested but always refused to identify). 'They knew who they were,' Nichols confided to his biographer, 'and they were furious with me.'[10] Nichols always suspected that Evelyn Waugh helped himself to the scenario of *Crazy Pavements* for his second novel, *Vile Bodies* (1930). Years later, Nichols found himself aboard the SS *United States* with Waugh as a fellow passenger. Waugh dismissed Nichols, by then in his fifties, as 'a poor old journalist',[11] so vain that he wept with disappointment that the weather was too bad for him to acquire a suntan. For his part, Nichols scoffed at this self-appointed grandee, a 'plebian figure with aristocratic pretensions' whom he dismissed as 'The Waugh of the Poses'.[12]

In 1932, the young editor of the downmarket *Sunday Chronicle*, James Wedgwood Drawbell, came up with an idea for a new feature and offered it to Nichols. 'Something new, something different,' trumpeted the paper, 'not gossip, not small talk, not society silliness, but real life, real people.' Although he never grubbed for gossip in the traditional manner, Nichols, an inveterate snob, seldom missed the chance to drop a distinguished name or two into his own weekly page. Drawbell, a bold innovator, promised Nichols the whole of page two of the paper with complete freedom to write what he wanted. Nichols felt instinctively that the *Chronicle's* leftish views were at odds with his own, and he was rather hoping for a better offer from the mass-circulation *Sunday Express*. But when Drawbell upped the money, Nichols signed. His friend Rebecca West wrote a flattering profile of him to launch 'Page 2', which ran without a break for fifteen years. Nichols came to hate the tyranny of a weekly column, and found filling it a strain. Although Drawbell honoured his promise of editorial freedom, he increasingly leaned on Nichols to write about 'names', preferably aristocratic and upper-class ones. One article, published with the heading 'Is Lady Astor a Liar?', led to Nichols being summoned to Cliveden where Lady Astor berated him for writing for 'that rag', adding that it was not a 'gentleman's paper'.[13] Nichols knew she was right. But his fear of poverty, and the security of the *Sunday Chronicle's* pay cheque, meant that his page of high-society gossip continued throughout World War II and into the peace.

Nichols's self-loathing finally reached breaking point at the start of 1947 when Drawbell published copies of his correspondence with Nichols in his journalistic memoirs. The letters demonstrated Drawbell's total domination of his columnist and his contempt for Nichols's feeble protestations about the column's gossipy content. 'Every single one of the letters I have received by this mail,' Nichols once wrote to Drawbell, '*implores* me not to drag in the names of "celebrities". Couldn't we have photographs of public lavatories for a change? Nobody would notice the difference... I believe the way to make our page sensationally different is to fill it with the bloodiest cartoons from Moscow and Munich, or with pictures of working men, and *not* with the old, old gang.'[14]

By then the *Sunday Chronicle* could claim that – thanks to celebrity gossip and pictures of 'the old, old gang' – 'Page 2' had boosted sales by 100,000 copies a week.

Getting those post-war glitterati pictures wasn't always easy, as one *Daily Mirror* photographer found to his cost. His quarry was Captain Robert Cecil, son of Lord Cranborne, Conservative leader in the House of Lords, and great-grandson of the Victorian Marquess of Salisbury, three times Tory prime minister. When dashing Captain Cecil of the Grenadier Guards, twenty-nine, married the stunningly beautiful Mollie Wyndham-Quin, twenty-three, at Westminster Abbey a week before Christmas 1945, the newspapers were gagging for the story. Their interest was all the keener when the Cecils decided to ban the national press from covering the wedding, so creating an air of intrigue which the papers did their best to exploit. Not only were reporters excluded from the service and the swanky reception that followed at Arlington House, the family's London townhouse, but photographers were explicitly banned from taking pictures of the newly-weds.

Every means was tried to thwart the press, it was observed later, short of a mosquito net. But one paper, the *Daily Mirror*, seeing the Cecil society wedding as a metaphor for toffs on the spree while war-weary workers still languished in the toils of austerity, determined to get their photographer inside to obtain a particular picture. The photographer, Tom Lea, had given some thought to his mission. He knew that many of the tenantry employed by the Cecils at their country home, Hatfield House, had been invited to London for the wedding and the ensuing beano. What Lea had in mind was to snap 'one beautiful incident', he explained, 'that would tell the story'.[15] But although he went to some trouble to gatecrash his way into the seat of the mighty, his single snatched picture of snooty young Captain Cecil glad-handing his estate workers not only blighted Lea's career but dealt the press a considerable blow on the question of intrusion into people's private lives.

News of the young couple's impending marriage had excited a lot of gossip column interest. Despite this, or perhaps because of it, the Cecil family had decided to hold the wedding away from the public gaze, as if that were possible when it involved one of the top families and the single most important church in a country yearning for a glint of glamour after six miserable years of war. Dozens of calls to the groom's family from Fleet Street in the weeks before the ceremony had been effortlessly swatted away; the Cecils had pulled strings to ban photographers from the Abbey's great west door, and the police had laid on officers to keep an eye on overzealous press representatives while ostensibly (like the brawny estate workers bussed down from Hatfield for the day) dealing with the crowds of accredited guests, their cars, limousines and taxis. Two photographers from the downmarket *Daily Graphic* who fetched up at the private reception at Arlington House to ask for a picture were turned down, shown the door and departed without demur. As they left, they nodded at Tom Lea going in, and may have smiled to themselves: in an attempt to pass himself off as an invited guest, he had dressed to the nines in his best suit, which he had adorned with the classic socialist emblem, a bright scarlet carnation buttonhole, bought in the Burlington Arcade on his way from the Abbey for three shillings (15p).

At the door, Lea hid his Leica camera under his tweed overcoat and mingled with the crowds. He sought out Cecil's best man, admitting that he was a photographer but telling him that he represented 'the paper of the times' because, as Lea later explained, 'I hoped he would think that it was *The Times* if he didn't like the *Daily Mirror*.'[16] Lea said he wanted permission to photograph the bride and groom. He was directed through the throng to Cecil's grandmother, Lady Salisbury, who pointed out the groom's mother, Lady Cranborne, 'the lady with a big feather in her hat'. But neither of these women was prepared to sanction a picture, so Lea buttonholed Cecil himself as he and his new bride walked down the great marble staircase. 'No, certainly not,' said Cecil when Lea asked for a picture. 'I would object most strongly.' Seeing Lea's dismay, he added he was very sorry, but 'it is not possible'.

A few moments later, in the reception room at the foot of the stairs, the newly-weds were shaking hands with a line of staff from Hatfield House when Lea stepped forward and, with a blinding flash, took his picture. Cecil, seeing Lea raise his camera, lunged at him, dealing him several blows to the head and crying, 'I told you "No"!' Tearing the camera from its strap round Lea's neck, Cecil hurled it to the ground and stamped on it repeatedly until it lay broken in several pieces. Two burly estate workers bundled Lea out of the house and into the courtyard, where someone brought him the remains of his camera and his spectacles. It turned out that this was not the first time that Cecil had lost his temper and lashed out; during the war he had been fined £5 for assault. When he appeared at Bow Street court a few weeks later, charged again with assault, the magistrate described his behaviour as 'ungentlemanly' and 'cowardly', and fined him £10 with £50 costs and another £135 for smashing the camera.

The wedding reception had taken place in a private house that was closed to the press. Lea had taken his picture despite being warned not to. The *Mirror*, said one commentator, might find it hard to believe that many decent English people abhor the type of publicity that fills the papers with well-known people; Lea himself had perhaps never met a bride and bridegroom who would regard his intrusion as an outrage. Captain Cecil was defending his bride from the insult of having her picture in the gutter press 'with the presumed inference that she had agreed to its appearance there'.[17]

Of course, the case was as much about class as it was about press intrusion. In the opinion of a magazine for the squirearchy, titled *Justice of the Peace and Local Government Review*, Lea had 'demonstrated his lack of elementary breeding' by taking his picture in a private house when forbidden to do so. The magazine said it sympathized with Cecil, even though he had broken the Victorian code of behaviour that regarded it as 'ungentlemanly' for such a man to strike a social inferior. The intrusion ('of the baser type of paper in particular') into private life is, the magazine harrumphed, 'an unmixed evil'. 'The learned magistrate's epithets of "cowardly" and "ungentlemanly" exactly fit these intruders, and are still more apt to the newspaper proprietors by whom they are employed.' (Lea sued for libel over this paragraph and lost.) 'Of course,' the magazine added,

> the evil goes still deeper, in the vulgar thirst for notoriety which (natural to the newly rich or recently ennobled) has afflicted many men and women in that section of the community where a tradition of *gravitas* might have been expected, but the rot (at present chiefly to be seen in the worst type of London newspapers and along the cruder fringes of 'society') will inevitably spread, both in London and in provincial circles, unless public opinion makes it plain that healthy English sympathies are against the sort of thing attempted by the *Daily Mirror* in this case.[18]

Meanwhile, in the Sunday papers, Godfrey Winn and Beverley Nichols continued to claw at each other with gentlemanly *gravitas*. Winn's relationship with Beverley Nichols was complex: whatever had passed between them when they first met soon curdled into mutual bitchery and distaste. By the mid-1960s, the rift was total. Winn was appalled when Nichols wrote a book excoriating Somerset Maugham for his treatment of his wife Syrie;[19] Winn numbered Maugham among his lovers and had been a frequent visitor to the Villa Mauresque, the novelist's home in the South of France. Nichols in turn was displeased when Winn launched a scarcely veiled attack on him in his autobiography the following year.[20] Winn quoted Gladys Cooper, complaining about 'all that stuff that is being written about Willie [Maugham] and such inferior muck, too'.[21] Nichols told his biographer that Winn had 'caused great harm to me behind the scenes', presumably in a professional sense, and confessed that he detested Winn as 'the worst kind of hypocrite'.[22]

When Winn collapsed and died while playing tennis in 1971, a friend told Beverley Nichols: 'We could hear the champagne corks popping for miles around.'

'Not champagne,' replied Nichols, 'but a good stiff celebratory gin.'[23]

And yet Winn, the first great sob-sister, had turned an important page in British journalism. With his irresistible appeal to women readers, Winn, encouraged by Hugh Cudlipp, had helped open up a new seam in popular newspapers by promoting the cult of the signed column. Where the *Mirror* led, others soon followed, including the broadsheets, which adapted the idea for a more sophisticated audience. Before long, imitation columns sprouted, covering subjects ranging from wine to motoring. But Winn and his ilk also pointed the way ahead for editors anxious to interest women readers, and as the 1940s ebbed the papers began to feature celebrities from the world of dress and fashion who now clamoured for gossip columnists' attention alongside the more familiar stars of stage, screen and radio. Riding in on this rolling wave came talented women writers like Marjorie Proops and Jean Rook. Their signed columns ran in parallel with the still-anonymous plugs and puffs of the gossip writers, who revelled in the new post-war mood of optimism and restlessness.

The old London social season was quietly shrivelling away, to be replaced by glitzy parties thrown by the very rich, attended by the very famous and lovingly chronicled by Hickey and Co. It was also the era of Lord and Lady Docker, a ludicrously rich pair of showily vulgar loungers with gold-plated Daimlers upholstered in zebra-skin ('mink is too hot to sit on'),[24] and the 'Margaret Set' of (often) idle but (invariably) wealthy young men who fawned on Princess Margaret, all of whose dreary doings were closely reported in the gossip pages. There were first-night parties and birthday bashes all over the West End, where new nightclubs, bars, hotels and restaurants were springing up each week, predictably opening in a flurry of publicity involving a well-known star or personality.

In the 1950s, Britain's royal family came to life, fleshed out not just in film, pictures and on television, but in gossipy (if invariably deferential) references in the papers. In the late 1940s, the wedding of

Princess Elizabeth to Philip Mountbatten had excited a nation weary from war. Fleet Street editors soon realized that the royals offered all the elements of a real-life soap opera, with the young, new Queen as its star. As one social historian commented, 'the monarch was processed into a super personality in whom...the audience naturally possessed proprietary rights.'[25] The Queen's coronation in 1953 brought the biggest newspaper sales boom in history. It was clear that royal stories sold papers. Arthur Christiansen, editing the *Express*, ordered the features pages to be henceforward 'sprinkled with stardust'.[26]

The *Express's* deadly enemy, the *Daily Mail*, came late to the gossip game. Between the wars, it had looked flustered, unsure of how its middle-class readers would take to tittle-tattle, despite the dictum of the paper's legendary founder, Lord Northcliffe, that news was 'what people talked about in kitchen, parlour, drawing-room and over the garden wall; namely, other people'.[27] But when other papers began devoting increased space to gossip after World War I, Northcliffe had disapproved. Only when university-educated writers joined the *Mail* did Northcliffe relent. 'Get more names in the paper,' he had roared, 'the more aristocratic the better.'[28] After Northcliffe's death in 1922, the *Mail* had struggled to keep up with the altogether smarter *Express*, and had failed to put up any serious rival to William Hickey when Tom Driberg took over the column in 1933.

It was only in 1947 that the *Mail* launched a new diary page under the unlikely name of Paul Tanfield. Wartime paper restrictions had been eased, and with more space available the *Mail* decided to tackle Hickey head-on by featuring Tanfield on the back page. Lord Rothermere, chairman of Associated Newspapers, assigned his wife Ann to oversee the launch of the column and to appoint its editor. Lady Rothermere enlisted the help of one of her husband's executives, Bill Richmond, who immediately canvassed Douglas Sutherland at the *Evening Standard's* 'Londoner's Diary'. Would he be interested in the job? The two men had a bizarre audience with Lady Rothermere at her mansion overlooking Green Park; as Sutherland recalled, they were received in the long drawing room 'where she had taken up a pose reminiscent of Madame Récamier on an elegant Louis-Quinze chaise-longue'.[29] Lady Rothermere made it plain that she expected some hot, juicy scandal every day, although she was careful to stress that it needed to be legally watertight. Sutherland begged off the job, and the column, called 'Who, When and Where?', began life in the charge of Simon Wardell, flimsily disguised as Simon Ward. It had a baleful baptism: Bill Richmond, the *Mail* executive who had tried to head-hunt Sutherland, was seized by a fit of depression and blew his brains out with a twelve-bore shotgun after breakfasting at his London club.[30]

The column soon mutated into the Paul Tanfield page, and refashioned itself around Donald Edgar, a bright Oxford scholar and ex-prisoner of war recruited from the 'Peterborough' column at the *Telegraph*. His brief was not to dish dirt, but 'to write about people who were doing something interesting in a lively way, and consequently to provoke an interest in the paper other than hard news'.[31] But it was not a success. Some senior figures on the *Mail* pressed for more gossip, while the ascetic editor Guy Schofield wanted something more serious. It seemed to Edgar that the paper was adrift, unable to decide whether to compete head-on with the popular *Express* or try to become a cheaper *Telegraph*. Early in 1953 Arthur Christiansen solved Edgar's problem for him by poaching him to write for the *Express*.

Donald Edgar was one of Christiansen's big discoveries. He made a disastrous start, but quickly recovered to achieve a personal triumph with his reporting from Westminster Abbey at the Queen's coronation. From the Abbey's tented annexe, Edgar filed 'three columns of brilliant detail about the fidgets of the mighty, about the hip-flasks that were secretly swigged for breakfast, about the painting and the powdering and the impatient posturings that went on as the hours dragged by'.[32] It was Edgar who famously spotted the first signs of romance between Princess Margaret and Peter Townsend, when he saw her smilingly lift a stray wisp of fluff from the group captain's uniform.[33] His reward was the William Hickey byline.

With the help of just one assistant, Christopher Dobson, whose burly frame caused the pair to be nicknamed 'Poet and Peasant', Edgar himself wrote almost daily. Far from social snippeting, his column was often an account of a single experience that read like an adventure, observed through a fresh and original eye: perhaps a meal with a celebrity, a day at the races, a ceremonial occasion or (more than once) simply the passing scene. Edgar could be effusive: 'Oh, London!' he began once. 'I was drunk with the joy of you yesterday. Drunk with the bliss of being alive in London in May. It is a city of blossom and fresh green leaf. A city of sunshine and massed tulips. And also this week a city of expectancy...'[34] It was Edgar, as Hickey, who first spotted that the King's Road in Chelsea would become the highway of a new youth culture.

Edgar's Hickey framed a small, closed world, but the column caught the wide-eyed optimism of post-war Britain. It was redolent of a village newsletter, with its emphasis on money and aristocrats, tradition and a static social hierarchy. Lord Beaverbrook was delighted. 'He said you seemed to be having a wonderful time meeting all these people,' Christiansen reported to Edgar, 'and that the enjoyment came through. He said you were the first columnist he had had who seemed to like people. To tell you the truth, I was surprised the old man liked you liking people.'[35]

Under Edgar, the column crackled with names. Archbishop Makarios of Cyprus, television personality Gilbert Harding, conductor Sir Malcolm Sargent and former Prime Minister Clement Attlee seem staid subjects by modern standards, but Hickey regaled Britain with the minutiae of their lives. 'Met Eva Bartok at a preview of her new film *Special Delivery*,' he trilled after one of his more glamorous assignments. 'And since I hadn't seen her with Denholm Elliott before, I had this picture taken.'[36] He chronicled the butterfly-dance of a new generation of young royals. 'Gay 18 year old Princess Alexandra had quite a night out in wedding-happy Lisbon,'[37] Edgar reported in a front-page Hickey dispatch in February 1955. In November, following Princess Margaret's decision to break off her engagement to Peter Townsend, Hickey peered into his crystal ball. 'You will be telling the story of Princess Margaret and Peter Townsend not just this year, not just next year: you will tell it to your children as they grow up. You will, some of you, tell it to your grand-children when the new century comes in.'[38]

He was right. But the Queen's glamorous younger sister and the gossip-hounds of Fleet Street had not yet finished with each other.

13

The Princess and *Queen*

In February 1960, Princess Margaret, then twenty-nine, announced her engagement to Anthony Armstrong-Jones, a fashionable young photographer who had friends in Fleet Street. For all their fevered endeavours, not one gossip columnist had managed to detect so much as a whiff of what would be one of the biggest royal stories of the decade. The couple's courtship had been conducted in total secrecy, and they had become privately engaged the previous December. The betrothal, when it was formally announced, took everyone by surprise, including the newspapers. The gossip columnists were ridiculed for failing to break the news before the entire world knew. 'What a sell for the Press,' crowed Harold Nicolson, 'who missed the scoop!'[1] It was indeed a moment of exquisite satisfaction for the British Establishment, which took private delight in the public discomfiture of hackdom. 'One pleasing feature of the engagement,' purred the anonymous writer of the *Annual Register*, the po-faced logbook of British official life, 'was that the gossip writers of the press, who had so often pried so intrusively into Princess Margaret's private affairs, had entirely failed to forecast the event.'[2] Such *schadenfreude* was to prove sadly misplaced. Fleet Street's tattlers may have slunk away but they were, as the *Daily Mail*'s Bernard Levin recalled, 'from the moment of this exposure of their missed scoop determined to have their revenge'.[3]

For years, Princess Margaret had conducted a highly public affair with Group Captain Peter Townsend, a dashingly handsome Battle of Britain hero who joined the royal household during the war and became equerry to her father, King George VI. The fact that Townsend was married with two children, and lived with his wife near Windsor Castle, had caught the attention of the press in the autumn of 1948 when he and the Princess danced at an official function in Amsterdam until three in the morning. Townsend divorced his wife in 1952, and by the following summer he and the Princess were being 'romantically linked' in the London gossip columns, even though, apparently to discourage the affair, Townsend had been given a diplomatic posting in Brussels. Despite this, the couple's romance blossomed to the point at which marriage was a distinct possibility. Only after the intervention of the Archbishop of Canterbury did Margaret, 'mindful of the Church's teaching' on divorce, break it off. Now, five years later, with the Princess finally apparently set to marry not only a commoner but a man with a real, if raffish, career, Britain's stuffily grand royal family appeared ready to take a great leap forward into the modern world.

But no sooner had the royal engagement been announced than there came the unmistakable murmurs of muttered dissent. They began in the 'William Hickey' column in the *Daily Express* and concerned the groom's choice of best man, Jeremy Fry. In the finest whispering tradition of the gossip column, Hickey leaked the odour of suspicion, putting Fleet Street on red alert and causing the newspapers to wrestle with the dilemma of whether or not to tell the nation about something in Fry's past that might cause embarrassment all round. Someone had tipped Hickey off that eight years earlier, Fry, then in his late twenties, had been convicted of a homosexual offence in London. Hickey asked Buckingham Palace if the royal family knew about this, and received a lips-pursed 'no comment' in response. But within a matter of hours, Fry announced he was withdrawing as best man, 'on doctor's advice'. Hickey, who had predicted Fry's withdrawal because 'he had not really recovered from a severe bout of jaundice', peered again into his crystal ball: 'I see Prince Philip, eyes glinting. He seems to be rather upset about something. Who is this? It looks rather like Commander Richard Colville, Palace press secretary. He is scolding everyone in sight. Enter Tony Armstrong-Jones. Unhappy and perplexed'.[4] Fry, a member of the wealthy chocolate family, was on a skiing holiday in Switzerland when he was abruptly ordered home by the Palace to convalesce following a genuine attack of jaundice. At a stroke, he was dumped as best man, but the public remained in the dark.

When the news finally broke the following Sunday with the full unexpurgated story in the *People* – THE PALACE AND THE BEST MAN: HOW AN EMBARRASSING SITUATION FOR THE ROYAL FAMILY HAS BEEN ENDED –

the clamour of outraged morality, as playwright John Osborne recorded, was deafening, and threatened to become an issue of constitutional proportions.[5] In the event, one embarrassing situation was followed by another: several Scandinavian royals said they couldn't attend the wedding in May because of previous engagements, prompting much speculation that something was wrong. Even the republican *Guardian*, dismissing this as nothing more than 'healthy Hanoverian gossip', detected a spirit of 'spite for spite's sake – perhaps the obverse of gush for the sake of gush'.[6] Certainly, having toppled Jeremy Fry, the triumphant gossip columnists could wave aloft an unusually distinguished scalp, but if they felt their retaliation settled a score with the British Establishment, they were wrong. The Fry affair merely served as the preamble to the biggest upset ever experienced in London's gossip world. And the William Hickey page would turn out to be one of the bloodiest casualties.

The Fry fiasco was classic Hickey fare. Royalty, wealth, success (Jeremy Fry was making a fortune on his own account, as an entrepreneurial engineer) and sexual illicitness in a milieu of upper-class toffs: it had all the ingredients for a vintage Hickey parable. It offered the millions of *Express* readers in 'never had it so good' Britain a glimpse of a life to which they might aspire. The newspaper historian A. C. H. Smith has likened Hickey's world to the 'charmed spectacle'[7] defined by the Victorian constitutionalist Walter Bagehot a century before, offering readers a 'theatrical show of society' to compare with their own humdrum lifestyles.[8] Smith outlined the small, closed cardboard world that Hickey created, a parallel universe to the real one, populated by royals, aristocrats, the ruling and governing elite, and anyone with money. Of course it also included the raggle-taggle legions of starlets, fashion models and their leering escorts who had become public figures only because they were written about in gossip columns: 'a shadow society [in which] Hickey people, at work and play, enjoy a power over their own style of life undreamed of by other classes'.[9] No sooner had Hickey and his cohorts wiped Fry's blood from their knives than their shadow society was exposed as a sham and their methods of gossip-gathering denounced as outrageous and intrusive.

Their nemesis was Jocelyn Stevens, the well-connected owner of *Queen* magazine who, as a wealthy young playboy, figured in gossip columns throughout the 1950s. He hated them, as did his friends who, as Stevens explained, 'were being almost daily rubbished by these columnists using their favourite weapons of intrusion and inaccuracy'.[10] As the campaign against Jeremy Fry gathered momentum in late March 1960, Stevens assembled a seven-page feature in *Queen* lacerating the gossip writers as 'The Friendless Ones'. 'They go where they are not asked,' Stevens began. 'They live in a world which exists only in their fertile imaginations; they are supplied with information by your friends; they have a language, a code, an attitude as unreal as the news they deal in.'[11] But having put the story together, Stevens hit a snag. His lawyers advised him not to sign it because he risked being charged with malice. Stevens immediately hit on the idea of persuading *Queen*'s 28-year-old theatre critic, Penelope Gilliatt, to sign the feature. He persuaded, she signed. This single broadside became the most remarkable and influential journalistic campaign of the 1960s, and a landmark in the decade's swinging media culture.

Masquerading as the blameless Mrs Gilliatt ('she had never appeared in a gossip column,'[12] he explained), Stevens lambasted the gossip-grubbers for a want of ethics, a limitless effrontery disguised as the public's right to know and a know-all manner. He tore open the seedy way in which their informants passed on snippets of tittle-tattle in exchange for money, and scoffed at the PR men who, for a fee, specialized in 'creating' gossip-column characters. Stevens denounced the grubbing methods of Hickey in the *Express* and his (equally mythical) rival Paul Tanfield in the *Daily Mail* as brazen, ingenious and practically invincible. If harassment and betrayed confidences failed to drag a story from one of their victims, there were back-door methods: children cornered and questioned, neighbours and colleagues bribed, subterfuges devised, bullying, impertinence – anything for a line or a quote. 'The tenacity and fatuity of the gossip columnist on the scent of his gossip,' foamed Stevens, 'provides a new variant of Oscar Wilde's view of hunting: the unbeatable in pursuit of the unspeakably dull.' But beyond the journalistic knockabout, Stevens articulated an altogether more serious concern: that the illusory, glamorous world of such columns was socially mischievous. 'There is a point where people's natural taste for small-talk can be exploited and perverted,' Stevens declared, 'and a good many of our gossip columns are way over the line:

their assumptions are jaundiced, materialist and smug, and the picture of the world that they project is morally as well as factually dishonest.'

Stevens illustrated his argument with cruelly drawn vignettes of various gossip reporters, reserving particular bile for Peter Baker (alias William Hickey) – 'decidedly touchy [with] a grand sense of his own importance' – and Alan Gardner, editor of the *Mail's* 'Paul Tanfield' page: 'a florid-faced little man who specialises in broken marriages, lost jobs and petty rows in the film world,' snorted Stevens. 'He noses out failure with the same single-minded concentration that Hickey brings to the pursuit of success.'[13]

On the day *Queen* went to press, Jocelyn Stevens received a frantic telephone call from Penelope Gilliatt to say that her husband, Dr Roger Gilliatt, a consultant neurologist, had accepted Tony Armstrong-Jones's invitation to replace Jeremy Fry as best man at the wedding. 'You must stop the feature,' she said. Stevens told her it was too late. By the time Princess Margaret walked down the aisle at Westminster Abbey three weeks later, all the columnists exposed by *Queen* magazine had been fired.

The *Mail's* editor, William Hardcastle, who later became the first presenter of BBC Radio's *The World at One*, went further than his rivals, not only sacking Alan Gardner but replacing the 'Tanfield' column altogether two years later with a new gossip feature named, like Hickey, after another historical diarist, Charles Greville. Hardcastle and the paper's owner, Lord Rothermere, signed up Quentin Crewe, *Queen's* assistant editor, who agreed to take the column on provided he could ignore royalty, divorces, family rows, pregnancies and other assorted misfortunes. His criterion was one of intelligent interest. But such a lofty aspiration was difficult to meet; compared with Hickey, who was still starstruck, the struggling newcomer sounded earnest and lacking in humour. Old hands at the *Mail* pressed for more to interest women, more toffs and more scandal from the Chelsea set; and before long even Hardcastle was pleading with Crewe to lighten up. After a row about a picture of Princess Alexandra, Hardcastle fired him on the spot, but Crewe returned, at Rothermere's insistence. Shortly afterwards William Hardcastle himself left the paper, followed for a second time by Crewe, who was unhappy at being moved from the 'Greville' page by Hardcastle's replacement, Mike Randall. Reflecting years later on what went wrong, Quentin Crewe admitted that he had failed to find a real voice for Charles Greville. 'Much of the trouble lay in the near impossibility of shaking off the old patterns or rather the expectation of them,' he wrote. 'In eschewing the fabric of a popular newspaper's gossip column, we had nothing to build with that might not perfectly well have appeared on other pages, in the news columns or among the features.'[14]

While London started to swing, gossip writers sought to change with the liberating mood of the 1960s. The Jeremy Fry affair was a watershed, marking the beginning of the end for the old-fashioned gossip column with its nose, as well as its eye, to the keyhole. 'It was absolutely terrible,' recalled Nicholas Tomalin, who left the 'Hickey' column shortly before the Fry affair. 'There I was, with Gaitskellite pretensions and with terribly high principles and guilt about the integrity of journalism, going along to lunch after lunch to talk to corrupt little dollies who whipped out their notebooks to tell me the news of the latest divorces in high places. They sold their friends for a free lunch and anything for a few quid... Very nasty.'[15]

Both the *Mail* and the *Express,* the two big mid-market titles, abandoned their penchant for prying open the intimate details of private lives, and turned instead to the altogether more wholesome, if trivial, fads and fancies of the age. But just as this fresh wind seemed to be blowing away the unsavoury whiffs of Fleet Street's inveterate keyhole peepers, a few cryptic lines sown in the glossy *Queen* magazine's gossip column in the high summer of 1962 were destined to reap the greatest political whirlwind of the age.

The item appeared in the week that John Profumo, the war minister in Macmillan's Conservative government, had threatened to resign over the scrapping of the Blue Water missile project. What appeared in *Queen* wasn't a paragraph, or even a sentence, merely a fragment, but it packed all the power of a nuclear device. It was written by the magazine's associate editor, Robin Douglas-Home, nephew of the Foreign Secretary (and later Prime Minister) Lord Home. As a member of Princess Margaret's social set, Douglas-Home had impeccable Establishment connections and contacts, and he kept his ear as close to the ground as any gossip writer in London for his regular column headed 'Sentences I'd Like to Hear the End of'. On the last day of July, he ran these puzzling (if seemingly innocuous) words: '...called in MI5 because every time the chauffeur-driven Zil drew up at her *front* door, out of the *back* door into a chaffeur-driven Humber slipped...'[16]

No one knows who whispered this story to Douglas-Home (he swallowed a suicidal overdose of pills in 1968, when he was thirty-six). It may have been someone in the swinging Chelsea set, with whom he mixed, or he may have heard it from an anonymous source on the telephone. It's possible that it came from Stephen Ward himself, a characteristic indiscretion rather than a deliberate leak. The point was that, although the tale was getting on for a year old, it was true, or at least the thrust of it was; some of the detail was not.

In the summer of 1961, Jack Profumo, then forty-eight, conducted an extramarital affair with Christine Keeler, a call-girl of twenty who was also sleeping with Russian spy Yevgeny Ivanov, the assistant naval attaché at the Soviet embassy in London. Their various toings and froings at a flat in Wimpole Mews (with Captain Ivanov driving his limousine himself, Profumo not in his ministerial Humber but at the wheel of his own Mini) promised all the ingredients of high farce. The paths of a senior British cabinet minister and the Russian spy must have crossed, or very nearly, during the few short weeks in which Miss Keeler was seeing both men. This ragged little wisp of gossip, with neither a beginning nor an end, would eventually weave the biggest scandal story of the 1960s, a tale of high jinks in high places, with illicit sex, spies, political intrigue, crime, passion, lies and the law all bubbling in the stew together. In their reinvestigation of the affair in the 1980s, Anthony Summers and Stephen Dorril pointed out that Ward was appalled when the newspapers finally broke the story, and tried desperately to protect Profumo from exposure. Whoever blabbed to Douglas-Home handed him the most devastatingly accurate morsel of scandal in gossip-column history.

Macmillan's government was already twitchy when *Queen* set its story afloat. Two major espionage cases, the Portland spy ring and the Vassall affair, were still fresh in the memory. In the Vassall case, two newspaper reporters had been jailed for contempt of court for refusing to reveal their sources, and relations between Fleet Street and Whitehall were in low water. But what followed changed them entirely. The *News of the World* was already investigating a high-class call-girl ring used by top people, organized by a fashionable but dissolute West End osteopath, Stephen

Ward. Ward, an indiscreet man, boasted openly to journalists about his flamboyant sex life, in particular the wild parties he threw at his country cottage, rented from Lord Astor on his estate at Cliveden. The *News of the World*'s crime reporter Peter Earle had heard about Ward, and had put together a dossier based on what he had been told about Keeler and her friend, Mandy Rice-Davies. So when the paper's chairman Sir William Carr dropped into the editor's room, shut the door carefully and checked behind the curtains before whispering: 'Make some very discreet inquiries about a scandal involving a girl and a minister,' Stafford Somerfield could reply that he already had.[17] He reached into his desk drawer and produced Earle's 3,000-word memo on the case.

The affair between Profumo and Keeler began when they met at one of Ward's Cliveden weekends in July 1961, and was soon picked up by the British intelligence service, MI5. They prompted the cabinet secretary, Sir Norman Brook, to speak to Profumo, warning him of the potential risks, but although Profumo wrote Keeler a hastily scribbled note on War Office stationery, fobbing her off ('Darling,' it began, and it was signed 'Love J'), it wasn't until December that the affair was finally ended. The world might never have heard anything of it – despite the encrypted hint dropped by *Queen* in its gossip column the following summer – but for a violent incident in December 1962 outside Ward's flat, when one of Keeler's spurned West Indian lovers, Johnny Edgecombe, blasted the front door with a revolver. When Ward asked her to leave, Keeler felt threatened and vulnerable, and poured out her tale of sexual and political intrigue to a circle of Ward's associates, claiming that Ward had asked her to pump Profumo for a delivery date of nuclear warheads to West Germany. When a former Labour MP, John Lewis, heard this tale, he passed it on to George Wigg, another Labour MP and an expert on defence issues; Wigg had been humiliated in Parliament by Profumo and saw his chance to take his revenge. But as Wigg began to compile a dossier on the affair, Keeler started talking to the newspapers. In January 1963, with the help of one of Ward's journalist friends, Paul Mann, she gave the tabloid *Sunday Pictorial* all the intimate details of her affair with Profumo, and claimed that the minister had left himself open to 'the worst type of blackmail – the blackmail of a spy'.[18] The paper offered her £1,000 for the story and Profumo's 'Darling' letter. Although Keeler agreed to the deal, Ward intervened and managed to persuade the *Pictorial* to drop the story, claiming that it contained material inaccuracies and would inevitably attract a major libel suit.

The fear of writs kept all the papers quiet, even though by now both Fleet Street and Westminster were buzzing with rumours. Then, early in March, an obscure weekly newsletter, *Westminster Confidential,* run by the expatriate American journalist Andrew Roth, ran a thinly veiled account of the scandal, mentioning 'a letter, apparently signed "Jack", on the stationery of the Secretary for W–r'.[19] Most of Roth's readers were MPs, so the affair soon became common knowledge in Parliament. Roth had apparently been fed this juicy morsel of gossip by a right-wing Tory MP, Henry Kerby, a former MI6 officer then employed by MI5 as a parliamentary informant.[20] When Johnny Edgecombe's trial opened at the Old Bailey a few days later, he was charged with the attempted murder of Christine Keeler, but Keeler herself had vanished, fuelling speculation that she had been pressurized to keep quiet.

The dam could not hold. Using parliamentary privilege, which protected him from libel writs, George Wigg rose to his feet in the Commons and, without naming Profumo, challenged the Conservatives to deny rumours involving 'a member of the government front bench'. Within hours, Profumo had been forced to the House to make a personal statement, a device that, by convention, put him on implicit trust to tell the truth. He lied. He acknowledged meeting Keeler on various occasions between July and December 1961, but explicitly denied an affair with the fateful phrase: 'There was no impropriety whatsoever...' The Prime Minister Harold Macmillan, while harbouring private doubts, took Profumo at his word. George Wigg was less forgiving and went on BBC Television's *Panorama* programme to allege that Ivanov and Ward were security risks. As the police continued to probe, Ward became an increasingly isolated figure, abandoned by his friends and associates and struggling to rescue his dwindling osteopathy practice. He frantically tried to convince assorted politicians of his innocence, writing to the Home Secretary and the Labour leader Harold Wilson, and claiming that Profumo was lying about the nature of his relationship with Keeler. At Wilson's request, Macmillan agreed to set up a government inquiry into the security implications of the affair, but when Profumo cut short a foreign holiday to give evidence, he realized the game was up. In early June he resigned, admitting in a letter to Macmillan that he had lied.

The press, now unfettered, hit all the buttons at once. For days, the papers were awash with stories about the affair and about the unsavoury goings-on in London high society. Everything that Fleet Street had held back, for fear of a rerun of the Vassall case, was now (as one observer put it) 'splashed safely, and with a high sense of vindication, across the front pages. The British reading classes lapped it up.'[21] To add still further spice, there was the trial of Keeler's second black lover, Lucky Gordon, who was charged with assaulting her; the arrest and trial of Stephen Ward himself for living off the earnings of prostitution; and the appearance in the *News of the World* of Keeler's 'confessions', for which the paper had paid £23,000. Profumo himself had gone, but the government came under increased pressure for failing to act sooner. An inquiry by Lord Denning into the security aspects of the Profumo affair, published in September, concluded that there had been no security leaks and blamed the scandal on Stephen Ward and a hysterical press. Nevertheless, Profumo's resignation and disgrace led to the government's downfall in the 1964 general election, engulfed by a landslide that had been started by a single tiny pebble of gossip.

Although Fleet Street had more than an inkling of the scandal from the outset, alerted by the paragraph in *Queen*, the newspapers cowered in the face of legal threats from Profumo and his advisers. The *Sunday Pictorial* had Keeler's version at an early stage, initialled by Keeler herself, page by page, as the paper's reporters wrought her hesitant recollections into tabloid prose. The *News of the World* knew the gist of it, since Keeler had gone there from the *Pictorial* in the hope of a better offer, only to be told the paper wasn't interested in an auction for the story. It was only when George Wigg drove enough of the story into the public domain, shielded by parliamentary privilege, that the press took its cue. Wigg said that every MP and journalist at Westminster had heard the rumours, but the papers had hitherto shown themselves willing only to wound, not to kill. 'These great press lords,' he went on, 'these men who control the great instruments of public opinion and of power, do not have the guts to discharge the duty that they are now claiming for themselves.'[22] In fact, less than a week earlier, Beaverbrook's *Daily Express* had ventured to link Profumo and Keeler by splitting its front page between an (erroneous) splash story about the minister's offer to resign, and a big, three-column pouting photograph of Keeler over the story of her disappearance as a witness in the Edgecombe trial. When an enraged Macmillan telephoned Beaverbrook at home to complain, Beaverbrook explained that as he was an old man, no one at the *Express* took any notice of him any more. Having fobbed off the Prime Minister, Beaverbrook telephoned the *Express* office and congratulated the editor. 'It was a fine front page today,' he barked. 'Give us more of that.'[23]

It was all very well for Wigg to bait the press for its gutlessness. But the early 1960s had been traumatic times, with the *Daily Telegraph* and the *Daily Mail* ordered to pay record libel damages over articles published in July 1961 about a fraud squad investigation into a firm run by one John Lewis, the same ex-Labour MP to whom Christine Keeler was to tell her lurid tale about Profumo. There was a new fearfulness about running exposés, and a greater inclination to camouflage alleged wrongdoing in encrypted innuendo and, of course, gossip items. The government had been gravely embarrassed by the Vassall spy case, which had just ended with the jailing of two journalists for refusing to name their sources, so what was the *Sunday Pictorial* to do with Keeler's story? The pressure on them grew in March, with Andrew Roth's piece in *Westminster Confidential*; some journalists suspected it might be a trap to lure Fleet Street into printing it. THAT WAS THE GOVERNMENT THAT WAS! ran the headline, a parody of David Frost's new TV satire show. It detailed the rumour, by now somewhat embellished, of how two girls had been pitched into the limelight because of a shooting incident involving a West Indian, and how the story had been offered to two Sunday papers. One of the choicest bits of the story, it went on, was the letter signed 'Jack'.[24] It was incendiary stuff, but no one in Fleet Street was yet ready to put a spark to the tinder. It was only Keeler's disappearance at the start of the Edgecombe trial in mid-March that finally presented the papers with an opportunity to thrust her into the public glare. Even then, only the *Express* dared to hint at her links with Profumo, juxtaposing her picture with the (apparently unrelated) story about the minister's offer to resign. Of the paper's 13 million readers, scarcely a few hundred, mostly in London's West End, would have understood the message encoded in the *Express*'s front page. It was a kind of secret signal, to show (even if only to a handful of people) that the paper really did know of the link between the 'model' and the minister.

Readers of the recently launched satirical magazine *Private Eye* might have expected the inside track on such a political scandal, smacking of sex, security and Establishment hypocrisy. Although circulation more than doubled in the 'Profumo summer' of 1963, the magazine actually offered very few insights into the story. There was a double-spread drawn by cartoonist Timothy Birdsall, headed 'The Last Days of Macmillan' and showing the Prime Minister as a Roman emperor, lying by a swimming pool attended by naked girls. Journalists were portrayed as a gaggle of geese, but the real clue lay in the motto above the pool ('Per Wardua ad Astor'), a touch that, however puzzling to the uninitiated, brought Stephen Ward himself scurrying into the *Eye*'s Soho offices in the mistaken belief that the magazine had discovered the full story. According to the *Eye*'s historian, Patrick Marnham, although Ward did brief the editor, Richard Ingrams, and managing director, Tony Rushton, about what was going on, 'very little of it appeared in the subsequent paper'.[25] The magazine contented itself with largely cryptic references to Keeler ('Miss Gaye Funloving, the 21 year old "model"'), Ivanov ('Bolokhov'), Lord Astor and Profumo himself (mentioned variously as 'Mr Montesi' or 'Profano'). As Marnham explained, by referring to the rumours in this way *Private Eye* was saying nothing that anyone could understand unless they had already heard the rumours themselves, 'but it was enough that those who had heard them could find this written confirmation, however garbled, for the magazine to win its first reputation as an important source of gossip'.[26] Everyone else, of course, remained as flummoxed as ever.

Imperceptibly, however, Profumo's lie was beginning to break the surface. When Edgecombe's trial ended (he received seven years' imprisonment on an amended charge of possessing a pistol with intent to endanger life), the *Daily Sketch* interviewed the girl who had not got away, Keeler's friend Mandy Rice-Davies. Her ghosted account of 'the top-drawer life we had been leading among the Peers and the VIPs' concealed Profumo's identity, but spoke of a 'well-known man [who] brought a huge bottle of perfume, swathed in wrappers, from Fortnum and Mason's'.[27] It was as though the paper was nervously clearing its throat, but afraid to speak. No matter what Fleet Street gossip said, in the fearful climate of the day, no newspaper lawyer was going to risk the unsubstantiated word of a wide-eyed nineteen-year-old against that of a government minister.

Their newspapers' judgment seemed vindicated when, a few days later, Profumo made his personal statement to MPs in which he flatly denied sleeping with Christine Keeler. But the pressure built up further when the missing model turned up on holiday in Spain and signed a contract with the *Daily Express*. For £1,400, she unfolded the story of her disappearance and posed for the paper's photographer in leather boots, short skirt and tight sweater. Her account of her meetings with Profumo squared blamelessly with his. 'I have met Mr Profumo on several occasions,' she said. 'He was most courteous and gentlemanly...'[28] The whole effect was like a jigsaw, jerkily put together piece by piece. And even when Keeler's confessions in the *News of the World* seemed to reveal the full, complete unsavoury picture, they also had the effect of triggering still more rumours, just as lurid, of an expensive high-class call-girl ring, involving (it was said) at least four cabinet ministers, a member of the royal family and organized orgies of unheard-of depravity.

Under the heading 'Profumo Case Rocking Palace Set', the *Washington Post*'s gossip writer, Dorothy Kilgallen, disclosed that police searching the flat of one of the people in the case had found a photograph showing a key figure frolicking with a group of women. 'All were nude except for the gentleman in the picture who was wearing an apron. And this is a man who has been on extremely friendly terms with the very proper Queen and members of her immediate family!' squealed Kilgallen. The Americans, alerted by one New York paper that the Profumo–Keeler affair apparently involved '[o]ne of the biggest names in American politics',[29] were looking on in goggle-eyed amazement. *Newsweek*, trumpeting 'The New Pornocracy', said the affair had lifted the lid on 'a sort of World Parliament of prostitutes, whore-mongers, sex deviates, orgy-prone highbinders, and libidinous Soviet agents'.[30] Britain's *Daily Mirror*, traditional guardian of working-class morality, for once sounded an all-inclusive blast, with a headline that demanded to know WHAT THE HELL IS GOING ON IN THIS COUNTRY?

But if Fleet Street's gossipmongers really were little more than a squalid crew of keyhole-peepers, they had evidently been peeping through the wrong keyholes. They should, and could, have nailed this story. Some of the principal characters were well known to the gossip columnists, not least Profumo himself, whose wedding on New Year's Eve in 1954 to the beautiful actress Valerie Hobson was widely covered by the diaries of the day. 'The Profumos had an almost ostentatiously Quiet Wedding,' purred one gossip writer, 'no film stars, no producers, no directors, no political names'.[31] This was the kind of Fleet Street fluff fed to millions of gossip readers every day by writers trying to create the illusion of easy familiarity with the starry world of high society. But if the columnists had no reason to suspect Profumo of anything racier than a roving eye, they should have known that Stephen Ward was an altogether darker character.

Ward had flitted on the London social scene throughout the 1950s, and knew and mingled with several Fleet Street journalists. He had been linked with rumours of a Mayfair call-girl ring as early as 1951, when the *Daily Express* was tipped off, almost certainly by John Lewis, then an ambitious Labour MP, who hated Ward for having seduced his wife. One of Ward's media cronies, Freddy Mullally, a former Sunday newspaper reporter turned PR man, stormed into the *Express* editor's office and persuaded him to drop the investigation. Not long after this, Ward's teenage protégée, Vickie Martin, whom he had befriended while sheltering from the rain in a West End shop doorway, was launched into Mayfair society with much press ballyhoo, becoming not only the toast of London but the darling of the gossip writers, who hailed her as 'the Golden Girl', 'the Girl from Nowhere' and 'the Girl with No Past'. By the time she was killed in a car crash in 1955, Ward was hobnobbing with the raffish Lord Astor, who was so impressed with Ward's healing hands on his injured back that he recommended the osteopath to his wide circle of society friends. As Ward's practice flourished, he became a frequent guest at Astor's country house, Cliveden, and for a peppercorn rent of £1 a year was allowed the use of the estate cottage in return for being on call if Astor or his guests needed the services of an osteopath. 'The cottage is big enough to entertain Ward's friends,' one Fleet Street gossip writer reported, 'and what a lovely line they can shoot at dinner parties . . . the Cliveden tag makes the Ward retreat unbeatable in the U-stakes!'[32]

Ward's fashionable contacts were extended further still when he joined the men-only Thursday Club, founded by the young society photographer Baron Nahum. Politicians, Fleet Street editors and journalists, businessmen, tycoons and even royalty (Prince Philip was a member) met each Thursday at Wheeler's Oyster Bar in Soho to enjoy a good lunch, conversation and gossip. Risqué stories about women were bandied about, and Ward's reputation as the escort of a string of London's most beautiful girls flourished.

Undoubtedly, Ward's highest-placed contact in Fleet Street was Sir Colin Coote, then editor of the *Daily Telegraph*, whom Ward had treated for chronic lumbago. Coote had turned from a patient into a friend, inviting Ward to make up a four at bridge, and had hired him not as an osteopath but as an illustrator for his paper after seeing some portraits Ward had sketched for a magazine. In 1960, when Ward hit on the idea of visiting Moscow to draw the Soviet political leaders, he sought Coote's help in obtaining a visa. Over lunch at the Garrick Club, Coote introduced Ward to Captain Ivanov, a newly arrived Soviet diplomat who had recently toured the *Telegraph* offices on a routine courtesy call. The two young men hit it off at once, and Ward introduced Ivanov to his circle of friends. Perhaps, with all these high-powered contacts and acquaintances in the social, political and media worlds, it was hardly surprising that Stephen Ward might confidently have considered himself scandal-proof.

Just a few weeks after that first murmur in the *Queen* gossip column, Ward was at the glittering opening of John Aspinall's Clermont Club, at which his reputation as an osteopath who procured girls for wealthy clients was being openly discussed. Names were being bandied about, including those of Profumo and Keeler, when another government minister, Christopher Soames, chimed in: 'So what? At least it's a girl. You too could have her for five pounds a go.' As Phillip Knightley and Caroline Kennedy put it in their investigation of the affair, '[i]f a senior Minister in Macmillan's Government knew of Profumo's relationship with Christine Keeler, how much longer could it be kept from the public?'[33] Not long, as it turned out. Two months later, Fleet Street was abuzz with rumours, and MI5 was hearing how Keeler had hawked her story round the Sunday papers.

With all the opportunities the newspapers had to gather not just gossip but hard facts about the twilight world of Stephen Ward,

Profumo's humiliating confession that he had lied about his relationship with Christine Keeler should have been Fleet Street's finest hour. But the most they could claim was that they had known the story all along. Only the tiny one-man newsletter *Westminster Confidential* could boast of having broken the story ahead of the field. The mainstream press had sat on the story, afraid to run with it in the post-Vassall climate of intimidation, and only joined in the general clamour of vindication when Keeler's story broke in the *News of the World*. These were feverish months in Fleet Street, with the hot breath of scandal blowing from several directions at once. On top of the Profumo–Keeler affair came gossip that more well-known people in public life were about to be named in two loosely related stories of depravity in high society. Keeler herself had lifted the lid on a tale about an orgy in London at which one distinguished male guest waited on the others clad only in a frilly apron and a black mask. Meanwhile, there was growing speculation about the identity of a man whose headless photograph had featured in the sensational divorce of the Duke and Duchess of Argyll, a case heard in Edinburgh that spring. 'The more rich and influential people I met,' Keeler mused, 'the more amazed I was at their private lives.'[34] It was hardly surprising, in such an overheated climate, that panic gripped the ranks of the British Establishment.

As a beautiful young debutante (she was Deb of the Year in 1930), Margaret Whigham was gossip-column fodder throughout the 1930s. She knew the three most popular columnists of the day, Driberg as Hickey, the Marquis of Donegall and Lord Castlerosse, who all went to the same parties. 'It is amazing,' reported the *Sunday Chronicle*, 'how she had leapt into the forefront of every social event of consequence during the past twelve months... she has suddenly become the most photographed girl in the country.'[35] However, the Polaroid photograph that featured in her divorce was not that of a sparkling ingénue but a middle-aged woman, naked except for a three-stranded pearl necklace, performing fellatio on an unidentified man, whose head had been cropped from the picture. The woman was plainly the Duchess of Argyll (as she had become in 1951, when she divorced her first husband), but whoever the headless man was, expert anatomical evidence demonstrated that it certainly wasn't the Duke. The couple's marriage had disintegrated because the Duchess relished a hectic social life, while the Duke (as his wife put it) just enjoyed 'poking around in his bloody garden'. Granting the Duke his divorce in a blistering 40,000-word judgment that took four and a half hours to deliver, Lord Wheatley described the Duchess as 'a completely promiscuous woman'. The judge found that she had committed adultery with three named men and a fourth unnamed one, the naked and headless man in the photograph.

Putting a name to the mystery suspect became a national pastime, and although the papers refrained from bandying names themselves, they did fan the mood of excited expectation. One name that wafted into the frame of public speculation was that of yet another government minister, Duncan Sandys, the son-in-law of Winston Churchill. At a stormy cabinet meeting on 20 June, Sandys confessed that he was rumoured to be the headless man and, although claiming to be innocent, offered to resign. To clear the air, Sandys persuaded Harold Macmillan to allow him to testify to Lord Denning, the Master of the Rolls, who was looking into the security aspects of the Profumo affair. Denning also examined Christine Keeler's startling tale of a prominent public figure being the man in the black mask who had waited on guests at an orgy while carrying a note that said: 'If my services don't please you, please whip me.' Denning found that, far from being a one-off affair, such exotic parties were regular events, and that while sometimes the masked man's appearance was nothing more than a comic turn, on other occasions it was followed by 'perverted sex orgies' at which 'guests undress and indulge in sexual intercourse one with the other: and indulge in other sexual activities of a vile and revolting nature'.[36]

When the permissive society dawned, it caused an unprecedented moral upheaval among Britain's sexually timid newspapers. The shenanigans of the 1960s forced Fleet Street to redraw boundaries of taste and decency that had remained more or less fixed for over a century. Even so, it was another thirty years before the newspapers ended the guessing game about the infamous headless man. Although Duncan Sandys had been one of the lovers of the Duchess of Argyll, the man in the photograph was not him, we were told, but the swashbuckling Hollywood actor, Douglas Fairbanks Jr.

14

Princely Peccadilloes

Successive Princes of Wales have endured their share of modern media scrutiny, discovering as young men that Fleet Street's searching beam can scour with as much heat as light. After all, they held a title that over seven centuries has gathered around it a penumbra of glamour and romance, that special mystique unique to the office of Prince of Wales that has, for two centuries past, mesmerized the British reading public. If, as Walter Bagehot observed, princely marriages rivet mankind, princely peccadilloes seem every bit as spellbinding. People are transfixed by the doings, particularly the sexual shenanigans, of an heir to the throne waiting in enforced idleness. In the 1970s, Prince Charles was dismayed to find his 'secret' trysts on the royal train with Lady Diana Spencer splashed in the tabloids. Half a century before, his Uncle David, the twentieth century's first Prince of Wales (later Edward VIII), woke to find his pleasure-seeking splattered in the press. 'I see David continues to dance every night & most of the night too,' his father, George V, harrumphed to Queen Mary in August 1925, apparently having peeked at the cheekier newspapers. 'What a pity they should telegraph it every day. People who don't know will begin to think he is either mad or the biggest rake in Europe, such a pity!'[1] Eleven years later, the year that the new King abdicated, the Lord Chief Justice, Lord Hewart, railed against the 'infamous abyss' of personal journalism. This prompted the radical press commentator, Hamilton Fyfe, to compare the proletarian *Daily Mirror* with the hard-boiled New York tabloids, which ran 'pages of ill-natured gossip about [the King] and Mrs Simpson, which, whatever his own desire had been, would have made it impossible for him to stay'. But, as Fyfe pointed out, the King's romancing of a twice-divorced American arguably elevated gossip to the status of news. 'The unwise hushing-up of the affair for so long,' Fyfe reflected, 'had sharpened appetite for any information about it.'[2]

But it was the Victorians nearly a century before who first fired the appetite of the British masses for royal gossip. When, early in the morning after their marriage in 1840, Queen Victoria and Prince Albert were spotted walking in the grounds of Windsor Castle, many of the papers remarked on the brevity of the wedding night. 'Strange that a bridal night should be so short,' commented the diarist Charles Greville, and the royal-watching newshounds even set the tale in verse:

> If *we* were satisfied with lying
> From twelve to eight, I cannot see
> Why meddling fools should now be trying
> To bring discredit upon *me*.[3]

Although such salacious journalistic scrutiny was designed to shock and wound her, the young Queen laughed at such impudence and confounded the prying hacks by quickly falling pregnant with her first child, followed, in short order, by another and another until the royal brood stood at nine. Her eldest son Bertie, the Prince of Wales, soon showed signs of developing a rakehell disposition, to the delight of court gossips and servants who wafted smuts of tittle-tattle towards the ever-attentive royal-watchers on the newspapers.

One of their most productive sources was a teenage chimney-sweep known as Boy Jones. On at least six occasions, he managed to penetrate the defences of Buckingham Palace to hide in the royal apartments for days on end. On his first such foray in December 1840, a few days after the birth of the Princess Royal, Jones was discovered skulking under a sofa in a room adjoining the Queen's bedchamber. Marched in manacles to a neighbouring police station, Jones was questioned by a group of Privy Councillors, who were hurriedly assembled for the purpose and who remarked on his repulsive appearance. 'He repeatedly requested,' *The Times* reported, 'that the police should address him in a becoming manner, and behave towards him as they ought to do to a gentleman anxious to make a noise in the world.'[4] Testifying before a magistrate as Edward Jones, he explained that he had entered the Palace through an unfastened window, hidden for two days in an empty attic, sat on the throne during the night (his fingerprints were found on the arms and an impression of his bottom on the cushions) and had pinched and eaten a meat pie from the royal larder, 'the property of Our Lady the Queen'. Dubbed 'In-I-Go Jones' by a tickled popular press, he was sentenced to three months in the House of Correction, where a regime of treadmill and oakum-picking failed to cool his exploratory ardour. Shortly after his release, he was caught in the Palace again, explaining to a startled royal page that he wanted to see what was going on there 'so that he could write about it'.[5] He was as good as his word, not only tossing scraps of gossip to the papers but contributing squibs to the newly founded *Punch* magazine in the form of spoof court circulars.[6] By mid-century, the papers boasted quasi-royal correspondents accredited at court.

In 1860, when not yet nineteen, the Prince of Wales toured Canada and the United States, giving the New World its first experience of a modern celebrity. Crazed trophy-hunters pilfered items of his clothing; by the time he arrived in New York City, according to one versifier, they had

> Torn his bed-clothes to strips, – every fool keeping one,
> To remember the linen the Prince slept upon.[7]

North America was gripped by Prince of Wales mania, all the more remarkable because the object of it all was a virtual unknown. Hitherto Bertie's parents had kept him firmly out of the public eye. Queen Victoria habitually scooped up and garlanded herself with any pro-royal acclamation, and she resented interlopers, even her own son, muscling in on her act. For years she had sequestered him and suppressed his role; his American tour only went ahead because she found him increasingly intolerable to have at home. Now Bertie burst from his cocoon to become an obsession. The Canadians hailed him and fell at his feet. Newspapers lionized him, and hustlers purloined his picture to endorse advertisements for pork and beans and cider. You couldn't even sit down to a meal in a restaurant, reported one London journalist, without having his portrait loom dimly from beneath the gravy.[8] It was an extraordinary reception for a young man, who was unknown both to the public and to the journalists whose articles paved his progress. Unbriefed and unguided, they knew nothing of his personality, piques or passions; rumours of a grave demeanour, physical delicacy, social ineptitude and an aversion to women were demolished only when the press saw him on the hoof, laughing and joking, sparklingly at ease, especially in the company of pretty girls.

At a gala ball for 3,000 in Boston, the Prince danced with a string of stunning young women, including one nameless beauty described by Kinahan Cornwallis in the *New York Herald* as 'the most lovely girl I ever saw'. After seventeen dances, an exhausted Prince staggered into supper at 1 a.m., murmuring to one Bostonian lovely: 'I don't have half enough of this sort of thing [at home], you know.'[9] But back in London, readers of *The Times* were offered only bleak official accounts of the royal progress, filed by its correspondent Nicholas Woods. Royal tittle-tattle only started to rattle the following year, when Bertie visited Germany, ostensibly to attend the Prussian Army's autumn military manoeuvres. The real purpose of the visit was for Bertie to meet a potential wife, the very young and beautiful Princess Alexandra of Denmark. The prying German press had realized this and had already 'taken it up', as Bertie complained to his mother, while forecasting a rift between the Prussian and British courts if the marriage went ahead. The meeting between the two amorous royals was supposed to be in secret, but thanks to the gossiping papers their cover was blown. 'We were known immediately,' Bertie reported ruefully. The couple regarded each other politely, but it was no love match.

Bertie returned to Cambridge, where he was enrolled as an undergraduate. There, he was not entirely displeased to find that the talk in his circle concerned his recent loss of virginity, while he was on a short training tour with the Grenadier Guards at the Curragh Camp in Kildare. Some of his drunken fellow officers smuggled an 'actress' called Nellie Clifden into the camp and into the Prince's bed. His initiation into the facts of life quickly became the talk of the London clubs, as was the whisper that an appreciative Prince had arranged for Nellie to be spirited to England on his return. The story soon reached the ears of George Byng, the 7th Viscount Torrington, a minor courtier and talkative London barfly who fed titbits of royal gossip to *The Times* under the byline 'Your Windsor Special'. While doing duty as a lord-in-waiting, he mentioned it to the Prince's father Albert, adding that Bertie's dalliance with Nellie explained his reluctance to get engaged to Princess Alexandra. Albert relayed the ruinous news to the Queen, sparing her what she described in her journal as the 'disgusting details';[10] he also turned for advice to the Prince's old mentor, Baron Stockmar, living in Coburg, who could only suck his teeth and confirm that some of the Continental newspapers had already printed stories about Bertie and his Irish 'actress'. The London papers would soon follow suit.

Too distressed to confront his son face to face, Albert sat down and wrote to Bertie 'with a heavy heart upon a subject which has caused me the greatest pain I have yet felt in this life'.[11] The scandal was already the talk of the clubs; Nellie Clifden was making boastful appearances at London dance halls where, apparently to her huge amusement, she was being burlesqued as 'the Princess of Wales'. Worst of all, wrote Albert, what if she were pregnant? No matter that someone else may be the real father, Albert warned Bertie, but were he to deny it

> she can drag you into a Court of Law to force you to own it & there with you in the witness box, she will be able to give before a greedy Multitude disgusting details of your profligacy for the sake of convincing the Jury, yourself cross-examined by a railing indecent attorney and hooted and yelled at by a Lawless Mob! Oh horrible prospect, which this person has in her power, any day to realize! and to break your poor parents' hearts![12]

For the moment, however, the Prince was spared the gossiping pens of Fleet Street. Nevertheless his father's letter came as a jolt, and he realized that he would be forced into marrying Alexandra in order to protect the throne from an ugly public scandal. Bertie expressed remorse, admitting his indiscretion but claiming that the Nellie affair was over. Albert, ailing but determined to spare the Queen further distress by ordering Bertie to Windsor, ordered a special train to take him to Cambridge where, walking together in chill November rain, father and son conducted a heart-to-heart confessional. Bertie promised not to reoffend; Albert confirmed his forgiveness and promised not to persecute the subalterns who had corrupted his son.

On his return to Windsor, Albert's health deteriorated sharply. Bertie was at his father's bedside when he died a few days before Christmas 1861. The heartbroken Queen blamed 'the dreadful affair at Curragh' for Albert's death. The press, whose attention had been diverted by the royal passing as well as by the prospect of war in America, remained silent on the subject of the rampant heir, even though rumours about the Prince of Wales (according to a source at Eton) 'have been freely circulated that [Bertie's] conduct is becoming loose'.[13] Within eighteen months, however, the Prince had married his Danish princess Alexandra, known as Alix, and settled into his new London home at Marlborough House with an annual allowance of £100,000.

With Albert consigned to his mausoleum, the Queen plunged into the deepest mourning. There was little change in Bertie's behaviour. With his wife happily bringing up a growing family, Bertie went on the spree. London by night offered a range of dubious diversions to the young Prince and his companions, wilder members of the aristocracy, young bloods and heavy swells, all eager to escape the confines of Victoria's stuffy court. Bertie's bed-hopping 'Marlborough House Set' was prime gossip fodder for scandal sheets like the short-lived *Tomahawk*, one of Bertie's particular tormentors and a distant precursor of *Private Eye*. Launched in 1867 by Arthur à Beckett, son of one of the founders of *Punch*, *Tomahawk* promised to 'wield a hatchet with a very sharp edge'[14] and guyed the Prince mercilessly over his pleasure-seeking ways. But the Prince took care that none of his circle caused a scandal, knowing that certain papers were constantly on the lookout for spicy royal stories.

The racy tales of high life that did appear seem to have intrigued the public rather than offended them, and fuelled the demand for royal snippets of eye-watering banality. Even the dullest princely activity, as the magazine *Punch* pointed out, became the inevitable target of scribblers. Things would get worse, *Punch* warned him, to the point where he couldn't 'even take a bath without a paragraph being published recording that event, and telling us at what temperature you bathed'. Bertie himself might recoil from the publicity, but it was a burden he had to bear. 'A cat may look at a king,' the magazine observed, 'and a toad may look at a prince.'[15] But in early 1870, it became apparent that Bertie had left the warning unheeded and was breasting deep and dangerous waters; rumours of his indiscretions had already reached the ears of the Queen in far-flung Balmoral, and when the Mordaunt scandal broke they were impossible to hide any longer.

The Mordaunts were socially prominent in London and in Warwickshire, where they had their country seat. Lady Harriett

Mordaunt, the attractive 21-year-old wife of Sir Charles Mordaunt MP, had just given birth to her first child, a daughter, but the baby's vision was impaired and it seemed the little girl might grow up blind. Harriett Mordaunt, mortified and in the throes of profound post-partum depression, blamed herself and tearfully confessed to her husband that he was not the child's father. She had behaved wickedly, Harriett sobbed, and had taken numerous lovers 'often, and in open day'. She named two of the Prince's closest friends, Lord Cole and Sir Frederic Johnstone, as well as Bertie himself. Sir Charles had suspected a liaison between his wife and the Prince ever since the latter had written her a harmless letter some eighteen months before the birth of her child, Violet. Now Harriett Mordaunt suggested that Violet's eye affliction might have been caused by a venereal infection that she had contracted from young Lord Cole. Mordaunt sued for divorce, rifling his wife's escritoire to find her diary and various communications from the Prince of Wales, including a handkerchief, a valentine and a handful of letters. These were leaked, not to one of the mainstream London papers, or even one of the contemporary scandal sheets hawked around the capital, but to the staidly provincial *Birmingham Post,* which risked proceedings for contempt of court by publishing them. In its first mention of what became known as 'The Warwickshire Scandal', the *Post* hinted at its sources, pointing out that 'among those who admit the story to be undeniable are many personal friends of the unfortunate husband.'[16] In fact, the correspondence was perfectly innocuous and had the effect of casting Bertie in an unwontedly favourable light.

Harriett's parents (it was her mother, Lady Louisa Moncrieffe, who famously warned, 'Never comment on a likeness') believed their errant daughter was mad, and had her examined by a series of doctors, one of whom assured them that she was, indeed, insane. Accordingly, a jury found Lady Mordaunt 'utterly unfit' to plead in divorce proceedings, but after interminable legal wranglings – the case holds the record as the most protracted and most expensive in the annals of the English divorce court – Sir Charles finally got his decree, citing only one co-respondent, Lord Cole. Harriett, now socially ruined, lost her looks, ran to fat and found herself pilloried in verses of coarse doggerel:

> This lady's appetite
> It really is enormous,
> But whether right or wrong,
> The papers will inform us.
> She is fond of veal and ham,
> To feed she is a glutton.
> She got tired of Charley's lamb,
> And longed for royal mutton.[17]

The Prince did, in fact, appear in court, but he was not cross-examined and his testimony revealed nothing. He firmly denied that he and Lady Harriett had been improperly familiar, and whilst this assurance was accepted by the Establishment press, there were uneasy rumblings among the radical papers. *Reynolds News* led the assault.

> If the Prince of Wales is an accomplice in bringing dishonour to the homestead of an English gentleman; if he has assisted in rendering an honourable man miserable for life; if unbridled sensuality and lust have led him to violate the laws of honour and hospitality – then such a man, placed in the position he is, should not only be expelled from decent society, but is utterly unfit and unworthy to rule over this country, or even sit in its legislature.[18]

The Mordaunt affair provided the Victorian press with all the spicy ingredients of a Roman holiday: sex, royalty, wealth, intrigue and uncovered correspondence between high-profile members of the leisured classes. The Queen complained in her journal that her son's 'intimate acquaintance with a young married woman' had been 'publicly proclaimed' amid 'an amount of imprudence which cannot but damage him in the eyes of the middle and lower classes, which is to be lamented in these days when the higher classes, in their frivolous, selfish and pleasure-seeking lives, do more to increase the spirit of democracy than anything else'.[19] Harriett herself remained in an asylum for the rest of her life and died in 1906. Many years later, the society hotelier Rosa Lewis, visiting Longleat, paused before a portrait of Violet, Marchioness of Bath, the grand woman that Harriett's little girl had grown to become. The scandal would have blown over, Rosa Lewis declared, had 'certain people' not written letters and if Sir Charles Mordaunt ('the dirty tyke') had observed basic decencies and accepted his wife's adultery without complaint. As the old Duchess of Jermyn Street snappily put it: 'No letters, no lawyers and kiss my baby's bottom.'[20]

While Fleet Street had feasted on the indelicate details of the Mordaunt case, most newspapers refrained from personally criticizing Bertie. But in New York, the Irish journalist Justin McCarthy launched a scathing attack in *Galaxy* magazine on the 'profligate' Prince as 'dull, stingy and coarse', a royal roisterer whose tastes ran not to 'high art' but to 'little theatres where vivacious blondes display their unconcealed attractions'.[21] Bertie was hissed at Ascot as the tide of public scorn rose. The mutterings, once distant, were beginning to surface in the mainstream press, orchestrated by bolder editors and increasingly outspoken journalists, whose barbs and broadsides no longer portrayed Bertie as an heroic young heir but a vain and incompetent hell-raiser. The Prince, however, now in his gay thirties, seemed unabashed, and roistered on. He loved women, he loved horses, and he loved food, drink and cigars, all in extravagant measure. He feared boredom above everything, and when in 1876 events threatened to drag him back to the divorce court witness box in the Aylesford case, at least they furnished a diversion from the dull royal round. This scandal was smothered when Lord Hartington ('Harty Tarty' of the frivolous 'fast' social set that Queen Victoria so despised) threw the Prince's letters to Edith Aylesford into the fire. 'The result,' wrote Bertie's dandy friend, the Earl of Hardwicke, inventor of the polished silk hat, 'is that no Public Scandal will take place.'[22]

Stifling scandal in the papers was critical. As Prince of Wales and society's leader, Bertie continued to conduct numerous discreet affairs, but these were not the casual couplings of twentieth-century permissiveness, rather the result of chess-like strategy and patience and a quicksilver capacity to seize an opportunity. For society women, public scandal, especially of the printed sort, meant social ruin. Avoidance of scandal was the first commandment of society's sexual code; for breaking it there was one penalty and no appeal: social banishment. The Victorian double standard eventually readmitted errant husbands, but no divorced person of either sex could be asked to court. As Anita Leslie, the granddaughter of one of the luminaries of Bertie's Marlborough House set, pointed out, marriage was the cement holding together the entire social edifice. 'To sin in secret was one story,' she explained,

> to shake the home by getting into the newspapers or law courts another. Naturally intent on preserving itself and its good times, Society turned pitilessly on those who tumbled openly into trouble. Behind the few hundreds constituting the Prince's Set lay stern middle-class England, where Puritan tendencies had become solidified. The toiling hungry workers hardly came into the picture. They didn't care if the gentry carried on, all they wanted was enough to eat.[23]

The puritan tendencies of middle-class England were galvanized again in the early autumn of 1890, when the newspapers seized on Bertie's other great recreational penchant – gaming – and fashioned one of the most painfully public scandals of the High Victorian era. Although everyone involved had been sworn to secrecy, rumours of what had gone on at Tranby Croft, the Yorkshire home of wealthy shipowner Arthur Wilson, soon began to trickle out. A Jewish journalist heard the story and sold the details to a paper called the *Pelican*. Edmund Yates, editing the rival *World*, commented enviously, 'You have got hold of a big thing.'[24] It was certainly too big to keep secret. Bertie and some friends had been Wilson's guests during the Doncaster race meeting; to while away an evening, they had played baccarat, which had been ruled illegal because it was a game of chance and not skill. The Prince of Wales ignored such pettifoggery and never travelled without his own personalized baccarat counters. In the course of play at Tranby Croft, one of the Prince's circle, Sir William Gordon-Cumming, a lieutenant-colonel in the Scots Guards who had served in the Zulu wars, had been observed cheating. Several guests saw him, using sleight of hand, slyly increasing his stake as soon as he realized he had won a coup, so multiplying his winnings. From the outset, Gordon-Cumming consistently and indignantly denied the charge, but in a moment of weakness, pressed by the Prince and two other members of the party, he had signed a promise never to play cards again. He explained that he had done this out of desperation to avoid a scandal that would inevitably damage someone and quite possibly the Prince of Wales. Now impossibly compromised, Gordon-Cumming demanded a retraction and apology from his accusers, and when this was refused launched an action for slander against them.

Once again there was the delicious prospect of Bertie being forced to testify on oath in a court of law. The army could have stifled the case by holding an inquiry or court martial, but the fact that Gordon-Cumming had hurried to a solicitor and sought redress through the civil courts removed that option. The Prince blamed the adjutant-general, the army's top legal officer. 'If he had acted promptly and decisively at the beginning,' Bertie complained, 'all this public scandal and especially in the press would have been avoided.'[25] Advised by friends, the Prince was convinced that he had been pitched into the affair through no fault of his own, and was doubly aggrieved because it was mainly his money that the cheating Gordon-Cumming was supposed to have won. At Marlborough House, the Prince's personal secretary, Sir Francis Knollys, egged on his master in attempts to thwart Gordon-Cumming's efforts to obtain a hearing in a civil court. However, this proved counter-productive when articles appeared in the papers at home and abroad, criticizing Bertie and railing at his private card-shuffling cronies.

Many of those present at Tranby Croft had consulted society solicitor George Lewis, to whom the upper classes habitually turned when social or marital disaster threatened. Lewis blamed Gordon-Cumming for trying to prejudice public opinion by giving false and misleading statements to the press, an early example of the black art of spinning. These briefings, which appeared first in the *Hawk*, then in the *World*, *Truth*, the *Star* and other papers, created a public web of intrigue all the more compelling for the fat figure at its centre. 'It is a curious, complicated, ugly fin de siècle drama of the "great" world,' Henry James wrote to Robert Louis Stevenson, 'with the extraordinary stamp of vulgarity on it that is on everything the Prince of Wales has to do with.'[26]

Having been tried in the press for months, the case finally opened in June 1891, with the Prince present throughout the evidence. His own testimony in the witness box was lacklustre, his words mumbled and largely inaudible. As the proceedings dragged on, he became increasingly tense and nervous; there were rumours that Bertie himself was the real cheat, and that Gordon-Cumming was a hapless scapegoat, a victim of a conspiracy, his lawyer insisted, to save the Prince from a public scandal. Both in court and outside, the mood throughout the nine-day trial was in Gordon-Cumming's favour. When the jury found against him, there was angry hissing from the gallery. Bertie was booed by the crowd at Ascot (where he had been betting on horses as the jury deliberated) and he was attacked in the radical press as 'a wastrel and whoremonger' as well as a gambler. Even *The Times* inveighed at length against the future king's devotion to baccarat and the gaming table. As the controversy bubbled on, Queen Victoria fretted about her son's behaviour and its impact on the monarchy, complaining that it was 'the light which has been thrown on his habits which alarms and shocks people so much, for the example is so bad'.[27] Certainly, the Prince's name had been sullied by the Tranby Croft scandal.

In the 1890s it was perhaps Bertie's misfortune to be the first Prince of Wales to endure the close scrutiny of the new and vigorous popular press. His affair with yet another titled married woman, Lady Brooke, had become common knowledge. She had supplanted Lillie Langtry in Bertie's affections, and while Lady Brooke was scarcely the most discreet of mistresses – she was talked about, sniggeringly, as 'the babbling Brooke' – she was undoubtedly a stablilising influence on the future king. By the time Queen Victoria died in 1901, Bertie had mellowed. His old roistering ways had mutated into a private regime of dutiful circumspection, and his life of kingship would be scandal-free. But a new Prince of Wales was waiting in history's wings, to foxtrot his way through one of the most extraordinary royal scandals ever while Fleet Street looked dumbly on.

15

A Perfect Avalanche of Muck and Slime

In November 1936, ten months after the death of Bertie's son King George V, a retired Whitehall mandarin, Dr Thomas Jones, sat down to write to his American friend, Dr Abraham Flexner, at Princeton. 'There is only one topic in London,' Jones reported, 'Mrs Simpson. All our papers are silent and rumour is busy.'[1] For some years, the playboy Prince of Wales, now the uncrowned Edward VIII, had been having an affair with an American married woman, the divorcee Wallis Simpson. Every gossip writer in London knew that the Prince had been wooing Mrs Simpson, but it had been a convention since his grandfather's rakehell days that royal foibles were off-limits, because etiquette dictated that the royals themselves were unable to respond. So while the newspapers rustled with the respectful sussurations that traditionally precede a coronation, they were holding back an avalanche of royal scandal, a more sensational story than the crowning of a new king, and one too big for them to handle or even hint at.

A crowded half-century had passed since the Victorian press had goaded Bertie over his dalliance with Lillie Langtry, the *Sporting Times* (aka *The Pink 'Un*) famously announcing one week that there was 'nothing whatever between the Prince of Wales and Lillie Langtry' and following up the next week with the apparently unrelated observation, 'Not even a sheet.'[2] While the new king seemed unabashed about his friendship with Mrs Simpson and was perfectly relaxed about squiring her in public, the government squirmed with embarrassment. Sixty years before the appearance of Downing Street spin doctors, no word of guidance was issued by Baldwin's mortified cabinet to enlighten or direct the papers, which created a perilous vacuum. Word of the royal romance involving the lady from Baltimore had flashed across the wires to the United States, and by the summer of 1936 the story was red meat in the American press. But in Fleet Street, there was muddle and confusion. For two full months, scarcely a hint of the royal romance crept into the British papers. The King appeared to think this pact of silence was in deference to him, and up to a point it was. But despite what he wrote many years later, there was no 'gentleman's agreement'.

The British press was aware of his affair from the very outset, and the gossip writers and royal-watchers of the late 1930s were overwhelmed by information leaking from the various royal households. The problem was that both the writers and the written-about were in uncharted waters. In 1936, the love life of the reigning monarch was generally regarded as taboo, and reporting on it was an extremely grave matter. What was more, because custom and practice had effectively curtained off the King's sex life, no one knew what the penalties might be in the event of a breach.

Sitting on such a hot story was always going to be an uncomfortable ordeal for Fleet Street's finest. In June, an Australian scandal sheet, *Smith's Weekly*, ran an exclusive, reporting that Edward planned to marry, but naming his bride-to-be as Alexandrine, a wholesome Scandinavian princess aged twenty-one and the niece of the King of Denmark. The *Daily Mirror* picked up the story and toyed with it, nervously floating the odd gossip paragraph and prompting the *Express* to go so far as to print the princess's picture without hinting at why it was doing so. Under the headline AMERICA HAS CHOSEN HER AS OUR KING'S BRIDE, the *Sunday Referee* was emboldened to print Alexandrine's horoscope. 'An opportunity should occur during the next twelve months,' trilled the paper, 'for an outstanding brilliant marriage to an eminent member of a friendly foreign State.' Only one British paper got the story right, and printed it. The paper was the now-forgotten *Cavalcade*, a weekly news magazine modelled on the American *Time*.

With its distinctive red cover featuring a big close-up shot of a personality in the news, *Cavalcade* ('Accurate, Brisk, Complete') offered news-starved Britain the inside track on the royal romance every week for sixpence. It was fresh on the market. The launch issue in February 1936 gave a detailed account of the death of the old king and the accession of the new one. The tone was bright but sober. 'No screaming headlines,' noted the country's best-known journalist, Hannen Swaffer, who wrote in approvingly after the first issue saying he had found it so interesting 'that I will allow you to put me on the free list'.[3] The popular press barons Beaverbrook and Rothermere joined in the congratulations. *Cavalcade* was class. Also in the mix, unusually, were letters critical of the paper and its contents, particularly its breathless *Time*-style three-dotter prose. The biographer G. R. Parkin admitted that *Cavalcade* was 'something different... and disgustingly void of brassières and brazen hussies'.[4] Certainly, the brassières were off. Without trumpeting the fact, and burying it towards the back of the paper, it ran a full-frontal, studio-posed shot of a naked woman, for no other reason than that she looked terrific, tasteful not vulgar.

Aside from the King and Mrs Simpson, there were other scoops, chased up by other papers, such as a cover story about the encroaching deafness of the Prime Minister, Stanley Baldwin. The story was true, but it was the King who was deaf to reason. Courtiers had signalled their worries to Downing Street about the new king's unconventional habits, his impatience with protocol, his indiscretions, extravagances and deteriorating relations with Palace officials. The King's private secretary quit, but before he went he begged the Prime Minister to warn the monarch about the risks he was running, while admitting that against such an overmastering passion for Mrs Simpson reason was unlikely to prevail. Baldwin, preoccupied with the raging political storm over Italy and Abyssinia, shrank from confronting the King about the consequences of his affair. Twice the court circular announced that Mr and Mrs Ernest Simpson had dined at St James's Palace. The Baldwins were among the guests on one of these occasions. Baldwin, dull and provincial, was startled to see Mrs Simpson at one end of the table and the raffish Lady Cunard, one of the wealthiest hostesses in London, at the other. But on this, and on the other manifestations of the King's infatuation, the gossip columns remained silent.

In August, the uncrowned King went to Greece on a yachting holiday. The party included Mrs Simpson, who by now had instituted divorce proceedings against her husband. Following the tradition dating from Victorian times, the Palace asked the press to respect the King's privacy on holiday. By and large, Fleet Street meekly complied. But at *Cavalcade*'s offices in the Strand, the editor William J. Brittain tossed caution aside. For weeks, his magazine had unflinchingly reported Mrs

Simpson's increasing encroachment into royal life. The King canoodling with an American divorcee on board a luxury yacht in the Mediterranean just a few months into his reign was a massive story, and Brittain was determined to tell it.

He had made a mistake in July, running a story that the King would take his holiday at a rented villa in the South of France, accompanied by Mrs Simpson and her svelte, charming husband. To make amends to his readers, Brittain went nap on the royal cruise aboard the yacht *Nahlin*, printing gossipy stories and splashing on the cover of *Cavalcade* an intimate close-up shot of the king and Wallis aboard a launch. The result of this enjoyable, if slightly indecorous, holiday was that the names of the King and Mrs Simpson were firmly linked in the world's press. But in Britain, the media (*Cavalcade* apart) remained silent. Even old Fleet Street sweats were unsure about how to react. The admiring Hannen Swaffer, for one, confessed to some bemusement at the blanket coverage in *Cavalcade*, bemusement verging on bewilderment at Mrs Simpson's rocketing promotion to celebrity status. His reaction was the universal one of the man in the street. 'Who is she, anyway?' he demanded.[5] Within a few months, she would become the most notorious woman in the world, the woman who had stolen the Fairy Prince.

He was rich gossip-column meat indeed. Throughout the 1920s, he had cut a dash through London society, the young fair-haired heir to the throne, shyly good-looking, eligible, relaxed, informal, clubbable and, so far as most of his future subjects knew, available. In fact, since the closing months of the Great War, he had been conducting a more-or-less discreet affair with an older, married woman, Mrs Freda Dudley-Ward. The romance surfaced publicly from time to time, but no one in 'society' seemed affronted since Mrs Dudley-Ward's marriage, having produced two young daughters to whom she remained devoted, was a polite charade. Nightclubs were the couple's favourite resort. 'Saw the Prince of Wales dancing round with Mrs Dudley Ward,' wrote Lady Cynthia Asquith in 1918, 'a pretty little fluff with whom he is said to be rather in love.'[6] At first, certainly, the boyish Prince was abjectly smitten, but the royal ardour cooled and in the summer of 1929 he met the beautiful American, Thelma, Lady Furness. From that point, the Prince's affections were shared between two married women, a singular fact that, like every other particular of the Prince's colourful private life, languished unpublished by the deferential British newspapers.

In the early 1930s, both women were unceremoniously dumped in favour of Mrs Simpson, who (with and without her husband) spent more and more time at the Prince's home, Fort Belvedere, just outside London. In New York, it was Maury Paul, as Hearst's society columnist 'Cholly Knickerbocker', who first scented something. 'Over in London,' he wrote in May 1934, 'the Prince of Wales, who once was noted as the frequent dancing partner of Lady Furness, now is tripping the light fantastic with a Mrs Simpson. And the air becomes frigid whenever Lady Furness and Mrs Simpson happen to meet – which, fortunately, is not often.'[7] Fleet Street knew of her existence, but believed her to be no more than one of the Prince of Wales's close women friends. Later that summer Mrs Simpson was on the French Riviera when he was there, and in 1935 in Budapest he and she danced a number of rumbas together. By the end of that year, stories were appearing in the American papers about Mrs Simpson's association with the Prince. When the Simpsons received an unexpected invitation to stay at the home of Sir Robert Vansittart, then permanent under-secretary at the Foreign Office, it seemed for a moment that the dam was about to burst. Something unnerved Mrs Simpson, who quickly realized that she had been invited for the purposes of official scrutiny at close quarters. Vansittart, she wrote later, 'was looking me over, dissecting me, no doubt, in the light of what he had been reading about me in his Foreign Office digest of the overseas press'.[8]

The year turned, the old king's health faltered, and the Prince and Mrs Simpson continued to step out on the town. In mid-January Harold Nicolson, a friend of the Duchess of York (later the Queen Mother), met the couple at the first night of Noël Coward's *Tonight at Eight-Thirty* and noted his impressions of Mrs Simpson ('bejewelled, eye-brow plucked, virtuous and wise') while confessing to feeling ill at ease in the company of this 'nice woman who has flaunted suddenly into this absurd position.'[9] By early summer Edward, now king, was making clear to those within the charmed circle of the court that he intended to marry her. 'You all think this is a great joke,' warned the wife of one courtier, 'but I'm not so sure it is.'[10] At a royal dinner party in late May, Mr and Mrs Simpson appeared in public for the last time, their names on the guest list, which was published in the court circular the following morning, looming all the more conspicuously by coming last. Fleet Street continued to look the other way. 'It was ironic,' one Palace insider remembered, 'that the Press which had steadfastly restrained itself from linking HM's name with Mrs Simpson was now obliged to do so at his insistence.'[11]

But while the British papers dithered, across the Atlantic that court circular had an instant, galvanizing effect. American journalists were back on Mrs Simpson's trail. On 8 June, *Time* magazine reported that she was 'known to the world press as King Edward's favourite dancing partner, his companion on numerous holiday occasions'. A month later, a second court circular, reporting another of the King's regular dinner parties, again supplied a complete guest list. The last of the twenty names was that of Mrs Simpson. Alone, without Ernest. On 13 July, *Time* reported that Lloyd's had shortened the odds against the King's marriage from 11–1 to 5–1. The following week the same magazine ran two pages of pictures of Mrs Simpson and her house. On 21 July, Ernest Simpson spent the night at the Hôtel de Paris in Bray with a woman who was not his wife. Fleet Street seethed with rumour. The diarist Sir Henry 'Chips' Channon was dismayed to note: 'The Simpson scandal is growing.'[12]

The news that the King had chartered Lady Yule's luxury yacht *Nahlin* for a summer cruise broke in the *Daily Mirror* on 30 July. The *Telegraph* followed up a few days later with a list of guests. It included the Mountbattens, Lady Cunard, Duff Cooper and Lady Diana Cooper, and the King's old friends Lord and Lady Brownlow. Mrs Simpson's name did not appear. The king flew to Calais a few days later to join the Orient Express for the journey south to the Adriatic coast where the *Nahlin* was moored. Travelling incognito, as Duke of Lancaster, he stopped off in Salzburg on the way, where a press photographer snapped him with Mrs Simpson. The camera was seized by the police and later released. When the British press ran the picture, it cut Mrs Simpson out. But on 11 August, the 'Londoner's Diary' in the *Evening Standard* announced that Mrs Simpson was in the party: 'Mrs Ernest Simpson is the former Miss Wallis Warfield and comes from Baltimore.'

Beaverbrook was the one who had provided these tiny nuggets of information, according to Bruce Lockhart, the journalist who wrote the diary item. Beaverbrook had given strict instructions to the editor, Percy Cudlipp, that every precaution was to be taken to protect the source. 'Cudlipp not even to tell me,' Lockhart noted in his diary. 'Paragraph to be read by Cudlipp to him over private line.'[13] Five days later, on 16 August, the *Sunday Referee* splashed a massive ten-inch picture on its front page of the king and Mrs Simpson. The journalists' magazine, *World's Press News,* reported two official requests from Buckingham Palace asking Fleet Street to publish as little as possible about the King's holiday. Rothermere's *Sunday Dispatch* explained to its readers on its front page WHY THERE ARE NO PICTURES OF THE KING.

> His Majesty... like many of his subjects, is on holiday. Photographs and stories of his shore excursions on the Dalmatian coast are being sent to English newspapers in great numbers. Unless these contain matter of proper national interest – such as the whereabouts of the King – the *Sunday Dispatch* will not publish them, believing that its readers realize and respect the King's natural desire for occasional respite from the public attention focused upon his movements by responsibility and tradition.[14]

The *Daily Express* was unimpressed by this lofty tone, and the next day published a picture of the King rowing a dinghy round the *Nahlin.* He was pictured alone. But the American papers showed that Mrs Simpson was sitting in the stern. She had been cropped out of the British pictures; the *Express* evidently knew more than it was letting on. Some papers had recently printed pictures of Princess Catherine of Greece, hinting at possible marriage to Edward. Driberg, in his 'Hickey' column in the *Express* on 20 August, seemed to be inviting his readers to look between the lines: 'Girl whose name has been most often mentioned as queen-to-be denies truth of story indignantly. Well, maybe it's someone else...' In fact, the King was driving through the streets of Athens with Mrs Simpson by his side. No British newspaper printed any pictures. But by the time Edward returned to London, English readers of *Time* magazine and the British weeklies *Cavalcade* and *News Review* knew the story of the royal romance aboard the *Nahlin.* So did Mayfair and so did Fleet Street, for whose special enlightenment a sailor from the yacht dictated a log of proceedings. A dog-eared copy of this document made the rounds of the newspaper pubs and clubs.

17. Godmothers of gossip: Louella Parsons (left) and Hedda Hopper, all smiles for once.

18. Roy Blackman and the *Daily Mirror* gossip team of 1960. A notice on the office ceiling read: 'Start the day with a smile. It costs nothing.'

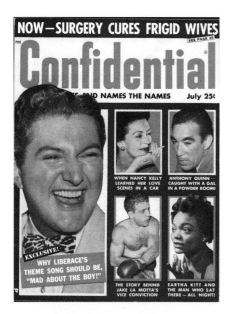

19. *Confidential*'s 1957 cover story exposing Liberace as a closet homosexual. The 'Kandelabra Kid' won $40,000 in libel damages, even though the story was true.

20. Fred Newman, 27, Oxford-educated gossip editor of the *Daily Sketch* in 1960, with the paper's Scottish stunt-girl Rosemary McLellan. She was a fashion writer who turned prankster, gate-crashing the Miss World contest, for example, to manufacture a story. 'Our policy,' explained Newman, 'is to entertain.'

21. Jack Profumo makes his bed and sits on it as the scandal breaks in 1963.

22. Christine Keeler, the most photographed woman in Britain as Stephen Ward's trial opens at the Old Bailey in 1963.

23. Pip Pip! *Private Eye*'s Grovel, based on Nigel Dempster of the *Daily Mail*.

24. Former beauty queen Joyce McKinney, star of the Mormon missionary 'sex-in-chains' case, flaunts her charms.

25. Rapid getaway: Peter Bessell MP (in passenger seat), star witness at Jeremy Thorpe's trial in 1978, runs the media gauntlet.

26. No peace from the Press: Lady Diana Spencer lives up to her 'shy Di' image when doorstepped outside her Kensington flat in 1980, the year she became engaged to the Prince of Wales.

27. Jeffrey Archer and Andrina Colquhoun, whose affair was first reported in a Fleet Street gossip column.

28. Who's that girl? Monica Lewinsky braves the US media at the height of the scandal over her liaison with President Clinton.

29. Matt Drudge, the original cyber gossip columnist.

30. Shy no more: a troubled Princess of Wales outdazzles the rest of the Royals even when mobbed by Fleet Street's finest on a visit to the ballet in 1996.

Cavalcade continued to run with the story. In early October, it described how the King had driven fifty miles from Balmoral to Aberdeen station to meet Mrs Simpson off the London train. When other guests left the castle after one of the King's house-parties, it reported, Mrs Simpson remained, along with Mr and Mrs Herman Rogers, another American couple who were friends of the Simpsons. In New York, it was open season on the woman from Baltimore. *Liberty* magazine ran off 2.5 million copies of an issue hailing Mrs Simpson as 'The Most Envied Woman in the British Empire'; commuting New Yorkers gaped at placards proclaiming 'The Yankee at the Court of King Edward' in a new paper, the *New York Woman,* which sold 100,000 copies at 15 cents a time. 'While the outcome, no doubt, will be a victory for the Throne,' speculated the paper, 'the King, quite evidently, is the most helpless of creatures, a man over 40 [he was 42] who has fallen desperately in love.'[15] The Balmoral party broke up. The King returned to Buckingham Palace, Mrs Simpson to her new house in Regent's Park. Ernest Simpson moved from Bryanston Court to the Guards' Club.

In mid-September, the editor of *The Times,* Geoffrey Dawson, returned from holiday to find a stream of letters and newspaper cuttings from America trickling into the office about the King's affair with Mrs Simpson. The stream gradually swelled to a flood, Dawson recalled, 'and the letters began to include a number which were abusive and contemptuous of the British Press for its silence and others which were frankly distressed'.[16] Some of Dawson's American correspondents enclosed a cutting of one particular story headed 'Edward will wed Wally', and asking why the British public were not as much disturbed as they themselves. About a month later, Dawson received a nine-page typewritten letter from a Briton residing in America who complained that the King's antics, as reported by the US press, had reduced Britain's image in the eyes of the average American to 'a dizzy Balkan musical comedy attuned to the rhythm of Jazz'. To be blunt, this correspondent added, where George V had been an invaluable asset to British prestige abroad, Edward VIII was proving to be an incalculable liability.

The letter continued: 'For several months now,

the American public has been intermittently titillated with unsavoury gobbets of news about the King and Mrs Simpson; but in the course of the last three or four weeks there has come a perfect avalanche of muck and slime. The American public are notorious for the manner in which they can be suddenly swept by a 'craze' on this or that subject. The prevailing 'craze' today is the King and Mrs Simpson: the popularity of the theme is no doubt in large measure attributable to the fact that the lady is American. First we had the news dispatches, suitably and abundantly illustrated by photographs; Mrs Simpson accompanies the King on a yachting cruise, Mrs Simpson accompanies the King when he goes to consult a Vienna ear specialist, Mrs Simpson accompanies the King to Balmoral, Mrs Simpson accompanies the King on the train back to London, the ubiquitous Mrs Simpson is in the King's company on every conceivable occasion. If the American 'news-hawk' happens to be slightly malicious he will point a contrast between the King and Mrs Simpson 'merrymaking' at Balmoral while the 'grief-stricken' Queen Mary prepares to leave Buckingham Palace. Then comes the juicier pieces of outright scandal. One journal facetiously suggests that Mrs Simpson's aid be enlisted in the collection of the British War Debt to the United States. Another gives the alleged details of a conversation in which the Prime Minister reproves the King for his carryings on, and the latter curtly tells him to mind his own business. Another asserts that Queen Mary is being ousted from Buckingham Palace in order to clear the way for Mrs Simpson's installation as the King's official hostess.

Another popular weekly magazine with a circulation of over two million publishes a sensational article about 'the most envied woman in the British Empire'. A chain of newspapers with a huge circulation is now publishing in daily instalments a popular 'biography' of 'the most talked of woman in the world'. Advertisements in railway trains and other places scream out exhortations to buy this or that publication to get the inside story about the King and Mrs Simpson. Distinguished Britons landing on American shores are beset by pressmen who ask them what the British people think about it all; and the next day appear accounts describing with malicious glee how the distinguished Britons struggled amid confusion and embarrassment to evade the question.

Nor can one simply ascribe this campaign of defamation, which is gathering volume like a careering snowball, to the sensational proclivities of the American press; for George V was never in my experience the subject of such publicity. As a matter of fact a sober newspaper like the *New York*

Times, which has consistently sought to promote good relations with Britain, until quite recently eschewed Mrs Simpson's name from its columns as rigorously as the British press; but it has now given up this voluntary censorship as useless and prints copious news about Mrs Simpson on its front page, although in less febrile accents than the sensational press.[17]

The anonymous letter, rotundly signed 'Britannicus in Partibus Infidelium', concluded that the greatest service Edward could render his country would be to walk out of his job. Newspaper editors seldom set much store by anonymous letters, but in this case Dawson did an extraordinary thing. He immediately drove to Buckingham Palace, left a copy for the King, then went on to 10 Downing Street to give a copy to the Prime Minister. This flurry of activity has suggested to at least one historian[18] that the Britannicus letter was a put-up job, the result of a secret deal between Dawson and an unknown correspondent, to fuel the opposition to the King. But, crucially, it flagged up the possibility of abdication, and Dawson and Baldwin swiftly manoeuvred to bring about the downfall of the new king in the belief that he was simply not up to the job.

The political twists and turns leading up to Edward VIII's abdication, involving Prime Minister Baldwin, the Archbishop of Canterbury and other Establishment figures, fall outside the scope of this account of how the affair played in the press and, in particular, Fleet Street. But there can be little doubt that the protracted silence of the British newspapers, broken only by the increasing tumult in the American press, brought the abdication crisis to a head. As one observer put it: 'Never since the battle of Saratoga has the US made so signal contribution to a major event in British history.'[19] One of the principal players in the drama being played out behind the scenes was Lord Beaverbook, the buccaneering Canadian millionaire who owned the *Daily Express,* then the biggest-selling paper in Britain. Beaverbrook took the King's part in the crisis because although the young monarch was not yet a close friend, Beaverbrook knew him slightly and sympathized (in the judgment of A. J. P. Taylor) with 'a human being being harassed by the established order'.[20] Beaverbrook's role in damming the Fleet Street flood was pivotal; the self-imposed dumbfoundedness of the British press created a vacuum and set in motion a train of events that altered the succession to the throne. But Beaverbrook was further motivated by his hatred for Baldwin, who did not share his enthusiasm for the *Express*'s crusade over Empire Free Trade, and who had won the 1935 general election by lying about Britain's need to rearm against Hitler. Despite the clamour over the King's affair with Mrs Simpson, Beaverbrook believed that the manoeuvres to force him out began in early 1936, before Edward had let it be known that he was in love with the woman and was determined to marry her. The King's freewheeling lifestyle, distaste for the chores of kingship and dislike of stuffy Establishment figures and politicians had upset many in positions of power who, as the calamity loomed, were not prepared to come to his rescue. 'He would not go to church,' Beaverbrook observed, 'and he would go to nightclubs.'[21] No wonder neither the Prime Minister nor the Archbishop of Canterbury wanted Edward to reign as king.

In Fleet Street, rumours about the King's involvement with an American divorcee took root in January shortly after his accession, when one of the papers published a photograph of a group of Edward's friends watching a ceremonial parade from a window at St James's Palace. Most of the faces were familiar figures from London café society, but Mrs Simpson's was not. Although her identity was soon discovered, it appears to have excited little public curiosity, because there was no word about her in the mainstream daily press. With this exception: her name did appear regularly in the court circular as a dinner guest of the King, usually (although not always) with that of her husband, the stolid Ernest.

It was at about this point that an obscure political scandal sheet added its small but intriguing contribution. The *Week* was a small-circulation briefing paper, a sort of serious political precursor to *Private Eye*. Its smudged brown typewritten pages were run off on a second-hand duplicator in a garret in Victoria Street; its influence beyond its mainly London-based subscribers was zero. But it was read in high places. One of the King's closest advisers, Lord Mountbatten, was a subscriber, and shortly after the death of George V in January 1936 had commended it to the new King. Using a go-between, Mountbatten had persuaded the *Week*'s editor, the Communist Claud Cockburn, to supply him with a potted autobiography ('the King wants to know who you are,' Cockburn was told). Then, everything went quiet. Months passed. The clamour over the Simpson affair grew ever louder in the American press. Cockburn mentioned this excited foreign coverage in the *Week* but frivolously, suggesting that the Americans were deviously trying to distract attention from the realities of the Spanish civil war. 'The *Week* became at times quite governessy,' wrote Cockburn's wife, Patricia. 'Its tone was that of some grave editor of *The Times* complaining that the gossip column was invading the news pages.'[22] But as the turmoil over Edward and Mrs Simpson deepened, Cockburn realized that with the British newspapers gripped by discretional lockjaw, the King was losing the propaganda war. They were determined to show responsibility, delicacy, restraint and the Best Possible Taste, Cockburn recalled, if it was the last thing they did before total paralysis gripped them. 'In the suffocating silence,' he added, 'the trend was running strongly against the King.'[23]

Mountbatten's go-between, another left-wing journalist, John Strachey, reappeared and made Cockburn an extremely juicy proposition. Mountbatten, it seemed, had conceived the idea that if certain sensational 'inside information' could be suddenly forced into the open, the trend might possibly be reversed in the King's favour. Cockburn was naturally intrigued, especially when Strachey explained that there were facts about the whole affair that the mainstream newspapers and periodicals would be most unlikely to print. On the other hand, it had been noted in royal circles (Cockburn knew that the *Week* had become required reading at Fort Belvedere) that on several occasions in the past the paper had succeeded in securing wide publicity for matters thought 'not fit to print'. Mountbatten, Strachey added, believed that if he could present the King with this concrete possibility, the King might agree to try it.

Would Cockburn 'in principle' be prepared to publish 'certain facts' if they reached him from Fort Belvedere? Strachey was blunt. He warned Cockburn that such 'facts' would immediately be denied by the cabinet, and that the resulting row would be certainly appalling and possibly catastrophic. The King himself, Strachey added, as yet knew nothing of this proposal. Cockburn didn't hesitate. While being a passionate opponent of the monarchy, he detested Baldwin's government still more, and, after all, 'My enemy's enemy is my friend.'

'I accepted, of course,' wrote Cockburn, many years later, 'and anyway it looked as though whatever happened we should have a lot of fun.'[24]

Baldwin returned from holiday in October to find a rising tide of indignation against the American press, together with growing bewilderment from people at home who had heard, and in some cases read, the stories and who now wanted to know if they were true. Some demanded action against the 'libels' in the US papers. In America itself, the belief grew that the British press had been gagged by official censorship. News that imported copies of *Time* magazine had been mutilated by its British distributor fuelled this assertion. A couple of MPs asked questions in the Commons, but since it was the magazine's own agents doing the mutilating, the government was able to deny imposing official censorship. The *Morning Post* explained the silence of the British newspapers, but only after the crisis had blown over and the King, by then living in exile with Mrs Simpson, had been replaced:

> It is no part of the function of the press to publish gossip possibly injurious to such an institution as the monarchy. At the time when the King's friendship for Mrs Simpson passed from the region of vague rumour for that of substantial fact, the friendship seemed to be a matter of private rather than public life. It concerned the man rather than the King.
>
> The British press very properly ignored it. It was not prompted to do so by any influence outside. It was not – and could not have been – compelled to do so by any form of censorship, official or unofficial. The reason was to be found in the general sense that the King, who must bear a greater public burden than any man, was of all men most entitled to have his private life kept private.[25]

In the autumn the *News Chronicle* splashed the news that Mrs Simpson was seeking a divorce. In itself, the news was meaningless to most British readers, who continued to be kept in the dark. Other papers printed the report, but kept it small. Matters moved swiftly when Beaverbrook's *Evening Standard* learned that the case was listed at Ipswich for 27 October. The *Standard's* editor Percy Cudlipp consulted Beaverbrook about publishing this information ahead of the case. Cudlipp had already been offered 'revelations' about the King's affair with Mrs Simpson and had turned them down. But now that the relationship seemed to be edging into the public arena, it was time to reconsider. Beaverbook's view was that since Mrs Simpson's name had become known to the British public, together with her links to the King, publication of her divorce hearing was warranted. But he advised Cudlipp to wait. Beaverbrook put a call through to Mrs Simpson's solicitor, his friend Theodore Goddard, who immediately asked to see him. The two met that evening. Goddard anxiously sought privacy for his client, but Beaverbrook made no promises. Word evidently got back to Mrs Simpson, for very shortly the King telephoned Beaverbrook and asked to see him. 'Name your own time,' the King had said, leaving Beaverbrook with the distinct impression that the matter was pressing. The following day, the *Week* ran the first of its abdication scoops.

Plans were afoot, it reported, for 'a social bomb to be exploded under the King. The ideal method envisaged by those planting the bomb would be for a reference to be made from the pulpit to "the very different standards of conduct set to his subjects by the late King".'[26] What could this possibly mean? As it turned out, the *Week* was weeks ahead of the game.

Two days later, on Friday, 16 October 1936, Beaverbrook went to the Palace.

The King 'calmly and with considerable cogency and force'[27] asked Beaverbrook to help stifle all advance news of the Simpson divorce and to limit publicity after it. He explained that Mrs Simpson was ill, unhappy and distressed by the thought of her impending notoriety. The King, explaining that her problems stemmed from her association with himself, felt duty-bound to protect her. Beaverbook said he would fix it, not just in his own papers but in Fleet Street as a whole. News coverage would be confined to a report of the unhappy woman's divorce, making no mention of her friendship with the King.

Beaverbook called on Esmond Harmsworth, chairman of the Newspaper Proprietors' Association. 'There and then,' Beaverbrook recalled, 'we arranged a plan of campaign. Most of the British newspapers consented without much difficulty to the policy of discretion. Sir Walter Layton of the *News Chronicle* hesitated, but I went to see him, and after consideration he took the same line as the other newspapers.' Beaverbrook also squared the Scottish and Irish papers, and even *Paris-Soir* in France, explaining to them that while not wishing to hamper their journalistic activities, the aim was 'to escape, as far as possible, the publication of unjustifiable gossip concerning the King'.[28] Years later, Beaverbrook tried to justify this extraordinary self-muzzling by explaining that at this point in the crisis he had no idea that the King planned to marry Mrs Simpson.

Late in October, the New York popular papers made a sensational splash with front page headlines an inch and a half high: KING *WILL* WED WALLY. Three thousand miles away, what should Fleet Street do? For the editor of Beaverbrook's *Express*, Arthur Christiansen, it was a quandary. The story was unsigned, but Christiansen, Beaverbrook's *wunderkind*, knew that the author of the piece was William Randolph Hearst, owner of the *New York Journal*, who had recently visited Edward at Fort Belvedere. 'Within a few days,' the *Journal* announced, 'Mrs Ernest Simpson of Baltimore, USA, will obtain her divorce decree in England, and some eight months thereafter she will be married to Edward VIII, King of England.'[29] The Boston *Record* went even bigger on the story, running headlines five inches tall: KING SETS JUNE FOR WEDDING TO MRS SIMPSON.

The country town of Ipswich, chosen because of its remoteness from London, thronged with American reporters, detectives and lawyers, to the surprise of the judge in particular, who had expected little if any interest in this undefended and unexceptional divorce case. So many people turned up on 27 October that tickets of admission were issued. The hearing was a shambles, an unedifying media scrum. Photographers trying to get pictures of Mrs Simpson entering the court were hustled away by unprecedented numbers of police. Movie cameramen were forbidden to set up near the court, and a group of them, who the previous day had booked into a room overlooking the court, were greeted at the door on arrival by a polite police inspector. One American reporter from a New York paper, arriving without a ticket, scrambled over an eight-foot wall into the court precincts, only to land in the arms of a policeman. In the court itself, several seats were deliberately left empty, the seats that Mrs Simpson faced while giving evidence. Reporters, about thirty of them, could only see her back. At 2.17 p.m., with the customary flourish of trumpets, Mr Justice Hawke arrived. *Simpson* v *Simpson* was under way.

The case lasted just nineteen minutes. The judge duly granted a decree nisi, and Mrs Simpson was swiftly ushered out. The reporters all bolted for the door with such a racket that the ushers bellowed for silence. The newspapermen complained afterwards that they had been locked in until Mrs Simpson's car had gone. Once released, they surged into the street, scything through a crowd of gaping townsfolk. In the back room of a nearby shop, a transatlantic telephone link was being held open. Within moments, the story was crackling down the wire to New York. Outside, it was the photographers' turn to be thwarted. When Mrs Simpson had been hustled into her waiting car, photographers planning to follow her found a police car blocking the street. The only picture to make it on the day was of other photographers trying to get into the court.

While some Fleet Street reporters took a verbatim note of the evidence for the information of their editors, none of it appeared in print. Thanks to an Act of Parliament passed ten years before, reports of divorce proceedings were restricted so as to forbid the publication of unsavoury evidence. All that appeared in the British papers were the bald facts of the case, positioned modestly at the foot of the column on an inside page under such discreet headings as 'Undefended Divorce Case at Ipswich Assizes'. But in America, the case was billed as a sensation. 'King's Moll Reno'd in Wolsey's Home Town' was the startling headline in one paper. According to the London correspondent of the *Chicago Daily Tribune*, 'Mention of Mrs Simpson for the first time in all London newspapers this morning gave a fillip to the gossip about the 40 years old American woman and her friendship with King Edward VIII of England, a friendship which, on a word from the strong Newspaper Proprietors' Association here, most London editors have barred from print.'[30] But the gossip was still mainly confined to the fashionable West End of London. 'We discussed rumours, now current everywhere that the King means to marry Mrs Simpson,' was a typically informed view from one political insider.[31] Millions of ordinary people, on the other hand, had still never heard of Mrs Simpson, and the publication of low-key paragraphs about her divorce case aroused no curiosity.

The truth about the King and Mrs Simpson was only revealed to a bewildered Britain when the Bishop of Bradford, Dr Blunt, made a speech attacking the King and urging him to be more of a Christian, like his father. The press took its cue and the whole extraordinary story tumbled out. The new king planned to marry a twice-divorced American woman, having first raised her to the peerage as Duchess of Lancaster. 'It is a remarkable fact,' boomed *The Times*, 'that the American campaign of publicity so long and so widely ignored...has now reached a point at which it goes far beyond that side of His Majesty's life which may justly be held to be private.'[32] Incredulous, the *Morning Post* 'shrank from believing that there was solid foundation for the current gossip, because if it were true the gravest injury to every national and imperial interest must result'.[33]

All the morning papers on 11 December sold out. The evening papers, stuffed with pages of pictures stored in every office in Fleet Street, broke all sales records. People walked along the streets reading them, gawping at the grainy images of their King cavorting with Mrs Simpson at Ascot, in restaurants, on board *Nahlin*. At midnight, the King was driven at top speed out of the gates of Buckingham Palace, his lined face caught in the flashlights of the waiting cameramen. Mrs Simpson, meanwhile, slipped out of London unobserved, in a car driven by the King's own chauffeur. At Newhaven, in the early hours, a mysterious veiled woman, wrapped in furs, boarded the boat for Dieppe.

The year of three kings, 1936, reminded Malcolm Muggeridge of the strange and tragic Philip Page, one-time 'Mr Gossip' of the *Daily Sketch*, once a theatre critic but by the mid-1930s washed up at the *Standard* where he contributed only the occasional paragraph. 'His harmless vanity was to have known everyone intimately,' Muggeridge remembered, adding that whenever this knowledge was put to the test it needed heavy reinforcement by reference to the cuttings files.[34] Page crowned his dyed black hair with a bowler hat and wore an overcoat with a velvet collar, whatever the weather. In one other way, too, Philip Page was unique. 'He alone of us all believed in what we were doing,' Muggeridge explained, 'seeing each Diary paragraph as a sacrificial offering laid on the altar of social rectitude.'[35] When George V died on that fateful January day, Muggeridge found him at his desk in tears, staring at a silver half-crown piece bearing the old king's image.

16

Godmothers of Gossip

Reporting on Hollywood, a town (and an industry) that gulps gossip as a drowning man gulps air, has always been a finely tuned business. Once, film stars and show-business reporters coexisted in state of armed truce; the relationship was symbiotic and, on the whole, friendly, but the ever-present threat of atomic meltdown kept the two sides wary and respectful. Before and after World War II, in Hollywood's golden age, two women, Louella Parsons and Hedda Hopper, controlled the source and supply of virtually all the gossip about movies and movie stars. 'Their columns were the first thing we looked at every morning,' Bob Hope recalled, 'to see what was going on.'[1]

But behind the celluloid fantasy, it was an ugly, bitching business; Parsons and Hopper became all-powerful and were just as famous as the stars they wrote about. Hopper's column ran in the *Los Angeles Times* from 1928 for nearly thirty years. She had trained and worked as an actress, and played herself in such films as *Sunset Boulevard* and *The Oscar*. As a gossip writer, she became so powerful, both as a journalist and as a Hollywood fixer and socialite, that she described her home on Tropical Drive in Beverly Hills as 'the house that fear built'.[2] Parsons, her great rival, was syndicated by the Hearst group; she also wielded enormous influence and appeared in several movies. All Hollywood quaked at the thought of what these two women might print. Producers, directors, established stars or budding starlets, all would have to pass muster sooner or later. 'If you were out of favour,' remembers Mamie Van Doren, Queen of the B-movies, who detested Parsons, 'you might as well get on the bus back to Podunk because you were never going to do more than wait on tables, pump gas, or become a hooker or a producer's wife.'[3] In his portrait of 1940s Hollywood, where he lived as a student, Otto Friedrich declared: 'It is almost impossible now to realise the power once exercised by Mrs Parsons and her rival Hedda Hopper, but in the 1940s these two vain and ignorant women tyrannised Hollywood.'[4]

Parsons was already twice divorced when she was hired by the *Chicago Tribune* in 1910. She wrote film scenarios in her free time and claimed to have invented the movie gossip column while she worked at the Chicago *Record-Herald*, serving up her daily helpings of 'live current gossip, such as everyone from property boy to film president likes to read'.[5] Her style in 'Seen on the Screen' was idiosyncratic; by the 1920s it had moved beyond parody with her references to 'madcap Mabel Normand', Mary Pickford 'the golden child' and 'the irresistible Charlie Chaplin'. When she moved to Hollywood in 1924 to write for Hearst, a story circulated that Parsons had got the job in mysterious circumstances. It was said that she had witnessed Hearst shooting dead film director Thomas Ince on board Hearst's yacht *Oneida* while cruising off the California coast. According to the gossips, Hearst had discovered Ince *in flagrante delicto* with Hearst's mistress, the actress Marion Davies. An even more lurid version of events claimed that Hearst had found Miss Davies with the 'irresistible' Charlie Chaplin, had started shooting wildly and had killed Ince by mistake. Parsons, also a guest aboard *Oneida*, had been sworn to secrecy (so the story went) and was handed her column as a pay-off. In fact, Ince appears to have died of too much food and drink (the official cause of death was listed as angina), and at the time of his death Louella Parsons was apparently thousands of miles away in New York.

Nevertheless, for all its whimsical wrong-headedness, the story might well have made it into one of Hollywood's gossip columns and been signed by either Louella Parsons or Hedda Hopper. Both churned out the same kind of flat-footed prose, littered with mistakes, misrepresentations and errors of judgment; in the 1950s, for example, Louella assured her readers that Ronald Reagan had no political ambitions. Her worst professional moment was a lost scoop about Clark Gable's marriage to Carole Lombard. The couple had promised her an exclusive but eloped instead and called a press conference. Parsons never got over the betrayal. She was successfully schmoozed by the young and handsome Orson Welles over *Citizen Kane*, a thinly disguised attack on William Randolph Hearst himself. At the end of a five-course lunch, served in Welles's satin-lined dressing room, Parsons asked him, on behalf of her 30 million readers, if his new movie dealt with Hearst. Of course not, replied Welles. The film was entirely a work of fiction. Parsons believed him.

After a press preview, Hedda Hopper turned to Welles and said: 'You can't get away with this.'

'I will,' Welles retorted.

Prompted by Hearst himself, who had read Hopper's column, Louella Parsons dashed to a special screening, accompanied by two lawyers. In a flurry of telephone calls, she threatened as many RKO board members as she could reach with the wrath of her master. 'Mr Hearst says if you boys want private lives,' she hissed, 'I'll give you private lives.'[6]

The controversy found Parsons at the height of her powers and celebrity, but in the early days of working for Hearst much of her copy was froth and gloop, with an extravagant coating of glitter. 'Never looked lovelier', Louella's gushing vignette of Marion Davies, became a catchphrase. But once in Hollywood as motion-picture editor of Hearst's Universal News Service, Parsons struck a darker note by digging for stories that pried directly into the private lives of stars. Her revelation that the film star Tom Mix had fathered five children to a woman who was not his lawful wife set the new tone for greater candour in reporting the film industry. By the late 1920s, Parsons had firmly latched on to what she sensed was a growing public appetite for dished dirt.

Throughout the 1930s, Parsons wrote as though she had the whole of Hollywood in her bony grip. She was always passionately protective of the movie industry, never missing an opportunity to bang the Hollywood drum. Film actors who accepted parts in stage shows were rubbished in her column. She meddled endlessly in casting decisions, scoffing at any she disagreed with, and long after she had lost her own figure she commented unblushingly on any actress she considered overweight or who looked flaky. 'The buxom, blonde Mae West, fat, fair and I don't know how near forty has come to Hollywood,'[7] she once trumpeted. (Debbie Reynolds remembered Louella turning up wearing a strapless dress over a Merry Widow undergarment 'and everything pushed up. We weren't ever sure we wouldn't have another opening, another show.')[8] Stars who snubbed her were banned from her column;

if they begged for forgiveness, they were readmitted only by promising Parsons a scoop. In her far from frank memoirs in 1944, she declared that her greatest exclusive was the Mary Pickford–Douglas Fairbanks divorce, which she claimed 'shook the United States'. Pickford believed that Parsons had betrayed her by printing it. Like all driven journalists, Parsons over-hyped stories. Describing another scoop, the tale of Ingrid Bergman's illegitimate baby, Parsons identifies her contact only as 'a man of great importance not only in Hollywood but throughout the United States', who telephoned her in the middle of the night to whisper: 'Louella, Ingrid is going to have a baby.'[9] There is a momentary flicker of doubt, but Parsons prints it anyway. She was right. The tale was true. Her informant? Probably Hearst. Or Howard Hughes.

Parsons considered herself versatile enough to try her hand outside the gossip field. She covered Tunney–Dempsey prize fights in New York and Philadelphia, and in 1926, with the likes of Damon Runyon and James Thurber, reported the celebrated Hall–Mills murder trial in Somerville, New Jersey, one of 200 gaping, gasping correspondents whose copy, put into book form, would have made a shelf of novels twenty-two feet long.[10] But she was a gossip woman at bottom, with a gossip woman's attention span. She thought, ate and supped in paragraphs, trilled in squibs in her whiny little voice, tossed scraps of smut, generalizations and misunderstandings at a hungry public. She relied on her notoriously defective memory, which she called 'the old bean'. To Parsons, facts weren't sacred, or even respected. 'Louella's enthusiasm for running down a story,' wrote her biographer George Eells, 'did not extend to the tedium of cross-checking. For Hearst, the bulldogging of a story was what counted, and for Louella that was part of the romance of being a newspaperwoman.'[11]

Such reckless buccaneering had, by the mid-1930s, confirmed Louella Parsons as the uncrowned Queen of Hollywood, with a syndicated column running in 600 papers, a reputed 20 million readers, a networked radio show, *Hollywood Hotel*, a mansion in Beverly Hills and a chauffeured Rolls-Royce. In 1937, her third husband, Dr ('Docky') Harry Watson Martin, a hard-drinking urologist specializing in venereal diseases, signed a $30,000 contract with Twentieth Century-Fox to treat its studio staff for any nasty little rashes and worse, so tightening Louella's grip on the industry's favours still further.

It seemed an unpropitious moment for a rival to surface, but when she did, Hedda Hopper caused quite a stir in the piranha pool. After a shaky start, this failed jobbing actress ('Queen of the Quickies,' jibed Parsons), fifty-three years old, divorced and a single mother, launched a full-throttled challenge for Parsons's crown and began an on-off gossip feud that sent crossfire crackling across Hollywood for nearly twenty years. Hopper's weapon was bare-nailed bitchery. 'The minute I started to trot out the juicy stuff,' she recollected, 'my phone started to ring.'[12] Hopper landed an early blow in 1939, scooping news of the divorce plans of the President's son, James Roosevelt, literally by jamming her foot in his door and yelling so loudly that he finally appeared in his dressing-gown, demanding to know what the ruckus was about. Hopper later recounted that, having authenticated the story, she phoned her editor at the *Los Angeles Times* shouting: 'Stop the presses! Whatever that means!'[13]

Hopper was at pains to distinguish herself from her rival. Whereas she was flamboyant, blonde and still slender (in her acting days, she reputedly possessed the best legs in New York), Parsons was a dumpy, frowsty brunette. Whereas everyone suspected that beneath an outer crustiness Louella concealed a soft centre, Hedda Hopper (real name Elda Furry) was flashy and brittle, a chrome-coated exterior concealing a heart of ice. Where Parsons sloshed about for the leavings of love lives, Hopper cracked down on union racketeers using the kind of ripe language normally reserved for bar-room barracking. 'There would be a crusade,' one of her secretaries, Patsy Gaile, a one-time actress, told Hedda's biographer, George Eells. 'About anything – all kinds of things – that's what made it so fascinating. Trivial things, but behind all this folderol there was a solid set of values.'[14] She worked hard to create a persona of small-mindedness, but in reality her powerful dynamism fuelled a rise to fame and fortune.

The industry, of course, connived at the rivalry between the two columnists and even encouraged it. 'Hedda Hopper's Hollywood' flourished. In 1940, she earned more than £110,000, and when, the following year, she signed with the *Chicago Tribune* and the New York *Daily News* syndicate, her gossip column added 5.75 million new daily and 7.5 million new Sunday readers in New York alone. The feud with Parsons soon lost its synthetic quality, and became earnest and personal. From under her extravagant hats (a gimmick that quickly mutated into a trade mark) Hopper was thumbing her nose at Hollywood's Old Contemptible. 'She's trying to do in two years,' Parsons complained, 'what it took me thirty years to do.'[15] But she was wrong. Unlike Parsons, Hopper felt impelled to pontificate on affairs in the wider world, not just the Hollywood village. After Pearl Harbor, and despite her Quaker background, she repudiated her earlier isolationist stance and cheered on the war effort, the gung-ho clamour of the times drowning out the inescapable fact that by temperament, education and experience she was scarcely equipped to offer any useful analysis of the issues she wrote about.

Like Parsons, Hedda Hopper schmoozed her favourites (Judy Garland, Alan Ladd, Tyrone Power, Clark Gable and Howard Hughes) while picking fights with adversaries like Merle Oberon, Marlene Dietrich and her old enemy Joan Bennett, who once ordered her chauffeur to deliver a live skunk to Hopper's house. Joseph Cotten threatened to 'kick her up the ass' if she repeated a suggestion that he had been caught in the back of his car straddling the teenage Deanna Durbin; when she did, he publicly delivered a well-aimed punt up the Hopper derrière. If Orson Welles was Louella Parsons's *bête noire*, Hedda Hopper's was Charlie Chaplin. In 1943, she broke the story of Chaplin's protégée Joan Barry falling pregnant with his baby. From the end of the war, two years later, the reactionary demon within her seized control, and she became increasingly political and rabidly conservative. In the feverish atmosphere of the early 1950s, she was so bellicose in her support for anti-Communist witch-hunts that she was gagged by the House Committee on Un-American Activities and publicly rebuked by the editor of the New York *Daily News* for 'trying to settle international affairs'.[16] She made a fool of herself, to be sure (that same editor ridiculed her call for a boycott of Judy Holliday and José Ferrer), but in flaunting her prejudices she was at least being honest with her readers, a quality that counted when the lights went down on old Hollywood in the late 1940s. Louella, on the other hand, who never really let go of that glittering land of make-believe, had trouble accepting the new and grittier generation of movie-makers who, in turn, wrote her off as a quaint anachronism. The two warrior queens made up in the end, and produced volumes of memoirs in their decline. Parsons was content to remangle her collection of clichés, while Hopper showered vitriol over everyone, attracting a $3 million libel suit from Michael Wilding, which she lost. She died of double pneumonia in 1966, followed six years later by Louella Parsons, who by then was senile and demented.

Perhaps it was never true that these ageing gorgons could make or break careers in Hollywood, although as the British film actor David Niven allowed, they certainly wielded, and often misused, their enormous power. 'Only Hollywood could have spawned such a couple,' Niven reminisced, 'and only Hollywood, headline hunting, self-inflating, riddled with fear and insecurity, could have allowed itself to be dominated by them for so long.'[17] Created by Hollywood, fawned on, then feared and despised, no wonder these two tough old broads succeeded in becoming stars in their own right.

17

Winchell

If any one spot might fairly lay claim to have been the cradle of the cult of modern media celebrity, it would be Table 50 at the fashionable Stork Club in New York. Between the twentieth century's two world wars and beyond, it was permanently reserved for Walter Winchell, America's most celebrated gossip writer. It was, as he put it, 'the New Yorkiest place in New York', a command post from which he ran a vast network of informants, sifting their tips and titbits before relaying the results to the 50 million Americans – two-thirds of the adult population – who read his syndicated column every day or listened to his nationally networked radio show. He spied through the keyholes of the great and the good, and for the first time America's masses were offered the chance to gape at the private frailties of public people. His breathless, impudent paragraphs echoed changing social attitudes and punctuated his homespun definition of democracy as a state in which 'everybody can kick everybody else's ass'.[1]

Walter Winchell single-handedly created celebrity journalism. His impact on modern culture was seismic, yet his gossip columns were written as ephemeral chaff; when revisited today, they are almost entirely meaningless. According to his biographer Neal Gabler, they were meant to self-destruct almost as soon as they were read. 'Their function was to let the reader be ahead of the curve, but as soon as you read them, you knew millions of people were in the know, too. You had to wait for the next one and the next one. The process repeated endlessly.'[2] In the 1930s and 1940s Winchell helped fashion the modern culture of celebrity and as the undisputed king of keyhole journalism he wrought the tabloid obsession with the 'right to know' every detail of someone's private life. Ernest Hemingway trumpeted him as 'the greatest newspaper man that ever lived'.[3] In his heyday, Winchell was credited with drawing between a third and a half of all the readers of the Hearst press with his Broadway column in the New York tabloid, *Daily Mirror*, the most widely read, oft-quoted and frequently purloined of any newspaper column in American history. The veteran BBC broadcaster Alistair Cooke likened Winchell to a freak of climate, like a tornado or electric storm, in his ability to strike and cause whirling damage before darting away over the horizon.[4]

Scavenging for gossip, Winchell coined gold in the gutter as well as new words for the language – 'slanguage' – so that people who fell in love, married, had children or were divorced, were 'on fire' or 'that way', 'middle-aisled', 'storked' or 'blessed evented', 'melted', 'Reno-vated' or 'Parised'. His hunting grounds were the nightclubs of Manhattan to which, in the era of booze and bullets, gangsters, thieves, gunmen, racketeers and their crooked associates swarmed by night to (another Winchellism) 'make whoopee'. Winchell chiselled big paragraphs from little incidents, stringing them together with ellipses, the three-dotter device that gave them ticker-tape urgency.

> The Dudley Field Malones (she was Edna Johnson of Ziegfeld's 'Louie, the 4teenth') anticipate a blessed event in Dec... Peggy ('Flying High') Mosely, an eyeful, will Lohengrin it with a Wall St lad who has plenty... The Irving Netchers (Townsend's brother) were secretly blasted in Chi[cago] last wk... Helen Henderson, ex-'Follies' femme, who divorced Bob Rice of Geo. Olsen's crew to weld the rich Aaron Benisch, only to phffft with Aaron and be resealed to Rice, was melted from him last month... Mr Moody, who gets heavy fees to tour the country and tell bankers how good American business is, laid off nine stenogs on Satdee... Don't the police know that one of the $1,500,000 jool crooks nabbed in the Commodore Hotel raid is a well-known Vth Ave. wholesale jeweller? If so, why not reveal his real tag?[5]

Gossip had never been this shiny and brittle before.

Winchell sprang from New York's bawling East Side in 1897, the son of second-generation Jewish immigrants. A dunderhead at school, he wound up in vaudeville as a song-and-dance man, or (another word he coined) 'hoofer'. From the obscurity of travelling shows, he made his break into journalism. It was an unlikely fling at fame. Backstage of every theatre is a bulletin board carrying messages for the performers. In 1919 there appeared on the bulletin boards of the Pantages vaudeville circuit a page of typewritten chit-chat pecked out by Winchell on a portable given to him by his new bride Rita. It was headed 'Newssense' and amounted to little more than a jumble of disconnected items of gossip assembled by a busybody, but the actors and acrobats who read it were tickled by it. One thing led to another: the *Vaudeville News* in New York picked up Winchell's feature; he launched a new weekly column in New York's sleazy *Evening Graphic;* it blossomed into a daily; then a syndicate bought it; and finally Winchell was hired, at a princely price, by the great William Randolph Hearst. Winchell's years as a small-time hoofer had served him well. As essayist Heywood Broun remarked, as Winchell's career took flight he only dropped his pumps for his pen when his message had taken form within his soul.[6]

Winchell's gossip was journalism as vaudeville. Show business, like his Harlem childhood, had ingrained in him raw experiences of fear, humiliation and resentment, and he applied these experiences in his column. He realized early on that as a purveyor of free publicity in the first era in history to boast a tabloid culture, he was someone to be courted and revered. 'What do you know that I don't know?' was Winchell's stock greeting, and he never flinched from discovering an answer. At the *Evening Graphic,* his editor Fulton Oursler thought Winchell's column was 'nothing to write to Chaucer about' – journalist-turned-playwright Ben Hecht once likened his stuttering prose to 'a man honking in a traffic jam'[7] – but admitted that it exuded reader appeal. 'It was personal,' explained Oursler, 'it was intimate.'[8] The idea of signing Winchell was to outshout the *Daily News* and *Daily Mirror* in the lurid New York tabloid wars. To Oursler, Winchell's real value (at $75 a week) was not so much his column as his contacts. Oursler reckoned that someone with such an overstuffed Roladex would be able to alert the city – or home news – desk to stories they might otherwise have missed.

Winchell's beat was Broadway. It was such a fertile gossip patch, especially at night, that comparisons have been drawn with the coffee-house London of the eighteenth century. Whilst New York never produced a Dr Johnson, Winchell might have laid claim to the title of Broadway's Boswell. For over three decades, what happened on

Broadway's primrose path defined America to the world: brassy, sassy, knowing, sleazy, breezy, with all the cocksure confidence of the jazz age. Winchell saw and heard it all, and chronicled it to a rapt and receptive nation. At the peak of his powers in 1940, his column was running in 1,000 newspapers across America, his audience (via radio and newspaper) was reckoned at 50 million in a country of 130 million.

Of course, there were legions of other columnists, but Winchell was unique outside the entertainment trade papers in making Broadway his exclusive domain. When he launched his column, 'Your Broadway and Mine', in September 1924, he did so as an innocent, mingling with a largely urbane circle of show people, chorus girls, prize fighters, restaurateurs, journalists and politicians who gathered nightly at Billy LaHiff's chophouse. But there was another Broadway of which Winchell knew virtually nothing, the darker, more sinister world of speakeasies, gangsters, gamblers and idle playboys. He determined to infiltrate it and write about it in his column. Winchell recruited guides to this gloomy netherworld, including Sime Silverman of *Variety* and a harpy hustler and 'hostess' called Texas Guinan. The move soon paid off. It led him into uncharted regions that he described in vivid vernacular: speakeasies became 'hush-houses', hard liquor 'giggle-water', showgirls 'torso tossers' and mistresses 'keptives'. In the toils of Prohibition, Winchell disclosed to an awestruck public a parallel universe to their own, where bootleggers and their kin drank unlimited quantities of bad liquor, gorged on bad food and smooched on impossibly small dance floors, all at outrageous prices, with a share of the profits being siphoned off by Federal agents and corrupt police officers. It was deliciously dangerous stuff.

Some of what Winchell wrote got him into trouble. He was called a 'vulture', an 'outlaw' and a 'blab-boy'; the actress Ethel Barrymore, with whom he conducted a highly public feud, thought it was 'a sad comment on American manhood that Walter Winchell is allowed to exist',[9] but Winchell was unrepentant. He seldom retracted or backed down, and he dealt ruthlessly in his column with anyone who tried to tangle with him. 'He is diabolically clever and utterly fearless,' wrote one admirer; 'he writes what he pleases and doesn't appear to care a chorine's cuss for anybody. He despises the thugs who run the night clubs and the drunken imbeciles who infest them, and says his say about them and makes no bones about it.'[10] Meanwhile Winchell's life had come to imitate his art. He became the fast-talking, gun-toting wiseguy in the image of Cagney, Raft and Bogart, cruel and vindictive, the hard-boiled newspaperman flicking his snap-brimmed fedora at critics. With unprecedented recklessness, he would reveal in his column what the Secretary for War had told the President, which Broadway actor had left his wife the night before, and who was being blackmailed by gangsters: their sins and scams were his juiciest meat throughout the 1930s. Hearing that some gangsters were moving in on him, Winchell reportedly hired his own bodyguard, but it was unnecessary; the hoodlums were coming merely to tell Winchell that they were fans. Winchell, ahead of the curve, had recognized that just like film stars, politicians and other gossip-column fodder, gangsters too liked nothing more than to see their names in print.

His readers loved it, but serious journalists were appalled. One, Heywood Broun, accused Winchell of 'smutting over a great tradition'.[11] Others complained that the smaller, cheaper papers had ceased to deal in journalism and had switched to entertainment; as such, they had more in common with the motion picture industry than with the serious press. Like the movies, the tabloids were visual, first and last. Recognizing this, William Randolph Hearst staked the success of his tabloid *Daily Mirror* on bigger, sharper, more exciting pictures. Murder trials were promoted as the tabloid equivalent of movie blockbusters, examples (argued the tabloid antagonists) of a new and distorted view of life. 'Sentimentalise everything,' bemoaned one critic as the Twenties roared, 'with cynicism just beneath. In place of the full life, or the good life, or the hard life of experience, fill the mind with a phantasmagoria where easy wealth, sordid luxury, scandal, degeneracy, and drunken folly swirl through the pages in an intoxicating vulgarity.'[12] Walter Winchell's gossip was part of the mix.

Then, as now, the media were mesmerized by personalities. On the silver screen, in magazines and in the New York tabloids, personalities were bankable; they sold. When Winchell launched himself in 1924, he challenged, then defied, a taboo, crossing into unknown territory by writing candidly about the private lives of public figures. He was encouraged by Texas Guinan, an inveterate gossip herself, a woman (in Damon Runyon's portrait of her alter ego Missouri Martin) who 'tells everything she knows as soon as she knows it, which is very often before it happens'.[13] Winchell's early columns of prurient tittle-tattle caused a sensation. 'People could scarcely believe what they saw in print,' recalled New York press agent Bernard Sobel, an old Broadway hand. 'All the old secrets of personal sex relations – who was sleeping with whom – were exposed to the public gaze... If Winchell were to keep talking this frankly, no one would be safe.'[14]

Winchell certainly kept talking. Traditional journalists complained of an affront to privacy, but there was no doubt that Winchell had identified something new in the American national consciousness that transcended voyeurism. The raffish stateliness of old Broadway had been swept away, and with it any remnants of professional modesty. Now, as one Broadway-fancier pointed out, 'a press increasingly soliciting the masses was avid for the juicy detail, and stars revealed their thoughts, which tended to be commonplace, on love and the meaning of life.'[15] Hollywood's dream factory had fuelled a new phenomenon of celebrity which, linked to growing American urbanization, was starting to change the way people thought about people. Old concepts of community were being eroded and supplanted by new concepts of society; Winchell's gossip offered a social currency that bound this new national order together, a sort of glue redolent of the old order of neighbourhoods, intimacy and mutual regard. It put the bluebloods on their guard and for once empowered the economically weak against the rich, powerful and privileged. Winchell had stormed a citadel, breached its defences and now beckoned Mr and Mrs America to follow him into its hitherto impregnable heart. When Hearst tempted Winchell to join the New York *Daily Mirror* in 1929, 200,000 of his *Graphic* readers switched papers with him and did just that.

Enthroned at the Stork Club's Table 50, Winchell dined for free, held court and handled as many as fifty phone calls a night from his web of tipsters and narks. The club's shady owner, the bullet-scarred Sherman Billingsley, fawned on Winchell as, with 'the instincts of a shit-house rat',[16] he schmoozed a ragbag of entertainers, politicians, socialites, robber barons, sportsmen and visiting European aristocrats. It was at Table 50 that Grace Kelly whispered too Winchell word of her engagement to Prince Rainier; it was there to that Lana Turner and Artie Shaw announced their divorce. But it was always Winchell's call; his column fodder, no matter how grand, approached or sat unbidden at their peril. In the kaleidoscope of gossipdom, these supplicants were either acknowledged or ruthlessly cut, blanked out by poisonous feuds and Winchell's magisterial judgments, which consigned those who had upset or betrayed him to his dreaded 'Drop Dead List'. When the Duke and Duchess of Windsor turned up at the Stork, Winchell snubbed their request to meet him, complaining that the royal couple had been too cosy with Hitler for his liking.

Winchell prospered; as early as 1929, when Wall Street crashed, he was making $500 a week from his Hearst column and boasted about his bloated balances, flipping open his bank book and inviting his friends to 'take a gander at that'.[17] He earned it. Haunted by the fear of failure, he worked furiously to satisfy the column's insatiable appetite for material. He had manic energy and often worked around the clock, claiming that he didn't count a day productive without seeing or talking to fifty or sixty contacts. He never went to bed before dawn or rose before noon. When he complained to his friend and mentor Mark Hellinger that he couldn't get any sleep, Hellinger reminded him that Edison only slept four hours a night, 'and he invented the electric light'.

'Yeah,' Winchell shot back, 'but he didn't have a column to write.'[18]

In the early 1930s, Winchell began his weekly radio broadcast, which propelled him from being America's best-known journalist to national stardom. As the Depression deepened, newspaper circulation faltered while wireless ownership soared, and Winchell caught the wave. 'Like a tornado,' Alistair Cooke reported, 'Mr Winchell comes roaring out of the air at his listeners every Sunday evening at nine o'clock, and to 25,000,000 Americans he is as impressive as the voice of a prophet.'[19] He wobbled at first, thinking he would flop 'because I talk too fast',[20] but his curiously high-pitched, rasping, driven style electrified the airwaves. Winchell's opening words each week – 'Good evening Mr and Mrs America and all the ships at sea' – became his signature.

Cooke once dropped into Winchell's studio to watch him work. 'He tore at his tie; he pushed his hat back; he talked in a frenzy for fifteen minutes and tore for the tape just in time to bid a frantic goodnight to Mr and Mrs America.'[21] It sounded like a three-ring circus – indeed, the show was structured like a vaudeville bill – but behind the machine-gun fusillade Winchell used what became his weekly 'Lucky Strike Dance

Hour' to back the artful Democrat President, Franklin D. Roosevelt, in his New Deal crusade to get America working again. Winchell enjoyed special access to the White House, staying behind after press conferences for tête-à-têtes with the President in his private office. Here, Winchell would regale him with his funniest jokes and spiciest gossip. In return, Roosevelt fed him with titbits of insider government information. Winchell became the President's most vocal advocate, pushing his radical reforms and rallying support for his policies at home and abroad, in particular American intervention in Europe. Roosevelt's programme stirred Winchell's instinctive social liberalism, and also meant he could wave the patriotic flag too.

As early as 1933 he began a roistering campaign against Hitler, alerting America, which was preoccupied with the Depression at home, to the danger in Europe. When the Nazis invaded Poland, Winchell cabled the British Prime Minister Neville Chamberlain, suggesting that Britain should declare war not on Germany but on Hitler personally. Winchell's conduit to the White House, his Falstaffian lawyer Ernest Cuneo, was sitting with him at the Stork when Winchell announced his decision to wire Chamberlain. Cuneo, according to Winchell's biographer Neal Gabler, 'thought it took enormous gall for him to believe that Chamberlain or Kennedy would want advice from a gossip columnist'.[22] Through the US ambassador in London, Joseph P. Kennedy, Chamberlain explained that such a move would be constitutionally impossible.

Traditionalists scorned Winchell's pretensions as a news commentator, believing that they represented a further coarsening of the American media culture. But Winchell seemed to think nothing of it. It was, he felt, simply an extension of Hearst's razzmatazz approach to journalism, like hiring a hula dancer to gyrate on the cathedral steps, drawing the biggest crowds to sample the serious stuff within. Actually, Hearst disapproved of his star gossip man straying into serious debate. For one thing, Hearst's own political creed was completely at odds with Winchell's, which created a tension that wound tighter and tighter over the best part of a decade. In the spring of 1938, Hearst angrily messaged all his editors: 'Please edit Winchell very carefully and leave out any dangerous or disagreeable paragraphs. Indeed, leave out the whole column without hesitation, as I think he has gotten so careless that he is no longer of any particular value.'[23]

Yet at his peak, Winchell was hailed as a national icon as well as a folk hero. He created a new journalistic form, extending the boundaries of what is news to include the most private behaviour of public personalities. He reigned as the undisputed emperor of gossip, swatting away criticism of his ethical standards as so much humbug. 'As if this or that newspaper cares a continental about ethics,' he wrote in early 1932, 'in these wild days of thefting each other's circulation ideas, plans and all the other malaaaarkey that passes for tradition – haw!'[24] While the sobersides of the newspaper establishment continued to fret about the new cult of gossip – Winchellism – 'endangering the good name of journalism'[25] (as Marlen Pew bewailed in *Editor and Publisher*), there was also the question of image. Both Broadway and Hollywood had seized on Winchell as a model for stereotype journalists, fast-talking, wisecracking, cynical, fedora-crowned, unscrupulous snoopers, or 'journalistic gangsters', as Pew saw them. This was in fact very much how Winchell promoted himself, but he claimed that it was an act '[s]o that people won't think I'm a columnist'.[26] He acted it to the full, neglecting his wife and surrounding himself with glamorous actresses and a string of showgirls girls eager for a break and a mention in his column or on the air. 'The problem with having a mistress,' he reflected, 'is not the screwing part. It's having to eat dinner twice in one night.'[27] Not that Winchell flinched from his extramarital adventures. 'Sex,' he pointed out, 'is the most fun you can have without laughing.'[28]

Winchell has been judged a baleful influence on news and newspapers. True, he savoured of much that was disreputable: working for Hearst and his distasteful tabloids offered, in the venomous view of Ambrose Bierce, 'all the reality of masturbation',[29] and there were sinister links with the Mafia and with J. Edgar Hoover, chief of the FBI. Winchell's conceit was limitless and, harnessed to his powers to make or break, could create a towering and overbearing monster. St Clair McKelway, a writer who scrutinized Winchell's columns for the *New Yorker* in 1940, believed their effect was pernicious; gossip, he argued, had infected the regular news from home and abroad even in the most conservative newspapers. McKelway detected 'gossip-writing techniques' in the way important national and international affairs were being reported and concluded that it was the fault of one man: Walter Winchell. Yet by the end of the same decade, two New York historians were garlanding him as 'the reporter who has done more to rouse the conscience of America against intolerance and totalitarianism than any other journalist of his time'.[30] Others felt his contribution to public discourse amounted to little; as E. B. White complained, reading Winchell was like crawling home from nightclubs 'carrying a basket of fluff'.[31] As Walter himself might have mused: orchids one day, scallions (spring onions) the next.

It was Winchell's fate to be crowned the first celebrity journalist at the dawn of the celebrity age. He was the man for the hour, a hustler hack who stepped into the limelight at the dawn of the 1920s and who flourished like an exotic desert bloom during the thirteen-year drought of Prohibition. The 1920s were destined to be big news, dizzying years of history-making events, big crimes, big trials, big stars, a sulphurous brew that fostered not just gossip columns but a new pitched battle of brawling tabloids on the New York streets. The irreverent *Daily News* set the pace, but when Hearst leaped in with his *Mirror* in 1924 it was all-out war, with the papers sinking to the occasion and Winchell leading the charge. Columnist Westbrook Pegler, who derided Winchell as 'a gent's room journalist', likened the Hearst style to 'a screaming woman running down the street with her throat cut'[32] and it certainly seems that Winchell's contributions to the *Mirror* were often more sound and fury than substance: 'The Sig Thayers (Emily Vanderbilt) romance has wilted already,' began his debut *Mirror* column in June 1929. 'As soon as they get their respective decrees, Sonny Whitney and Mrs Edgar Warburton will be sealed.' This, as Winchell's critic McKelway pointed out, was half true. 'The first item was correct, the second incorrect, and contained a misspelled name,' he explained, 'but it was gossip and it was good gossip.'[33]

Not that the poacher was anxious to turn gamekeeper. When Winchell's own privacy was threatened by the *Saturday Evening Post* in 1938, he threw a fit. 'No, sir!' he roared at writer J. P. McEvoy. 'You can say anything you like about me, but you've got to keep my family out of this.'

'But Walter,' McEvoy protested, 'you've made a national reputation and a tremendous fortune out of other people's private affairs.'

'That's different,' Winchell replied. 'That's business.'[34]

In the end, Walter Winchell faded out. Television made his column and his radio show seem quaint and ultimately redundant. In the 1950s and 1960s he lost his grip on the new national mood and was reduced to buying space in the trade press, begging newspaper publishers to run his column. His private life spiralled too: his second wife left him, his drug-addicted son Walter Jr shot himself dead and he had his daughter Walda committed to an asylum after a bungled suicide attempt. After the war, the famous columnist who had been on back-slapping terms at Roosevelt's White House became the scourge of liberal America, a ranting right-winger who threw his weight behind Senator Joseph McCarthy's Communist witch-hunt, becoming more paranoid and erratic as he slid towards self-destruction. When he died of cancer in 1972, alone and forgotten, his daughter was the only mourner at the funeral.

The man who dispensed or denied fame at Table 50, who invented the cult of fleeting media celebrity, became a victim of its rules. But in redefining the role of the press, Walter Winchell bequeathed a curious legacy, placing the media at the centre of events that once they merely reported. In 1935, Winchell covered the trial of a German immigrant carpenter, Bruno Hauptmann, for the kidnap and murder of the infant son of America's heroic aviator, Charles Lindbergh. In an early example of media frenzy, some five hundred reporters and photographers covered the spectacle, with Winchell, who turned in 70,000 words of copy, turning tragedy into entertainment. Since then, such trials have become a rite of celebrity culture; sixty years later, the O. J. Simpson case, attended by batteries of star writers and gossip-gleaners, would furnish the live-as-it-happens rolling news age with a roaring echo of the case that helped forge the Winchell legend.

18

Snoops and Privacy

Part of the function of the press has always been to pry. As George Orwell suggested, a fair definition of news is simply that it is information someone wants to conceal; everything else is just public relations.[1] Gossip-gleaners have always operated on both sides of the divide, but it is the unedifying business of disclosure – what one might describe as un-concealment – that has produced both the juiciest gossip and the most distress; one man's disclosure is often another's invaded privacy. Treading this fine line in pursuit of a story has been the undoing of many a journalist. Pressure to find the story is enormous, but so are the lengths to which the unscrupulous are prepared to go. Press invasion of privacy has a history as long and as colourful as the press itself; intrusion, subterfuge, duplicity, deception, false representation, eavesdropping, none is the exclusive invention of the tabloid age. Only with changing public attitudes to such antics in the mid-twentieth century did the press confront the privacy issue.

Between the wars, the papers clamoured for 'human interest' stories behind sensational murder trials, often picking up the defence lawyer's bill in return. When the louche seductress Alma Rattenbury committed suicide in 1935 after her Old Bailey acquittal on a charge of murdering her cuckolded husband, the crime novelist Francis Iles complained that 'Mrs Rattenbury was, for all practical purposes, hounded to her death by reporters.'[2] Journalists staked out the house in London where she had been taken after the trial and, although police cleared the street of a hostile crowd, the reporters refused to move. When the wretched woman finally emerged to be bundled into her doctor's car, one reporter shouted: 'If you take her [home] to Bournemouth, we'll follow you there!'[3] The King's abdication the following year and the 'outing' of Mrs Simpson as his mistress stoked the debate to a new intensity. The editor of the *Daily Mirror*, Cecil Thomas, wondered aloud what newspapers were really for and whether they should print only 'nice' news. 'The truth is,' he declared, 'the London Press is already far too niminy-piminy, too nice altogether, too refined, too ready to leave out, too reluctant to print without fear or favour. So refined, in fact, that some newspapers would rather not give the news than tell their readers the truth.'[4]

In 1962, one of nature's greatest gossips, the novelist Evelyn Waugh, made a huge fuss about a harmless paragraph that had appeared in the *Sunday Telegraph* concerning the circumstances in which he had turned down the offer of a CBE. Waugh decided (wrongly) that he had been betrayed to the paper's diarist, Kenneth Rose, by Lady Pamela Berry, wife of the *Telegraph*'s editor-in-chief, at whose house he had lunched and discussed the invitation. Furiously, Waugh denounced Lady Pamela as 'little Miss Judas Sneakhostess' and 'Lady Randolph Grubstreet',[5] recalling a controversy from the late 1920s involving what the newspapers called 'sneak guests' – impoverished young men who sold gossip to Fleet Street. Waugh's complaint was about an item devoid of sexual content, but the 'sneak guests' of the 1920s were hell-bent on dishing some dirt. The hoo-ha began when *The Times*, which then employed no gossip writer, diarist or columnist, whipped up an agitation against what it called the practice of columnism, publishing a letter signed by 'A London Hostess', which deplored this 'new and dangerous tendency in our social life' and complained that her hospitality was being abused by these sneaks who tattled to the press about what her guests had been up to. 'What was at one time mere idle and comparatively harmless chatter (written in many cases with no personal knowledge of the people concerned),' the letter continued, 'has lately developed in certain quarters into a regular system of spying, followed by the publication of the most deplorable hints and insinuations.'[6]

Of course, far from being new and dangerous, the gossiping tendency could be traced back at least to Roman times. In any case, many London hostesses of the time were anxious for publicity, if only to reassure their creditors, and some were known to devise devious ruses in order to get mentioned, in some cases bribing go-betweens with contacts in Fleet Street. A Labour minister in Ramsay Macdonald's government, J. H. Thomas, described these gossip-grubbers as 'pin money' journalists, but according to one gossip columnist who wrote in response to *The Times*'s affronted hostess, there was more at stake than that. 'Anyone who is suspected of contributing paragraphs to the Press is pursued, flattered, and bribed to a well-nigh incredible degree,'[7] he wrote, adding that swanky gifts, free meals and first-class return train tickets to country house shooting parties were among the blandishments on offer. The Bishop of Durham joined in, deploring the modern appetite for personal gossip but pointing out that demand created supply. 'The vanity of the sneak-host,' he boomed, 'is hardly less prolific than the sordid enterprise of the sneak guest.'[8]

What this controversy did was to illuminate some subtle social changes, not just a keener taste for spicy gossip but a loosening of the stays of discretion and good manners. To the old guard, trade in gossip, like the increased bandying of first names to propose instant intimacy, was as much a regrettable feature of slacker social rules as the growing disregard for notions of privacy and privilege. Gentlemen's clubs were a good example. The long-standing point of honour that nothing said within a club's walls would be repeated outside had been abandoned, and confidences now babbled in the streets of St James's like rainwater, while gossipy books and chatty memoirs spilled off the presses. It was inevitable, as *The Times* observed with dismay, that popular newspapers should not remain unaffected by 'this growing neglect of reticence and personal and family privacy'. Such quaint notions of discretion continued to unravel throughout the 1930s. When one the Mitford girls ran away to Spain in 1937 to marry without parental consent, her brother-in-law, Peter Rennell Rodd, fulminated against the *Daily Express* for running the story against the wishes of the family, adding that privacy was essential if matters weren't to be made even worse.[9]

In the space of two generations, the keyhole peepers of the press had stormed the citadel of Edwardian domestic decorum. In the early years of the twentieth century, to protect their privacy and to keep the public paragraph-writers in check, society ladies often hired their own. These were usually women with Fleet Street connections, a sort of cross between gossip writer and press agent, poacher and gamekeeper concurrently, who would supply the papers with details of her ladyship's clothes, movements and entertainments, arrange for the woman's photograph to be published and, whenever the chance arose, slip in paragraphs that would vex her rivals. The rewards were modest: a little money or clothing, plus some extra scraps of gossip to feed to the papers about other, sometimes rival, society women. From polite society's point of view, this self-service system of setting paragraphs afloat was flexible, reliable and cheap. It virtually guaranteed privacy as well as a burnished reputation and a flattering public profile.

But in the world of society columns, as in almost every other facet of British social life, the Great War changed everything. 'Before the war,' explained gossip writer Patrick Balfour, 'people had greater freedom within society's ranks, because the social columnists were all outside them. Thus were they able to keep up a reputable face to the world. Their ignominious money intrigues and their scandals never saw the light of day.'[10] And not just their intrigues and scandals but their indecorous behaviour, too. Balfour himself incurred the wrath of a prominent politician's wife who demonstrated in a public restaurant that she could touch her toes. When he published a paragraph about it in his column, the woman was furious, contending that it held her up to public ridicule. But the genie was out of the bottle. The old deference, guaranteeing immunity from the impudence of social inferiors, was crumbling. By the early 1930s, gossip writers were all over London, recording the preening and pratfalls of the great and the good. As Patrick Balfour observed in 1932, people who wanted to preserve their pre-war reputation had to be twice as careful as they were then. 'You dare not behave like a fishwife in somebody's drawing room. There may be a social columnist present, who will record your antics. Before the war, you could do these things; but it is different now.'[11]

Of course, despite the worries of a few London hostesses and their unwelcome sneak guests, most gossip writers did their social rounds by invitation rather than stealth. Gossip-gathering was no longer a question of pressing eyes and ears to keyholes, as the Edwardians did. The so-called Harriet affair exposed such low practices. In those *Upstairs Downstairs* days, it was the servants who were blamed. In January 1911, this letter appeared in *The Times* under the heading 'Scandalmongers':

Sir: My butler who is leaving my service recently advertised for a situation and in reply received a letter of which I send you a copy. It is difficult to believe that anyone with the slightest pretensions of being a lady should descend to methods mean and contemptible. Such methods throw an enormous temptation in the way of servants, besides exposing them to actions for slander should they fall into the trap ... It appears one's servants are to be bribed to repeat all the tittle-tattle they hear, when no doubt it will be worked up into something 'spicy' by the spurious journalist ... [12]

The writer, signing himself 'Householder', enclosed the letter to his butler. This was signed 'Harriet'. Harriet said that she had noted the butler's advertisement in the *Morning Post*, and explained that she would be 'pleased to hear from you if you have half an hour to spare once or twice a week and would care to turn it into cash by writing me a long gossipy letter about well-known people in English Society who stay in the houses where you are employed. I pay liberally and settle each month.' 'Harriet' added that the material would be sold to American newspapers which, she said, 'insist' on having information of this kind. 'To give you an idea of what I buy,' she went on, 'I may say that just now anything about Lady Gerard and the De Forests is "good copy" on account of the slander case between them now coming on; also about the Dillon jockey on account of the Marie Lloyd divorce suit, in which he is co-respondent.' And for good measure, 'Harriet' asked the mortified butler to put her in touch with any of his friends on the staffs of Lord Howard de Walden (then figuring in a libel suit), the King's grocer Sir Thomas Lipton, or the sovereign's mistress Alice Keppel, not forgetting talkative restaurant employees at Claridges, the Savoy, the Gaiety, the Waldorf and the leading London clubs.[13]

The Times itself, in a maidenly fit of the vapours, fired off an indignant leader at what it identified as 'a new pest of society', an organized system of paid snoops in the servants' halls of the mighty which would shock and disgust everyone, especially women. The paper made it clear that in its opinion the whole wretched business was the fault of the essentially caddish Americans whose press, the *Globe* sneered next day, was 'the most degraded form of journalism', adding that attempts by the likes of Harriet to bribe the servants added a new terror to private life. The *Evening Standard* congratulated *The Times* for revealing 'the sordid secrets of a sordid trade' and thought such exposure may, at least, 'cause those ladies and gentlemen who are accustomed to flavour their talk with current tittle-tattle to be more careful what they say now that they know there may be a paid sneak behind their chair'.[14] Curtis Brown, the London representative of (and supplier of gossip to) various American papers, disclosed that he too had received a similar letter from Harriet, 'except that the precious news offered to me was to be gathered by "quite an army of girl friends in the best of the various English society sets"'. He denied that 'this particularly obnoxious specimen of scandal-mongering had its origin in America',[15] but as the campaign grew, evidence emerged of an undeniable American appetite for English society chit-chat. A West End physician disclosed to *The Times* a 'disgusting' letter he had received from an American woman journalist, soliciting 'any amount of [society] scandal, for which I pay most liberally.' The (unnamed) journalist was anxious to have first refusal of 'rumours of any *causes célèbres*, divorces &c., and also to know of the financial shifts and difficulties of any well-known people', adding that 'the class of public for whom I cater are particularly interested in any scandal affecting the Royal Families [sic].'[16]

'Harriet' was partially unmasked by other newspapers as a Miss Harriet Churchill of Birmingham, but *The Times* claimed that this was not her real name. She had apparently worked as a journalist in that city for some years, taking frequent holidays (presumably on the proceeds of her gossip gleanings) which she spent hunting with friends. But it soon transpired that it wasn't just the servants that Harriet Churchill had in her sights. The teenage daughter of a peer sent *The Times* a copy of a letter that Harriet had written her the previous autumn:

> *Chestnut Cottage, Ladywood Road, Birmingham*
> 28 September 1910
>
> Madam,
>
> As the English correspondent of several American papers, I purchase large quantities of gossip about well-known people and anecdotes – amusing or malicious, preferably both!
>
> I pay *liberally* and never under any circumstances disclose the names of my correspondents.
>
> I am wondering whether it would be possible to induce you to become one of them, sending me a weekly, or later on, perhaps, bi-weekly, letter containing ten or twelve pieces of gossip and anecdotes?

You will of course understand that nothing which has appeared in the English Press is of any use; also that it is only the *latest on dits* and previous information of rumoured *causes célèbres* with the reported co-respondents' names, financial difficulties, &c., of well-known people which it is worthwhile sending me, as anything that has already appeared in rival papers when my letters or cables arrive my editors of course 'scrap' at once (*i.e.* consign to the W. P. B.).

For this reason I have hitherto paid quarterly, but after Christmas I can if you prefer it arrange to pay monthly, at the end of the month *succeeding* the month in which any news or anecdotes sent me by you appeared; I do not know for six weeks after I send my letters how much of my stuff has been used – it all, as I said, depends on whether I have been forestalled in any of it by correspondents of rival papers.

If you are inclined to consider my proposal to become one of my regular 'scouts' I would suggest that you send me ten or twelve specimen pieces of gossip and anecdotes about the following people: Prince Francis of Teck, Lord Winterton, Lord Anglesey, Lord Howard de Walden, Lord Curzon of Kedleston (Americans are particularly interested in gossip about his re-marriage), Sir Ernest Cassel, Sir Thomas Lipton, Mrs George Keppel, Duke and Duchess of Marlborough, Lord and Lady Sackville and Miss Sackville-West, Lord Kitchener, Lady Crewe, Sir Arthur and Lady Hardinge, Sir Charles and Lady Hardinge.

Any gossip or anecdotes à propos of the rumoured intention of King George and Queen Mary to discourage the reception of American *nouveaux riches* in English Society.

Also anything amusing about Anglo-American peeresses is always welcomed by my readers.

Yours cordially,

(Miss) HARRIET CHURCHILL

If you write please say if you prefer payment by cheque, notes, or postal orders.[17]

The letter offers an extraordinary glimpse into the world of the Edwardian tabloid journalist. But it has an unmistakably modern echo, with its promise of money and secrecy, its insistence on exclusivity, a sort of A-list of current celebrities in the public eye and the idle snooper's presumption that others will do the work on his or her behalf and (at least at first) for nothing.

By the 1950s, the figure of the snooping newspaper reporter was becoming a familiar caricature. The playwright John Osborne, who had briefly worked as a reporter on technical journals between school and National Service, was obsessed by what he considered to be the evils of gutter journalism, and he sketched out some ideas for a piece on this theme even before making his name with *Look Back in Anger* in 1956. The material was eventually reworked into his musical play, *The World of Paul Slickey* (1959), a critical and commercial flop that parodies the self-loathing of a Fleet Street gossip columnist lost in a maze of sexual intrigue. Osborne dedicated the play 'to the liars and self-deceivers; to those who daily deal out treachery'.[18] An even seedier figure, a cynical reporter called Stanley, appears in Osborne's short play *Under Plain Cover* (1963), but this time drawn from life. The story (Osborne called it 'a light *cadenza* on the clash of public prurience and private innocence')[19] is based on a real one from 1955, when Harry Procter, chief investigator for the tabloid *Sunday Pictorial*, exposed the accidentally incestuous marriage of siblings in the Midlands under the two-inch-high headline, I MARRIED MY BROTHER. By a happenstance, Osborne, the angry young man of British theatre and twice married, stumbled into the public debate over press intrusion almost by accident when he took up with the flame-haired writer Penelope Gilliatt, whose name had appeared over the *Queen* magazine exposé of gossip columnists the year before. As the best-known playwright of his generation, young, successful and affluent, John Osborne felt permanently under siege from nosy newspaper reporters; having guyed the gossiping trade in *The World of Paul Slickey*, he might have anticipated a heavy return of fire. It wasn't long in coming.

With his mistress, the doe-eyed costume designer of *Slickey*, Jocelyn Rickards, Osborne had found an ideal country retreat, The Old Water Mill at Hellingly in Sussex. Curiously, their happy discovery in 1961 coincided with Osborne's decision to dump one used mistress in favour of a new one, so it was with the scourge of Fleet Street, Penelope Gilliatt, at the wheel of her new Triumph Herald, that Osborne was driven through the night to what both had hoped would be their new adulterous fastness. In fact, as they turned into the narrow lane leading to the house, they drove into the jaws of a tabloid stake-out. 'Our path was blocked by dozens of cars; we were dazzled by battalions of light from all directions,' Osborne recalled. 'Figures and faces advanced on the little roadster. Hemmed in by cameras, microphones, flashlights, notebooks, we stumbled our way across the creaky, narrow bridge that straddled the stream beside the Mill. We were pelted with questions by a couple of dozen reporters and cameramen.'[20]

Someone had blown the whistle.

Worse, Osborne's gay actor friend Anthony Creighton had drunkenly asked the rest of the press corps into the house, and some were the worse for wear. Coverage of the famous runaways extended far beyond Osborne's detested gossip columns; the couple were real news, and accounts of their arrival at the playwright's remote 'love-nest' (the kind of deliciously illicit retreat Osborne had coveted ever since first hearing the expression as a youngster) were splattered over the news pages of the popular papers. *The Times* and *Guardian* ignored the story; Osborne himself sneered at the 'louche behaviour of the footman's paper',[21] the *Telegraph*, which gave it double the space accorded by either the *Mail* or the *Express*, running it on its middle page opposite the leading articles. The *Spectator's* Cyril Ray was stunned:

> I have always thought that one measure of a newspaper's dignity is whether *any* of its stories could have been undertaken by *any* member of its staff without his feeling ashamed of himself and his calling... I should have thought that a paper with the *Telegraph's* pretensions to gentility would have hesitated before even exposing the lowliest of its staff to having to report that he was told, 'She doesn't want to talk to you. Nor do I. Now go away.[22]

The newspaper historian Francis Williams complained of 'a disgrace to journalism... one of the most disreputable and degrading examples of what passes in Fleet Street for newspaper enterprise I have come across in years.'[23]

Osborne recoiled from the journalist's life; he admitted to the necessary cheekiness of spirit but also conceded that 'my irreverence was not the pushy, imperturbable kind necessary to a young reporter. Even at the highest level, it seemed a striving, unrelenting pursuit, untroubled by inner life or dignity.'[24] Osborne considered the popular British press to be predominantly lower middle class, never able to 'restrain their spite against someone who must surely be of their own kind'.[25] The result was a mutual dislike and hostility lasting forty years.[26] He believed that papers like the *Mail*, *Express* and *Telegraph* traduced and vilified him constantly, rubbishing his work and his personal life with 'a vindictive, retributive energy that arrogantly disputes the possibility of natural decency'.[27]

Surveying Fleet Street's best-known 'professional snoopers [and their] dumb twaddling', Osborne ridiculed in particular the *Mail*'s Nigel Dempster as 'an Australian coxcomb who assumes the airs of a floor-walker lately fitted from Fortnum's for colonial chippiness and demoted to the counter of a Jermyn Street shirtmaker, from which he jumped into the arms of a Duke's daughter: a bizarre alliance of patrician beauty and fawning braggart'.[28] But the name Dempster first loomed large in the gossip pages of the 1970s, an era in which the tattling trade became sharper, nastier and more cut-throat than ever, in which the gossip-guzzling public demanded glitz with everything.

19

Sex and the Body Politic

Gossip curdled in the 1970s, and ceased to be any kind of journalistic confection. The candyfloss world of 1960s columnists like the *Mail*'s Charles Greville and Ephraim Hardcastle of the *Sunday Express* began to seem unreal and Utopian, viewed through a telescope from the start of a new century, because the conventions of the gossip column had long since mutated into something much more complex. In the mid-1960s, a typical Hardcastle column would be exclusively 'social', concerned only with the marriages, broken marriages, engagements and so on of a comparatively small circle drawn from London 'society'. Many, indeed most, of the names mean nothing at all today, having blown away like so much chaff, but *haut ton* and high society are constant themes running through the crumbly little paragraphs like veins of silver. 'They are basically "inside stories" about people and events,' observed the sociologist Stuart Hall at the height of the Swinging Sixties, 'inconsequential stories about consequential people.'[1]

In the 1970s, the protocol changed completely, with a growing demand for scandal that, particularly in the mid-market circulation battle, Fleet Street was happy to satisfy. The appetite for keyhole peeping, barely suppressed since the *Mail* and *Express* cleaned up their gossip columns in the wake of the 1960 Jocelyn Stevens exposé in *Queen* magazine, returned more keenly than ever. The continuing post-war decline in deference encouraged better-educated journalists (playwright Arnold Wesker's 'anonymous little Farts of Fleet Street')[2] to target and challenge Establishment figures whose standing in national life had for so long guaranteed them immunity. Perhaps the trend was inevitable as anti-Establishment proprietors like the Australian Rupert Murdoch strengthened their grip on the British media, but what could scarcely have been foreseen was the flowering of the new celebrity culture. By the end of the decade, gossip had moved out of its ghetto and on to the front pages, offering an increasingly star-struck readership a bewildering array of inconsequential stories about equally inconsequential people. Rock singers and film stars, television actors and radio disc jockeys, nightclub owners and fashion models, all jostled for attention in Fleet Street's new 'popocracy'.

The *Mail*, the first middle-market paper to recognize the stirrings of this phenomenon, was relaunched as a tabloid in 1971 by the new editor, David English. The paper's strategy was to attract women readers ('Every woman needs her *Daily Mail*'), so English hired an American, Suzy Knickerbocker, to write the paper's gossip at a reported fee of £1,000 a week. When this experiment failed, she was replaced by Paul Callan, an Old Etonian poached from the 'Londoner's Diary' at the *Evening Standard*, with a brief to concentrate on stories about marital rifts, a direct throwback to the discredited ways of the late 1950s. As one Fleet Street commentator remarked, Paul Slickey was back at the typewriter.

In the early 1970s, *Daily Mirror* boss Hugh Cudlipp had predicted that the old-style gossip column was finished; the dawn of the permissive society meant that no one was interested any longer in who was sleeping with whom. Rupert Murdoch, on the other hand, realized that permissiveness actually sharpened the public's taste for sexual scandals, packing his *Sun* with unprecedented amounts of titillation. Paul Callan too showed that sex – and especially celebrity sex – continued to sell newspapers. The new *Zeitgeist* meant a new freedom for gossip writers. When Callan discovered that a Tory minister had visited a sex show in Brussels, he ran it in his column as his lead story. No one complained. 'In the mid-Sixties,' Callan recalled, 'a story like that about a minister of the crown would have caused questions in the House, no end of trouble. But there wasn't a peep. Not even a letter.'[3] In the summer of 1972, Callan ran a paragraph reporting an alleged affair between a married musician and a woman music critic. This prompted the journalist Peter Paterson to warn gossip writers against a return to the 'personalised, prying, intrusive style of writing which caused gratuitous distress to the people singled out for comment, and which dwelt heavily on the matrimonial disasters of people well-known to the public'.[4] This criticism so gravelled Callan that he resigned his job at the *Mail* and moved (temporarily) to broadcasting, returning to Fleet Street within eighteen months to write gossip for the *Mirror*.

In October 1973, English hired Nigel Dempster, then on the Hickey column at the *Express*, to start a new gossip page. Dempster had been taking pot-shots at the *Mail*'s Charles Greville team in *Private Eye*'s 'Grovel' column, to such effect that he was finally offered their job. Dempster had worked under Richard Berens, who edited Hickey in the early 1970s with great panache. Berens was 'just an Old Etonian shit', reflected Ross Benson, another *Express* diarist, 'with a quarter of a million in the bank and a lot of style'.[5] Dempster also had a public-school background (he left Sherborne at the age of sixteen) and married into money; his second wife is Lady Camilla, wealthy daughter of the late Duke of Leeds. His early career included stints as hospital porter, 'the youngest broker in the history of Lloyds',[6] New York nightclub doorman and vacuum cleaner salesman. Perhaps to his own surprise, Dempster's switchback career has so far kept him more or less anchored at the *Mail*, despite regular announcements that he is 'leaving'. He has a high opinion of his market value. When Robert Maxwell offered him the editorship of the *Mirror* diary, Dempster demanded £3,000 a week plus a £250,000 transfer fee. 'It's ridiculous that Captain Bob can't afford a great column,' declared the self-proclaimed Greatest Living Englishman, 'but I was quaking in my boots that he might accept my offer.'[7] Sometimes he is beset by self-doubt: when the *Mail*'s proprietor Lord Rothermere rubbished his column as tasting like 'an old, cold fried potato',[8] Dempster complained that he couldn't carry on, but that was in 1979, since when he has outlasted and in some cases outlived every other diary editor in London.

In the spring of 1975 it was Nigel Dempster who landed the scoop that Lady Antonia Fraser, the Roman Catholic wife of a Tory MP and a best-selling historical novelist, was having an affair with the left-wing playwright Harold Pinter. When Pinter's wife, the actress Vivien Merchant, sued for divorce, naming Lady Antonia, Dempster illustrated the story with smiling pictures of six of her previous lovers. In splashing details of Lady Antonia's private life across its pages, the *Mail* was regarded as having achieved a sort of journalistic breakthrough, something to rival the 1960s saga of that other playwright, John

Osborne, and his mistress Penelope Gilliatt. 'He *is* Paul Slickey,' insisted a BBC producer who worked with Dempster. 'He is proud of it. He is proud of being disliked.'[9] Dempster's demonization among the upper classes made his name.

The editor of *The Times*, William Rees-Mogg, vented his dislike of Dempsterism, accusing the *Mail* and *Express* diaries of 'straight scandalmongering',[10] but Dempster countered that 'the function of a gossip column is to generate news',[11] having already admitted that his function in particular was 'to spy for my readers'.[12] The socialite Arianna Stassinopoulos, an occasional target of gossip herself in the early 1970s, complained that amid the 'mincing, self-congratulatory, condescending, laboriously trivial and fathomlessly dull revelations about nonentities... real people get hurt'.[13] Dempster, however, was unrepentant. Hailing the revival of the monster of old-style gossip-writing, he proclaimed himself Dr Frankenstein. 'I am responsible,' he boasted, 'for the re-emergence of the genre.'[14]

Nigel Dempster once justified his keyhole columns by likening them to a social crusade. He listed his targets: 'Politicians, people who feed off the House of Lords, people who feed off inherited wealth, all those rich aristocrats whose money was made from Lancashire coal mines. People who maltreat waiters. People who seek money, fame, power, public approval. I am the defender of the public. It is my great joy and pleasure to show that the privileged are not what they claim to be. There's been criticism of my material,' he acknowledged, 'but don't forget we are dealing with highly resourceful and powerful people.'[15] He is a puzzling figure, complex and contradictory, bombastic yet insecure. But over nearly thirty years, he has become the best-known gossip writer in the world. When Dempster started in the business in the mid-1960s, gossip was corralled in the gossip columns. 'Now,' he explained, 'it's on page one, it's on page one hundred, it's everywhere.'[16] That's largely down to Dempster.

He cultivates an image of unruffled urbanity, but he has all the brawling instincts of a street fighter. That's vital in such a litigious area of journalism; no one could dominate the gossip heap without a glint of steel and a dash of poison. He has lost many friends as a result of plying his trade, but he has also made new ones along the way; these included Princess Margaret, about whom he published an admiring biography in 1981. They do not seem to have included his one-time boss, Vere Harmsworth. 'What Dempster writes in his column,' the *Mail* supremo reportedly declared in 1977, 'is one third lies, one third truth and the other third he works up from some social tit-bit or other he is given.'[17] Nevertheless, Dempster has had more than his fair share of scoops; what he would not or could not print on his page in the *Mail* often used to appear in *Private Eye's* 'Grovel' column. It was here, in 1974, that he first floated a paragraph about Princess Margaret's affair with young Roddy Llewellyn. It was there too, in November 1975, that he ran another about Norman Scott and the Liberal Party leader, Jeremy Thorpe, a typical 'Grovel' fragment that was to signal Thorpe's spectacular downfall: 'A Mr Norman Scott has sent me some very curious material concerning his close friend, the Liberal leader Jeremy Thorpe. If Mr Thorpe would send me my usual fee, £5, I will send him the dossier and say no more.'[18]

The Thorpe affair was the first political sex scandal to topple a national party leader in modern times, and it was also the one that introduced allegations of criminal violence into British politics. Throughout the 1970s, 'Grovel' printed items that forced the pace for Fleet Street, but this one, with its unspoken hint of a homosexual relationship, was problematic. The story was a confusing jigsaw, which only made sense in the context of the two men's affair. But, fearful of the consequences from a wrathful political establishment, none of the newspapers was prepared to print the fact that Thorpe was gay. Police officers investigating the mysterious shooting of Norman Scott's Great Dane Rinka on Exmoor knew that the case involved serious criminal misbehaviour, but the Director of Public Prosecutions hesitated, while Fleet Street continued its stately dance round the edges of the story. The touchpaper smouldered for nearly three more years. Only when the police leaked details of the allegations against Thorpe to *Private Eye* in August 1978 was the DPP persuaded to act. Even then Thorpe tried to sue the magazine for criminal libel in an attempt to create a diversion from the continuing police investigation into his activities.

Thorpe's relationship with Norman Scott, a former male model, turned into one of Britain's greatest political scandals, with Thorpe accused of conspiring to hire a hit man to kill Scott and his dog. Scott, a sponger and a drifter with an interest in horses, found life difficult to cope with: everything and everyone seemed to him to conspire against him. Thorpe had befriended him in the early 1960s, helped him find a job and somewhere to live; also (according to Scott) he slept with him at various addresses, including the home of Thorpe's mother. In 1962, Thorpe sent Scott an affectionate note, making reference to Scott's ambition to study dressage in France and concluding with the infamous line: 'Bunnies *can* (and *will*) go to France.' Scott became obsessed with his glamorous, powerful benefactor, but when Thorpe wearied of the relationship and tried to disentangle himself, he realized that he risked being blackmailed and sought the advice of the Liberal MP, Peter Bessell. To Thorpe's dismay, Bessell discovered that Scott possessed a cache of letters from Thorpe. By 1968, Thorpe, now Liberal Party leader, was looking for a way in which to deal with Scott for good. According to Bessell, Thorpe suggested the 'ultimate solution', killing him off.

Then to everyone's surprise, Jeremy Thorpe got married. His wife Caroline was astonished to receive a telephone call at home in which Scott ranted about his homosexual relationship with her husband. He also rang Peter Bessell, threatening to give his story to the Sunday papers. But it was not until 1971 that Scott seriously began hawking his tale around Fleet Street. Not only would no national newspaper touch it, but when Scott made allegations against Thorpe at a coroner's inquest in North Wales, where he rented a cottage, these, too, were dismissed as the ravings of a lunatic. Early in 1974, a *Sunday Times Magazine* profile of Jeremy Thorpe failed to mention his homosexuality. *The Times*, tipped off about Thorpe and Scott, was not interested. Neither was the *People* or the *Sunday Mirror*. All of them thought that Scott was deranged. In any case, Thorpe's political fortunes were rising, and following the election in February 1974 it seemed as if he might hold the balance of power in the new Parliament.

Only after a bizarre series of events on a remote part of Exmoor did the papers grasp the scale of the story. In October 1975 the airline pilot Andrew Newton met Scott by arrangement in Barnstaple and drove him to Porlock Hill, accompanied by Scott's Great Dane bitch, Rinka. There, Newton pulled a pistol, shot the dog dead and turned the gun towards Scott. Either the gun jammed or Newton merely wanted to scare him, but in any event Newton drove away, leaving Scott weeping hysterically over the body of his dead dog. The incident was reported by the local newspaper, the *West Somerset Free Press*, which garnished it with a flip comment from Jeremy Thorpe about hunting dogs on moorland. The story attracted the attention of the *Private Eye* journalist Auberon Waugh, who lived in Somerset and who loathed Thorpe. Waugh made a mental note of it, but it was mid-December before his story about 'rumours of a most unsavoury description'[19] appeared. He was beaten to it by the 'Grovel' gossip column in his own magazine, which had run the gnomic fragment about Scott's letters in mid-November. In any case, it quickly became academic, because in January a Devon news agency was tipping off Fleet Street about Scott's forthcoming appearance at Barnstaple magistrates' court. Scott himself said he deliberately fiddled his dole in order to get caught, so guaranteeing himself a hearing in front of the local bench. Once in the dock, watched by reporters from most of the national papers, he seized his chance and blurted out the seventeen words that unleashed the gathering storm: 'I am being hounded by people all the time because of my sexual relationship with Jeremy Thorpe.'

There was uproar in the packed courtroom. Thorpe, advised by his formidable lawyer Lord Goodman, issued a categorical denial. But the *Daily Mirror* then splashed a story that changed the way the whole affair was perceived: according to the *Mirror*, the South African authorities might have concocted the Thorpe–Scott connection in order to discredit Jeremy Thorpe. The paper speculated that Gordon Winter, a journalist spying for BOSS, the South African security service, might have manipulated events behind the scenes. The story exposed Winter as a secret BOSS agent who had 'campaigned for five years to push the Jeremy Thorpe story into the headlines'.[20] The motive was political. The South Africans, with their far-right apartheid regime, detested left-of-centre politicians like Thorpe. The story struck a chord in 10 Downing Street, where the Labour Prime Minister Harold Wilson had convinced himself over a period of years that he too was the victim of a South African smear campaign. The *Daily Mail* found out where the ex-Liberal MP Peter Bessell was living in California, and within a day all the London papers were staking out his beachside house, demanding his version of events and his role in them. When Scott threatened to leak some of his correspondence with Thorpe – including the 'bunnies' letter

– the Liberal leader pre-empted him by publishing the letters himself in the *Sunday Times* in May 1976.

The *Daily Mirror* promptly whisked Norman Scott to London and offered him a deal for his story, to be unfolded to the paper in the course of a thirteen-day debriefing. For this, Scott, suddenly the hottest property in Fleet Street, would be paid £1,000 a day. But Scott failed to last the course, fleeing back to Dartmoor after just three days closeted with *Mirror* reporters in 'an awful hotel' in London. Thorpe, embarrassed at the appearance of the 'bunnies' letter in the *Sunday Times*, continued to deny that he had ever had a homosexual relationship with Scott, or that he had arranged hush money or hired a hit man to kill his dog. But when it became clear that he had lost the support of Liberal MPs, Thorpe resigned as party leader. By then, Wilson had also quit as Prime Minister, ending his lengthy period in office in a sensationally sudden and baffling way. Within a few weeks, he had briefed a pair of astonished BBC journalists, Barrie Penrose and Roger Courtiour, claiming that the British security services had plotted against him and had suspected him of being a Soviet agent. Democracy itself was in grave danger, he told them, from anti-democratic agencies in South Africa. Norman Scott, he went on, was a South African agent. Wilson urged Penrose and Courtiour to investigate the role of Peter Bessell and Gordon Winter in the 'international conspiracy' against Jeremy Thorpe. As for Rinka, '[n]o one would have guessed,' Penrose and Courtiour wrote later, 'that this tiny incident of the shot dog was the key to why an established Prime Minister resigned when he did.'[21]

Jeremy Thorpe's troubles multiplied in April 1977 when Andrew Newton was released from prison after serving half of a two-year sentence for shooting Rinka. Newton sold his story to the London *Evening News*, claiming that he had been hired to murder Norman Scott. He failed to say by whom, since the paper had refused to stump up the £150,000 demanded by Newton to name names, but in a follow-up story that autumn Newton referred to 'prominent Liberals'. Penrose and Courtiour, desperate to stave off any more scoops that might damage the impact of their own investigations, ran a story in the *Observer*, explaining how a prominent Liberal named X (the paper would not identify Thorpe for fear of attracting a libel writ) had tried to persuade Peter Bessell to mastermind Scott's murder. This story finally pushed Thorpe into facing his accusers, and he called a press conference at which he again denied a sexual relationship with Norman Scott. When the BBC reporter Keith Graves asked point-blank if Thorpe had ever had a homosexual relationship, the press conference disintegrated in a barrage of shouting.

In January 1978, the *Daily Mirror* began serializing Penrose and Courtiour's book, *The Pencourt File*. The *Observer* (which had originally bought the serial rights) had decided that Thorpe was innocent and that the story linking him and Scott was too big a legal risk. When Thorpe failed to sue the *Mirror* for libel, the mood in Fleet Street changed. Editors who had taken Scott for a madman and Penrose and Courtiour for half-baked conspiracy theorists thought again. What if they had been right after all? When in February the *Sunday Times* ran a two-page story on 'The Scott affair: the dog, the gun and the money', Thorpe knew that he could no longer rely on the crucial support of the 'serious' papers. Early in August, detectives arrested Jeremy Thorpe, former Liberal leader, MP and Privy Counsellor, and charged him with conspiracy and incitement to murder Norman Scott.

The story that emerged at the committal proceedings in Minehead was reported in full because one of Thorpe's co-defendants had opted to waive the rules that usually restrict pre-trial publicity. The feeling among experienced crime reporters was that the case against the accused was cut and dried. The story had all the elements of soap opera: sex, murder, power, money, secrecy, betrayal and revenge. At the centre of the drama stood Jeremy Thorpe, one of the best-known politicians of his generation, and his secret gay lover, the unstable and obsessive Norman Scott. When their relationship soured, Thorpe bought Scott's silence with weekly 'retainers' paid by Peter Bessell. As Thorpe's political career prospered, and the possibility arose of a cabinet seat, he became increasingly worried that Scott would return to haunt him. Thorpe told Bessell and one of his co-defendants, a gay banker friend called David Holmes, that Scott's execution was the only answer. It would be, Thorpe reportedly claimed, 'no worse than shooting a sick dog.' Nothing happened, however, until Bessell had emigrated to California and Holmes (helped by a couple of Welshmen, George Deakin and John Le Mesurier) hired Andrew Newton to murder Scott. This all seemed straightforward enough, but in May 1979, at the end of what the newspapers billed for the umpteenth time as 'The Trial of the Century', Thorpe and his co-accused were cleared on all charges. As Thorpe emerged triumphant from the Old Bailey, astonished newspaper editors the length of Fleet Street were tearing up their expensively researched background articles, which had been predicated on verdicts of Guilty, and were ordering hasty rewrites.

One of the more enduring legacies of the Thorpe case was the way in which it paved the way for reforming the long-established Fleet Street tradition of 'buying up' witnesses at sensational criminal trials. It emerged that the *Sunday Telegraph* had done an extraordinary deal for Peter Bessell's exclusive story. Under the terms of their agreement, Bessell would have received £50,000 if Thorpe had been convicted, but only £25,000 if he was cleared. Later, one of the jurors revealed that this 'double your money' deal had prejudiced the crown case, and the *Sunday Telegraph* was subsequently severely censured by the Press Council for flagrantly breaching the guidelines on such 'buy-ups'. These rules dated back to the Moors murders trial in 1966 when one of the main prosecution witnesses admitted being under contract to the *News of the World*. The press has habitually promised to stick to its code of self-regulation, a promise invariably broken in the course of such lurid cases as the Yorkshire Ripper killings of the 1970s and the Cromwell Street murders, for which Rosemary West stood trial in 1995. In both these instances, several papers and broadcast media competed to sign up key witnesses. In 2002, the Labour government's Lord Chancellor, Lord Irvine, finally announced plans to outlaw such payments, arguing that the 'pernicious practice' of papers paying witnesses for the stories is at its 'most dangerous' when payments 'are made conditional on the accused being found guilty'.[22] The worry is that such witnesses might exaggerate their evidence to guarantee a guilty verdict; they might also withhold evidence in order to make their stories more newsworthy. Bessell's astonishing deal with the *Sunday Telegraph* was a major milestone on the long road to legislation.

His acquittal notwithstanding, Jeremy Thorpe was destroyed by the Scott affair. In the early 1960s, when the pair first met, homosexual acts were still illegal in Britain, and although decriminalized in 1967, gay sex still carried a stigma, which the red-top tabloids in particular exploited at every opportunity. Thorpe dropped out of political life, while Scott resumed his ramshackle existence, apparently dividing his time between Ireland and Devon. Peter Bessell died in 1985.

With the Thorpe case exposing such sexual hypocrisy at the heart of the British Establishment, the tabloids had sharpened their appetite for political sex scandals, and in 1983 they brought down the Conservative Trade Secretary, Cecil Parkinson, a married man whose mistress and former secretary, Sara Keays, had become pregnant with his child. Parkinson's problem was that his behaviour in private was at odds with his party's policy of restoring 'family values'. When the press began to sniff around his affair with Miss Keays, they did not know that Parkinson, having promised to divorce his wife and marry her instead, had then changed his mind. In September 1983, at the Tory party conference in Blackpool, Parkinson suddenly resigned as party chairman, the post in which he had organized Margaret Thatcher's landslide election victory earlier in the year. 'Why,' wondered 'Grovel' in *Private Eye*, 'was Cecil Parkinson asked to step down as Tory Party Chairman? I can assure readers that it had nothing whatever to do with his marital difficulties which have recently caused raised eyebrows in Tory circles. Now comes the news that Parkinson's fun-loving secretary Ms Sarah [sic] Keays is expecting a baby in three months time.'[23]

Parkinson issued a statement the same day admitting the affair, the first in a series of indiscretions by high-profile Conservatives throughout the 1980s and 1990s that earned them an unsavoury reputation as the party of sleaze. No sooner had Thatcher's successor, John Major, launched his 'Back to Basics' campaign in 1993, for example, than Steven Norris, Tory MP and transport minister, was exposed as having no fewer than five mistresses. Another Conservative MP, Tim Yeo, a junior minister, resigned when the *News of the World* reported that he was the father of a love child from an extramarital affair with a single mother. At the same time, senior Tories were urging a tough line on single mothers drawing state benefits; the press could scarcely conceal its glee.

There was an element of farce in these exposés that was missing in the Thorpe case, which had by and large been presented as a serious crack in the face of the British Establishment. These revelation, however, all smacked of red-faced, pants-down knockabout, a theme echoing a vintage sexual roustabout from the late 1970s that again extended the boundaries of tabloid taste into uncharted territory. This was the bizarre case of Joyce McKinney. Curiously, this, too, had its origins on bleak moorland in the West Country, specifically an isolated cottage on the northern rim of Dartmoor National Park, hidden down a farm track with only stray sheep and a knifing wind for company. In the late summer of 1977, Miss McKinney, a busty American blonde, rented the cottage, telling the farmer who owned it that she wanted peace and quiet to write a novel. But within a matter of weeks, the press had laid siege to her remote hideaway, and Joyce McKinney was under arrest.

The so-called 'sex-in-chains' case cheered up Britain no end when the story broke in that post-Jubilee September. Miss McKinney, a 29-year-old former beauty queen, was suddenly the most infamous woman in Britain. The extraordinary shenanigans on Dartmoor sent the press into a frenzy. It seemed that Miss McKinney had kidnapped her former boyfriend, the clean-cut Mormon missionary Kirk Anderson, aged twenty-one, and driven him down to Devon. Once inside the cottage, she had held him captive, promising his freedom only if he agreed to marry her. While he was thinking this over, the former Miss Utah sought to encourage him not just with sex, but sex in chains.

Kirk Anderson, told police that he and Joyce McKinney had had a brief affair in Salt Lake City, the Mormon world headquarters. When he ended it she stalked and harassed him, smashing his windows, slashing his car tyres and even following him when he moved from Utah to California. Failing to shake her off, Anderson persuaded the Mormons to post him to Britain, but McKinney followed him across the Atlantic, pursuing him from East Grinstead to Reading and finally to Ewell in Surrey. Here, outside the Mormon church, McKinney pounced. With her friend Keith May posing as a potential convert, McKinney managed to entice Kirk Anderson into the street, where he was chloroformed and forced into a getaway car at the point of an imitation gun. Back in Devon, he was handcuffed, manacled and strapped to a bed.

No one doubted that sexual intercourse had taken place. But when McKinney appeared in court, the point at issue was that whilst Kirk Anderson claimed to have been the victim of forced sex, McKinney claimed that the shackles were merely instruments of bondage games. On the third night of captivity, the missionary testified, he was completely spreadeagled. 'When she came into the room there was a fire in the fireplace and she put some music on. She was wearing a negligée. She came to me as I lay on the bed.' Anderson said that although McKinney wanted sex again, he did not. McKinney returned with Keith May. Anderson was tied down on his back to the four corners of the bed using chains, ropes and padlocks. McKinney tore off the missionary's pyjamas and had sex with him.

During his testimony, Anderson referred to a bizarre accessory of his own, a special one-piece undergarment that functioned as a kind of male chastity belt. Anderson explained that he had burned the article, which was sacred to a Mormon, because McKinney had violated it. Joyce McKinney argued a very different version of events, saying that Kirk Anderson had made love willingly, and that the sex and bondage games had been designed to solve his sexual difficulties. In Utah, she had prayed for 'a very special boy' to come into her life. In a phrase that made headline-writers around the world weep with joy, she declared: 'I loved Kirk so much I would have skiied down Mount Everest in the nude with a carnation up my nose.'

Before the case came to trial, McKinney and May jumped bail and flew to America, heavily disguised. It was a farcical final chapter in an episode that had plastered a leering smile on the face of newspaper readers everywhere, and convinced the Fleet Street tabloids (if they needed convincing) that what their readers wanted first, second and last, was sex. Sex, secrets and scandal would no longer be trapped between the lines of old-style gossip columns. They would spill out across the splashes, trickle down through news and features, and saturate the red-tops from front page to back. One effect of this dam-burst of the late 1970s was to leave the gossip pages themselves in the doldrums. The same people, a familiar *galère* of Llewellyns and Goldsmiths, rotated round the gossip carousel. As Alan Rusbridger, later to become editor of the *Guardian*, lamented, 'an air of demoralisation does appear to have set in amongst today's gossip columns.'[24] What was needed was a dusting of glitter to restore the sparkle. 'Goddammit!' Beaverbrook might have exclaimed. 'Don't bother with people who know or do anything of interest. Just write about people who are famous.'

20

Gossip by Appointment

For the last twenty years, the tabloids have done just that. Led by Rupert Murdoch's celebrity-obsessed *Sun*, the hordes of Fleet Street swarmed to the gates of the famous and nearly-famous to construct a new national order, Thatcher's Britain ruled by a new cultural elite. Almost anyone on television – soap stars, game show hosts, footballers, fashion models, pop singers, people who for years had scurried in the foothills of the gossip columns – now found themselves swept to the commanding heights of a popular cultural explosion. The tabloids sagged with increasingly intrusive stories and pictures about these grinning new icons, whose hold on public attention derived almost exclusively from their status as celebrities, as defined by the American writer Daniel Boorstin: they were known for their well-knownness.[1]

By the 1990s, the private doings of public figures had spilled over into the serious mainstream press. As the twentieth century turned, many of the popular papers were offering not just one gossip feature but several. In the early 1980s, it was Murdoch's *Sun* that first fixed on TV as a source of glittery tittle-tattle, especially the soaps, where the boundaries of fact and fiction were easily blurred. But in an age in which tired old British warhorses like *Coronation Street* were being overtaken by glossy American newcomers like *Dallas* and *Dynasty*, driven by fantasies of glamour and wealth, it became apparent that viewers and readers wanted more than the usual froth and puffs from television's PR people. 'What I want to know,' the *Sun*'s feisty features editor Wendy Henry reportedly demanded, 'is who's fucking who.'[2] While the papers proceeded to dish the dirt on their TV heroes, an extraordinary royal soap opera was playing out in real life, a drama that mesmerized, enthralled, shocked and saddened in turn over two decades, engulfing the royal family in unprecedented scandal and threatening the very foundations of the British monarchy.

After the humiliations of the abdication nearly half a century before, Fleet Street was determined to get the inside story about the girl the Prince of Wales was going to marry. The first gleam of discovery came in September 1980, when the *Sun* spotted Prince Charles with a shy young Lady Diana Spencer near Balmoral and splashed the romance on the front page. Shortly afterwards came an exclusive report in the *Sunday Mirror* that the couple had twice met secretly at night aboard the royal train in a railway siding in Wiltshire. The Queen, who (everyone assumed) did not read gossip, 'blew her top' and in vain demanded a retraction of this 'totally false story',[3] which was flatly denied by the Palace. But the secret was out, and the papers laid siege to the fairytale princess-in-waiting at her flat and at the kindergarten in Pimlico where she worked. The royal romance became a gossip geyser. In an age of declining deference, diminishing class consciousness and growing republican disrespect for royalty, it was hardly surprising that Prince Charles's search for a bride who might one day be queen prompted a very British media frenzy, which scarcely faltered when the couple finally announced their engagement the following February.

What was new was the amount of personal tittle-tattle about the couple that slopped over the brim of the gossip columns and on to the news pages. In Diana, stunning, fresh and (so far as the world knew) in the first delirious flush of a royal romance, Fleet Street had uncovered an international superstar. The pictures clinched it: she was extraordinarily beautiful and knew how to love the cameras. 'Her talent for reacting to a lens, for projecting herself as a purely aesthetic phenomenon, was unparalleled in royal memory,' recalled Nigel Dempster. In their book on the royal marriage, Dempster and Peter Evans suggested that Prince Charles couldn't quite understand his new bride's sensual allure. 'It quickly became known in Palace circles as the Upstage Problem, or simply the Problem,' they reported. 'Before Diana, Charles was popular,' one friend explained. 'After their marriage he was second best. Everything Diana did, from buying a bag of sweets to having her hats retrimmed to show more of her face, became news.'[4]

In a sense, Diana had lived her whole life on the edge of the public glare. When she was six, her parents split up. An enterprising gossip columnist heard that Diana's mother had left home for another man and telephoned the house. 'One day she was just not here any more,' one of the servants told him, but in fact the separation had been mutually agreed in advance, because her mother had fallen in love with the wallpaper heir Peter Shand Kydd, whom she later married.[5] In the 1970s, it was Diana's older sister Sarah who attracted the gossip writers when the Prince of Wales romanced her, and she later enjoyed a brief affair with Gerald Grosvenor, the fabulously wealthy future Duke of Westminster. Now it was Diana's turn to step into the media spotlight, an experience she found both exhilarating and terrifying. The press pack, having discovered the address of her Kensington flat, staked it out around the clock; having discovered the phone number, they began calling from early morning until late at night, badgering her flatmates for information. Diana herself was hounded by reporters and photographers at every turn, going to extraordinary lengths to shake them off. Whilst she coped with good humour most of the time ('I simply treat the press as though they were children'), there were moments when the pursuit became too much and she was reduced to tears. Diana's mother wrote to *The Times,* asking Fleet Street editors 'whether, in the execution of their jobs, they consider it fair to harass my daughter daily, from dawn to well after dusk? Is it fair to ask any human being, regardless of circumstances, to be treated in this way? The freedom of the press was granted by law,' added Mrs Shand Kydd, 'by public demand, for very good reasons. But when these privileges are abused, can the press command any respect, or expect to be shown any respect?'[6] The papers apologized, but didn't draw back. Di-mania had arrived.

Even the Queen was powerless to stem the tide. 'I wish you would go away,' she hissed at a press posse camped outside Sandringham in January 1981, hoping to glimpse 'shy Di'.[7] When the media revved still harder, following the wedding of Charles and Diana six months later, the Queen summoned every national newspaper editor to Buckingham Palace to plead with them for an end to the harassment of her new daughter-in-law. The Princess of Wales, as she had become, was being driven to distraction by the paparazzi, freelance photographers selling pictures of the rich and famous that were often snatched in unguarded moments. Barry Askew, then editor of Rupert Murdoch's *News of the World,* drew gasps when he told the Queen that he thought the press had a right to cover Diana's activities, whether she was attending a film première or buying wine gums. Kelvin MacKenzie, the new editor of Murdoch's *Sun*, boycotted the meeting altogether, pleading a prior engagement with his boss, which he considered more important. Whilst most of Fleet Street reined in their royal newshounds as a result of the Queen's intervention, the respite was only temporary. At Christmas 1983, she again angrily rebuked the media for staking out Sandringham.

Like TV soaps and bingo – another Fleet Street craze of the time – the royals represented rich pickings for the popular press, and competition between the papers was intense. In the needle match between the *Daily Mirror* and the *Sun*, for example, the two titles vied to outdo each other every Monday with a front-page story from their royal correspondents. 'Don't worry if it's not true,' MacKenzie told his reporter Harry Arnold, 'so long as there's not too much of a fuss about it afterwards.'[8] The point was that royal stories sold papers. Although much of what the tabloids were printing about Charles and Diana was nonsense, at first no one in the media had any inkling of the way in which the 'fairytale' marriage was unravelling. But by the mid-1980s, whispers and murmurs about Prince Charles and his friend Camilla Parker Bowles were becoming impossible to ignore. Early in 1987, the Queen Mother complained to the *News of the World* columnist, Woodrow Wyatt, about the way the press were treating her grandchildren and Prince Charles in particular. According to the Queen Mother, rumours of a split with Diana were rubbish. 'We are very vulnerable,' she told Wyatt, 'and it is rather fraught having the gossip writers at you the whole time.' She recalled that when she was the Duchess of York in the 1920s, 'nothing of that kind ever appeared in the newspapers'.[9]

The royal marriage had in fact gone wrong straight away, partly because of the incompatibility of the participants, partly because of the baying media. Only a few months after the wedding, a plainly pregnant Diana was photographed on a beach in the Bahamas, wearing a bikini. Yet the more the Waleses complained about media intrusion, the more Diana seemed to relish her new role as, in the words of the *Sun*'s Harry Arnold, 'the world's number one cover girl'.[10] The tabloids, sniffing enormous commercial possibilities, now detected a new public appetite for stories that combined sex and royalty, and proceeded to feed it.

Royal reporting changed. Deference was dead, and what remained of the journalistic discretion that had shielded earlier Princes of Wales, the rakehell who became Edward VII and the effete playboy Edward VIII, shrivelled and died too. In the 1980s, editors cast aside any lingering inhibitions and printed what their royal-watchers saw and heard, gossip included, reckless of any consequences from the Palace. One rumour followed another: the pregnant Princess of Wales had fallen downstairs, she was suffering from an eating disorder, and so on. These stories were reported in a strident, almost jeering tone, contrasting with the old, reverential royal hush. As the Queen's biographer Ben Pimlott commented, by the ravening 1980s, 'media hunger had turned the bemused, half-resisting, half-co-operating, ill-equipped dynasty into a circus.'[11]

Joined in the royal soap opera by the Duchess of York – the extrovert redhead Sarah Ferguson had married Prince Andrew in 1986 – Diana nevertheless seemed strangely detached from Charles. 'Separate breakfasts, separate timetables, separate friends,' observed the young royal-watcher Andrew Morton in 1987. 'These days the Prince and Princess of Wales are leading active, interesting, but totally independent lives.'[12]

It was Morton who, five years later, finally tore the mask from Charles and Diana's sham marriage with the publication of his book *Diana: Her True Story*.[13] It not only confirmed many of the gossipy tales that had sloshed around in the tabloids during the 1980s, but it also offered new and terrifying insights: Diana, while pregnant, had hurled herself down a staircase at Sandringham; she had slashed her wrists with a razor; and she had submitted to psychotherapy. It portrayed her as an emotionally overheated woman trapped in a loveless marriage to a cold and indifferent husband, sick and despairing beneath the hostile surveillance of the frosty Windsors. The book's appearance in the summer of 1992 signalled another media frenzy as the tabloids, locked in yet another circulation war, competed with each other for more and more lurid royal stories. Round 1 went to the *Daily Mirror*, which in August pulled off a spectacular scoop by publishing pictures of a topless Duchess of York, separated but not yet divorced from the Duke, lounging beside a swimming pool and having her toes sucked by her 'financial adviser', the Texan John Bryan. The rival *Sun* hit back by publishing the transcript of telephone pillow-talk that had taken place in 1989 between the Princess of Wales and her car salesman friend, James Gilbey, who called her by the pet name 'Squidgy', a detail that led the press to dub the affair Squidgygate. In November came what many thought the most embarrassing leak of all, another illicit tape, this one known as Camillagate, on which the Prince of Wales was heard talking on the telephone, indiscreetly and at length, to his mistress, Mrs Parker Bowles. A month later, to no one's surprise, the Palace announced that the Prince and Princess of Wales were to separate.

The royal hoopla of the early 1980s, when Diana burst on to the scene, coincided with a big shake-up on Fleet Street's main gossip columns. The diaries at *The Times*, the *Guardian*, the *Express* and the *Daily Star* all changed hands, leaving only Nigel Dempster seemingly immovable at the *Mail*. Ritual insults were traded. 'Nigel churns out rubbish,' said Richard Compton Miller, the new Hickey at the *Express*. 'He writes about his old cronies every day, and the world has left him behind.'[14] Peter Tory, the new man at the *Star*, considered Dempster and his other rivals out of date, still trying to chronicle a non-existent café society. 'Nigel,' he added, 'has become a museum piece and lost his fight.'[15] In fact, Dempster was enjoying something of a purple patch; not only was he hearing the first worried whispers about Charles and Diana from 'my friends in the royal family',[16] but also about marital disharmony among the upper ranks of Margaret Thatcher's Conservative government. In 1983, Dempster's 'Grovel' gossip column at *Private Eye* had exposed cabinet minister Cecil Parkinson's affair with Sara Keays. A few months later, in the *Mail*, Dempster ran a titbit of tittle-tattle that, on the face of it, seemed harmless enough, but which turned out to have catastrophic consequences for the Conservative Party and another of its brightest stars.

Dempster's gossip fragment about Jeffrey Archer, the one-time MP turned blockbusting author, and 'former deb Andrina Colquhoun, 31, [who] acts as his hostess and makes no secret of her admiration for Archer'[17] went virtually unnoticed when it appeared in February 1984. It smouldered undisturbed for a year and a half before flaring up again, this time on Compton Miller's 'Hickey' page, in a piece about Archer's appointment as deputy chairman of the Conservative Party in September 1985. The paragraph was pointed out to Archer's wife, Mary, who had known of her husband's liaison with Ms Colquhoun but who believed it had virtually fizzled out. The Hickey piece prompted Mrs Archer to confront her husband, who, after admitting that the affair was continuing, promised it would stop. Archer's private embarrassment followed one of the regular outbursts of public discontent about the way gossip columns snoop and pry into people's lives. 'In some ways, gossip columns are a little like pornography,' fulminated the commentator Paul Johnson. 'People turn to them despite their better judgment, knowing that they are yielding to a sleazy impulse.'[18] Nonsense, replied Peregrine Worsthorne, then editor of the *Sunday Telegraph*. Everyone recognized that tittle-tattle was a vital part of the political process 'in the sense of determining public reputations and therefore affecting political appointments'.[19]

Six months later, Jeffrey Archer was appointed deputy chairman of the Conservative Party. At his trial for perjury and perverting the course of justice in 2001 in the wake of the Monica Coughlan affair, Archer was sentenced to four years in jail. 'Gossip columns!' snapped Mary Archer to an interviewer after the case. 'What are they for?' In the Archer case, they seemed to have dislodged the first brick in a towering wall of deceit that tottered and fell, engulfing one of Britain's best-known political celebrities in a maelstrom of disgrace and humiliation. It is questionable whether it would happen now. Extramarital affairs are hardly shocking any more, although politicians like Archer are still judged more harshly than film or television stars because their indiscretions call their character and judgment into question.

There is an overarching irony to the scandals that beset the younger royals. It was the media, and the vigorous, brash, gossipy popular newspapers in particular, that had earned the Windsors unprecedented public esteem in the pre-Diana era of the 1960s and 1970s. In 1960, the Queen made a speech courting the press, in the hope of improving relations between the royal family and Fleet Street, which had been distinctly chilly in the run-up to the marriage of her sister, Princess Margaret. The Queen's speech was a watershed. 'The silent barrier across which royalty and the press usually regard each other warily as they go about their separate jobs, was crossed for the first time,' reported the *News of the World*. 'Some people have suggested that, if the essential mystique of royalty is to be retained, the press should not get to know them too well.'[20] The warning went unheeded. More informal, less reticent coverage certainly glamorized the royals and enhanced their popularity. But by the end of the 1960s, so much daylight had been let in that the essential magic seemed all but dispersed, and what little remained vanished with the help of television. In 1969, Richard Cawston's documentary film *Royal Family* offered the viewing millions their first glimpse of the Windsors' intimate family life. 'To those who say "it started the rot",' a former Palace press secretary told Ben Pimlott, 'it is possible to reply, "how long could the curtains be held in place?"'[21] But it sent a strong signal to Fleet Street that perhaps the fusty old media protocols were crumbling. Kenneth Rose, who wrote the *Sunday Telegraph*'s genteel gossip column under the pseudonym 'Albany' for more than thirty years, thought the scene in the film showing the Duke of Edinburgh cooking sausages on a barbecue kindled a public curiosity that would prove insatiable. 'And whereas at that stage you could still keep the British press under control,' he added, 'you couldn't stop the paparazzi.'[22] Nearly thirty years after the BBC screened Cawston's film, it was the paparazzi, chasing Diana and her new lover Dodi Al Fayed at high speed through the streets of Paris, who were initially blamed for her death when the couple's car crashed in 1997.

Notwithstanding her brother's impassioned 'blood on their hands' speech, what actually caused the accident was a commonplace: the driver was drunk. But there remained an uneasy feeling that Diana had been a victim of the modern form of fame, the 'frenzy of renown'; that her fans and followers, hungry for her image, for gossip about her flawed fairytale life, were somehow complicit in her death. 'I killed her,' lamented one unnamed mourner, 'I hounded her to death. I followed her every movement. I gave her no peace. For I bought the papers. I read the stories and I looked at the photographs.'[23]

Like other celebrities of the late twentieth century, Diana had inhabited a house of mirrors, in which the press, with its cameras and flashguns, had fashioned her into an icon for her age. She craved this attention, but like so many others who seek public adulation she also recoiled from it. In marrying a man born to be king, Diana signed up to a life of celebrity, and must have known that in sealing this pact she was surrendering most of her rights to privacy. She was one of the few women in the world who could guarantee an appearance in the papers whether she wanted it or not, and whatever the result, Diana saw it. 'I read everything that's written about me,' she once admitted.[24] In her devastating *Panorama* interview less than two years before her death, she said she still found the worldwide media interest in her daunting and phenomenal, 'because I actually don't like being the centre of attention'.[25] But journalists knew that Diana was a skilled manipulator of the media. For nearly a decade, she briefed the papers about her troubles, either through friends or by talking directly to favoured journalists, such as James Whitaker of the *Mirror* and subsequently, moving upmarket, Richard Kay of the *Mail*. Very few of the stories about her stricken marriage leaked out from unverifiable sources. They were mostly planted or inspired by Diana herself. As David Montgomery, chief executive of Mirror Group Newspapers, pointed out, 'a lot of the stuff that had been criticised for being not true and for being scurrilous was absolutely bang on, and the reason it was bang on is because it came from her.'[26]

21

Greedy for it

Diana, Princess of Wales, wasn't the first to apply a double standard to fame and the media. Most people who get their names in gossip columns are there because they want to be. Far from shrinking from the modern media onslaught, most of the gossiped-about have no desire for privacy; on the contrary, they court publicity, prancing and dancing into the criss-cross searchlights of fame. For these people, there is just no such thing as bad publicity. More than anything else, they want to be written up, quoted and pictured, because what they crave above all is attention. Gossip columns are the natural habitat of these exotic creatures. They fetch up there thanks to a mixture of hard-faced self-assertion, sheer chutzpah and, increasingly, the machinations of their public relations people. These are the stage managers of gossip, the faceless ones who, on their clients' behalf, try to place positive stories, stifle negative ones and exercise as much control as possible over what actually appears. In 1990, when Donald Trump dumped his wife Ivana, both hired expensive personal publicists to promote their versions of the split. It's a technique borrowed from show business, and it amounts to sorcery of sorts. In London and in Hollywood, PRs and press agents plant speculative stories of coming projects and contracts, often nothing more than wish-lists, in the hope that at least some of them will come true. Copy approval – they ask to see what the columnist has written before it appears in the paper – is often sought but rarely, if ever, given. But haggling is common: how will the story be played, what topics can and cannot be broached, and can the client tweak the quotes?

Gossip columns are rich alluvium for the PR industry, which has created and sustains an entire parallel universe of spin in which many journalists happily collude. Gossip writers are lunched and dined at swanky restaurants; payola and other inducements are occasionally canvassed. Public relations people claim that numerous journalists rely on them for many, if not most, of their stories. These days, with the collapse of the old Fleet Street culture and its dead-eyed flickering-screen replacement, they may have a point. But their black arts are nothing new. Publicity people first appeared in the early twentieth century, when the booming popular press offered unprecedented scope for free puffs. Such were its pernicious practices that the American Congress considered outlawing press agents in 1913, but they proved to be unstoppable. At the pinnacle of the anthill, sleek public relations advisers counselled corporate clients, while below, hundreds – literally hundreds – of hucksters and hustlers scurried about, promoting to the press a motley array of performers and pleasure-providers, from ukulele players to nightclubs. PR mushroomed along with the mass media on which it fed. But this growth also coincided with the early stirrings of celebrity culture. From the dawn of the age of ballyhoo, the natural home for many PR-driven stunts and stories was the gossip column.

In New York, Walter Winchell sorted through a daily mountain of material from press agents, 'scores of items, pages of items, thick packets of items',[1] as his biographer Neal Gabler noted, but most of it was returned unused. 'I realized that competing to get into Winchell's column was like a third university to me,' press agent Gary Stevens told Gabler, 'because you were competing against four hundred other minds every day.'[2] It was a rough, tough business. According to another agent who represented a particular nightclub, unless he managed to get the club's name in the papers, the owner 'beat you up. He didn't fire you.'[3] Winchell and his fawning retinue of press agents regarded each other with mutual contempt, he for their craven sycophancy, phoniness and lickspittle desperation, they for his ultimate and absolute power and petty vengefulness. One agent who fouled up with a story for Winchell's column found himself peremptorily summoned to the Stork Club, where the great gossip gusher held court, to be told: 'You're on my shit list for one year.'[4]

They were, on the whole, an unprepossessing bunch, often failed journalists, bums and gangsters, scavenging for scraps of gossip, stories, even food scraps, ashamed of their humiliating grubbiness. In the early 1930s city editor Stanley Walker remembered hearing them 'curse their own strange calling... They do become ashamed of themselves at times, though the majority, if they keep at it long enough, manage to smother their consciences.'[5] But within the span of little more than a generation, this raggle-taggle crew had revolutionized the business of fame. In Britain as the 1950s closed, the journalist and historian Anthony Sampson, then writing the 'Pendennis' gossip column in the *Observer*, complained of the torrent of PR press releases and invitations designed to get someone's name into the papers:

'We're sure you'd like to come to a wine-tasting...'

'You'll be interested to hear that...'

'The brightest, gayest party of the year will be given at...'

'Celebrities of stage and screen are appearing...'

Astonishingly, it worked. 'A few weeks later,' Sampson observed, 'one notices the names creeping into print, the faces appearing on the television screen, and a reputation being established, with all the trappings of Fame.'[6] A handsome reward for a fistful of grimy PR handouts. When Tom Driberg was writing the 'William Hickey' column, he treated PR people with an amused disdain, noting wryly that, in his experience, women publicists often launched their speculative press releases with such quaintly courteous encomiums as 'Hoping for the favour of an insertion'.[7] (In our own times, gossip writers are more likely to encounter publicists face to face, especially if they are babysitting their clients for an interview.) But Driberg was a one-off: in his Hickey days, most newspaper gossip items appeared as the result of a trade-off, the kind of mutual exploitation of which Ogden Nash observed:

There are two kinds of people who blow through life like a breeze,

And one kind is gossipers, and the other kind is gossipees,

And they certainly annoy each other,

But they certainly enjoy each other,

Yes, they pretend to flout each other,

But they couldn't do without each other...[8]

Publicity and its flip side, privacy, are by no means a modern phenomenon. Throughout the nineteenth century, publicity was corroding the boundaries between private and public spaces, leaping to stardom as a symptom of popular modern culture with the rise of the mass media as the century closed. The publicity principle, roaring into public life in the shape of the New Journalism of the 1880s and 1890s, became all-pervasive. The American writer Henry James was obsessed with the way in which the late-nineteenth-century press intruded into private lives, with the 'insurmountable desire to *know*',[9] and he took steps to keep his own life as well shielded as he could. Like his friend Edith Wharton, he had a particular horror of common people satisfying their idle curiosity about the private lives of the rich or famous by gawping at the popular papers. He took pot-shots at this 'invasion of privacy' (he seems to have coined the phrase) in his published writings, and in his private notebooks attacked 'the impudence and shamelessness of the newspaper and the interviewer, the *devouring* publicity of life'.[10]

His loathing of the press sprang from an experience in Venice. A young American journalist, May Marcy McLennan, had written a letter to Joseph Pulitzer's New York *World,* describing in intimate detail 'the Venetian society whose hospitality she had just been enjoying'.[11] Her account was evidently a travesty, 'as long, as confidential, as "chatty",' James shudderingly recalled, 'as full of headlong history and lingering legend, of aberration and confusion, as she might have indited to the most trusted of friends'. It shed unfavourable light on the ways of American society people abroad, and caused, no doubt, much ribald amusement among the readers of what James lip-curlingly dismissed as Pulitzer's 'recording, slobbering sheet'.[12] James regarded this woman's shocking betrayal of private confidences as typical of 'that mania for publicity which is one of the most striking signs of our times'. Socially conservative, James was antagonistic to the emerging mass culture, equating it with cultural decline, 'the sinking of manners', as he put it, 'which the democratization of the world brings with it'.[13] The French political theorist Alexis de Tocqueville, observing American culture and society fifty years before, had blamed democratization for fostering a general inclination to intrude, and for blurring the line between public and private. 'The characteristics of the American journalist,' he commented, 'consist in an open and coarse appeal to the passions of his readers; he abandons principles to assail the characters of individuals, to track them into private life and disclose all their weaknesses and vices.'[14] On his first trip to the US in 1883, the poet and critic Matthew Arnold complained to his sister Frances about the 'blaring publicity of this place', which went 'beyond all that I had any idea of'.[15] As the lives of writers came under scrutiny from prying reporters who seemed more interested in their personalities than in what they actually wrote, James retreated to his 'blessed and uninvaded' workroom, out of sight of the media's eye. In the mid-1890s, James's compulsive aversion to prying journalists quickened, following the revelations in the trials of Oscar Wilde. Like Wilde, James was gay, but unlike him he had no desire to be wrenched from his closet into the blinding glare of scandal.

With this culture shift, in which traditional notions of deference, reticence and reverence were eclipsed by more transparency and candour, came the flowering of biography. From the dawn of the nineteenth century, there had been concerns about the searching beam of inquiry and the increasingly invasive character of biographical writing. As early as 1810, Samuel Taylor Coleridge had complained about what he called 'the cravings of worthless curiosity'.[16] By James's day, the journalist was refining the still relatively newfangled technique of the interview, 'about the only means,' one American writer noted in 1887, 'by which the public can learn some things which it has a distinct right to know and which it is the interest of designing persons to conceal'.[17] It was legitimate, the anonymous writer believed, for journalists to print private facts if they were in the public interest. But in practice, what happened was something different: whereas, ideally, the 'business of the newspaper is to furnish private people with the public news', the press actually tried 'to furnish the public with the news of private people'.[18] In the clamour over the 'right to know', it was time for some new definitions, beginning with where privacy begins and ends, so that the person being interviewed can have, as Henry James put it, 'the right to determine, in so far as he can, what the world shall know of him and what it shall not'.[19] An anonymous contributor to the *New Princeton Review* outlined a code of journalistic ethics, holding that a private conversation, off the record, enjoyed the same sanctity as private letters. 'An interlocutor,' the writer declared, 'has no more right to publish my correspondence than to ransack my drawers for private papers.'[20]

Three years later, two prominent American legal scholars, Samuel D. Warren and Louis D. Brandeis, later a Supreme Court justice, took the first step towards enshrining the privacy principle in a formal legal code.

'The press is overstepping in every direction the obvious bounds of propriety and decency,' they thundered in the *Harvard Law Review*. 'Gossip is no longer the resource of the idle or the vicious, but has become a trade, which is pursued with industry as well as effrontery.' Warren and Brandeis went on to stress the damaging impact of a sex-mad sensational press in 1890:

> To satisfy a prurient taste the details of sexual relations are spread [and] broadcast in the columns of the daily papers. To occupy the indolent, column upon column is filled with idle gossip, which can only be procured by intrusion upon the domestic circle. The intensity and complexity of life, attendant upon advancing civilisation, have rendered necessary some retreat from the world, and man, under the refining influence of culture, has become more sensitive to publicity, so that solitude and privacy have become more essential to the individual; but modern enterprise and invention have, through invasions upon his privacy, subjected him to mental pain and distress, far greater than could be inflicted by mere bodily injury.[21]

But if life in the late nineteenth century had indeed become so intolerable, there was, as the lawyers recognized, no real escape. They also acknowledged something more profound: that it was no longer tenable to claim a right to privacy based on the existing protection of private property rights. They grasped that publicity was neither a form of theft nor of defamation, and that privacy could best be protected through the common law right to 'intellectual and artistic property'.

James was intrigued by the lives of others, and he energetically wrote, read and reviewed biographies all his working life. His fascination stands at odds with his own hostility to biographical inquiry. But as the nineteenth century waned, so did Victorian concerns about privacy. Freed from repression, J. A. Froude and later Lytton Strachey blazed a trail towards the 'warts-and-all' biographies of the twentieth century. In James's story, the *Death of the Lion* (1894), the narrator is a journalist who resigns his job as a protest at his paper's new 'personal' approach. The incoming editor Pinhorn embraces the innovative New Journalism technique of the interview, in which the journalist witnesses his own encounter with his celebrity subject, in this case a famous novelist.

James's narrator guys Pinhorn as one whose 'sincerity took the form of ringing door-bells and whose definition of genius was the art of finding people at home'.[22]

There is an echo here of Edmund Yates and his weekly newspaper the *World*, which for six years in the late 1870s and early 1880s featured the popular 'Celebrities at Home' column. Yates always described the celebrity's home in great detail, regarding it not just as a convenient location for the interview but as an extension of the personality of the interviewee. So the style and ornament of Mark Twain's house in Connecticut, for example, offered 'a delightful peep into the inner recesses of his character'.[23] Encounters like this paved the way towards an abundance of interviews with literary celebrities in the 1890s, often illustrated by photographs of the writers in their homes. Readers of such magazines as the *Idler* and the *Strand* may not have read any of the author's books, but seeing him or her pictured at home in these popular weeklies somehow confirmed the public status of the literary celebrity. Prefiguring *Hello!* and *OK!* by a good hundred years, Yates set the tone of celebrity tat-mags, stressing the sanctity of the private sphere ('Soap Queen Welcomes Us into Her Beautiful Home') while at the same time thoroughly violating it. The late Victorians portrayed their printed excursions to the homes of writers as 'pilgrimages' to 'literary shrines'. In his 1898 tale *John Delavoy*, Henry James mocks such journalistic promotion of literary stars through his characterization of an editor planning a posthumous piece on a dead novelist but interested only in 'anecdotes, glimpses, gossip, chat; a picture of his "home life", domestic habits, diet, dress, arrangements – all his little ways and secrets'.[24] The editor's keenness is sharpened by the fact that the novelist kept his private life intensely private; it is, in fact, the point of the piece.

James's personal resentment of prying reporters recalled his unhappy time as a correspondent with the New York *Tribune* in the 1870s, when he submitted chatty columns from Paris. Two years after Matthew Arnold inveighed against the New Journalism, T. P. O'Connor, who had recently launched the *Star* evening paper in London, came to its defence, asserting that its 'more personal tone'[25] would reveal truths obscured by the 'effete' old impersonal journalism. 'For the proper development of a newspaper,' barked W. T. Stead, 'the personal element is indispensable.'[26] Henry James's most significant contribution to the debate was his short comic novel, *The Reverberator* (1888), written as he was lamenting the 'extinction of all sense between public and private'[27] in the new journalistic culture. The novel's hero is George Flack, the young Paris-based correspondent of the society newspaper that gives the story its resounding title. Flack (the Americans later stole the name to describe twentieth-century press agents) is the ruthless personification of the brash New Journalism, and he unblushingly outlines his vision of the gossip pages of the future:

> The society-news of every quarter of the globe, furnished by the prominent members themselves (oh, *they* can be fixed – you'll see!) from day to day and from hour to hour and served up hot at every breakfast-table in the United States: that's what the American people want and that's what the American people are going to have . . . I'm going for the inside view, the choice bits, the *chronique intime*, as they say here; what the people want's just what ain't told, and I'm going to tell it. Oh they're bound to have the plums! That's about played out, anyway, the idea of sticking up a sign of 'private' and 'hands off' and 'no thoroughfare' and thinking you can keep the place to yourself . . . it ain't going to continue to be possible to keep out anywhere the light of the Press.[28]

Echoing through George Flack's pious conceit that he knows 'what the American people want' is the self-proclaimed boast of the snake-oil salesman through the ages. Henry James for once agrees with W. T. Stead who, in his 1886 essay on the future of journalism, debunked the 'journalistic assumption of uttering the opinion of the public' as 'a hollow fraud'. In reality, as Stead noted, most of what the average journalist knows about the public is concocted 'in the office, in the club, or in the drawing-room'.[29]

In *The Reverberator*, Flack's inamorata, Francie Dosson, rejects him in favour of Gaston Probert, a member of a Frenchified American family that despises the vulgar clamour of newspaper publicity. But when Francie discloses Probert family secrets to her cast-off lover, he plasters them in print all over his newspaper. As in James's better-known novel *The Bostonians*, a journalist, having provoked hostility, proceeds to thrive on it: a metaphor for the impact of the American 'invasion of privacy' on a conservative European culture. In his working notebook,

James records that he decided to set his tale in Paris rather than in London because he wanted to find 'people today in Europe who would really be so shocked'[30] by the intrusive antics of Flack's newspaper. In London, as James pointed out, polite society had already become numbed; papers like Yates's *World* and Labouchere's *Truth* 'stare one in the face... [England] is in short also a newspaperized world'.[31]

The idea for the story came from the May McClellan episode that James witnessed in Venice. He was struck by the way her two columns of gossip, filed from Italy to an American newspaper, bounced back to Europe with the reverberation of a bomb, much to the hapless Miss McClellan's horror. James recognized the burgeoning print media's capacity to circulate scandal over great distances with enormous speed, unlike the spoken word. From the 1860s onwards transatlantic telegraphy and the telephone had started to shape a fledgling global news network; distances were collapsing with the advance of each technological innovation, and by 1898 Henry James, noting that the press 'fairly bristles with revelations of them', conceded that the globe was 'fast shrinking, for the imagination, to the size of an orange that can be played with'.[32] Hand in hand with the kind of technological advances that sent George Flack's scandal copy crackling across continents and back in *The Reverberator,* came the earliest signs of the journalist's need to grasp possibilities at once. He could cleverly decipher clues contained in hotel registers and other documentation, the kind of gumshoe journalism that Dickens would have recognized, but he had now also mastered the information resources of a new post-Victorian technology, the know-how he obtained, as the story explains, 'by a kind of intuition, by the voices of the air, by indefinable and unteachable processes'.[33] Flack exploits his esoteric skills as a kind of journalistic sorcerer, a dealer in scandals and spells.

Throughout the closing years of the nineteenth century, Fleet Street practitioners of the New Journalism were accused of importing insidious American techniques. At the *World,* for example, Edmund Yates found himself charged with practising 'the worst principles of American journalism' and, by extension, of being 'un-English'.[34] Certainly Yates and his companion New Journalists seized on such transatlantic innovations as the interview and the 'scarehead' (vivid headline) for effect, but more importantly they fed a new appetite – a furious greed – for publicity through they way they dished up gossip and scandal. Fame – the word derives from the Latin *fames,* meaning hunger or famine – cries out to be satisfied; there can be no doubt that this greed was magnified by the clamouring popular culture taking hold in the United States. The American sociologist Richard Sennett tells us that the late-nineteenth-century fascination with 'personalities' expressed a need to preserve a nugget of intimacy as a defence against the onslaught of impersonal modern urban life. This fascination was, and still is, fuelled by a sense of 'untouchability', in which celebrities are seen to be beyond the reach of both press and public, a kind of quarantine enjoyed by literary lions like Henry James, the media stars of the day. '[He] has never been interviewed,' crowed Florence Brooks in the New York *Herald,* claiming that he submitted to 'that profane rite, an interview' at her hands when he returned to America in 1904. 'It is one of his cherished habits to keep out of the sort of gaze that follows the limelight,' she explained, adding that while James portrayed himself as a shy, solitary recluse, it was precisely his refusal to court publicity that created the public's interest in him.[35]

James, as his biographer Leon Edel notes, had already seen the handwriting on the wall, having forecast a twentieth-century press obsessed with tittle-tattle. Under the guise of 'Names Make News', it would 'make capital of people's privacy, increasingly weaken the laws of libel, and increasingly turn themselves into journals of gossip'.[36] For James, such corruption was well advanced. Already 'the newspapers and all they contained were a part of the general fatality of things, of the recurrent freshness of the universe, coming out like the sun in the morning or the stars at night.'[37]

22

Frenzied and Breathless

In America, gossip got glossy in the 1950s. *Confidential* magazine, a garish tabloid reporting the misdeeds of Hollywood celebrities, sold on news-stands and in supermarkets across the nation, boasting a circulation at its peak of 10 million. When it launched in 1952, it laced the familiar Tinseltown gossip with a dash of poison. It was the idea of a flamboyant publisher of raunchy magazines, Robert Harrison, who had spotted a national craze. In the early 1950s, the Senate hearings into mob corruption in government were mesmerizing America. People couldn't get enough of the unfolding scandal, crowding into bars where the hearings were playing on TV so as not to miss a minute of the drama. Harrison hit on the idea of combining the gossip column format of Louella Parsons and Hedda Hopper with the hunt-'em-down exposé flavour of the Senate hearings. 'Behind-the-scenes stories, inside, gossipy facts,' declared Harrison, recalling his formula. 'That's what America wanted.'[1] And that's what America got, thanks largely to the endorsement of the grandfather of US gossip, Walter Winchell.

Winchell's career was fading. As television boomed, his old inky style seemed dated and irrelevant. He had made a serious error of judgment in 1951, when the black singer Josephine Baker made a fuss over the poor service she received at the Stork Club in New York, and accused its owner Sherman Billingsley of racism. Winchell sided with Billingsley, his friend and mentor, incurring the wrath of the liberal elite who, by marginalizing him, dealt him another damaging blow. Robert Harrison saw a way of pulling America's best-known gossipmonger on board by running articles in *Confidential*, backing the beleaguered Winchell, who loved the favourable publicity. In return, Winchell went on television trumpeting *Confidential*, holding up a copy to the camera and urging people to buy it. 'From then on,' Harrison recalled, 'this thing flew.'[2]

The public thirsted for the magazine's rich, dangerous brew of gossip and scandal, and by 1957 *Confidential* had become the best-selling magazine in America.

The format, familiar today, was ground-breaking then. Instead of stroking the oversized egos of Hollywood stars and studios, *Confidential* dished the dirt. It had never happened before. No one, for example, had had the nerve to take on the crooner Frank Sinatra who, according to a classic *Confidential* article, munched breakfast cereal between bouts of lovemaking. 'He had the nation's front page playboys dizzy for years trying to discover the secret,' *Confidential* reported, 'Ava Gardner, Lana Turner, Gloria Vanderbilt, Anita Ekberg. How does that skinny little guy do it? Vitamins? Goat glands? Nope – Wheaties.' One of Sinatra's conquests described how, after excusing himself from the bedroom for the fourth time, the 'unbelieving babe could plainly hear the crunch, crunch, crunch of a man – eating Wheaties'.[3] When Sinatra read it, he went berserk.

Then there was film star Robert Mitchum, billed by *Confidential* in June 1955 as 'The Nude Who Came to Dinner'. 'The menu said steak. There was no mention of a stew... and the party boiled over when one guest was not only fried – but peeled!' *Confidential* reported. At a dinner party in Hollywood, Mitchum had stripped naked and coated himself with ketchup, reportedly saying: 'This is a masquerade party, isn't it? Well, I'm a hamburger, well done.' According to the magazine, '[t]he hamburger began dancing around the room, splattering the walls and all who came near.'[4] Mitchum reacted with fury, and denied the story point-blank. 'If I were a catsup tosser,' he drawled, 'I wouldn't get invited to parties. And that would be tough. I just love parties.'[5]

Confidential spawned several imitators, with copycat titles like *Suppressed, Exposed, Inside Story* and *Hush-Hush*. All of them feasted on the sexual peccadilloes of the stars and exploited the neuroses of the age, in redneck crusades against Communists, blacks ('His Passion for Blondes: Will it Destroy Sammy Davis Jr.?' wondered *Hush-Hush* in 1955) and, in particular, gays. Rock Hudson, famous for playing hunky romantic leads, had successfully concealed his homosexuality for years, even though it was an open secret in Hollywood studio circles. When Fred Otash, a private investigator hired by *Confidential*, went to the head of Columbia Pictures, Harry Cohn, with a tape of Hudson and his wife Phyllis Gates discussing how to hide or 'cure' his sexual orientation, Cohn was mortified. 'Rock is one of our biggest stars,' he pleaded. 'If that stuff gets out, you'll ruin us.'[6] Cohn cut a deal that smothered the Rock Hudson story in exchange for dirt – 'the goods' in the parlance of the day – on lesser celebrities like Rory Calhoun who, as a youth, had been in trouble for stealing a car.

With the flamboyant entertainer Liberace, 'the heart-throb of 40 million women' but secretly gay, *Confidential* found itself facing a $20 million lawsuit over an exclusive story it ran in 1957 headed 'Why Liberace's theme song should be "Mad About the Boy" '. This described, in uninhibited detail, how 'the Kandelabra Kid' had made advances to a handsome young press agent in Ohio, California and Dallas, Texas. Liberace sued for libel, denying he was homosexual. He eventually won $40,000 damages by proving that he was not in Dallas at the time of one of the alleged assaults. (In 1959, in London, he sued the *Daily Mirror* for libel over an article by columnist Cassandra, who had called him 'this deadly, winking, sniggering, snuggling, chromium-plated, scent-impregnated, luminous, quivering, giggling, fruit-flavoured, mincing, ice-covered heap of mother love'.[7] Liberace won that one, too. Another £8,000 for the old Kitten on the Keys.)

Although millions of readers cheered it on, *Confidential* had powerful enemies. The heads of six major Hollywood studios banded together with a view to putting the magazine out of business, but lost their nerve. Then a group of prominent movie figures, including actor Ronald Reagan, formed a committee 'to expose people connected with smear magazines', receiving a valuable boost when the California attorney-general Edmund Brown pledged support. Brown counted among his friends stars like Frank Sinatra and members of the Kennedy political clan, who knew that *Confidential* had 'the goods' on their philanderings. In 1957, *Confidential*, its owner Robert Harrison and assorted contributors were indicted by Brown and the State of California, and charged with conspiracy to commit criminal libel. Ever the showman, Harrison's response was defiant. 'I love it,' he declared, adding that his lawyers were ready to subpoena every top-line star who had ever appeared in *Confidential*. 'Can you imagine those stars on the witness stand?' Harrison roared. 'They'll have to testify that the stories about them are true!'[8] But as the date set for the hearing approached,

Hollywood fell silent. Stars left town, took vacations or went into hiding to avoid being subpoenaed. Some witnesses vanished too, and two were found dead in suspicious circumstances. Once cocksure, Harrison was now becoming twitchy and refused to go to California to stand trial. So the case went ahead without him, *Hamlet* without the prince, but with enough big Hollywood names to keep America engrossed for weeks.

First up for a public shaming was one of the biggest TV stars of the 1950s, Desi Arnaz, husband of Lucille Ball of *I Love Lucy* fame. 'Does Desi Really Love Lucy?' *Confidential* had queried, before continuing: 'Arnaz is a Latin Lothario who loves Lucy *most* of the time but by no means *all* of the time. He has, in fact, sprinkled his affections all over Los Angeles for a number of years. And quite a bit of it has been bestowed on vice dollies who were paid handsomely for loving Desi briefly but, presumably, as effectively as Lucy.'[9] This scandalous tale had been fed to *Confidential* by Hollywood's best-known madam, flame-haired Ronnie Quillan, who testified that the magazine had paid her $1,200 for 'the goods' on Arnaz. He had denied the story, but Quillan knew it was true because, with two of her 'vice dollies', she had serviced Arnaz herself. Testifying in a figure-hugging white dress and gold slingbacks, Quillan explained that Robert Harrison of *Confidential* had recruited her to supply dirty stories about the stars. But although her evidence cast Harrison and his scandal sheet in a sleazy light, it was television's cutest husband Desi Arnaz and Hollywood itself that came off worst.

Next came actress Maureen O'Hara. *Confidential* had run a story about her indulging in a steamy 'necking session' with a mystery man at Grauman's Chinese Theater, the famous Hollywood movie house. Miss O'Hara claimed the report was inaccurate and libellous, producing her stamped passport to prove that she was abroad at the time. But again, *Confidential* wouldn't roll over and produced no fewer than three witnesses, including Grauman's former assistant manager who had flashed a torch in the darkened auditorium to discover Miss O'Hara, blouse undone, sprawled across her companion's lap. Blow after blow rained down on the prosecution case as the magazine was able to prove that what it printed was true. The beautiful black star Dorothy Dandridge, who had been awarded $10,000 damages over a

Confidential story headed 'What Dorothy Dandridge Did in the Woods', bitterly regretted her decision to give evidence against the magazine. The defence identified the bandleader Dan Terry as the source of the story and produced an affidavit in which he confirmed being the man in the woods with whom Dorothy Dandridge did it. *Confidential,* cheeky as ever, asked for its $10,000 back.

The *Confidential* trial was humiliating Hollywood. The prosecution's strategy, to expose the magazine as sleazy, scurrilous, trashy and corrupt, seemed to have backfired. Witness after witness had taken the stand, only to be identified as a *Confidential* source and to confirm that what the magazine had written was true. Then the tide turned. The judge ruled that any further testimony had to relate to the few articles already read into the record by the prosecution. This effectively scuppered Robert Harrison's plan to call a string of celebrity witnesses in his defence. After listening to six weeks of testimony and a further fortnight of deliberations, the jury reported deadlock. Emotionally and financially exhausted, Harrison couldn't face another trial and struck a deal with the attorney-general's office: all charges to be dropped in exchange for *Confidential* cleaning itself up. No more dirt, no more scandal, no more juicy gossip. *Confidential* would 'eliminate exposé stories on the private lives of celebrities' promised newspaper ads that were booked as a condition of the deal. But the sugar-coated substitute flopped, and although *Confidential* hobbled along for more than a decade the magazine eventually folded. Robert Harrison parted company with the emasculated *Confidential* after just three issues, with the gloomy prediction: 'This keyhole stuff is dead.'[10] In fact, he couldn't have been more wrong.

The notorious *National Enquirer* rekindled the flame.

The *National Enquirer* started life in 1926 as the *New York Enquirer,* a tabloid published on Sunday afternoons. By the early 1950s it was moribund muddle of sports and theatre news, with a circulation of just 17,000 and a full-time staff of one. When Generoso Pope, a young publisher with Mafia links, bought it for $20,000 in 1952, he turned it into a scandal magazine, but unlike *Confidential,* launched the same year, it was not an immediate success. This was partly because money was tight and there were no profits to invest, and partly because of Pope's exotic personal habits. 'Although Mr Pope spent most of the day at the paper,' recalled one of his writers, Reginald Potterton, 'he rarely left his office. He was accessible only to key executives, to his barber who called once a week, and to an intermittent procession of pinkie-ringed male visitors who arrived in twos and threes wearing white-on-white and expensive silk-shot suits.'[11] In 1957, witnessing a crowd of rubbernecks at a car crash, Pope was struck by their fascination with gore and hired editor Carl Grotham to serve it up thickly in the *Enquirer*. 'If a story is good,' boasted Grotham, 'no matter how vile, we'll run it.'[12]

Grotham was as good as his word. Gruesome tales, accompanied by blood-spattered pictures illustrating terrible crimes, were all grist to the *Enquirer's* grisly mill. 'Teenager Twists off Corpse's Head to Get Gold Teeth' was one headline. 'I'm Sorry I Killed My Mother, but I'm Glad I Killed My Father!' was another. The *Enquirer's* lensmen routinely raided morgues to snatch pictures of the dead, pulling the corpse from its drawer, photographing it and closing the drawer again. 'Imagine the anguish, the despair and hatred generated towards the *Enquirer* by the family and friends of the deceased when they saw their loved ones plastered through the pages of what was then the most terrifying tabloid in the country,' wrote ex-*Enquirer* reporter George Bernard. 'Not a very pleasant business.'[13] When Elvis Presley died in 1977, the magazine sent forty reporters swarming into Memphis, armed with cash to pay for dirt. A relative was paid $35,000 to take a photograph of the singer in his coffin.

In the *Enquirer's* heyday, money was never a problem. Gene Pope paid his 400 staff way over the odds, and he introduced profit-sharing and a retirement plan. On the other hand, he could be penny-pinching and dictatorial: he fired people for adjusting the office thermostat, or for opening a window. His annual net profit soared to some $20 million, even when he splashed out $1 million on the world's tallest Christmas tree in Lantana, the palm-fringed town in Florida where the *Enquirer* was headquartered. After Pope's death in 1988 and the arrival of a new owner, circulation stalled and by the mid-1990s the *Enquirer* and its rivals looked beached. Then the O. J. Simpson case broke. Not only did it dwarf any other story in modern tabloid history, but the way it was reported, with the *Enquirer* leading the pack, profoundly changed the whole of the American media. O. J. Simpson's trial for the murder of his ex-wife Nicole Brown Simpson and her friend Ron Goldman riveted not just tabloid readers but the entire nation and beyond. In the wake of the killings, the *Enquirer's* sales shot up by 10 per cent. The magazine consistently beat off the competition to break new angles, even earning praise from the staid *New York Times* for its 'aggressiveness and accuracy'.

But a curious thing was happening: the scandal was playing big in the mainstream media too, with gavel-to-gavel coverage of the trial on CNN, and reporters from the so-called serious papers elbowing in on what, ten years earlier, would have been exclusively tabloid turf. For the *Enquirer* and its bedmates, this was bad news. People didn't need to buy a tabloid to find out the latest in the case: it was all over the TV news, the *New York Times* and the *Washington Post.* Tabloid circulation fell back; in the scramble for sales, the *Enquirer's* arch-rival, the *Globe,* sided with Simpson, declared his innocence and claimed he had been framed. With the rest of the media as obsessed with the case as the so-called scandal sheets, it seemed that tabloid topics were now mainstream: the *Enquirer,* once the polecat of the media pack, was suddenly legitimate.

If the *Enquirer* sold millions with mean and nasty, in Britain there were signs of a trend from the nice end of the gossiping trade with the launch in 1988 of *Hello!* magazine. With its carefully posed, pin-sharp colour pictures and anodyne interviews, celebrities who featured in the magazine's glossy pages knew that not only would it not dig for dirt, but it would put them in control. 'Gossip was therefore transformed,' recalled one former Fleet Street editor, 'from a whisper over the garden wall (and its furtive equivalent in the tabloid columns) into a scream for attention on the spot-lit drawing room sofa.'[14] *Hello!* quickly earned a reputation for paying fees the size of telephone numbers for its treacly interviews with the rich, royal or famous; the magazine's aristocratic Mrs Fix-It and star interviewer, the Uruguayan Marquesa de Valera, was said to travel the world laden with cash stuffed into designer suitcases to clinch her deals. In 1990, when the Duchess of York posed with Prince Andrew and their second daughter Eugenie, *Hello!* paid a reported £250,000 to run some seventy pictures over forty-eight unrelenting pages. The deal also gave the magazine its most celebrated front-page headline: 'The Duke and Duchess of York Grant Us the Most Personal of Interviews and for the First Time Ever Throw Open the Doors of Their Home and Invite Us to Share Their Intimate Family Moments'.

The obsequious, high-camp breathlessness appealed to stars and star-struck alike. Imitators appeared, with rat-a-tat titles like *Here!*, *Now* and *Enjoy!*, but it was the lower-life *OK!* magazine ('Geri Gets Hot with New Man Damian') that overtook the other newcomers to challenge the pre-eminence of aristocratic *Hello!* ('Norway's Royal Wedding – A Fairytale Ending for Princess Martha Louise's Love Story'). One of *OK!*'s editors teased that she concentrated on famous people that the public really cared about, not necessarily Prince Joachim of Denmark. With its less reverential tone, *OK!* never quite matched the fairytale feel of *Hello!* But *Hello!*'s obsession with family values seemed to define the new morality of the early 1990s by remaining scandal-free, with no grainy paparazzi pictures and absolutely no adulterous sex. It subjected stars to what one sociologist, Stuart Hall, called a 'personalising transformation', a public domestication that brought them down to earth by picturing them in the privacy of their own homes, with their alarmingly bright carpets, gleaming kitchen sinks and conservatories the size of cathedrals.

By the century's end, however, the glitter was fading in the face of aggressive competition from a new breed of less deferential celebrity weeklies like *Now* and *Heat*. Sales slumped, budgets were slashed, and there was talk of unhappiness among the stars to whom *Hello!* had pandered so eagerly. When *Hello!*'s billionaire Spanish publisher, Eduardo Sanchez Junco, met *OK!*'s owner, Richard Desmond, in Madrid, they agreed to call a truce in the bidding war for celebrity exclusives between the rival titles; after overtaking *Hello!*'s circulation figures in the late 1990s, *OK!*, too, was feeling the heat. In 1999, it reportedly paid David and Victoria Beckham £1 million to persuade them to share their most private moments with the nation after what it billed as 'The Wedding of the Decade'. It sold a record 1.6 million copies.[15]

In America, too, the *National Enquirer* and its tabloid imitators seem to be in decline. They still sell at special magazine stands in supermarkets, filling stations and pharmacies, but in much smaller numbers than they used to in their 1960s and 1970s heyday; the *Enquirer*, which once sold more than 5 million copies, now sells fewer than 2 million. Thirty years ago, the typical 'tab' reader was a middle-aged, blue-collar woman. Today, she would be nudging eighty, while her daughters can gorge on gossip across a huge range of media outlets, from *People* magazine to the E! Channel and tabloid television. It seems that journalism no longer regards news and information as its primary function. It's all about entertainment.

In the days before exclusive £1 million magazine deals, stars of stage and screen regarded the gossiping trade as an occupational hazard, rather than an opportunity to tap into a fortune. The cereal-crunching Sinatra and even Mitchum coated in ketchup would probably have considered the idea beneath their dignity. In Hollywood, there was a philosophical acceptance among the movie colony that all publicity was good publicity. In any case, as most of them knew, it was really all a game. Some of the stars even caught the tabloid bug themselves. Back in the 1950s, when *Confidential* was trashing Tinseltown with its lurid exposés, the magazine ran a piece about the comedian Groucho Marx chasing girls. He ignored it. But when, a month or so later, *Confidential* implied that his television quiz show was crooked, Groucho sent the editors a threatening letter. 'Gentlemen,' he announced. 'If you continue to publish slanderous pieces about me, I shall feel compelled to cancel my subscription.'[16]

23

tittle-tattle.com

NEWSWEEK KILLS STORY ON WHITE HOUSE INTERN
BLOCKBUSTER REPORT: 23 YEAR OLD FORMER WHITE HOUSE
INTERN, SEX RELATIONSHIP WITH PRESIDENT

At 6 p.m. on Saturday evening, *Newsweek* magazine killed a story
that was destined to shake official Washington to its foundation:
a White House intern carried on a sexual affair with the President
of the United States!

The Clinton–Lewinsky scandal was the story that launched gossip into
the computer age. Monica Lewinsky was a perky young White House
intern (trainee) who had gossiped to her friend Linda Tripp that she had
conducted 'an intense sexual relationship' with President Bill Clinton.
Clinton, an inveterate womanizer, denied it, wagging his finger on
television to scotch any suggestion that he had 'sexual relations with that
woman, Miss Lewinsky'. The Presidential sex allegations were blasted
into the public arena in January 1998 by Matt Drudge, a young
maverick working alone at a cheap computer terminal in a shabby one-
bedroomed apartment in Los Angeles. Drudge called himself a
cybercolumnist, publishing items of gossip on his 'Drudge Report'
internet website. 'I don't call it journalism,' he once explained. 'I go
where the stink is.'[1]

What became known as Monicagate, his stinkiest story to date, had
started as a *Newsweek* exclusive that was so hot that it was still
unpublished. But Drudge had somehow learned the details, either from
a *Newsweek* mole or by hacking into the magazine's computer system.
When he posted his version on the net, nearly half a million people tried
to log on, sending the site crashing. For four days, Drudge sweated it

out in his room at the scuzzy end of Hollywood Boulevard, waiting for someone to smash down his barricaded door or for the story to be picked up and legitimized by the mainstream media. When, at last, *Newsweek* ran an on-line version of it, confirming the details, the story made front-page news around the world.

Monica Lewinsky was twenty-one when she and Clinton began their affair in November 1995. It continued on and off for eighteen months, with secret meetings in the Oval Office and in a windowless hallway just off it, where Monica administered oral sex to the President. Although Monica became emotionally involved, Clinton merely regarded her attentions as a pleasant distraction from affairs of state, and the liaison might have just fizzled out had it not been for Monica meeting Linda Tripp. Tripp disliked Clinton and his liberal Democrat administration, and had considered writing a book about her own experiences as a former White House employee. She knew that Clinton was a serial philanderer, and that various women from his past had claimed some form of sexual entanglement with him. These included a hotel receptionist, Paula Jones, who claimed that the President had made lewd advances to her in 1991. As Jones was suing Clinton over the alleged encounter, Linda Tripp was worried that she might be subpoenaed to give evidence. So when Monica Lewinsky confided her affair with Clinton, Tripp decided to preserve her confessions on tape to back up her story. In October 1996, Tripp began secretly recording Monica's conversations and persuaded her to keep the now famous navy-blue dress, which had been stained with Presidential semen during one of the couple's clandestine encounters at the White House.

Monica Lewinsky was startled to discover the existence of these tapes when FBI agents confronted her at a Washington hotel on 16 January 1998. Also present were officials from the Office of the Independent Counsel (OIC), Kenneth Starr, who was investigating Clinton and his wife over their role in a failed land deal, the so-called Whitewater scandal. Lewinsky was told that unless she cooperated with the OIC's investigation, she could be prosecuted for perjury. The following day, unaware that Monica had been interviewed, Clinton testified on oath at a hearing in the Paula Jones case. When Lewinsky's name was put to him, he admitted receiving gifts from her and agreed that he may have given her a hat pin, but he denied categorically ever having had sexual relations with her. But *Newsweek* knew different, having also been briefed by Linda Tripp, and would have run the story but for the intervention of the OIC, who persuaded the magazine to hold off for fear that publication might compromise a deal with Lewinsky. Enter Matt Drudge.

For all his repeated denials ('I want you to listen to me, I'm going to say this again: I did not have sexual relations with that woman, Miss Lewinsky'), Clinton became increasingly mired in the scandal. Eventually he changed his story, admitted that he had had 'an inappropriate relationship' with Monica, and apologized for 'a critical lapse of judgment and a personal failure on my part'. Kenneth Starr's report to Congress on whether Clinton had committed perjury in the Paula Jones case was, like Matt Drudge's *Newsweek* leak, posted on the internet, so that surfers worldwide, children included, could read about the President's sexual dalliances with Lewinsky in intimate detail. Starr's report listed several grounds for impeachment, but Clinton was subsequently cleared at his Senate trial, having come perilously close to being removed from office. 'Like Osama Bin Laden in his cave,' noted one commentator, 'Drudge had made the White House quake.'[2]

How did gossip get this good, so potent, so dangerous? Matt Drudge, now thirty-five, grubbed for it (literally) when he worked for seven years at the CBS gift shop in Los Angeles. He unearthed what he calls 'information gold' in photocopier bins, mainly top-secret TV ratings material, which he traded with a small network of e-mail correspondents in the early 1990s. He spiced up this data with gossip from the network's back lot and, as his mailing list grew longer, found that people were sending in titbits of their own. These he recycled along with items cherry-picked from the papers and TV shows. By 1995, he was ready to launch 'The Drudge Report'.

Drudge has an agenda. He is a conservative who voted for George W. Bush, which is one reason why he is disliked by the Washington press liberal elite. Unlike Watergate, a Presidential scandal driven by questions of national security and abuse of power, Monicagate was driven by sex. As New York gossip writer Jeanette Walls pointed out, it was the stuff of gossip columns. 'Yet because the scandal dominated the news for months, Matt Drudge, who never studied journalism and had never worked for a news organisation, became one of the best-known reporters in the country. Matt Drudge was the personification of how scandal had hi-jacked the news,' she added, 'and those in the establishment media hated it.'[3] Moreover, Drudge represented a threat to the American journalistic elite. 'His only credential,' complained Tom Shales of the *Washington Post*, 'is his computer.'[4] Six months after his Clinton scoop, Drudge, in his trade-mark Winchellesque fedora, faced his critics at the National Press Club in Washington. Like Lincoln Steffens, he had seen the future and it worked: it was called the internet, it was Drudge's medium and it would be a great equalizer. Anyone who owned a laptop and a modem could be a publisher and a reporter, or, as Drudge preferred, a 'citizen reporter'. He relished the day when everyone in America would have an equal voice, and the country would be 'vibrating with the din of small voices'.[5]

Drudge characterizes gossip on the net as a 'fight for eyeballs', because there is so much of it. It's edgy, with a whiff of danger, because it flouts constraints, it can be as sleazy as it likes; and, best of all, it's free. 'The Drudge Report' itself, still apparently hammered out on a budget-level 486 Packard-Bell computer, downloads in implacably primitive monochrome and remains typographically crude. He claims 4 million hits a day, more than 100 million a month. Today (May 2002) it's dull, dull, dull. Lead story: 'Man Files Lawsuit against Bush for 9/11 Intelligence Failures'. But most people use Drudge as a stepping stone to other news and gossip sites, including virtually all the national British newspapers. Drudge himself is more of a filter than a reporter; he doesn't actually go out there for gossip, but he does, in a way, legitimize it. During Monicagate, members of Kenneth Starr's investigation team e-mailed him stories that Drudge turned round and posted on his site: the stained blue dress, Bill's cigar and Monica pleasuring the President while he was on the phone to members of Congress. That way, the stories broke into the public domain and became fair game for the conventional press, who could report the gossip as allegations. The fact that Drudge is a one-man operation, with no staff and no sponsors, provides him with protection of a sort: who is going to swat away something that small? But he's not completely fireproof. Someone in the White House planted a false story about a named staffer whose 'spousal abuse past' had been 'covered up'. Drudge ran it without checking, was challenged, retracted, corrected and apologized within twenty-four hours. It was too late. The man and his wife launched a $30 million lawsuit, not against the fruit-fly Drudge but against his hugely wealthy internet service provider, AOL. Oops. Drudge concedes that he gets 20 per cent of his stories wrong. There again, real journalists foul up too.

In America, Drudge has caught an updraught caused by the end of the old *entente cordiale* between government and a pliant press. In the old pre-Watergate days, a reporter would find something out and be expected not to write about it. The deal was that in exchange for access, the reporter would show discretion. 'A media that once dealt in quiet signals,' critic Adam Gopnik noted in the mid-1990s, 'now sounds loud and acts mean.'[6] The arrival of Drudge has meant sounding louder and acting meaner than ever. Not that such brutal scrutiny is new, of course; in the mid-1870s, American newspapers were hungrily hawking detailed accounts of sex scandals in high places. The New York *Sun* tagged President-to-be Grover Cleveland 'a coarse debauchee who might bring his harlots to Washington... a man leprous with immorality'.[7] For the first half of the twentieth century, such lusty explicitness was stifled by a mixture of moral ambivalence and a growing respect for the Presidential office. Journalists also worried about safeguarding their freedom of speech, guaranteed under the First Amendment. So although American newspapers knew about President Kennedy's many affairs, they didn't write about them. Most editors admired him and what he stood for. Even when relations between the press and Kennedy's successor, Lyndon Johnson, soured over, no newspaper blew the whistle on Johnson's well-documented womanizing. But as the social revolution of the 1960s engulfed the media, attitudes to sexual hypocrisy changed. A growing mistrust of authority figures, part of the death of deference, put journalists back on the scent of scandal.

But if the post-Clinton American press has taken its cue from Matt Drudge, the British media was already out in front, plastering gossip from front page to back, and not just the tabloids. 'All the newspapers are putting it on their front pages now,' explains Simon Walker from PeopleNews.com ('1,000 pages of celebrity gossip, updated 20 times a day'), adding that what used to languish in the diary columns is now 'all over the cover of the *Daily Telegraph*'.[8] But by and large, this is not the type of scandalous gossip to topple prime ministers or presidents. It is low-grade candyfloss about B-list celebrities which, on the tabloid agenda at least, has overtaken hard news entirely. Dumb or what? And is it any wonder that newspaper sales across the board have slumped?

The cyber-gossips claim to point to the future, with their obsession with the grinning faces of the famous. 'They're people on telly,' says Catherine Ostler of PeopleNews.com, 'and we want to know what they're up to.' The website boldly claims to have created a new genre: people news. 'This is the really interesting media story of our time,' says Walker, 'the fact that people just love this kind of stuff. We reckon that with all the TV, magazines, newspapers and chatting, people spend over an hour a day doing stuff that is people news. It's gossip, it's people-based lifestyle news, it's entertainment news and it's fun.'[9] But 'people news', far from being a new genre, is rooted in the New Journalism of the Victorians. What is new is the reckless certainty with which these new frothing websites distinguish fame from greatness (or perhaps fail to), a distinction that has hastened the decay of fame into mere notoriety.

Our Edwardian ancestors grasped the 'people news' concept; in 1905, the American Edith Wharton in her novel *The House of Mirth* lamented 'a world where conspicuousness passed for distinction, and the society column had become the roll of fame'.[10] To glance at PeopleNews.com a century later is to run a finger down today's roll of fame, to encounter no great statesmen, soldiers or philosophers, no real achievers, or even Lord and Lady Muck, but a gruesome *galère* of tack, the reverse of alchemy in which all that glitters turns to dross. 'What happened,' says Hollywood writer Richard Schickel, 'was that the public ceased to insist that there be an obvious correlation between achievement and fame.'[11] We are spellbound by our own feeble-mindedness as we pick through this celebrity guff, as guiltily embarrassed to read it as those who write it, it seems. 'The journalism I have always been involved in isn't really worthy or useful,' concedes PeopleNews editorial director Jane Procter, who leaped aboard the celebrity gossip dot.com bandwagon from editing *Tatler* for nine years. 'I mean, knowing that Brooklyn Beckham's baby clothes have been sent on to Johnny Vaughan's child is not going to find a cure for cancer – but it amuses me. The fact that Michelle Pfeiffer hates blue M&Ms doesn't matter,' she adds, 'but it rivets me.'[12]

The unstoppable deluge of dot.com gossip may have swept into Britain, but its origins are essentially American. Like so much US pop culture, it is informal and aggressive, but – critically – it is fast ('updated twenty times a day' at a click). Speed, the quality that distinguished US reporters from the British in the cut-throat race for news as long ago as the American civil war, is still of the essence. As newspaper historian Joel H. Weiner explains, it is part of being American to want to get there first, which is why an obsession with news came to characterize American life and journalism from the 1830s onwards.[13] Gossip about the rich and famous appealed to American fancy because the country lacked an established upper class. Reporters who were sent snooping by James Gordon Bennett to fill the columns of his New York *Herald* with the 'floating gossip, scandal and folly' of the day often found their way barred because, as one outraged observer put it, 'to submit to this kind of surveillance is getting to be intolerable'.[14] No longer. Just click on a column near you. Idle curiosity satisfied in nanoseconds. A triumph of attitude over content.

All this dot.com froth and scum has fuelled a debate in the serious print media, which have become infected with the same virus. Pausing occasionally to scourge themselves for joining in the obsession with tittle-tattle and sensation, the more expensive papers then return to it unabashed. Where will it lead? Already, gossip has overtaken news on the tabloid agenda; that has happened as a result of more people getting their news from television and radio, and looking to their newspapers for entertainment rather than information. But the result is a coarsening of our culture. Like the estuarial pap swamping Britain's popular mainstream television channels, it's loud, in-yer-face and larky, but ultimately worthless. What has happened to newspaper gossip in the space of an average lifetime mocks a prediction made in the early 1930s by the American-born gossip fan, R. D. Blumenfeld, editor-in-chief of the *Daily Express*. 'Everyone is interested in the doings, habits and peculiarities of other people,' he asserted, 'and if they are celebrities, his interest is so much the greater. [But] in years to come the Press will use this feature more scrupulously, and certainly with more taste than has been the tendency of late.'[15] As Winchell might have said: phffft!

So gossip gurgles on. In terms of old-style columns, it seems a shrunken commodity; in the *Express*, the once-mighty 'Hickey' page, as intrusive and vulgar as 1950s chrome tail-fins, is now reduced to a single orphaned column. (Hickey as a fully fledged *Express* entity was unceremoniously killed off fifteen years ago; his coffin was borne along Fleet Street, accompanied by a jazz band and a gloating Nigel Dempster, his so-called rival from the *Mail*.) Dempster himself still diarizes daily, nearly thirty years after his debut, still orbiting his own never-never land, while at the *Mirror*, the scribbling trio known as 'The 3 a.m. Girls' squeal around London, trying to get themselves photographed with celebrities and making sexual mischief. *They* are the story, the celebrities merely bit-part mushes.

Newspaper scandal, on the other hand, has flourished, by and large for the public good, and remains a great leveller of reputation. Putting down the mighty from their seats is a democratic triumph, especially in an age in which personal dissembling in public life has reached an art form. It satisfies a particularly British strain of *schadenfreude* to watch pontificating politicians, oversexed sportsmen and smug television personalities being upended by one of the cheaper Sunday papers and their cheeky banana skins.

All of us live in a tabloid world, a world in which all human endeavour is magnified to shock-horror dimensions, good or bad, black or white, with few shades of in-between. Gossip provides the popcorn of light relief. Forget wars, or rumours of wars. Here is today's dose of which celebrity is doing what to another celebrity. Maybe gossip about the unhappy lives of the stars helps us contend with our own ordinariness. All of us (but women in particular) seem to enjoy reading about rich people who apparently have it all, but who actually lead tormented lives.

We no longer seem to care too much for the real world, with its trials and tribulations. It seems we would rather be poking our noses into other people's business, truffling for that juicy morsel of gossip and scandal. And the more we uncover, it seems the louder we clamour for more.

Notes

Introduction
1 *Daily Telegraph*, 11 January 1998.
2 *Spectator*, 13 April 1985.
3 *Telegraph* magazine, 22 September 2001.
4 *Times 2*, 13 November 2001.
5 Oscar Wilde, 'The Soul of Man Under Socialism' in *Fortnightly Review*, February 1891.
6 *Sunday Telegraph*, 25 November 2001.
7 Quoted in Margery Bailey, *Boswell's Column* (William Kimber, London, 1951).
8 Aldous Huxley, 'English Snobbery' in *The Olive Tree and Other Essays* (Chatto & Windus, London, 1936).
9 R. D. Blumenfeld, *The Press in My Time* (Rich & Cowan, 1933).
10 Andrew Lycett, *Ian Fleming* (Weidenfeld & Nicolson, London, 1995).
11 Diary entry, 1–2 January 1936, in John Bright-Holmes (ed.), *Like It Was*: *The Diaries of Malcolm Muggeridge* (Collins, London, 1981).
12 Diary entry, 6 November 1930, in Nigel Nicolson (ed), *Harold Nicolson: Diaries and Letters 1930–39*, (Collins, London, 1966).
13 Robert Wernick in *Smithsonian*, February 1993.
14 Ambrose Bierce, *The Unabridged Devil's Dictionary* (University of Georgia Press, Athens, Ga., 2000).
15 T. H. White, *The Age of Scandal* (Jonathan Cape, London, 1950).
16 Mrs Delarivier Manley, *The New Atalantis,* (ed.), (Ros Ballaster, Pickering & Chatto, 1991).
17 George Bernard Shaw, *Sixteen Self Sketches* (Constable, London, 1949).
18 Quoted in Shaw, *Sixteen Self Sketches.*
19 Arianna Stassinopoulos in *The Times*, 28 November 1975.
20 Richard Schickel, *Intimate Strangers: The Culture of Celebrity* (Doubleday, New York, 1985).
21 George Harrison died of cancer in November 2001.
22 Quoted in *Dallas Morning News*, 12 October 1997.
23 Quoted in *Daily Telegraph*, 27 October 2001.
24 *Daily Telegraph*, 3 June 2002.

1: Puffs, Parsons and Paragraphs
(pages 11–30)
1 Horace Walpole, *Letters to the Countess of Ossory* (Arthur L. Humphreys, 1903) Vol. I.
2 Ibid.
3 *Morning Post*, 24 August 1776.
4 Quoted in E. S. Turner, *Unholy Pursuits* (Book Guild, Lewes, 1998).

5 Alfred Spencer (ed.), *Memoirs of William Hickey* (Hurst & Blacket, 1919) Vol. I.

6 Quoted in Wilfrid Hindle, *The Morning Post 1772–1973* (Routledge, London, 1937).

7 *Morning Post*, 14 November 1776.

8 *Gentleman's Magazine*, February 1777.

9 John Taylor, *Records of My Life* (Edward Bull, London, 1932), Vol. I.

10 James Boswell, *The Life of Samuel Johnson*, John Canning (ed.), (Clarendon Press, Oxford, 1964) Vol. IV.

11 T. H. S. Escott, *Masters of Journalism* (T. Fisher Unwin, London, 1911).

12 Horace Walpole, in *The Last Journals of Horace Walpole*, Francis Stewart (ed.) (Bodley Head, London, 1910), Vol. II.

13 Thomas Macaulay, *Critical and Historical Essays* (Longman, Green & Co., 1898) Vol. VIII.

14 *London Spy*, Part II (December 1698).

15 Ben Jonson, *The Staple of News*, Act I, Sc. IV.

16 Quoted by J. B. Muddiman, *A History of English Journalism*, (Longman Green & Co., London, 1908).

17 Quoted in Raymond Snoddy, *The Good, the Bad and the Unacceptable* (Faber & Faber, London, 1984).

18 C. S. Lewis, 'English Literature in the Sixteenth Century' in *Oxford History of English Literature*, (OUP, Oxford, 1954), Vol. VII.

19 Quoted in Lewis, *English Literature in the Sixteenth Century*.

20 Charles Nicholl, *A Cup of News* (Routledge & Kegan Paul, London, 1984).

21 Ibid.

22 Alexander B. Grosart (ed.), *The Works of Gabriel Harvey* (London, 1884–5 no imprint), Vol. II.

23 Jonson, *The Staple of News*: note 'To the Readers'.

24 Jonson, *The Staple of News*, Act III, Sc. iii.

25 Ibid.

26 James Sutherland, *The Restoration Newspaper* (Cambridge University Press, Cambridge, 1986).

27 Quoted in Jeremy Black, *The English Press in the Eighteenth Century* (Croom Helm, London, 1987).

28 *Review*, 19 September 1704.

29 *Review*, 19 February 1704.

30 *Review*, 4 March 1704.

31 *Review*, 19 February 1704.

32 *Review*, 25 March 1704.

33 John Dunton (1659–1733) published some 600 books and pamphlets and is credited with authorship of the longest sentence ever printed in an English pamphlet, covering eight pages of his *Dying Groans from Fleet-Prison* (1726).

34 Quoted in Michael Shinagel, *Daniel Defoe and Middle-Class Gentility* (Harvard University Press, Cambridge, Mass., 1968).

35 G. M. Trevelyan, *English Social History* (Longmans, Green & Co., London, 1942).

36 Shinagel, *Defoe*.

37 Quoted in Shinagel, *Defoe*.

38 Jonathan Swift, quoted in *Bickerstaff Papers and Pamphlets on the Church*, Herbert Davies (ed.) (OUP, Oxford, 1957).

39 Ibid.

40 Jonathan Swift, quoted in *The Examiner and Other Pieces Written in*

1710–11, Herbert Davies (ed.) (OUP, Oxford, 1957).

41 *Review,* 14 December 1710.

42 *Review,* 21 December 1710.

43 *Moderator,* 10–14 July 1710

44 *Rehearsal,* 7–14 July 1705.

45 3 August 1705.

46 Daniel Defoe, *Introduction to a Supplementary Journal, to the Advice from the Scandal. Club* (September 1704).

47 Defoe, *Introduction.*

48 Introduction in *Defoe's Weekly Review of the Affairs of France,* Arthur Wellesley Secord (ed.) (facsimile edition, Columbia University Press, New York, 1938).

49 *Review,* Saturday, 15 April 1704.

50 *Review,* 20 August 1707.

51 John Gay, *The Present State of Wit* (1711), quote in M. Shinagel, *Daniel Defoe and Middle Class Gentility* (Harvard, 1968).

52 *Tatler,* 11 June 1709.

53 Gay, *The Present State of Wit.*

54 Ibid.

55 *Spectator,* 19 March 1711.

56 Introduction in Donald Bond, *The Spectator* (Clarendon Press, Oxford, 1965).

2: The Bubble of the Rabble

(pages 31–46)

1 Thomas Wright (1810–87) in *Caricature History of the Georges* (J. C. Hotten, 1868).

2 Robert Trevor to Stephen Poyntz, 21 December 1729, quoted in Jeremy Black, *The English Press in the Eighteenth Century* (Croom Helm, London 1987).

3 *Growler,* 15 February 1711, quoted in Black, *The English Press in the Eighteenth Century.*

4 *Tatler,* 29 September 1709.

5 Letter from Jonathan Swift to Joseph Addison, 22 August 1710.

6 Dr J. Doran, in *Notes & Queries,* 2nd series 70 (May 1857).

7 Paula McDowell, *The Women of Grub Street: Press, Politics, and Gender in the London Literary Marketplace 1678–1730* (Clarendon Press, Oxford, 1998).

8 Sarah Churchill (Duchess of Marlborough), *Private Correspondence* (Henry Colburn, London 1838), Vol. I.

9 G. M. Trevelyan, *English Social History* (Longmans, Green & Co., London, 1942).

10 Quoted in Fidelis Morgan, *A Woman of No Character* (Faber & Faber, London, 1986).

11 Morgan, *Women of No Character.*

12 Della Manley, *The Lost Lover* (1696).

13 *Female Spectator,* 1745, Vol. I, Book I.

14 Alexander Pope, *The Dunciad* in *The Works of Alexander Pope,* Vol. IV (John Murray, 1882).

15 Jonathan Swift in a letter to the Countess of Suffolk, 26 October 1731.

16 *The Character of a Coffee-House* (1673), quoted in Steve Pincus, 'Coffeehouses and Restoration Political Culture' in *Journal of Modern History,* V. 67, no. 4 (December 1995).

17 *Gentleman's Magazine,* 8 March 1735.

18 *True Patriot,* quoted in *Gentleman's Magazine,* January 1746.

19 Henry Coventry to Sir William Swann, 20 March 1674.

20 Quoted in Pincus, op. cit.

21 Quoted in *Quarterly Review,* CXVII, no. 351, April 1903.

22 James T. Hillhouse, *Grub-Street Journal* (Duke University Press, Durham, North Carolina, 1928).

23 Preface to *Memoirs of the Society of Grub-Street* Vol. I (London, 1737).

24 Quoted in Hillhouse, *The Grub-Street Journal.*

25 Quoted in Dr Michael Harris, *London Newspapers in the Age of Walpole* (Associated University Presses, London and Toronto, 1987).

26 Ibid.

27 *Gentleman's Magazine*, December 1766.

28 T. H. White, *The Age of Scandal* (Jonathan Cape, London 1950).

29 Ibid.

30 Ibid.

31 Dennis Griffiths (ed.), *The Encyclopaedia of the British Press* (Macmillan, London, 1992).

32 Source unknown.

33 Source unknown.

34 Quoted in Isaac D'Israeli, *Calamities and Quarrels of Authors* (Frederick Warne & Co., London, 1881).

35 Source unknown.

36 Quoted by Philip Gosse, *Dr Viper: The Querulous Life of Philip Thicknesse* (Cassell, 1952).

37 Ibid.

38 Philip Thicknesse, *Memoirs and Anecdotes*, Vol. 3 (Printed privately, 1791).

39 Quoted by Philip Gosse, *Dr Viper.*

40 Ibid.

41 The earliest eye-witness account of a public execution, that of Charles I in 1649, is by an unknown writer.

42 Margery Bailey, *Boswell's Column* (William Kimber, London, 1951).

3: A Scandalous Profession
(pages 47–68)

1 *Vanity Fair*, May 2002.

2 E. S Turner, *Unholy Pursuits: The Wayward Parsons of Grub Street* (Book Guild, Lewes, 1998).

3 Edward Ward, *A Trip to Jamaica* (1698) (Facsimile Text Society, New York, 1993).

4 Diary entry, 3 April 1829, in Sir Walter Scott, *Journal*, W. E. K. Anderson (ed.) (Clarendon Press, Oxford, 1972: first published 1890, Vol. II.).

5 Diary of John Baker, 11 December 1776.

6 John Taylor, *Records of My Life* (Edward Bull, London, 1832).

7 Ibid.

8 Quoted in Turner, *Unholy Pursuits*, Ch. 4.

9 *Morning Post*, 21 February 1786.

10 Quoted in Turner: *Unholy Pursuits*, Ch. 9.

11 Ibid.

12 Oliver Goldsmith, *The Citizen of the World*, quoted in G. A. Cranfield, *The Press and Society* (Longman, 1978).

13 Quoted in Cranfield, *Press and Society.*

14 Benjamin Franklin, 'On Scandal' in *Complete Works of Benjamin Franklin* (Putnam, New York, 1887).

15 Quoted in Fintan O'Toole, *A Traitor's Kiss: The Life of Richard Brinsley Sheridan* (Granta Books, 1997).

16 H. R. Fox Bourne in *Gentleman's Magazine*, November 1887.

17 *Gentleman's Magazine*, June 1838.

18 Charles Lamb, 'Newspapers Thirty-Five Years Ago' in *Charles Lamb, Last Essays of Elia* (Dent, London, 1897).

19 *Fraser's Magazine*, March 1836.

20 F. Knight Hunt, *The Fourth Estate* (David Boyne, London, 1850).

21 11 July 1838.

22 M. H. Spielmann, *History of 'Punch'* (Cassell & Co., London, 1895).

23 Charles Greville, *The Greville Memoirs* (Longmans, Green and Co., 1909) Vol. IV.

24 Quoted in Greville, ibid.

25 Charles Lamb, 'Newspapers Thirty-Five Years Ago', in *Last Essays of Elia* (Dent, London 1897).

26 Quoted in H. R. Fox Bourne, *English Newspapers: Chapters in the History of Journalism* (Chatto & Windus, London, 1877), Vol. I.

27 *John Bull*, 17 December 1820.

28 *John Bull*, 25 February 1821.

29 *John Bull*, 16 September 1821.

30 Diary entry, in 25 April 1821, Francis Bamford and Duke of Wellington (eds.), *The Journal of Mrs Arbuthnot* (Macmillan, London, 1950).

31 *John Bull*, 3 March 1822.

32 Myron Brightfield, *Theodore Hook and his Novels* (Harvard University Press, Cambridge, Mass., 1928).

33 *John Bull*, 17 December 1820.

34 Letter among collection of Croker papers at University of Chicago, quoted in Bill Newton Dunn, *The Man Who Was John Bull* (Allendale Publishing, London, 1996).

35 William Makepeace Thackeray, *Pendennis* (Garland Publishing, 1991), Ch. 34.

36 Revd R. H. Dalton Barham, *The Life and Remains of Theodore Edward Hook* (Richard Bentley, London, 1853).

37 'Theodore Hook' in A. J. A. Symons, *Essays and Biographies*, Julian Symons (ed.) (Cassell, London, 1969).

38 Quoted in R. H. M. Buddle Atkinson and G. A. Jackson (eds.), *Brougham and His Early Friends* (privately printed, 1908).

39 Quoted in J. A. Roebuck, *The London Review and the Periodical Press* (1835). Cited in Arthur Aspinall, The Social Status of Journalists at the Beginning of the Nineteenth Century in Review of English Studies (1945), Vol. 21.

40 Samuel Carter Hall, 'Theodore Hook and his Friends' in *Atlantic Monthly*, April 1865.

41 Emily Cowper to George Lamb, *c.* February 1821, in *The Letters of Lady Palmerston,* Tresham Lever (ed.) (John Murray, London, 1957).

42 *The Times*, 22 April 1822.

43 Quoted in Editors of *The Age, The Spirit of the Age Newspaper for 1828* (A. Durham, London, 1829).

44 *Age*, 1 January 1832.

45 *Satirist*, 21 December 1835.

46 *Satirist*, 14 October 1838.

47 *Satirist*, 7 July 1839.

48 Mrs Sumbel, *Memoirs of the Life of Mrs Sumbel, late Wells* (Chapple, London, 1811).

49 Henry Crabb Robinson's MS diary, 1812.

50 *The Times*, 21 February 1789.

51 William Cobbett, *Cobbett's Political Register*, 4 January 1817.

52 *Morning Post*, 9 February 1789.

53 *Morning Post*, 10 February 1789.

54 Charles Knight, *Passages of a Working Life* (Bradbury & Evans, London, 1864).

55 Le Marchant's MS Journal (1833) cited in Aspinall, *Social Status of C19th Journalists.*

56 Donald J. Gray, 'Early Victorian Scandalous Journalism' in *The Victorian Periodical Press: Samplings and*

Soundings, Joanne Shattock and Michael Wolff (eds.) (Leicester University Press, Leicester, 1982).
57 Ibid.
58 Madeleine House (ed.), *Letters of Charles Dickens* (1974), Vol. III.
59 *Town,* 2 June 1838.
60 *Town,* 28 March 1840.
61 *Town,* 14 October 1837.
62 *Town,* 30 May 1840.
63 *Town,* 18 April 1838.
64 *Town,* 4 August 1838.
65 *Town,* 26 January 1842.
66 *The Times,* 23 November 1838.
67 *Crim-Con Gazette,* 25 August 1838.

4: Blackmail and Lady Blessington
(pages 69–77)
1 James Grant, *The Great Metropolis* (Saunders & Otley, New York, 1837).
2 R. G. G. Price, *A History of Punch* (Collins, London, 1957).
3 Ibid.
4 W. M. Thackeray, 'Half-a-Crown's Worth of Cheap Knowledge' in *Fraser's Magazine,* March 1838.
5 W. M. Thackeray, 'The Adventures of Philip' quoted in Nigel Cross, *The Common Writer* (Cambridge University Press, Cambridge, 1985).
6 Henry Chorley, quoted by Prudence Hannay, in *Genius in the Drawing-Room,* Peter Quennell (ed.) (Weidenfeld & Nicolson, London, 1980).
7 Quoted in Michael Sadleir *Blessington D'Orsay – a Masquerade* (Constable, 1933).
8 Quoted in Sadleir, ibid.
9 *Age,* 23 August 1829.
10 *Age,* 24 September 1829.
11 *Age,* 11 October, 1829.
12 Quoted in J. Fitzgerald Molloy, *The Most Gorgeous Lady Blessington*

(Downey & Co., London, 1896).
13 *Maclise Portrait Gallery* (Chatto and Windus, London, 1883).
14 *Satirist,* 31 July 1831.
15 Michael Sadleir (1888–1957), author of *Blessington–D'Orsay: A Masquerade* (Constable, London, 1933). His best-known work was the 1940 novel *Fanny by Gaslight.*
16 Sadleir, *Blessington–D'Orsay.*
17 *Crim-Con Gazette,* 4 May 1839.
18 Letter from Charles Dickens to Countess of Blessington, 16 January 1846, quoted in R. R. Madden (ed.), *The Literary Life and Correspondence of the Countess of Blessington* (T. C. Newby, London, 1855), Vol. I.
19 Dickens to Lady Blessington [?] 30 January 1846 in Letters of Charles Dickens.
20 Ibid.
21 Dickens to Lady Blessington, 9 February 1846.
22 Ibid.
23 Donald J. Gray, 'Early Victorian Scandalous Journalism' in *The Victorian Periodical Press: Samplings and Soundings,* Joanne Shattock and Michael Wolff (eds.) (Leicester University Press/University of Toronto Press, 1982).
24 Edmund Yates, *Recollections and Experiences* (Richard Bentley & Son, London, 1884), Vol. I.
25 Laura Smith, 'Society Journalism: Its Rise and Development', in *Newspaper Press Directory* (1898).

5: Yates and his *World*
(pages 78–85)
1 *The Times Literary Supplement,* 6 February 1998.
2 *Illustrated Times,* 19 July 1856.
3 Mrs Steuart Erskine (ed.), *Twenty*

Years at Court (Nisbet, London n.d.), quoted in Kennedy Jones, *Fleet Street and Downing Street* (Hutchinson, London 1920).

4 Edmund Yates, *Recollections and Experiences* (Richard Bentley & Son, London, 1884).

5 *The Times*, 20 January 1912.

6 James D. Symon, *The Press and its Story* (Seeley Service, London, 1914).

7 Quoted in 'Class and Clique Journalism' in H. R. Fox Bourne, *English Newspapers: Chapters in the History of Journalism* (Chatto & Windus, London, 1887).

8 Edmund Yates, *Fifty Years of London Life: Memoirs of a Man of the World* (Harper & Brother, New York, 1885).

9 Edmund Yates, 'Summer Days' in *Temple Bar*, III (1861).

10 Joseph Hatton, *Journalistic London* (Sampson, Low, London, 1882).

11 *Inverness Courier*, 2 September 1858.

12 Ralph Straus, *Sala: The Portrait of an Eminent Victorian* (Constable, London, 1942).

13 *World*, 8 July 1874.

14 Quoted in Raymond L. Schults, *Crusader in Babylon: W. T. Stead and the Pall Mall Gazette* (University of Nebraska Press, Lincoln, 1972).

15 *Morning Advertiser*, 3 April 1884.

16 *Pall Mall Gazette*, 3 April 1884.

17 Quoted in Hesketh Pearson, *Labby* (Hamish Hamilton, London, 1936).

18 Hatton, *Journalistic London*.

19 Quoted in Schults, *Crusader in Babylon*.

20 President of the Institute of Journalists in a speech to Congress of Journalists, reported in *Daily Chronicle* and *The Times*, 22 September 1893.

21 In Leon Edel (ed.), *Henry James Letters:* Vol. III, 1883–1895 (Macmillan, London, 1981).

22 Yates, *Recollections and Experiences,* Vol. II.

23 T. H. S. Escott, 'Literature and Journalism' in *Fortnightly Review,* XCVII (1912).

24 *Gobemouche*: one who credulously accepts all news (*Shorter OED*), Vol. I.

25 *Inverness Courier*, 8 July 1858.

26 Edward Dicey, 'Journalism Old and New', in *Fortnightly Review,* LXXXIII (1905).

27 Quoted in Joel H. Wiener, 'The Americanisation of the British Press, 1830–1914' in *Studies in Newspaper and Periodical History*, Michael Harris and Tom O'Malley, (eds.) (Greenwood Press, Westport, Conn., 1995).

6: Not for Babes, Prudes, Idiots or Dudes

(pages 86–103)

1 *Weekly Rehearsal,* 27 January 1735.

2 *News-Letter*, 6 January 1763.

3 Quoted in Frank Luther Mott, *American Journalism* (Macmillan, Toronto, 1962).

4 Michael Schudson, *Discovering the News: A Social History of American Newspapers* (Basic Books, New York, 1978).

5 Quoted in Joel H. Wiener, 'The Americanisation of the British Press, 1830–1914' in *Studies in Newspaper and Periodical History*, Michael Harris and Tom O'Malley, (eds.) (Greenwood Press, Westport, Conn., 1995).

6 H. W. Massingham, 'The Great London Dailies: The Halfpenny Evening Press', in *Leisure Hour* (September 1892).

7 George Bernard Shaw, *Sixteen Self Sketches* (Constable, London, 1949).

8 W. T. Stead, 'Mr T. P. O'Connor MP' in *Review of Reviews,* November 1902.

9 *New Review,* October, 1889.

10 Evelyn March Phillipps, 'The New Journalism' in *New Review,* XXX, August 1895.

11 Quoted in Wiener 'Americanisation of the British Press' op cit.

12 Charles Dickens, *American Notes,* Granville, 1985 by Ch. 18.

13 Anon. [John Forster], 'The Newspaper Literature of America' in *Foreign Quarterly Review* (Chapman and Hall, 1843).

14 Quoted in Charles F. Wingate (ed.), *Views and Interviews on Journalism,* (F. B. Patterson, New York, 1875).

15 Quoted in F. M. O'Brien, *The Story of the* [New York] *Sun* (New York, D. Appleton, 1918).

16 Quoted in Wiener, 'The Americanisation of the British Press' in Harris and O'Malley (eds.), *Studies in Newspaper and Periodical History.*

17 Quoted in Don C. Seitz, *Pulitzer: Life and Letters* (Simon & Schuster, New York, 1924).

18 *New York World,* 17 June 1883.

19 Noel B. Gerson, *Lillie Langtry* (Robert Hale & Co., London, 1972).

20 Mark Twain, quoted in Gerson, *Lillie Langtry.*

21 Quoted in Don C. Seitz, *The James Gordon Bennetts, Father and Son: Proprietors of the New York Herald* (Bobbs-Merrill Company, Indianapolis, 1928).

22 Isabel Ross, *Ladies of the Press: The Story of Women in Journalism by an Insider* (New York, 1936).

23 Emma Mayer, 'Society Reporting Among the "400"' in *Editor & Publisher,* 12 December 1931.

24 Interview with *New York Times,* July 1905, quoted in Andy Logan, *The Man Who Robbed the Robber Barons* (W. W. Norton, New York, 1965).

25 Quoted in Egon Larsen, '*The Fine Art of Blackmail*' in *First with the Truth* (John Baker, London, 1968).

26 Ibid.

27 Logan, *The Man Who Robbed the Robber Barons.*

28 Ibid.

29 Edwin Post Jr quoted in Logan, *The Man Who Robbed the Robber Barons.*

30 Quoted in Logan, *The Man Who Robbed the Robber Barons.*

31 Quoted in Larsen, 'The Fine Art of Blackmail' in *First with The Truth.*

32 Quoted in Logan, *The Man Who Robbed the Robber Barons.*Quoted in Logan, *The Man Who Robbed the Robber Barons.*

33 Quoted in Larsen, 'The Fine Art of Blackmail', *First with the Truth.*

34 Ibid.

35 *New York Times,* 22 January 1932.

36 Quoted in Logan, *The Man Who Robbed the Robber Barons.*

37 Ibid.

38 Ibid.

39 Ibid.

40 James L. Ford, *The Brazen Calf* (Dodd, New York, 1903).

41 Richard Schickel, *Intimate Strangers: The Culture of Celebrity* (Doubleday, New York, 1985).

42 George W. S. Trow, *My Pilgrim's Progress: Media Studies 1950–1998* (Pantheon Books, New York).

43 Quoted in Eve Brown, *Cholly Knickerbocker: The Life and Times of Maury Paul* (Dutton, New York, 1947).

44 Ibid.

45 Ibid.

46 Ibid.

47 Quoted in Cleveland Amory, *Who Killed Society?* (Harper & Bros., New York, 1960).

48 Quoted in Jeanette Walls, *Dish* (Avon Books, New York, 2000).

49. Ibid.

7: Lillie Langtry and *Vanity Fair*
(pages 104–117)

1 Robert Rhodes James (ed.), *Chips – The Diaries of Sir Henry Channon* (Weidenfeld & Nicolson, London, 1967).

2 *Sunday Chronicle*, February 1928, quoted in Laura Beatty, *Lillie Langtry: Manners, Masks and Morals* (Chatto & Windus, London, 1999).

3 Lillie Langtry, *The Days I Knew* (G. Doran, New York, 1925).

4 *Vanity Fair*, 12 July 1877.

5 *Truth*, date unknown.

6 *Vanity Fair*, issue unknown.

7 Quoted in Leonard Naylor, *The Irrepressible Victorian* (Macmillan, 1965).

8 Ibid.

9 *Vanity Fair*, 26 January 1878.

10 *Vanity Fair*, 26 January 1878.

11 *Vanity Fair*, 2 March 1878.

12 *Vanity Fair*, 12 April 1879.

13 *Vanity Fair*, 19 April 1879.

14 *The Times*, 24 April 1879.

15 *Vanity Fair*, 14 December 1878.

16 *Town Talk*, 11 January 1879.

17 *Town Talk*, 12 April 1879.

18 *Town Talk*, 31 May 1879.

19 *Town Talk*, 7 June 1879.

20 *Town Talk*, 30 August 1879.

21 *Town Talk*, 30 August 1879.

22 *Town Talk*, 6 September 1879.

23 *Town Talk*, 4 October 1879.

24 *Truth*, quoted in Naylor, op cit.

25 *Vanity Fair*, 12 March 1884.

26 Quoted in Naylor, *The Irrepressible Victorian*.

27 Ibid.

28 Ibid.

29 Robert Buchanan, 'The Newest Thing in Journalism' in *Contemporary Review*, September 1887.

30 *Vanity Fair*, 23 July 1887.

31 *Vanity Fair*, 20 August 1887.

32 *Vanity Fair*, 2 October 1887.

33 Heinrich Felberman, *Memoirs of a Cosmopolitan* (Chapman & Hall, London, 1936).

34 James Brough, *The Prince and the Lily* (Hodder & Stoughton, London, 1975).

35 Quoted in Laura Beatty, *Lillie Langtry* (Chatto & Windus, London, 1999).

36 Bernard Falk, *He Laughed in Fleet Street* (Hutchinson, London, 1933).

37 Lillie Langtry, *The Days I Knew* (Hutchinson, London 1925).

38 Quoted in Beatty, *Lillie Langtry*.

8: The Bracing Sea of Sex
(pages 118–142)

1 Auberon Waugh, 'In Praise of Mr Nigel Dempster' in *New Statesman*, 5 December 1975.

2 Harry Procter, *The Street of Disillusion* (Allan Wingate, London, 1958).

3 *Town and Country Magazine*, 18: 345.

4 Thornton Hunt (ed.), *Correspondence of Leigh Hunt* (Smith, Elder & Co., London, 1862), Vol. I.

5 William Congreve, *The Way of the World*, V.v.

6 Anon., 'The Last of Criminal Conversation' in *Saturday Review*, 3 (1857).

7 A. C. Benson and Viscount Esher

(eds.), *Letters of Queen Victoria* (Murray, London, 1908), Vol. III.

8 Quoted in Lawrence Stone, *Road to Divorce – England 1530–1987* (OUP, Oxford, 1990).

9 W. T. Stead in evidence to the Royal Commission on Divorce, *Royal Commission on Divorce* (1912) Minister of Evidence.

10 *Royal Commission on Divorce,* (1912), Minutes of Evidence, Vol. II.

11 H. Montgomery Hyde, 'Whose Baby? A Matter of Paternity' in *A Tangled Web: Sex Scandals in British Politics and Society* (Constable, London 1986).

12 Quoted in John Collier and Iain Lang, *Just The Other Day* (Hamish Hamilton, London, 1932).

13 Letter from King's private secretary, Lord Stamfordham, to Lord Chancellor, 15 July 1922, PRO file LCO 2/775.

14 Robert Graves and Alan Hodge, *The Long Weekend* (Hutchinson, London, 1940).

15 Peregrine Churchill and Julian Mitchell, *Jennie, Lady Randolph Churchill* (Collins, London, 1974).

16 Quoted in Georgia Battiscombe, 'The Aylesford Affair' in Harriet Bridgeman and Elizabeth Drury (eds.), *Society Scandals* (David & Charles, Newton Abbot, 1977).

17 Letter from Queen Victoria to Prince of Wales, 10 March 1876, quoted in Anita Leslie, *Edwardians in Love* (Hutchinson, London, 1972).

18 Quoted in Anita Leslie, *Jennie: The Life of Lady Randolph Churchill* (Hutchinson, London, 1969).

19 Ibid.

20 Quoted in Leslie, *Edwardians in Love.*

21 Quoted in G. H. Fleming, *Lady Colin Campbell* (Windrush Press, Moreton-in-Marsh, 1989).

22 Ibid.

23 Ibid.

24 Quoted in G. H. Fleming, *Lady Colin Campbell.*

25 J. Goole, *The Contract Violated, or the Hasty Marriage* (1733), quoted in Stone, *Road to Divorce.*

26 [L. Simond], *A Journal of a Tour and Residence in Great Britain during the Years 1810 and 1811 by a French Traveller...* (New York, 1815), Vol. I, p. 34, quoted in Stone, *Road to Divorce.*

27 Stone, *Road to Divorce.*

28 Quoted in Arthur Aspinall, *Politics and the Press* (Home & Van Thal, London, 1949).

29 Ibid.

30 Stone, *Road to Divorce.*

31 Michael Harris, 'Trials and Criminal Biographies: A Case Study in Distribution' in R. Myers and M. Harris (eds.), *Sale and Distribution of Books from 1700* (OUP, Oxford, 1982), quoted in Stone, *Road to Divorce.*

32 Quoted in Stone, *Road to Divorce.*

33 Middleton v Middleton in Lawrence Stone, *Broken Lives: Separation and Divorce in England 1660–1857* (OUP, Oxford, 1993).

34 Westmeath v Westmeath in Stone, *Broken Lives.*

35 *Globe,* 18 May 1857.

36 Westmeath v Westmeath in Stone, *Broken Lives.*

37 Ibid.

38 Quoted in in Stone, *Road to Divorce.*

39 Sidney Low in *Royal Commission on Divorce* (1912), Minutes of Evidence.

40 Sir G. H. Lewis in *Royal Commission on Divorce* (1912),

Minutes of Evidence.

41 *Royal Commission on Divorce* (1912), Report Part XVII.

42 Ibid.

43 Sidney Low in *Royal Commission on Divorce* (1912), Minutes of Evidence.

44 C. P. Scott in *Royal Commission in Divorce* (1912), Minutes of Evidence.

45 Sir Charles Petrie, *Scenes of Edwardian Life* (Eyre & Spottiswode, London, 1965).

46 C. P. Scott in *Royal Commission on Divorce* (1912), Minutes of Evidence.

47 Quoted in *News of the World*, 14 March 1909.

48 Quoted in *News of the World*, 24 January 1909.

49 *Spectator*, 13 February 1909.

50 Footnote in Lord Morley, *Life of Gladstone* (MacMillan Company, New York, 1903), quoted in evidence to Royal Commission on Divorce (1910), Minutes of Evidence.

51 Gorell questioning C.P. Scott, editor of the *Manchester Guardian*, in evidence to the Royal Commission on Divorce, 21 December 1910.

52 Quoted in *Newspaper Press Directory* (1923).

53 W. T. Stead in evidence to the Royal Commission on Divorce (1910).

54 *Newspaper Press Directory* (1923).

55 Letter from King's private secretary, Lord Stamfordham, to Lord Chancellor, 6 March 1925, PRO file LCO 2/775.

56 *News of the World*, 8 March 1925.

57 Minutes of secret meeting on 7 April 1925 between the Home Secretary, Sir William Joynson-Hicks, and newspaper owners, HO45/12288.

58 Ibid.

59 *News of the World*, 8 March 1925.

60 Quoted in H. Montgomery Hyde,

Norman Birkett (Hamish Hamilton, London, 1965).

9: Daddy's Girls and Boys

(pages 143–159)

1 Beverley Nichols, *Crazy Pavements* (Jonathan Cape, London, 1927).

2 Ibid.

3 Nancy Mitford to Mark Ogilvie-Grant, 30 March 1930, quoted in Harold Acton, *Nancy Mitford: A Memoir* (Hamish Hamilton, London, 1975).

4 Jessica Mitford, *Hons and Rebels* (Gollancz, London, 1960).

5 Acton, *Nancy Mitford.*

6 Nancy Mitford to Mark Ogilvie-Grant, 11 April 1930, quoted in Acton, *Nancy Mitford.*

7 Ibid.

8 Nancy Mitford to Mark Ogilvie-Grant, 17 November 1930, quoted in Acton, *Nancy Mitford.*

9 Nancy Mitford to Mark Ogilvie-Grant, 11 April 1930, quoted in Acton, *Nancy Mitford.*

10 Nancy Mitford to Mark Ogilvie-Grant, 15 May 1931, quoted in Acton, *Nancy Mitford.*

11 Ibid.

12 Charlotte Mosley (ed.), *A Talent to Annoy* (Hamish Hamilton, London, 1986).

13 Ibid.

14 Quoted in Mitford, *Hons and Rebels*, p. 130.

15 Later the 2nd Lord Birkenhead.

16 Lord Birkenhead, *Lady Eleanor Smith – A Memoir* (Hutchinson, London, 1953).

17 Ibid.

18 Ibid.

19 Ibid.

20 Eleanor Smith, *Life's A Circus*

(Longmans, Green & Co., London, 1939).

21 *Sunday Dispatch*, 1 July 1928.

22 Quoted in Birkenhead, *Lady Eleanor Smith*.

23 Kenneth Young (ed.), *The Diaries of Sir Robert Bruce Lockhart*: Vol. I, (*1915–1938*) (Macmillan, London, 1973).

24 Birkenhead, *Lady Eleanor Smith*.

25 Ibid.

26 Nichols, *Crazy Pavements*.

27 Diary entry, 30 January 1934, in Virginia Woolf, *The Diary of Virginia Woolf:* Vol. IV, *1931–35* (The Hogarth Press, London, 1982), p. 200.

28 John Collier and Iain Lang, *Just the Other Day*, (Hamish Hamilton, London, 1932).

29 Diary Entry, 21 September 1943, in Robert Rhodes James (ed.), *Chips: The Diaries of Sir Henry Channon* (Weidenfeld & Nicolson, London, 1967).

30 Anita Leslie, *Cousin Randolph* (Hutchinson, London, 1985).

31 Quoted in Leonard Mosley, *Castlerosse,* (Arthur Barker, London, 1956).

32 *Daily Express*, 28 June 1932.

33 'The Years with Kinross' (4) in *Punch,* 16 August 1961.

34 Hugh David, *On Queer Street* (HarperCollins, London, 1997).

35 King George V, when told Beauchamp was gay, reportedly harrumphed: 'I thought men like that shot themselves.' Quoted in H. Montgomery Hyde, *The Other Love,* (Heinemann, 1970).

36 Balfour to 'Darling Mum', Paris, Whit Sunday 1926, in Kinross Papers (Acc 7638), National Library of Scotland.

37 Ibid.

38 'The Years with Kinross' (4) in *Punch,* 16 August 1961

39 Ibid.

40 Patrick Balfour, letter to his mother, 1 November 1927.

41 Patrick Balfour, letter to his mother, 1 November 1927.

42 Patrick Balfour, letter to his mother, undated.

43 'The Years with Kinross' (4) in *Punch,* 16 August 1961.

44 Bevis Hillier, *Young Betjeman* (John Murray, London, 1988).

45

46 'The Years with Kinross' (4) in *Punch,* 16 August 1961.

47 Ibid.

48 Lord Kinross to Patrick Balfour, 8 March 1932, in Kinross Papers (Acc 7638), National Library of Scotland.

49 Lord Kinross to Patrick Balfour, 11 March 1931, in Kinross Papers (Acc 7638), National Library of Scotland.

50 'The Years with Kinross' (5) in *Punch,* 23 August 1961.

51 'The Years with Kinross' (4) in *Punch,* 16 August 1961.

52 Patrick Balfour, *Society Racket* (John Long, London, 1933).

53 'The Years with Kinross' (5) in *Punch,* 9 August 1961.

54 Balfour, *Society Racket.*

55 Quoted in Collier and Lang, *Just the Other Day.*

56 Evelyn Waugh, *Vile Bodies* (Penguin, London, 1938).

57 E. M. Forster to Sibyl Colefax, 1 May 1934, Colefax MS Eng. *c.*1362, Bodleian Library, Oxford, quoted in Ross McKibbin, *Classes and Cultures: England 1918–1951* (OUP, Oxford, 1998).

58 Balfour, *Society Racket.*

59 Diary entry, 30 January 1932, in John Vincent (ed.) *The Crawford Papers: The journals of David Lindsay, twenty-seventh Earl of Crawford and tenth Earl of Balcarres 1871–1940 during the years 1892 to 1940* (Manchester, Manchester University Press, 1984).

60 Ibid.

61 Karl Silex, *John Bull At Home* (Harrap, London, 1931).

62 Paul Cohen-Portheim, *England, the Unknown Isle* (Duckworth, London, 1930).

63 Sir Robert Bruce Lockhart, *Friends, Foes and Foreigners* (Putman, London, 1957).

64 Beaverbrook in *Evening Standard*, 19 November 1926, quoted in Mosley, *Castlerosse*.

65 Quoted in Mosley, *Castlerosse*.

66 Quoted in George Malcolm Thomson, *Lord Castlerosse: His Life and Times* (Weidenfeld & Nicolson, London, 1973).

67 Later the *Weekly* (and later still the *Sunday*) *Dispatch*.

68 *Bystander,* 19 August 1936.

69 All Donegall's comments are from the unfinished MS of his unpublished memoirs, courtesy of the late Marchioness of Donegall.

70 Robert Graves and Alan Hodge, *The Long Weekend: A Social History of Great Britain 1918–1939* (Hutchinson, London, 1940).

71 *Sunday Dispatch*, 5 March 1933.

72 *Sunday Dispatch*, 28 May 1933.

10: Talk of the Town
(pages 160–168)

1 *Guardian*, 22 November 1973.

2 'The Case for Beelzebub' in Michael Foot, *Debts of Honour* (Davis Poynter, London, 1980).

3 *Times Literary Supplement,* 9 December 1973.

4 Anne Chisholm and Michael Davie, *Beaverbrook – A Life* (Hutchinson, London, 1992).

5 *Guardian,* 22 November 1973.

6 Douglas Sutherland, *Portrait of a Decade: London Life 1945–1955* (Harrap, London, 1988).

7 Howard Spring, *In The Meantime* (Constable, London, 1942).

8 Ibid.

9 Malcolm Muggeridge, *Chronicles of Wasted Time: Part 2, The Infernal Grove* (Collins, London, 1973).

10 *Evening Standard* 150th anniversary number, 21 May 1977.

11 Muggeridge, *The Infernal Grove.*

12 Ibid.

13 Ibid.

14 Ibid.

15 John Bright-Holmes (ed.), *Like it Was: The Diaries of Malcolm Muggeridge* (Collins, London, 1981).

16 Muggeridge, *The Infernal Grove.*

17 Ibid.

18 Ibid.

19 Ibid.

20 Ibid.

21 Ibid.

22 Ibid.

23 Harold Nicolson to Vita Sackville-West, 2 January 1930, in Nigel Nicolson (ed.), *Vita and Harold: The Letters of Vita Sackille-West and Harold Nicolson* (Weidenfeld & Nicolson, London, 1992).

24 Diary entry, 31 December 1930, in Nigel Nicolson (ed.), *Harold Nicolson: Diaries and Letters 1930–1939,* (Collins, London, 1966).

25 Ibid.

26 Diary entry, 2 April 1931 in

Kenneth Young, (ed.), *The Diaries of Sir Robert Bruce Lockhart: Vol. I, (1915–1938)* (Macmillan, London, 1973).

27 Ibid.

28 Diary entry, 22 August 1931, in Nicolson (ed.), *Harold Nicolson: Diaries and Letters.*

29 Diary entry, 9 May 1931, in Young (ed.), *The Diaries of Sir Robert Bruce Lockhart.*

30 Introduction to Young (ed.), *The Diaries of Sir Robert Bruce Lockhart.*

31 Ibid.

32 Lockhart was wrong. See his diaries.

33 Diary entry, 23 July 1936, in Bright-Holmes (ed.), *Like it Was: The Diaries of Malcolm Muggeridge.*

34 Muggeridge, *The Infernal Grove*, p. 62.

35 Ibid.

36 Diary entry, 13 April 1930, in Young (ed.), *The Diaries of Sir Robert Bruce Lockhart.*

37 Sutherland, *Portrait of a Decade.*

38 Quoted by Ron Hall in his introduction to *Nicholas Tomalin Reporting* (André Deutsch, London, 1975).

39 Ibid.

40 E. J. Robertson, quoted in Dennis Griffiths, *Plant Here the Standard* (Macmillan, London, 1996).

41 Quoted in Griffiths, *Plant Here the Standard.*

42 Quoted in Sir Robert Bruce Lockhart, *Your England* (Putnam, London, 1955).

11: Like Socrates, a Gadfly
(pages 169–187)

1 John Rayner, 'High Sex' in *London Magazine* (August–September 1977).

2 W. H. Auden, 'September 1, 1939' in Edward Mandelson (ed.) *The Complete Works of W. H. Auden* (Faber & Faber, London 1993).

3 Leo Abse, 'The Judas Syndrome' in *Spectator,* 20 March 1982.

4 Tom Driberg, *Ruling Passions* (Jonathan Cape, London, 1977).

5 Ibid.

6 Ibid.

7 Diary entry, 15 April 1932, in Kenneth Young (ed.), *The Diaries of Sir Robert Bruce Lockhart: Vol. I, 1915–1938* (Macmillan, London, 1973).

8 Tom Driberg, *Colonnade* (Pilot Press, London, 1949).

9 Ibid.

10 *Daily Express,* 12 May 1933.

11 Driberg, *Colonnade.*

12 Christopher Sykes, *Evelyn Waugh: A Biography* (Collins, London, 1975).

13 Evelyn Waugh to Lady Mary Lygon, [July? 1936] in Mark Amory (ed.), *The Letters of Evelyn Waugh* (Wiedenfeld & Nicolson, London, 1980).

14 Evelyn Waugh to Tom Driberg, [7 January 1937] in Amory (ed.), *The Letters of Evelyn Waugh.*

15 Tom Driberg, 'But whose names make what news?' in *Daily Telegraph,* 13 August 1975.

16 Peter McKay, 'Gossip' in Steven Glover (ed.), *Secrets of the Press* (Allen Lane Penguin, London, 1999).

17 Diary entry, 26 May 1942, in Michael Davie (ed.), *The Diaries of Evelyn Waugh* (Weidenfeld & Nicolson, London, 1976).

18 Driberg, *Colonnade.*

19 Tom Driberg, 'My Kind of Column' in Vivian Brodzky (ed.), *Fleet Street: The Inside Story of Journalism* (Macdonald, London, 1966).

20 Michael Foot, postscript to Driberg,

Ruling Passions.
21 *Daily Express*, 5 May 1938.
22 Francis Wheen, *Tom Driberg: His Life and Indiscretions* (Chatto & Windus, London, 1990).
23 Tom Driberg, *Beaverbrook: A Study in Power and Frustration* (Weidenfeld & Nicolson, London, 1956).
24 Driberg, *Ruling Passions.*
25 Quoted in Robert Edwards, *Goodbye Fleet Street* (Jonathan Cape, London, 1988).
26 Driberg, *Ruling Passions.*
27 *Daily Express*, 13 May 1937.
28 Driberg, *Ruling Passions.*
29 Ibid.
30 *Daily Express*, 21 January 1939.
31 *Daily Express*, 4 September 1939.
32 *Daily Express*, 17 March 1941.
33 *Daily Express*, 18 March 1941.
34 *Daily Express*, 18 April 1941.
35 *Daily Express*, 8 December 1941.
36 Driberg, *Ruling Passions.*
37 Ibid.
38 Arthur Christiansen, *Headlines All My Life*, (Heinemann, London, 1961).
39 Beaverbrook in evidence to the Royal Commission on the Press, 18 March 1948.
40 Douglas Sutherland, *Portrait of a Decade: London Life 1945–1955* (Harrap, London, 1988).
41 Baldwin's speech at an election rally, 18 March 1931.
42 Beaverbrook evidence to Royal Commission.
43 Christopher Andrew and Vasili Mitrokhin, *The Mitrokhin Archive* (Allen Lane, The Penguin Press, London, 1999).
44 Dennis Wheatley, *The Time Has Come . . . : The Memoirs of Dennis Wheatley. Drink and Ink, 1919–1977* (Hutchinson, London, 1979).
45 Leo Abse, 'The Judas Syndrome', in *Spectator,* 20 March 1982.
46 *Daily Mail,* 25 March 1981.
47 *Sunday Telegraph*, 20 June 1977.
48 *Sun,* 23 June 1977.
49 Driberg, *Ruling Passions.*
50 John Rayner, 'High Sex' in *London Magazine* (August–September 1977).
51 Driberg in his introduction to *Colonnade.*

12: Sprinkled with Stardust
(pages 188–200)
1 Quoted in Arthur Christiansen, *Headlines All My Life* (Heinemann, London, 1961).
2 Ibid.
3 Godfrey Winn, *The Infirm Glory* (Michael Joseph, London, 1967).
4 Ibid.
5 Ibid.
6 Quoted in Douglas Sutherland, *Portrait of a Decade: London Life 1945–1955* (Harrap, London, 1988).
7 Beverley Nichols, *All I Could Never Be* (Jonathan Cape, London, 1949).
8 Ibid.
9 Bryan Connon, *Beverley Nichols: A Life* (Constable, London, 1991).
10 Ibid.
11 Letter date January 1955 to Margaret and Harriet Waugh in Mark Amory (ed.), *The Letters of Evelyn Waugh* (Weidenfeld & Nicolson, London, 1980).
12 Connon, *Beverley Nichols: A Life.*
13 Quoted in Beverley Nichols, *The Unforgiving Minute* (W. H. Allen, London, 1978).
14 Quoted in James Wedgwood Drawbell, *Drifts My Boat* (Hutchinson, London 1947).
15 Quoted in H. Montgomery Hyde, *Privacy and the Press* (Butterworth,

London, 1947).

16 Quoted in Hyde, *Privacy and the Press.*

17 Ibid.

18 *Justice of the Peace and Local Government Review,* 26 January 1946.

19 Beverley Nichols, *A Case of Human Bondage* (Secker & Warburg, London, 1966).

20 Godfrey Winn, *The Infirm Glory* (Michael Joseph, London, 1967).

21 Ibid.

22 Connon, *Beverley Nichols.*

23 Ibid.

24 Quoted in *Spectator,* 15/22 December 2001.

25 Harry Hopkins, *The New Look* (Secker & Warburg, London, 1964).

26 *Daily Express* staff bulletin.

27 Quoted in Robert Graves and Alan Hodge, *The Long Weekend: A Social History of Great Britain 1918–1939* (Hutchinson, London, 1940).

28 Ibid.

29 Sutherland, *Portrait of a Decade.*

30 Ibid.

31 Donald Edgar, quoted in S. J. Taylor, *The Reluctant Press Lord* (Weidenfeld & Nicolson, London, 1988).

32 Arthur Christiansen, *Headlines All My Life* (Heinemann, London 1961).

33 Donald Edgar's obituary in *The Times,* 17 May 1996.

34 *Daily Express,* 12 May 1954.

35 Quoted in Donald Edgar's obituary in *The Times,* 17 May 1966.

36 *Daily Express,* 1 July 1955.

37 *Daily Express,* 12 February 1955.

38 *Daily Express,* 1 November 1955.

13: The Princess and *Queen*

(pages 201–217)

1 Diary entry, 28 February 1960, in Nigel Nicolson (ed.), *Harold Nicolson: Diaries and Letters 1945–1962* (Collins, London, 1968).

2 *Annual Register* (1960).

3 Bernard Levin, *The Pendulum Years* (Jonathan Cape, London, 1970).

4 *Daily Express,* 6 April 1960.

5 John Osborne, *Almost A Gentleman* (Faber & Faber, London, 1991), Vol. II.

6 *Guardian,* 10 April 1960.

7 Walter Bagehot, *The English Constitution,* (Kegan Paul, Trench, Trubner, London, 1929).

8 A. C. H. Smith, William Hickey: The Charmed Spectacle, *Paper Voices: The Popular Press and Social Change 1935–1965* (Chatto & Windus, London, 1975).

9 Ibid.

10 Joceyln Stevens, quoted in Nicholas Coleridge and Stephen Quinn (eds.), *The Sixties in Queen* (Ebury Press, London, 1987).

11 'The Friendless Ones' in *Queen* magazine, 13 April 1960.

12 Stevens in Coleridge and Quinn (eds.), *Sixties in Queen.*

13 'The Friendless Ones' in *Queen* magazine, 13 April 1960.

14 Quentin Crewe, *Well, I Forget the Rest* (Hutchinson, London, 1991).

15 Quoted in Ron Hall (ed.), *Nicholas Tomalin Reporting* (André Deutsch, London, 1975).

16 *Queen,* 31 July 1962.

17 Stafford Somerfield, *Banner Headlines* (Scan Books, London, 1979).

18 Quoted in 'The Profumo Affair' in *Scandal* (Orbis, 1990).

19 Quoted in John B. Thompson,

Political Scandal: Power and Visibility in the Media Age (Polity Press, Cambridge, 1999).

20 Quoted in The Profumo Affair in *Scandal*.

21 *Annual Register* (1963).

22 Quoted in George Bain, 'The Trouble With Journalists' in *Maclean's* (5 December 1994).

23 Quoted in Anne Chisholm and Michael Davie, *Beaverbrook – A Life* (Hutchinson, London, 1992).

24 Quoted in Clive Irving, Ron Hall and Jeremy Wallington, *Anatomy of a Scandal – A Study of the Profumo Affair* (Mill-Morrow, New York, 1963).

25 Patrick Marnham, *The Private Eye Story* (André Deutsch, London, 1982).

26 Ibid.

27 *Daily Sketch*, 16 March 1963.

28 *Daily Express*, 26 March 1963.

29 'New York *Journal-American*', quoted in Phillip Knightley and Caroline Kennedy, *An Affair of State* (Jonathan Cape, London, 1987).

30 Quoted in Knightley and Kennedy *An Affair of State,* p. 9.

31 Ibid.

32 Quoted in Anthony Summers and Stephen Dorril, *Honeytrap: The Secret Worlds of Stephen Ward* (Weidenfeld & Nicolson, London, 1987).

33 Knightley and Kennedy, *An Affair of State.*

34 Quoted in H. Montgomery Hyde, *A Tangled Web* (Constable, London, 1986).

35 Quoted in Margaret, Duchess of Argyll, *Forget Not* by (W. H. Allen, London, 1975).

36 Lord Denning, *Lord Denning's Report* (Cmno 2152, HMSO, London 1963).

14: Princely Peccadilloes
(pages 218–229)

1 Letter in Royal Archives at Windsor, Geo.V, CC 4 250, quoted in James Pope-Hennessy, *Queen Mary* (George Allen & Unwin, London, 1959).

2 Hamilton Fyfe, *'Pestering by the Press'* in *Fortnightly Review*, April 1937.

3 Quoted in Ronald Pearsall, *The Worm in the Bud* (Weidenfeld & Nicolson, London, 1969).

4 *The Times*, 3 December 1840.

5 *Annual Register*, December 1840.

6 Olga Venn, 'The Youthful Excesses of Mr Punch' in Leonard Russell (ed.), *The Saturday Book 1941–42* (Hutchinson, London, 1941).

7 R. J. de Cordova, *The Prince's Visit: A Humorous Description of the Tour of His Royal Highness, the Prince of Wales, through the United States of America, in 1860* (New York, 1861), quoted in Stanley Weintraub, *The Importance of Being Edward: King in Waiting 1841–1901* (John Murray, London, 2000).

8 *Illustrated London News*, 11 August 1860, quoted in Kinley Roby, *The King, the Press and the People* (Barrie & Jenkins, London, 1975).

9 Quoted in Weintraub, *The Importance of Being Edward.*

10 Ibid.

11 Ibid.

12 Ibid.

13 Ibid.

14 Quoted in Allen Andrews, *The Follies of King Edward VII* (Lexington Press, London, 1975).

15 Quoted in Roby, *The King, the Press and the People.*

16 *Birmingham Post*, 26 March 1869.

17 Quoted in Some Victorian Sex Scandals' in H. Montgomery Hyde, *A*

Tangled Web (Constable, London, 1986).

18 *Reynold News*, 20 Feburary 1870, quoted in Roby, *The King, the Press and the People*.

19 Quoted in Anita Leslie, *Edwardians in Love* (Hutchinson, London, 1972).

20 Quoted in Daphne Fielding, *The Duchess of Jermyn Street* (Eyre & Spottiswode, London, 1964).

21 *Galaxy*, March 1870, quoted in Weintraub, *The Importance of Being Edward*.

22 Quoted in Weintraub, *The Importance of Being Edward*.

23 Leslie, *Edwardians in Love*.

24 Quoted in 'Removed from the Army' in Horace Wyndham, *This Was the News* (Quality Press, London, 1948).

25 Royal Archives Add.MSS A.12/1752, quoted in the Rt. Hon. Sir Michael Havers QC, Edward Grayson and Peter Shankland, *The Royal Baccarat Scandal* (William Kimber, London, 1977).

26 Henry James to Robert Louis Stevenson, 18 February 1891, in Leon Edel (ed.), *Henry James Letters* (Macmillan, London, 1981), Vol. III.

27 Royal Archives Add. MSS U.32.

15: A Perfect Avalanche of Muck and Slime

(pages 230–246)

1 Thomas Jones, *A Diary With Letters 1931–1950* (OUP, Oxford, 1954).

2 The exact source of this much-quoted aperçu has eluded all modern writers on the affair, including this one.

3 Hannen Swaffer, Letter to *Cavalcade*, 8 February 1936.

4 G. R. Parkin, ibid.

5 Hannen Swaffer, letter to *Cavalcade*, 29 August 1936.

6 Lady Cynthia Asquith, *Diaries 1915–1918* (Hutchinson, London, 1968).

7 Quoted in Eve Brown, *Cholly Knickerbocker: The Life and Times of Maury Paul* (Dutton, New York, 1947).

8 Duchess of Windsor, *The Heart Has its Reasons* (Michael Joseph, London, 1956).

9 Harold Nicolson, in Nigel Nicolson (ed.), *Diaries and Letters 1930–39* (Collins, London, 1966).

10 Helen Hardinge, *Loyal to Three Kings* (William Kimber, London, 1967).

11 Ibid.

12 Robert Rhodes James (ed.), *Chips: The Diaries of Sir Henry Channon* (Weidenfeld & Nicolson, London, 1967).

13 Diary entry, 11 August 1936, in Kenneth Young (ed.), *The Diaries of Sir Robert Bruce Lockhart: Vol. I, 1915–1938* (Macmillan, London 1973).

14 *Sunday Dispatch*, 16 August 1936.

15 *New York Woman*, October 1936.

16 Dawson, private diary entry, quoted in John Evelyn Wrench, *Geoffrey Dawson and Our Times*.

17 Quoted in John Evelyn Wrench, *Geoffrey Dawson and Our Times* (Hutchinson, London, 1955).

18 Lewis Broad, *The Abdication Twenty-Five Years After* (Frederick Muller, London, 1961).

19 Ibid.

20 A. J. P. Taylor, Beaverbrook (Hamish Hamilton, London, 1972).

21 Lord Beaverbrook, *The Abdication of King Edward VIII* (Atheneum, New York, 1966).

22 Patricia Cockburn, *The Years of The Week* (Macdonald, London, 1968).
23 Claud Cockburn *Cockburn Sums Up* (Quartet, London, 1981).
24 Ibid.
25 *Morning Post*, quoted in Beaverbrook, *The Abdication of King Edward VIII.*
26 *Week*, 14 October 1936.
27 Beaverbrook, *The Abdication of King Edward VIII.*
28 Ibid.
29 *New York Journal*, 24 October 1936.
30 *Chicago Daily Tribune*, 28 October 1936.
31 Blanche Dugdale, *Baffy: The Diaries of Blanche Dugdale 1936–47* (Valentine, Mitchell, London, 1973).
32 *The Times*, 11 December 1936.
33 *Morning Post*, 11 December 1936.
34 Malcolm Muggeridge, *Chronicles of Wasted Time, Part 2 The Infernal Grove* (Collins, London, 1973).
35 Ibid.

16: Godmothers of Gossip

(pages 247–253)
1 Quoted by Richard Lemon, 'The Warrior Queens of Gossip' in *People* magazine, 13 May 1985.
2 Ibid.
3 Quoted on website www.mamievandoren.com/louella.htm.
4 Otto Friedrich, *City of Nets* (Harper & Row, New York, 1986).
5 George Eells, *Hedda and Louella* (Putnam, New York, 1972).
6 Quoted in Friedrich, *City of Nets.*
7 Quoted in Eells, *Hedda and Louella.*
8 Debbie Reynolds, quoted in Richard Lemon, 'The Warrior Queens of Gossip' in *People* magazine, 13 May 1985.
9 Quoted in Robert S. Sennett,

Hollywood Hoopla (Billboard Books, New York, 1998).
10 Charles Merz, *Bigger and Better Murders* (Victor Gollancz, Lonon, 1928).
11 Eells, *Hedda and Louella.*
12 Ibid.
13 Ibid.
14 Ibid.
15 Ibid.
16 Ibid.
17 David Niven, *Bring on the Empty Horses* (Hamish Hamilton, London, 1975).

17: Winchell

(pages 254–264)
1 Quoted in Neal Gabler, *Walter Winchell: Gossip, Power and the Culture of Celebrity* (Picador, London, 1995).
2 Quoted by Mitchell Freedman in *Newsday*, 20 November 1994.
3 Ernest Hemingway to Arnold Gingrich, 13 March 1933, in Carlos Baker (ed.), *Hemingway's Selected Letters: 1917–1961* (Scribner's, New York, 1981).
4 Alistair Cooke, 'Walter Winchell: An American Myth' in *Listener*, 20 November 1947.
5 Quoted in Gabler op cit.
6 Heywood Broun, *'It seems to Heywood Brown'* in *Nation*, CXXVII 3326 (3 April 1929), p. 391.
7 Quoted in Gabler, *Walter Winchell.*
8 Ibid.
9 New York *World*, 27 April 1930.
10 Charles W. Wilcox, 'Winchell of Broadway' in *Scribner's Magazine*, February 1931.
11 New York *World-Telegram*, January [?] 1932, quoted in Gabler, *Walter Winchell.*
12 'Tabloid Poison' in *Saturday Review*

of Literature, III, 30 (19 February 1927).

13 Damon Runyon, 'Romance in the Roaring Forties' in *More Than Somewhat* (Constable, London, 1950).

14 Bernard Sobel, *Broadway Heartbeat* (Hermitage House, New York, 1953).

15 John Mosedale, *The Men Who Invented Broadway* (Richard Marek, New York, 1981).

16 Quoted in Gabler, *Walter Winchell*.

17 Quoted in Mosedale, *The Men Who Invented Broadway*.

18 Writer–producer Jerry D. Lewis, quoted in Gabler, *Walter Winchell*.

19 Cooke 'Walter Winchell: An American Myth, Listener' in 20 November 1947, p. 893.

20 Quoted in Mosedale, *The Men Who Invented Broadway*.

21 Cooke, 'Walter Winchell: An American Myth', in *Listener*, 20 November 1947.

22 Gabler, *Walter Winchell*.

23 Quoted in 'Walter Winchell Off-Broadway' in *Ken* magazine 19 May 1938.

24 'Shoptalk at Thirty' in New York *Mirror*, 28 January 1932.

25 Marlen Pew in *Editor and Publisher*, 14 January 1933.

26 New York *Mirror*, 4 January 1933.

27 Quoted in Milt Machlin, *The Gossip Wars* (Tower Books, New York, 1981).

28 Quoted in Mosedale, *The Men Who Invented Broadway*.

29 Ibid.

30 Louis L. Snyder and Richard B. Morris (eds.), *A Treasury of Great Reporting* (Simon & Schuster, New York, 1949)

31 Quoted in Mosedale, *The Men Who Invented Broadway*.

32 Ibid.

33 St Clair McKelway, *Gossip: The Life and Times of Walter Winchell* (Viking Press, New York, 1940).

34 J. P. McEvoy, 'He Snoops to Conquer' in *Saturday Evening Post*, 13 August 1938.

18: Snoops and Privacy
(pages 265–274)

1 Quoted in *New Statesman*, 30 January 1937.

2 Quoted in the Rt Hon. Michael Havers QC, Peter Shankland and Anthony Barrett, *Tragedy in Three Voices: The Rattenbury Murder* (William Kimber, London, 1980).

3 *World's Press News*, 28 January 1937.

4 Auberon Waugh in 'The Theatre of Waugh' in *Sunday Telegraph*, 21 January 2001.

5 *The Times*, 25 November 1929.

6 *The Times*, 28 November 1929.

7 Bishop of Durham, speech to South Shields Rotarians, quoted in *Newspaper World*, 21 December 1929.

8 *The Times*, 4 December 1929.

9 Peter Rennell Rodd, letter to *The Times*, 3 March 1937.

10 Patrick Balfour, *Society Racket* (John Long, London, 1933).

11 Ibid.

12 *The Times*, 21 January 1911.

13 Ibid.

14 *Evening Standard*, 21 January 1911.

15 *The Times*, 24 January 1911.

16 *The Times*, 25 January 1911.

17 *The Times*, 30 January 1911.

18 John Osborne, *The World of Paul Slickey* (Faber & Faber, London, 1959).

19 John Osborne, *Almost a Gentleman* (Faber & Faber, London, 1991).

20 Ibid.

21 Ibid.

22 *Spectator*, 29 September 1961.

23 *New Statesman*, 29 September 1961.

24 John Osborne, *A Better Class of Person* (Faber & Faber, London, 1981).

25 *Spectator*, 2 May 1992.

26 *Spectator*, 30 May 1992.

27 Ibid.

28 *Spectator*, 5 June 1993.

19: Sex and the Body Politic
(pages 275–287)

1 Stuart Hall, 'The World of the Gossip Column' in Richard Hoggart (ed.), *Your Sunday Paper* (University of London Press, London, 1967).

2 Arnold Wesker, *Journey into Journalism* (Writers & Readers Publishing Cooperative, London, 1977).

3 Interview with Paul Callan, August 2002.

4 *New Statesman*, 1972

5 *Observer Magazine*, 19 August 1990.

6 *Observer*, 3 August 1975.

7 *News of the World*, 4 August 1985.

8 Quoted in *Private Eye*, 22 July 1988.

9 *Observer*, 3 August 1975.

10 *The Times*, 6 November 1975.

11 *The Times*, 14 November 1975.

12 Nigel Dempster in interview on BBC Television, 4 June 1975.

13 *The Times*, 28 November 1975.

14 *Observer*, 3 August 1975.

15 Ibid.

16 Quoted in *Sunday Times*, 2 August 1998.

17 Reported in 'Grovel', *Private Eye*, 22 July 1977.

18 *Private Eye*, 14 November 1975.

19 *Private Eye*, 12 December 1975.

20 *Daily Mirror*, 31 January 1976.

21 Barrie Penrose and Roger Courtiour, *The Pencourt File* (Secker & Warburg, London, 1978).

22 'Irvine to outlaw payments' in *Guardian*, 5 March 2002.

23 *Private Eye*, 7 October 1983.

24 *Guardian*, 19 April 1980.

20: Gossip by Appointment
(pages 288–296)

1 Daniel Boorstin, *The Image* (Atheneum, New York, 1962).

2 Peter Chippindale and Chris Horrie, *Stick it up Your Punter* (Heinemann, London, 1990).

3 Douglas Keay, *Royal Pursuit* (Severn House, London, 1983).

4 Nigel Dempster and Peter Evans, *Behind Palace Doors* (Orion, London, 1993).

5 Quoted in Dempster and Evans, *Behind Palace Doors*.

6 Quoted in Keay, *Royal Pursuit*.

7 Ibid.

8 Quoted in Chippindale and Horrie, *Stick It Up Your Punter*.

9 Sarah Curtis (ed.), *The Journals of Woodrow Wyatt* (Macmillan, London, 1998), Vol. I.

10 *Sun*, 16 January 1983.

11 Ben Pimlott, *The Queen* (HarperCollins, London, 2001).

12 Quoted in Jonathan Dimbleby, *The Prince of Wales* (Little, Brown & Co., London, 1994).

13 Andrew Morton, *Diana: Her True Story* (Michael O'Mara Books, London, 1992).

14 *News of the World*, 4 August 1985.

15 Ibid.

16 *Daily Mail*, May 1993, quoted in *Private Eye*, 21 May 1993.

17 *Daily Mail*, 17 February 1984.

18 *Spectator*, 13 April 1985.

19 *Spectator*, 20 April 1985.

20 Quoted in Christopher Browne, *The Prying Game* (Robson, London, 1999).

21 Ronald Allison, quoted in Pimlott, *The Queen*.

22 Kenneth Rose, quoted in Pimlott, *The Queen*.

23 Quoted in *Requiem, Diana, Princess of Wales 1961-1997. Memorials and Tributes* (Pavilion Books, London, 1997).

24 Diana, Princess of Wales, speaking to Lady Colin Campbell, quoted in Jeanette Walls, *Dish* (Avon Books, New York, 2000).

25 *Panorama* interview, BBC Television, 20 November 1995.

26 David Montgomery, quoted in Chris Hutchins and Dominic Midgley, *Diana on the Edge: Inside the Mind of the Princess of Wales* (Smith Gryphon, London, 1996).

21: Greedy for it
(pages 297–306)
1 Neal Gabler, *Walter Winchell: Gossip, Power and the Culture of Celebrity* (Picador, London, 1995).

2 Ibid.

3 Quoted in Gabler *Walter Winchell.*

4 Gabler, *Walter Winchell.*

5 Stanley Walker, 'Playing the Deep Bassoons' in *Harper's* monthly magazine, CLXIV (February 1932).

6 Anthony Sampson, 'Gossip, Glitter and Some Confessions' in *Encounter,* December 1959.

7 Introduction to Tom Driberg *Colonnade* (Pilot Press, London, 1949).

8 Ogden Nash, 'I Have it on Good Authority' from *I'm a Stranger Here Myself* (Little, Brown and Co., Boston, 1938).

9 Henry James, *Literary Criticism* (Literary Classics of the United States, New York, 1984) Vol. II.

10 17 November 1887, in Leon Edel and Lyall H. Powers (eds.), *The Notebooks of Henry James* (OUP,

Oxford, 1987).

11 New York *World,* 14 November 1886.

12 Preface to Henry James, *The Reverberator* (Macmillan, London, 1908).

13 17 November 1887, in Edel and Powers (eds.), *The Notebooks of Henry James.*

14 Quoted by David Shaw in *Los Angeles Times,* 18 August 1991.

15 Matthew Arnold, *Letters of Matthew Arnold 1848–88* (Macmillan, London, 1895), Vol. II.

16 Samuel Taylor Coleridge, 'A Prefatory Observation on Modern Biography' (1810), reprinted in James L. Clifford (ed.), *Biography as an Art: Selected Criticism 1560–1960* (OUP, Oxford, 1962).

17 'The Interview' in *New Princeton Review,* III (1887).

18 Ibid.

19 James, *Literary Criticism,* Vol. I.

20 Ibid.

21 Samuel D. Warren and Louis D. Brandeis, 'The Right to Privacy' in *Harvard Law Review,* IV, 5 (1890).

22 Leon Edel (ed.), *The Complete Tales of Henry James* (J. B. Lippincott, Philadelphia, 1963) Vol. IX.

23 'Mark Twain at Hartford' in Edmund Yates (ed.), *Celebrities at Home* (Office of the *World,* 1877–79), Vol. III.

24 Edel (ed.), *The Complete Tales of Henry James,* Vol. IX.

25 T. P. O'Connor, 'The New Journalism' in *New Review* I, 5 (1889).

26 W. T. Stead, 'The Future of Journalism' in *Contemporary Review,* November 1886.

27 Quoted in Richard Salmon, *Henry James and the Culture of Publicity*

(Cambridge University Press, Cambridge, 1997).

28 James, *The Reverberator*.

29 Stead, 'The Future of Journalism' in *Contemporary Review*, November 1886.

30 Edel and Powers (eds.), *The Notebooks of Henry James*.

31 Ibid.

32 James, *Literary Criticism,* Vol. I.

33 James, *The Reverberator*.

34 Edmund Yates, *Recollections and Experiences* (Richard Bentley & Son, London, 1884), Vol. II.

35 Quoted in Leon Edel, *Henry James: The Middle Years 1884–1894* (Rupert Hart-Davis, London, 1963).

36 Edel, *Henry James: The Middle Years 1884-1894*.

37 Quoted in Edel, *Henry James: The Middle Years*.

22: Frenzied and Breathless

(pages 307–315)

1 Quoted in Jeanette Walls, *Dish* (Avon Books, New York, 2000).

2 Quoted in Thomas K. Wolfe, 'Public Lives: *Confidential* Magazine; Reflections in Tranquillity by the Former Owner, Robert Harrison, Who Managed to Get Away With It' in *Esquire*, April 1964.

3 Quoted in Walls, *Dish*.

4 Ibid.

5 Ibid.

6 Ibid.

7 *Daily Mirror*, 26 September 1956.

8 Quoted in Walls, *Dish*.

9 Ibid.

10 Ibid.

11 Reginald Potterton, 'I Cut Out Her Heart and Stomped on it!' in *Playboy*, April 1969.

12 Quoted in Walls, *Dish*.

13 George Bernard, *Inside the National Enquirer: Confessions of an Undercover Reporter* (Ashley Books, New York, 1977).

14 Roy Greenslade, *Guardian*, 24 June 1996.

15 *Sunday Telegraph*, 15 August 1999.

16 Quoted by Arthur Sheekman in Groucho Marx, *The Groucho Letters* (Michael Joseph, London, 1967).

23: tittle-tattle.com

(pages 316–323)

1 Quoted in Jeanette Walls, *Dish* (Avon Books, New York, 2000).

2 John Sutherland, 'The Fight For Eyeballs' in *London Review of Books*, 1 October 1998.

3 Walls, *Dish*.

4 Quoted in James Bowman, 'Postmodern Journalism' in *The World and I*, 1 May 1999.

5 Matt Drudge, speech to National Press Club, Washington DC, 2 June 1998.

6 *New Yorker*, 12 December 1994.

7 Quoted by David Shaw in *Los Angeles Times*, 18 August 1991.

8 *Guardian* New Media, 18 September 2000.

9 Ibid.

10 Edith Wharton, *The House of Mirth* (Scribners, New York, 1905).

11 Richard Schickel, *His Picture in the Papers* (Charterhouse, New York, 1973).

12 Quoted in *Independent*, 17 October 2000.

13 Joel H. Wiener, 'The Americanization of the British Press, 1830–1914' in Michael Harris and Tom O'Malley (eds.), *Studies in Newspaper and Periodical History 1994 Annual* (Greenwood Press, Westport, Conn., 1995).

14 Quoted in Don C. Seitz, *The James Gordon Bennetts, Father and Son: Proprietors of the New York Herald* (Bobbs-Merrill Company, Indianapolis, 1928).

15 R.D. Blumenfeld, 'The Press of the Future' in R. D. Blumenfeld, *The Press in My Time* (Rich & Cowan, London, 1933).

Selected Bibliography

(All titles published in London unless otherwise stated)

Acton, Harold, *Nancy Mitford: A Memoir* (Hamish Hamilton, 1975)

Amory, Cleveland, *Who Killed Society?* (Harper & Bros., New York, 1960)

Amory, Mark (ed.), *The Letters of Evelyn Waugh* (Weidenfeld and Nicolson, 1980)

Anderson, W. E. K. (ed.), Sir Walter Scott, *Journal* (Clarendon Press, Oxford, 1972: first published 1890)

Andrew, Christopher and Mitrokhin, Vasili, *The Mitrokhin Archive* (Allen Lane/The Penguin Press, 1999)

Andrews, Allen, *The Follies of King Edward VII* (Lexington Press, 1975)

Argyll, Margaret, Duchess of, *Forget Not* (W. H. Allen, 1975)

Arnold, Matthew, *Letters of Matthew Arnold 1848–88* (Macmillan, 1895)

Aspinall, Arthur, *Politics and the Press* (Home and Van Thal, 1949)

Asquith, Lady Cynthia, *Diaries 1915–1918* (Hutchinson, 1968)

Bagehot, Walter, *The English Constitution* (Kegan Paul, Trench, Trubner, 1929)

Bailey, Margery, *Boswell's Column* (William Kimber, 1951)

Baker, Carlos (ed.), *Hemingway's Selected Letters: 1917–1961* (Scribner's, New York, 1981)

Balfour, Patrick, *Society Racket* (John Long, 1933)

Bamford, Francis and Wellington, Duke of (eds.), *The Journal of Mrs Arbuthnot* (Macmillan, 1950)

Barham, Revd R. H. Dalton, *The Life and Remains of Theodore Edward Hook* (Richard Bentley, 1853)

Beatty, Laura, *Lillie Langtry: Manners, Masks and Morals* (Chatto & Windus, 1999)

Beaverbrook, Lord, *The Abdication of King Edward VIII* (Atheneum, New York, 1966)

Benson, A. C. and Esher, Viscount (eds.), *Letters of Queen Victoria* (Murray, 1908)

Bernard, George, *Inside the National Enquirer: Confessions of an Undercover Reporter* (Ashley Books, New York, 1977)

Bierce, Ambrose, *The Unabridged Devil's Dictionary* (University of Georgia Press, Athens, Ga., 2000)

Birkenhead, Lord, *Lady Eleanor Smith – A Memoir* (Hutchinson, 1953)

Black, Jeremy, *The English Press in the Eighteenth Century* (Croom Helm, 1987)

Blumenfeld, R. D., *The Press in My Time* (Rich & Cowan, 1933)

Boorstin, Daniel, *The Image* (Atheneum, New York, 1962)

Bridgeman, Harriet and Drury, Elizabeth (eds.), *Society Scandals* (David & Charles, Newton Abbot, 1977)

Brightfield, Myron, *Theodore Hook and his Novels* (Harvard University Press, Cambridge, Mass., 1928)

Bright-Holmes, John (ed.), *Like It Was: The Diaries of Malcolm Muggeridge* (Collins, 1981)

Broad, Lewis, *The Abdication Twenty-Five Years After* (Frederick Muller, 1961)

Brodzky, Vivian (ed.), *Fleet Street: The Inside Story of Journalism* (Macdonald, 1966)

Brough, James, *The Prince and the Lily* (Hodder & Stoughton, 1975)

Brown, Eve, *Cholly Knickerbocker: The Life and Times of Maury Paul* (Dutton, New York, 1947)

Browne, Christopher, *The Prying Game* (Robson, 1999)

Bruce Lockhart, Sir Robert, *Friends, Foes and Foreigners* (Putnam, 1957)

Bruce Lockhart, Sir Robert, *Your England* (Putnam, 1955)

Buddle Atkinson, R. H. M. and Jackson, G. A. (eds.), *Brougham and His Early Friends* (privately printed, 1908)

Canning, John (ed.), James Boswell, *The Life of Samuel Johnson* (Methuen, 1991)

Chippindale, Peter and Horrie, Chris, *Stick it up Your Punter* (Heinemann, 1990)

Chisholm, Anne and Davie, Michael, *Beaverbrook – A Life* (Hutchinson, 1992)

Christiansen, Arthur, *Headlines All My Life* (Heinemann, 1961)

Churchill, Peregrine and Mitchell, Julian, *Jennie, Lady Randolph Churchill* (Collins, 1974)

Churchill, Sarah (Duchess of Marlborough), *Private Correspondence* (Henry Colburn, 1838)

Clifford, James L. (ed.), *Biography as an Art: Selected Criticism 1560–1960* (Oxford University Press, Oxford, 1962)

Cockburn, Claud, *Cockburn Sums Up* (Quartet, 1981)

Cockburn, Patricia, *The Years of The Week* (Macdonald, 1968)

Cohen-Portheim, Paul, *England, the Unknown Isle* (Duckworth, 1930)

Coleridge, Nicholas and Quinn, Stephen (eds.), *The Sixties in Queen* (Ebury Press, 1987)

Collier, John and Lang, Iain, *Just The Other Day* (Hamish Hamilton, 1932)

Congreve, William, *The Way of the World* in Herbert Davis (ed.), *Complete Plays* (University of Chicago Press, Chicago, 1967)

Connon, Bryan, *Beverley Nichols: A Life* (Constable, 1991)

Crewe, Quentin, *Well, I Forget the Rest* (Hutchinson, 1991)

Cross, Nigel, *The Common Writer* (Cambridge University Press, Cambridge, 1985)

Curtis, Sarah (ed.), *The Journals of Woodrow Wyatt*, Vol. I (Macmillan, 1998)

Daugherty, Sarah B., *Literary Criticism of Henry James* (Ohio University Press, Athens, Ga., 1982)

Davie, Michael (ed.), *The Diaries of Evelyn Waugh* (Weidenfeld & Nicolson, 1976)

Davies, Herbert (ed.), *Bickerstaff Papers and Pamphlets on the Church* (Oxford University Press, Oxford, 1957)

Davies, Herbert (ed.), *The Examiner and Other Pieces Written in 1710–11* (Oxford University Press, Oxford, 1957)

de Cordova, R. J., *The Prince's Visit: A Humorous Description of the Tour of His Royal Highness, the Prince of Wales, through the United States of America, in 1860* (New York: 1861)

Dempster, Nigel and Evans, Peter, *Behind Palace Doors* (Orion, 1993)

Dickens, Charles, *American Notes* (Granville, 1985)

Dimbleby, Jonathan, *The Prince of Wales* (Little, Brown & Co., 1994)

Drawbell, James Wedgwood, *Drifts My Boat* (Hutchinson, 1947)

Driberg, Tom, *Beaverbrook: A Study in Power and Frustration* (Weidenfeld & Nicolson, 1956)

Driberg, Tom, *Colonnade* (Pilot Press, 1949)

Driberg, Tom, *Ruling Passions* (Jonathan Cape, 1977)

Dugdale, Blanche, *Baffy:The Diaries of Blanche Dugdale 1936–47* (Valentine, Mitchell, 1973)

Edel, Leon (ed.), *The Complete Tales of Henry James* (J. B. Lippincott, Philadelphia, 1963)

Edel, Leon (ed.), *Henry James Letters:* Vol. III, *1883–1895* (Macmillan, 1981)

Edel, Leon, *Henry James: The Middle Years 1884–1894* (Rupert Hart-Davis, 1963)

Edel, Leon and Powers, Lyall H. (eds.) *The Notebooks of Henry James* (Oxford University Press, Oxford, 1987)

Edgar, Donald, *My Years of Fame as William Hickey* (John Clare Books, [n.d.])

Editors of *The Age*, *The Spirit of the Age Newspaper for 1828* (A. Durham, 1829)

Edwards, Robert, *Goodbye Fleet Street* (Jonathan Cape, 1988)

Eells, George, *Hedda and Louella* (Putnam, New York, 1972)

Erskine, Mrs Steuart (ed.), *Twenty Years at Court* (Nisbet, [n.d.])

Escott, T. H. S., *Masters of Journalism* (T. Fisher Unwin, 1911)

Falk, Bernard, *He Laughed in Fleet Street* (Hutchinson, 1933)

Felbermann, Heinrich, *Memoirs of a Cosmopolitan* (Chapman & Hall, 1936)

Fielding, Daphne, *The Duchess of Jermyn Street* (Eyre & Spottiswode, 1964)

Fleming, G. H., *Lady Colin Campbell* (Windrush Press, Moreton-in-Marsh, 1989)

Foot, Michael, *Debts of Honour* (Davis Poynter, 1980)

Ford, James L. *The Brazen Calf* (Dodd, New York, 1903)

Fox Bourne, H. R., *English Newspapers: Chapters in the History of Journalism* (Chatto & Windus, 1887)

Franklin, Benjamin, *Complete Works of Benjamin Franklin* (Putnam, New York, 1887)

Friedrich, Otto, *City of Nets* (Harper & Row, New York, 1986)

Gabler, Neal, *Walter Winchell: Gossip, Power and the Culture of Celebrity* (Picador, 1995)

Gerson, Noel B., *Lillie Langtry* (Robert Hale & Co., 1972)

Glover, Stephen (ed.), *Secrets of the Press* (Allen Lane Penguin, 1999)

Grant, James, *The Great Metropolis* (Saunders & Otley, New York, 1837)

Graves, Robert and Hodge, Alan, *The Long Weekend: A Social History of Great Britain 1918–1939* (Hutchinson, 1940)

Griffiths, Dennis, *Plant Here the Standard* (Macmillan, 1996)

Griffiths, Dennis (ed.), *The Encyclopaedia of the British Press* (Macmillan, 1992)

Hall, Ron (ed.), *Nicholas Tomalin Reporting* (André Deutsch, 1975)

Hamilton, Elizabeth, *The Warwickshire Scandal* (Michael Russell, Norwich, 1999)

Hardinge, Helen, *Loyal to Three Kings* (William Kimber, 1967)

Harris, Michael and O'Malley, Tom (eds.), *Studies in Newspaper and Periodical History* (Greenwood Press, Westport, Conn., 1995)

Harris, Michael, *London Newspapers in the Age of Walpole* (Associated University Presses, London and Toronto, 1987)

Hatton, Joseph, *Journalistic London* (Sampson, Low, 1882)

Havers, Rt Hon. Sir Michael QC, Grayson, Edward and Shankland, Peter, *The Royal Baccarat Scandal* (William Kimber, 1977)

Havers, Rt Hon. Sir Michael QC, Shankland, Peter and Barrett, Anthony, *Tragedy in Three Voices – The Rattenbury Murder* (William Kimber, 1980)

Hillhouse, James T., *The Grub-Street Journal* (Duke University Press, Durham, North Carolina, 1928)

Hillier, Bevis, *Young Betjeman* (John Murray, 1988)

Hindle, Wilfrid, *The Morning Post 1772–1937* (Routledge, 1937)

Hoggart, Richard (ed.), *Your Sunday Paper* (University of London Press, 1967)

Hopkins, Harry, *The New Look* (Secker & Warburg, 1964)

Hopper, Hedda, *From Under My Hat* (Doubleday, New York, 1952)

House, Madeline (ed.), *Letters of Charles Dickens,* Vol. III (Oxford University Press, Oxford, 1974)

Hunt, F. Knight, *The Fourth Estate* (David Bogue, 1850)

Hunt, Thornton (ed.), *Correspondence of Leigh Hunt* (Smith, Elder & Co., 1862)

Hutchins, Chris and Midgley, Dominic, *Diana on the Edge: Inside the Mind of the Princess of Wales* (Smith Gryphon, 1996)

Huxley, Aldous, *The Olive Tree and Other Essays* (Chatto & Windus, 1936)

Hyde, H. Montgomery, *Norman Birkett* (Hamish Hamilton, 1965)

Hyde, H. Montgomery, *Privacy and the Press* (Butterworth, 1947)

Hyde, H. Montgomery, *The Other Love* (Heinemann, 1970)

Hyde, H. Montgomery, *A Tangled Web* (Constable, 1986)

Irving, Clive, Hall, Ron and Wallington, Jeremy, *Anatomy of a Scandal: A Study of the Profumo Affair* (Mill-Morrow, New York, 1963)

James, Henry, *Literary Criticism* (Literary Classics of the United States, New York, 1984)

James, Henry, *The Reverberator* (Macmillan, 1908)

Jones, Kennedy, *Fleet Street and Downing Street* (Hutchinson, 1920)

Jones, Thomas, *A Diary With Letters 1931–1950* (Oxford University Press, Oxford, 1954)

Keay, Douglas, *Royal Pursuit* (Severn House, 1983)

Knight, Charles, *Passages of A Working Life* (Bradbury & Evans, 1864)

Knightley, Phillip and Kennedy, Caroline, *An Affair of State* (Jonathan Cape, 1987)

Lamb, Charles, *Last Essays of Elia* (Dent, 1897)

Langtry, Lillie, *The Days I Knew* (G. Doran, New York, 1925)

Larsen, Egon, *First with the Truth* (John Baker, 1968)

Leslie, Anita, *Cousin Randolph* (Hutchinson, 1985)

Leslie, Anita, *Edwardians in Love* (Hutchinson, 1972)

Leslie, Anita, *Jennie: The Life of Lady Randolph Churchill* (Hutchinson, 1969)

Lever, Tresham (ed.), *The Letters of Lady Palmerston* (John Murray, 1957)

Lewis, C. S., 'English Literature in the Sixteenth Century' in *Oxford History of English Literature*, Vol. VII (Oxford University Press, Oxford, 1954)

Levin, Bernard, *The Pendulum Years* (Jonathan Cape, 1970)

Logan, Andy, *The Man Who Robbed the Robber Barons* (W. W. Norton, New York, 1965)

Lubbock, Percy (ed.), *Letters of Henry James* (Scribner's, Boston, 1920)

Lycett, Andrew, *Ian Fleming* (Weidenfeld & Nicolson, 1995)

Machlin, Milt, *The Gossip Wars* (New York, 1981)

McDowell, Paula, *The Women of Grub Street Press: Politics, and Gender in the London Literary Marketplace 1678–1730* (Clarendon Press, Oxford, 1998)

McKelway, St Clair, *Gossip: The Life and Times of Walter Winchell* (Viking Press, New York, 1940)

McKibbin, Ross, *Classes and Cultures: England 1918–1951* (Oxford University Press, Oxford, 1998)

Marnham, Patrick, *The Private Eye Story* (André Deutsch, 1982)

Marx, Groucho, *The Groucho Letters* (Michael Joseph, 1967)

Merz, Charles, *Bigger and Better Murders* (Victor Gollancz, 1928)

Mitford, Jessica, *Hons and Rebels* (Gollancz, 1960)

Morgan, Fidelis, *A Woman of No Character* (Faber & Faber, 1986)

Morley, Lord, *Life of Gladstone* (MacMillan Company, New York, 1903)

Mosedale, John, *The Men Who Invented Broadway* (Richard Marek, New York, 1981)

Mosley, Charlotte (ed.), *A Talent to Annoy* (Hamish Hamilton, 1986)

Mosley, Leonard, *Castlerosse* (Arthur Barker, 1956)

Muggeridge, Malcolm, *Chronicles of Wasted Time: Part 2, The Infernal Grove* (Collins, 1973)

Newton Dunn, Bill, *The Man Who Was John Bull* (Allendale Publishing, 1996)

Nichols, Beverley, *All I Could Never Be* (Jonathan Cape, 1949)

Nichols, Beverley, *A Case of Human Bondage* (Secker & Warburg, 1966)

Nichols, Beverley, *Crazy Pavements* (Jonathan Cape, 1927)

Nichols, Beverley, *The Sweet and Twenties* (Weidenfeld & Nicolson, 1958)

Nicolson, Nigel (ed.), *Harold Nicolson: Diaries and Letters 1930–1939* (Collins, 1966)

Nicolson, Nigel (ed.), *Harold Nicolson: Diaries and Letters 1945–1962* (Collins, 1968)

Nicolson, Nigel (ed.), *Vita and Harold: The Letters of Vita Sackille-West and Harold Nicolson* (Weidenfeld & Nicolson, 1992)

Niven, David, *Bring on the Empty Horses* (Hamish Hamilton, 1975)

Osborne, John, *Almost a Gentleman* (Faber & Faber, 1991)

Osborne, John, *A Better Class of Person* (Faber & Faber, 1981)

Osborne, John, *The World of Paul Slickey* (Faber & Faber, 1959)

Pearsall, Ronald, *The Worm in the Bud* (Weidenfeld & Nicolson, 1969)

Pearson, Hesketh, *Labby* (Hamish Hamilton, 1936)

Penrose, Barrie and Courtiour, Roger, *The Pencourt File* (Secker and Warburg, 1978)

Petrie, Sir Charles, *Scenes of Edwardian Life* (Eyre & Spottiswode, 1965)

Pimlott, Ben, *The Queen* (HarperCollins, 2001)

Pope-Hennessy, James, *Queen Mary* (George Allen & Unwin, 1959)

Price, R. G. G., *A History of Punch* (Collins, 1957)

Procter, Harry, *The Street of Disillusion* (Allan Wingate, 1958)

Quennell, Peter (ed.), *Genius in the Drawing-Room* (Weidenfeld & Nicolson, 1980)

Rhodes James, Robert (ed.), *Chips – The Diaries of Sir Henry Channon* (Weidenfeld & Nicolson, 1967)

Roby, Kinley, *The King, the Press and the People* (Barrie and Jenkins, 1975)

Ross, Isabel, *Ladies of the Press: The Story of Women in Journalism by an Insider* (Harper & Brothers, New York, 1936)

Runyon, Damon, 'Romance in the Roaring Forties' in *More Than Somewhat* (Constable, 1950)

Russell, Leonard (ed.), *The Saturday Book 1941–42* (Hutchinson, 1941)

Salmon, Richard, *Henry James and the Culture of Publicity* (Cambridge University Press, Cambridge, 1997)

Schickel, Richard, *His Picture in the Papers* (Charterhouse, New York, 1973)

Schickel, Richard, *Intimate Strangers: The Culture of Celebrity* (Doubleday, New York, 1985)

Schudson, Michael, *Discovering the News: A Social History of American Newspapers* (New York, 1978)

Schults, Raymond L., *Crusader in Babylon: W. T. Stead and the Pall Mall Gazette* (University of Nebraska Press, Lincoln, 1972)

Secord, Arthur Wellesley (ed.), *Defoe's Weekly Review of the Affairs of France* (facsimile edition, 1938)

Seitz, Don C., *The James Gordon Bennetts, Father and Son: Proprietors of the New York Herald* (Bobbs-Merrill Company, Indianapolis, 1928)

Seitz, Don C., *Pulitzer: Life and Letters* (Simon & Schuster, New York, 1924)

Sennett, Robert S., *Hollywood Hoopla* (Billboard Books, New York, 1998)

Shattock, Joanne and Wolff, Michael (eds.), *The Victorian Periodical Press: Samplings and Soundings* (Leicester University Press, Leicester, 1982)

Shaw, George Bernard, *Sixteen Self Sketches* (Constable, 1949)

Shinagel, Michael, *Daniel Defoe and Middle-Class Gentility* (Harvard University Press, Cambridge Mass., 1968)

Smith, A. C. H., *Paper Voices: The Popular Press and Social Change 1935–1965* (Chatto & Windus, 1975)

Smith, Eleanor, *Life's A Circus* (Longmans, Green & Co., 1939)

Snoddy, Raymond, *The Good, the Bad and the Unacceptable* (Faber & Faber, 1984)

Snyder, Louis L. and Morris, Richard B. (eds.), *A Treasury of Great Reporting* (Simon

& Schuster, New York, 1949)

Sobel, Bernard, *Broadway Heartbeat* (Hermitage House, New York, 1953)

Somerfield, Stafford, *Banner Headlines* (Scan Books, 1979)

Spacks, Patricia Meyer, *Gossip* (Knopf, New York, 1985)

Spielmann, M. H., *History of 'Punch'* (Cassell & Company, 1895)

Spring, Howard, *In the Meantime* (Constable, 1942)

Stone, Lawrence, *Broken Lives: Separation and Divorce in England 1660–1857* (Oxford University Press, Oxford, 1993)

Stone, Lawrence, *Road to Divorce – England 1530–1987* (Oxford University Press, Oxford, 1990)

Straus, Ralph, *Sala: The Portrait of an Eminent Victorian* (Constable, 1942)

Sumbel, Mrs, *Memoirs of the Life of Mrs Sumbel, late Wells* (Chapple, 1811)

Summers, Anthony and Dorril, Stephen, *Honeytrap: The Secret Worlds of Stephen Ward* (Weidenfeld & Nicolson, 1987)

Sutherland, Douglas, *Portrait of a Decade: London Life 1945–1955* (Harrap, 1988)

Sutherland, James, *The Restoration Newspaper* (Cambridge University Press, Cambridge, 1986)

Sykes, Christopher, *Evelyn Waugh: A Biography* (Collins, 1975)

Symon, James D., *The Press and its Story* (Seeley Service, 1914)

Symons, Julian (ed.), *Essays and Biographies* (Cassell, 1969)

Taylor, John, *Records of My Life* (Edward Bull, 1832)

Taylor, S. J., *The Reluctant Press Lord* (Weidenfeld & Nicolson, 1998)

Thackeray, William Makepeace, *Pendennis* (Garland Publishers, New York, 1991)

Thompson, John B., *Political Scandal: Power and Visibility in the Media Age* (Polity Press, Cambridge, 1999)

Thomson, George Malcolm, *Lord Castlerosse: His Life and Times* (Weidenfeld & Nicolson, 1973)

Toynbee, Mrs Paget (ed.), *Letters of Horace Walpole* (Clarendon Press, Oxford, 1904)

Trevelyan, G. M., *English Social History* (Longmans, Green & Co., London 1944)

Trow, George W. S. *My Pilgrim's Progress: Media Studies 1950–1998* (Pantheon Books, New York)

Turner, E. S., *Unholy Pursuits: The Wayward Parsons of Grub Street* (Book Guild, Lewes, 1998)

Various, *Mr Punch in Mayfair* (Educational Book Company, [n.d.])

Vincent, John (ed.), *The Crawford Papers: the Journals of David Lindsay, twenty-seventh Earl of Crawford and tenth Earl of Balcarres 1871–1940 during the years 1892 to 1940* (Manchester University Press, Manchester, 1984)

Walls, Jeanette, *Dish* (Avon Books, New York, 2000)

Walpole, Horace, *The Last Journals of Horace Walpole* (Bodley Head, 1910)

Waugh, Evelyn, *Vile Bodies* (Penguin, 1938)

Weintraub, Stanley, *The Importance of Being Edward: King in Waiting 1841–1901* (John Murray, 2000)

Wesker, Arnold, *Journey into Journalism* (Writers & Readers Publishing Cooperative, 1977)

Wheatley, Dennis, *The Time Has Come...: The Memoirs of Dennis Wheatley. Drink and Ink, 1919–1977* (Hutchinson, 1979)

Wheen, Francis, *Tom Driberg: His Life and Indiscretions* (Chatto & Windus, 1990)

White, T. H., *The Age of Scandal* (Jonathan Cape, 1950)

Williams, J. B., *A History of English Journalism* (Longman Green & Co., 1908)

Windsor, Duchess of, *The Heart Has its Reasons* (Michael Joseph, 1956)

Wingate, Charles F. (ed.), *Views and Interviews on Journalism* (F. B. Patterson, New York, 1875)

Winn, Godfrey, *The Infirm Glory* (Michael Joseph, 1967)

Woolf, Virginia, *The Diary of Virginia Woolf: Vol IV, 1931–35* (The Hogarth Press, 1982)

Wrench, John Evelyn, *Geoffrey Dawson and Our Times* (Hutchinson, 1955)

Wyndham, Horace, *This Was The News* (Quality Press, 1948)

Yates, Edmund, *Fifty Years of London Life: Memoirs of a Man of the World* (Harper & Brother, New York, 1885)

Yates, Edmund, *Recollections and Experiences* (Richard Bentley & Son, 1884)

Yates, Edmund (ed.), *Celebrities at Home* (Office of *The World*, 1877–79)

Young, Kenneth (ed.), *The Diaries of Sir Robert Bruce Lockhart: Vol. I, (1915–1938)* (Macmillan 1973)

Index